PENGUIN BOOKS

FOR YOUR EYE ALONE

Robertson Davies was born and raised in Ontario and was educated at a variety of schools: Upper Canada College, Queen's University, and Balliol College, Oxford. He had three successive careers: first as an actor with the Old Vic Company in England, then as publisher of the *Peterborough Examiner*, and as a university professor and first Master of Massey College at the University of Toronto, from which he retired in 1981 with the title Master Emeritus.

He was without doubt one of the twentieth century's most distinguished men of letters, with more than thirty books to his credit, among them several volumes of plays as well as collections of essays, speeches, and belles lettres. As a novelist he gained fame especially for his Deptford trilogy; *Fifth Business*, *The Manticore*, and *World of Wonders*, and for his last five novels, *The Rebel Angels*, *What's Bred in the Bone*, *The Lyre of Orpheus*, *Murther & Walking Spirits*, and *The Cunning Man* (all available from Penguin).

His career was marked by many honors, including honorary degrees from twenty-six universities. His death in 1995 was marked by obituaries around the world.

Judith Skelton Grant, who selected and introduced these letters, is the author of the biography *Robertson Davies: Man of Myth*.

ROBERTSON DAVIES

For Your Eye Alone

Selected and Edited by JUDITH SKELTON GRANT

PENGUIN BOOKS

PENGUIN BOOKS
Published by the Penguin Group
Penguin Putnam Inc., 375 Hudson Street,
New York, New York 10014, U.S.A.
Penguin Books Ltd, 80 Strand, London WC2R 0RL, England
Penguin Books Australia Ltd, 250 Camberwell Road,
Camberwell, Victoria 3124, Australia
Penguin Books Canada Ltd, 10 Alcorn Avenue,
Toronto, Ontario, Canada M4V 3B2
Penguin Books India (P) Ltd, 11 Community Centre,
Panchsheel Park, New Delhi – 110 017, India
Penguin Books (N.Z.) Ltd, Cnr Rosedale and Airborne Roads,
Albany, Auckland, New Zealand
Penguin Books (South Africa) (Pty) Ltd, 24 Sturdee Avenue,
Rosebank, Johannesburg 2196, South Africa

Penguin Books Ltd, Registered Offices:
Harmondsworth, Middlesex, England

First published in Canada by McClelland & Stewart Ltd. 1999
First published in the United States of America by Viking Penguin,
a member of Penguin Putnam Inc. 2001
Published in Penguin Books 2002

10 9 8 7 6 5 4 3 2 1

THE LIBRARY OF CONGRESS HAS CATALOGED
THE AMERICAN HARDCOVER EDITION AS FOLLOWS:
Davies, Robertson, 1913–
For your eye alone : letters 1976–1995 / Robertson Davies ; selected and
edited by Judith Skelton Grant.
p. cm.
ISBN 0-670-89291-2 (hc.)
ISBN 0 14 20.0029 9 (pbk.)
1. Davies, Robertson, 1913—Correspondence. 2. Authors, Canadian—
20th Century—Correspondence. I. Grant, Judith. II. Title.
PR9199.3.D3 Z48 2001
813'.54—dc21   00-043899

Printed in the United States of America
Set in Bembo

In memory of my mother

Contents

PREFACE

Robertson Davies was marvellously Canadian, but certainly a Canadian like no other. His appearance – broad-brimmed hats, beard, formal suit, pocket watch and fob chain, large dark rings – was theatrical, and a little old-fashioned. His accent was as much the result of coaching while at London's Old Vic theatre in the late 1930s as it was of the Ontario of the 'teens and 1920s. He had earned his bread in many diverse occupations – actor, journalist, editor of a daily newspaper, master of a graduate college and professor of English and drama. While his novels took his reputation to a new level, he worked in many different genres with grace and ease – belles lettres, plays, ghost stories, essays and reviews, speeches, and libretti. Intriguingly, everything he did appeared to contain an element of performance. His audiences were charmed and fascinated, but he seemed to hold them at a distance. The acclaimed novels – remarkable works of story-telling and showmanship, full of lightly handled, far-ranging, amazing erudition, and wise assessments of human kind – did little to assuage their curiosity about the real Robertson Davies.

Finally, in this volume, we are able to see the private man.

I have selected these letters for their range, for their excellence, and for their revelations about Davies himself. Even when writing to people he had never met, Davies wrote "in his own voice." And to friends who had known him for much of his lifetime, he wrote candidly and from their shared private experience.

This volume covers the period 1976–1995, from his 63rd to his 83rd year, just before his death. In maturity, Davies had a truly remarkable breadth of knowledge and understanding to call upon. He was well read in myth, religion, and psychology. To the right recipient he would open himself frankly and directly, revealing his own beliefs and uncertainties, in passages which are often moving in their honesty and courage. When someone for whom he cared had suffered the death of a parent, a child, or a mate, or had contemplated suicide, Davies' response was sometimes treasured for years.

Canadian culture, particularly Canada's literature, was bred in his bone, and he wrote about it with an insider's perceptiveness to (and about) a large number of this country's writers, including Marian Engel, Margaret Laurence, Margaret Atwood, Josef Skvorecky, Mordecai Richler, Morley Callaghan, and Timothy Findley. In his letters he was appreciative of the pioneering role of writers like Callaghan in asserting the value and dignity of authorship. He revealed an astute sense of what mattered in particular books, whether it be an underlying theme or the creation of a strongly individual voice. He had a sharp (sometimes thin-skinned) sense of the deficiencies of critics, deriding their inability to write effectively, their use of ill-understood psychological concepts, their narrow notion of their trade, their arrogance, and their stubborn pursuit of ill-founded interpretations. On the other hand, what he had to say about another writer or about a critic often moved him to consider his own capacities and limitations with humility.

Although firmly rooted in this country (and firm in his opinions about national character, Separatism, senate reform, and the like), he was widely read in Western literature and history and especially drama. His deep engagement with theatre surfaces again and again in his letters. Quite apart from the casual references to the many evenings he gave to it every year, there are letters to actors and colleagues which reveal a thoroughgoing knowledge of the history of theatre and performance, and others that reflect his own passionate engagement with the stage as a playwright.

The past was always present in his mind – his personal past, Canada's past, the long past of Western culture – and his discussion of a particular issue characteristically drew connections with distant experience. His parents – Rupert, who died in 1967, and Florence, who died in 1948 – were often in his mind, and surface in his letters. Because his novels were rooted in memories of the four Ontario centres where he had grown up (the village of Thamesville, the town of Renfrew, the cities of Kingston and Toronto), a reader's or a translator's questions might elicit a new memory or a fresh reflection about one he had already drawn upon in his work.

His letters, strongly influenced by his feelings and also by his assessment of the character of the person to whom he was writing, are a joy to read. How could they fail to be, when he took such pleasure in selecting the right word, turning a phrase, finding the appropriate literary shape? Besides, as anyone who talked with him knew, he was used to thinking in paragraphs and developing the sweep of his thought. The letters he wrote are immensely various – sometimes warm and embracing, sometimes chatty or whimsical, sometimes philosophical and wise, sometimes sharp or sarcastic or frosty, sometimes formal – but they always have the engaging quality of good talk; they draw the reader immediately into Davies' inner world.

When I first approached Davies about writing his life in 1981, he urged me to retrieve his letters to Tyrone Guthrie and to Gordon Roper. To Guthrie – the founding artistic director of the Shakespearean Festival in Stratford, Ontario – he had written candid, private assessments of each summer's productions during the late 1950s and through the 1960s. As this was a venture to which he was passionately committed and which went on to become one of Canada's major cultural institutions, the letters promised to be fascinating. But they proved to be unfindable. The letters to Gordon Roper, a professor of English and an old Peterborough friend, on the other hand, had been carefully preserved. Roper was an early, sympathetic and astute reader of Davies' work. It was he who first recognized how profoundly Davies' thinking had been influenced by C. G. Jung, and his article on the subject early in 1972 had a strong impact on subsequent criticism of Davies' work. He was in the midst of writing the first book-length study of Davies and his work when he fell gravely ill. For several months in the summer and fall of 1972, the period when *The Manticore* was published and *World of Wonders* took shape, Davies opened his mind to this valued friend as he gradually regained his health. These letters, delightful, thoughtful, deliberately revealing, expose much of Davies' inward life – his moments of insecurity, his sudden rushes of inspiration, his surface preoccupations, his profound concerns.

A great many more letters came my way as I researched his life. There were splendid series of letters to a number of people, among them Horace W. Davenport, an eminent American physiologist, and Elisabeth Sifton, Davies' editor for fifteen years at The Viking Press in New York. Davenport often moved him to reflect about scientific and religious matters, while Sifton especially inspired him to consider his own and others' writing. There were sparkling single letters, too: to an actress about a performance he had attended, comparing it to those of others he had seen, to a magazine in mock desolation after an adverse review, to a freelance journalist about Harlequin romances.

Davies' own book reviews made it clear to me that he found value in the letters of people who interested him. He felt they gave depth to his understanding of their characters and illuminated corners of their minds and careers. The more I saw of his own correspondence, the more convinced I became that it offered similar insights. But when I raised the subject briefly once or twice, Davies was uncomfortable. As was the case in 1978, when I proposed to gather selections from his journalism for publication, he was not convinced that anything of value would emerge. On that occasion, he had been sharply aware of how quickly many of the pieces had been written, and he was apprehensive that readers would think that he was "pushing out old stuff" because he was "writing nothing new." In the case of his letters, he was also uneasy about violating his own and his friends' privacy, for, as he was prone to observe, "no man with a scrap of moral decency writes to his friends with one eye cocked at posterity."

But it was not only I who considered that Davies' letters were especially valuable. It was a rare individual who tossed away a letter from Robertson Davies. Indeed, I discovered that a fair number of his letters had been framed and hung. One friend had begun to save his letters as early as 1930, sharing the percipience of the American writer and academic John Espey (another friend from Oxford) who "decided from the start to save everything from Rob, certain that he would make his mark."

When I again raised the possibility of publishing a selection of correspondence early in October 1995, Davies had changed his mind. This time he greeted the idea with interest, possibly because he knew that many of his letters had already been lodged in public institutions across

North America. He was by now curious about the record he had created of his life through his letters. We discussed those which were already in hand and those that needed to be retrieved. He suggested several correspondents I had missed, and I asked about several others who were then added to the list. There, however, matters rested for a time, for he fell ill and died very soon afterward.

In due course, Davies' wife, Brenda, and his daughter Jennifer Surridge took over his literary affairs, and the project moved forward again. Institutions across Canada and a few key libraries in the United States checked their holdings and proved to have letters to correspondents Davies had not thought to mention – Canadian writers, the biographer Leon Edel, the publisher Alfred Knopf, and the journalist and essayist H. L. Mencken, for example. By the time I had pursued all the suggestions of possible correspondents and had sifted through the copies of business letters made by Davies' secretaries from 1942 to 1995, I had examined thousands of letters. Once a selection had been made, it was clear that there was more than enough excellent material for two volumes. The first, which reveals Davies finding his feet as a young man and as a writer, carries the tale of his life through the writing of the Deptford trilogy. This present volume discovers him in vigorous maturity, fully engaged in writing major novels, taking on new creative challenges, berating the wrong-headed critics behind their backs, and charming his correspondents. When I once suggested that a collection of his journalism be called "The Pleasures of Robertson Davies," he insisted that I use "Enthusiasms" instead. The vigour of that approach to life is evident right through these letters. We begin in 1976, with Davies in mid-career. . . .

Dear Mr. Pashley:

I am pleased that my Table Talk was stained with nothing worse than red wine: when I was a boy I used to borrow the plays of G.B. Shaw from the Public Library in Kingston, & they bore the marks of a reader who had used his pipe-stem as a bookmark, so that they bore unpleasing brown stains & stank of his spittle & Old Chum tobacco. They were also scribbled over in pencil by dissident readers, presumably clergymen. — But if you will encourage public libraries, those robbers of the literary poor, I can do nothing for you. — Yes, I can: go out, buy a decent copy of T.T. & paste this letter in it; & sell it to a rare book dealer (Hugh Anson-Cartwright is a soft touch) for $2 more than you paid.

Samuel Marchbanks.

SECTION

I

n 1976, the year he turned 63, Robertson Davies was at the peak of his powers. The warm American critical reception of the novels of the Deptford trilogy had by now established his reputation as a major novelist. Their success had attracted the first of a series of contracts with Penguin Books, which would see reprints of his books distributed worldwide. By 1976, too, Davies had become an established, respected figure at the University of Toronto. As the first Master of Massey College, he had made it a centre for intellectual gatherings and ceremonial events, and as a professor in the Drama Centre and in the Graduate Department of English, he had gained his colleagues' respect for his teaching. His earlier journalistic career – as editor of the *Peterborough Examiner* 1942–63, literary editor of *Saturday Night* magazine 1940–42 and 1953–59, and columnist for the *Toronto Star* newspaper syndicate 1959–62 – had provided him with a reviewer's familiarity with Canada's literary scene. His knowledge of the theatre was extraordinarily broad, the product of his lifelong enthusiasm for drama as playgoer, actor, director, playwright, collector, and professor. He had learned much from the works of Freud as a young man, but by 1976, he had become a thorough-going Jungian, capable of talking about complex psychological issues simply and clearly. He wrote with easy authority in a wide range of keys to correspondents of many sorts.

Davies was a very busy man. He found time for many commitments in addition to College administration, teaching, and the writing of novels. In the summers of 1976, 1977, and 1978, for example, he spent a week at the Wesleyan–Suffield Writers' Conference in Connecticut giving lectures and counselling students. He wrote and gave many speeches, collected for publication as *One Half of Robertson Davies* (1977). In the course of the 1976–77 university year, he wrote his last play, the full-length *Pontiac and the Green Man*, for the University's sesquicentennial celebrations (it drew scathing reviews). And he responded as well as he could to the many letters sent to him by readers and students studying his work.

His private life at this time had a regular rhythm: with his wife, Brenda, he spent weekdays living in the Master's Lodgings at Massey College, and weekends and university breaks at Windhover, their country house near Caledon East, an hour's drive from Toronto. Their three daughters, Miranda, Jennifer and Rosamond, were by now living independent lives. Both Jennifer and Rosamond had married, and Rosamond had four children. Theatre continued to be a great pleasure, and Davies and Brenda saw, on average, a play once every week or two, in Toronto, at the Shaw Festival in Niagara-on-the-Lake and the Stratford Festival (both an easy drive from Caledon East), and in London during jaunts abroad.

⌐

To J. G. MCCLELLAND

Massey College
University of Toronto
January 6, 1976

John Gordon McClelland (1922–), Canadian, was the president of McClelland & Stewart in Toronto, influential publishers of Canadian books. Although not Davies' chief Canadian publisher, he had brought out several of his books of essays and criticism.

Dear Jack:

Thanks for your letter of December 24; it did not reach me until December 31, and I did not have time to read the MS until last night. You ask for a comment you can use. Very well: here goes –

The theme of *Bear** is one of the most significant and pressing in Canada in our time – the necessity for us who are newcomers to the country, with hardly four hundred years of acquaintance with it, to ally ourselves with the spirit of one of the most ancient lands in the world. In our search for this spirit, we are indeed in search of ourselves.

There – that being done, let me say a few other things, not for quotation. I thought the book admirably written, spare and taut, with a good command of tone throughout; the changes from reality to fantasy are very well managed, and the pathos of the lonely woman is conveyed without too much agonizing and feminine self-pity. It reminded me of Margaret Atwood's *Surfacing,** because it explores the same ground – the search for healing in the wilderness – but I thought it a much better book as a work of art. I am not surprised Margaret Laurence and Adele Wiseman* urged you to publish it: it is, in the best sense, a woman's book, and they know what they are talking about. But – this must be put delicately – neither Margaret nor Adele, who are both dears, labour under the burden of a strong sense of humour, and when the book is published you had better prepare yourself for some explosions, not of outrage but of ribaldry.

Writing from my own recent experience,* I think you may run into a few things like this: MacSkimming will like the book and understand it; French will not like the book and won't understand it, and will be vulgarly jocose about it; Brian Vintcent will complain that it is elitist (not every woman has a bear, so why should any woman have one?) and will hint that bears are well-known to be homosexuals (like all sensitive people) and should not be bothered by importunate archivists. All critics, everywhere in Canada, will tell the whole plot in the course of what they think of as reviews, thereby spilling the beans. Gordon Sinclair* will declare that he has never slept with a bear, but served under a sergeant who was a bear in World War One. Pierre Berton* will have an evening of The Great Debate on the theme Why Not Bears? Peter Newman* will discover and publish the bear's Income Tax file. The Ontario Public Archives will be queried in the Legislature about what goes on there during lunchtime, anyway? The CBC will offer an hour-long (50 minutes, and 10 minutes of commercials) drama about Goldilocks, a social worker, who attempts to mend the marriage of Father Bear and Mother Bear, which has come to grief because Father Bear thinks Baby Bear looks altogether too much like Farley Mowat,* and wants to know what has been going on in the den when he was out looking for acorns and honey. Peter Gzowski* and 99 other TV and radio interviewers will lure Miss Engel to their studios and after a lot of humming and hawing, ask, "Now Marian, I hope you'll take this question as it's intended, but did you ever – really – let me phrase this carefully – *you know what I mean* – with a bear?" Judy LaMarsh* will ask a similar question, but not having read the book, will think it was a porcupine. The SPCA and the ecology people will protest against the sexual solicitation of bears, and the Gay Lib people will counter by asking what is wrong with a consenting bear, especially if it is a sailor-bear or a truck-driver-bear?.... All of this you and Miss Engel will have to endure philosophically. Where you will be driven to the uttermost pitch of endurance will be when the Society for the Advancement of Native Peoples – months after publication (slow readers because of the poor education imposed on them by unsympathetic governments) will demand that in the paperback the line "Shit with the bear" be changed to "Excrete with the bear, having first provided the bear with an ample supply of Face-Elle, preferably pink." You are all set for a lively Spring.

More seriously, I thought the book a fine treatment of a tricky theme – tricky because intercourse with a large animal is one of the commonest of feminine fantasies, and in a country like Canada one that is rarely given public voice. But it is recurrent in all mythologies, and its roots lie very deep. Men do not fantasize about large female animals, and books like *Wild Animals I Have Known** are quite free of such material – incidentally, Miss Engel must be prepared to meet ladies at cocktail parties whose names figure in Peter Newman's book who will think the popular work named above is the one she has written; rich women don't seem to read, and when they do, they don't read straight..... I wish you luck, and my congratulations to Miss Engel, whom I do not know, but whose work I have long admired.

Yours sincerely,

Rob.

PS: Of course this letter is for your eye alone.

To SIR JOHN GIELGUD

Massey College
University of Toronto
April 5, 1976

Sir John Gielgud (1904–) is a renowned English actor, director, and producer. Davies got to know him first in 1936 when Gielgud directed the Oxford University Dramatic Society in Shakespeare's Richard II *with Davies as his student stage manager.*

Dear Sir John:

Forgive me for taking so long to reply to your delightful letter of March 1: I have been laid low by pneumonia, and am just getting back to work. Your letter cheered me greatly at a time when I needed cheering, so thank you very much. How did *World of Wonders* come into your hands? It has not been published in the U.K., but has just appeared in the U.S., and is being greeted with kind words and large sales; I am delighted that its romance and the wonder of life give satisfaction, and apparently a kind of reassurance, to so many people. Not many authors nowadays seem to like life or think it rich, and often I feel very lonely and somewhat odd; but people – just readers who do not suffer from literary ennui and sourness of spirit – often agree with me.

No, I never knew [Sir John] Martin-Harvey* or worked for him in any capacity. Nevertheless he was a determining element in my growing-up (what Jungians call a "transformation-symbol") and I feel an affection and gratitude toward him. I wonder if you actors are often aware of the extraordinary influence you have on impressionable young people who encounter your work at a critical time in their lives? My parents were keen theatre-goers, and when I was twelve they took me to see JMH in *The Corsican Brothers*;* it bowled me over, for I was just at an age when I longed for a whiff of assurance that life was not as commonplace as it was in my school world, and there it was, provided by Dumas, and JMH – a world of wonders, indeed! I often wonder if the keen political reformers of our time have any conception of the need in people for some aristocracy of spirit and feeling, which is so inimical to their well-meant but determinedly dowdy notion of the world and of human society, but so necessary if there is to be any flowering of the spirit.

Anyhow, I became a Martin-Harvey fan, and saw him as often as I could. Inevitably, as I grew older and began to know everything, I thought I had outgrown him. I recall that as a schoolboy of 17 I went with a friend of mine to see a matinee of *The Only Way*;* we would go, we thought, and have a sophisticated giggle at the old man and the old play. But we were both soggy with tears before the end, and I really don't think I have ever felt I knew everything since that memorable afternoon.

Later, when I was at Oxford, I went up to London to see his farewell performance as Oedipus at Covent Garden. Startling combination of Greek splendour and nineteenth-century romanticism; it was

his voice, I think that was most impressive, because it was too melli-
fluous for the ferocity of Greek tragedy, but nevertheless revealed
things in the Greek story that one had not suspected as being part
of it.

So, you see, I never knew him, though I did at one time know his
son Michael,* and that was very revealing. JMH was a tyrant as a
father, and wrecked Michael, who was a pretty good small-part actor,
but best at grotesque comedy. (He looked extraordinarily like his
mother [Nina de Silva],* who was I believe a charming woman, and
a fine comedy actress, though perfectly awful as romantic heroines.)
In time I began to collect things relating to the theatre, and acquired
a large group – about 450 – of JMH's letters, and through these I
began to know him better. He was not, of course, the elegant melodrama hero or villain I had seen on the stage; just a nice man, much
plagued by gout, finances, and bewildered that the theatre world was
passing him by. He regarded himself as the inheritor of Irving's
mantle, and rejection of him was rejection of Irving* – which was
the rejection of all sane theatre art, and contrary to God's manifest
will. Poor man; it makes sad reading.

He was also an important figure in the history of the stage in
Canada; his tours were heroic in scope and the number of productions he carried. He gave us some very good Shakespeare – *Hamlet*
(with a Gordon Craig* setting), *Richard III*, a wonderful sly ogre – and
Canada's first professional production of a Greek tragedy – *Oedipus*,
directed by Reinhardt;* and of course he allowed twentieth-century
playgoers like me to peep into the past, and see *Corsican Brothers* and
The Lyons Mail and *The Bells*＊ in very good, coherent and artistically
sincere productions, as Irving had done them; there was a quality of
jocose terror in some of those things that I have never seen any other
actor achieve; he had a wolfish quality which presumably was a legacy
from Irving.

The passage in my novel,* about the Irving Centenary Matinee is
virtually all imagination; I had heard that JMH had wanted to be in
it, made rather an ass of himself, and had also been somewhat shoul-
dered aside by younger organizers. But otherwise I invented it; I hope

you did not mind being made part of the scene – though not identified by name – in the role of the actor who tried to comfort him. But if it rang true I am of course complimented.

Thanks for your recollections* of the trouble about *A Tale of Two Cities*; certainly he does not seem to have behaved very well on that occasion. I suppose one must make allowance for the devouring egotism of actors of the Irving era, and their followers; those extraordinary and electric personalities were bought at the cost of a very large chunk of human decency – and may well have been worth the price. It must have cost Martin-Harvey a great deal in the coin of ordinary good behaviour, the sort of fair-play philosophy that makes a man a good member of a club, the *ordinariness* without which life would be a series of rancorous confrontations – to be what he was. But when one counts that against what he was able to do for his audiences, perhaps the price was not too high.

It is now about a year since I saw you in *No Man's Land*.* Stunning! Real star acting, and a splendid change from all the *committee* acting we saw in London – performances of plays which had obviously reached the stage after a great deal of committee discussion among the actors (including, of course, all the understudies, in the interest of democracy) and a firm understanding that under no circumstances would any glimmer of romance assert itself. The stage owes something to this kind of work, but it has cost us much theatre magic.

You ask how I know some of the things I use in *World of Wonders*. Well, when the first volume of this trilogy (it was *Fifth Business*) came out, a New York journalist, Israel Shenker,* demanded to know how I knew that the Bollandists* write in purple ink. "I divined it," I replied, and he was somewhat miffed, because he had letters from them in purple ink and thought it was his little secret. One either twigs things about the past or one doesn't, and I have been lucky.

Again, my warmest thanks & all good wishes –

Robertson Davies

To RAYMOND MASSEY

Massey College
University of Toronto
[May 1976]

*Raymond Massey (1896–1983) was a
Canadian-born American who made a
considerable reputation as an actor on the
stage and screen in the United States. He
was a member of the family foundation
which established Massey College.*

Dear Ray:

Congratulations on *When I Was Young;** I had to wait till I had read
a pile of examinations before I could get at it, but I finished it last
night and it gave me extraordinary pleasure because apart from
reading about someone I knew, the book is such a good piece of
writing! You seem to have the things writers strive for years to attain
– simplicity, immediacy and economy. With the unerring skill of a
shingler you repeatedly hit the nail bang on the head. I hope the succeeding volume* is already well advanced, and you will have crowds
of people waiting for it.

Because I am understandably concerned about writing, will you
excuse me for saying that your book stands out among theatrical reminiscences, which tend to fall into two main categories: Solemn Mass
in Honour of Myself, and Twee Me, the Baby Genius. But you have
written a true and frank book about a recognizably real person. A
very great achievement.

I was particularly happy about the childhood chapters and the
picture they gave of Toronto at the turn of the century. When Vincent
[Massey]* wrote his reminiscences, I urged him to do another, small
book, which would be an affectionate picture of Toronto in the past,
but he never got around to it. His book, if I may say so, suffers in
comparison with yours, because yours shows us a man, whereas his
pointed out the salient features of somebody who seemed other than
the writer. He could not do otherwise, or didn't want to. When he
was preparing *What's Past Is Prologue* he showed me the MS and asked
for an opinion. I was stumped, but felt I must be honest about writing,
as it was my own job, and begged him to warm it up a bit. I was

driven at last to say, "Vincent, you must choose between being an author and being a gentleman!" He misunderstood me; he thought I wanted him to liven up the text with raunchy anecdotes. What I really meant was that he must allow himself to be an artist – which was a side of his character he kept very much under wraps, though it was there. But you have written like an artist, and I congratulate you most sincerely.

The College seems to have turned a corner. As you know, we have had our troubles with the discontent that has swept all universities, and which now seems to be quiescent for a while: we have also had problems with the University, for the President [John Robert Evans]* is not among our admirers, though he likes to use us when we are useful. The greatest blow this College ever suffered was when the University made it clear that it had never intended to do anything but the minimum about supporting us with money. The reasons were plain; they were short of money. Nevertheless, they had made prom-ises, and even a token of interest in keeping those promises would have been friendly. But at last we are receiving assurances from our former members and from outside the University, that we are fulfilling our ambition to be a serious and effective centre of research and advanced scholarship. A book I shall send you shortly is one evidence of this, and since the Gordon Lectures* we have been the centre for a very good economic discussion, related to the bicentennial of Adam Smith's *Wealth of Nations*.* As for finance, we are keeping our heads above water, and have hopes that we may even make some addition to our capital fund. I have been begging assiduously, and though I hate the work it seems at last as if it might come to something. Perhaps best of all, we now have a group of former Junior Fellows who beat the drum for us wherever they go. The accusations of preciosity and elitism that used to be made against us continue, but there are now contradictory voices. So – given another three hundred years – we should be well and truly established. I shall be retiring in a fairly short time, and I hope the next Master will bring the qualities I have lacked – better administrative method, a keen financial sense, and lots of others. But I have enjoyed it, even when the going was rough.

All good wishes to you both —

Rob

Sorry about the messy typing, but I did not want to dictate this: dictation doesn't really work for me.

To ELISABETH SIFTON

Windhover
Caledon East . . .
[August 1976]

Elisabeth Sifton (1939–) was senior editor at The Viking Press in New York. She became editor-in-chief (1978–84) and vice president of Viking Penguin and publisher of Elisabeth Sifton Books (1984–87). She was Davies' editor in New York from 1972 to 1987 and became a good friend.

Dear Elisabeth:

Many thanks for your kind letter of July 29; so glad your holiday rinsed and refreshed you. How I envy you; I have not had a chance for a mental wash-up and brush-up since 1970, though I have had what are laughingly called holidays – but they are never holy in the true sense, and no single day goes by without some wretched duty crying out to be done.

About Penguin, and a name for the Trilogy: I am rotten at names, but cudgelling my brain brings up these poor suggestions:

The Deptford Trilogy
Three Men of Deptford
The Fifth Business Trilogy

I don't care much for Number Two, and the others are jejune; as you may have heard a movie is mooted of *Fifth Business*, so perhaps some reference to it would be sensible.

Thanks also for your comments about my speech on Canadian
Nationalism;* it is a very hot topic here, and nationalism always brings
a lot of idiots into prominence who cannot see beyond the ends of
their noses. Of course we don't want to be eaten by the USA, but
anybody with any wits knows that small countries (and we are small
in population) must be linked with somebody, and the USA is the
obvious link for us, in economic matters; as for art and literature, they
are nationalist at their peril. I think myself lucky that in my lifetime
Canadian writers have ceased to be asked by publishers in NY to
change the venue of their stories to somewhere south of the border.
That certainly happened to me in connection with several plays. Our
independence is a dicey affair and can never be complete; who is
completely independent? We just don't want to be chawed down to
a nubbin.

As we seem to be linked ever closer as the years pass by perhaps I
had better let you know what I am doing. This summer I am very
busy preparing a series of special lectures* for next autumn (a named
lecture series at the University of Toronto) called *Masks of Satan:
Aspects of Evil in 19th and 20th Century Literature*. It proves to be about
the length of a small book, and takes a devil of a lot of work, but is
rewarding. Whether it would ever be of any use as a publication I
can't say, but Macmillan are interested, though cautious. It is basically
about the decline in public acceptance of religion in the past 150
years, the probable consequences of that, and the unexamined turn
toward a kind of dualism in the thinking of people who think at all.

I am committed to write a play [*Pontiac and the Green Man*] for production in the autumn of 1977, and must get at it soon. It is about
Major Robert Rogers* (of Rogers' Rangers) but in his character as a
playwright; did you know he wrote a play called *Ponteach; or the
Savages of America*? It is very pro-Indian. But the piece is to be a
comedy, and not an Advancement of Red Men as Opposed to Pink
Men diatribe. It is to have a lot of music, and a splendid cast, including my wife [Brenda],* for whom I am writing a great part; haven't
decided yet whether she is to have a wooden leg or a patch over one
eye; it is a sort of female pirate.

When these things are cleared away I shall set to work on another novel [*The Rebel Angels*], which might just possibly turn out to be another trilogy. Subject: money, the love thereof and the rich comedy that ensues therefrom. Setting: a university, because nowhere is money, and the greed for benefactions, so great. But I swear to you on the Holy Evangelists that it will not be another one of those books about the most trivial of faculty squabbles, filled with improbable characters; I expect a murder in it, and maybe two. It nags at me now and wants to be written but although I make copious notes I can't get at it soon. Possible title: *Hard Food for Midas* (from *The Merchant of Venice*). There have been several splendid university novels, and scores of mediocre ones, but I don't know of any on quite the theme I have in mind. If I can manage it, it will make *Fifth Business* seem a Tale for Tiny Tots.

Back to the grindstone now –
with admiration –

Rob. Davies

To NICHOLAS PASHLEY

[after November 12, 1976]

Nicholas Pashley (1946–   ), Canadian writer and Toronto bookseller, was at the time a stranger to Davies. He had read a copy of The Table Talk of Samuel Marchbanks *from the Yorkville branch of the Toronto Public Library.*

Dear Mr. Pashley:

I am pleased that my *Table Talk* was stained with nothing worse than red wine: when I was a boy I used to borrow the plays of G. B. Shaw* from the Public Library in Kingston, & they wore the marks of a reader who had used his pipe-stem as a bookmark, so that they bore unpleasing brown stains & stank of hot spittle & Old Chum tobacco. They were also scribbled over in pencil by dissident readers, presumably clergymen. – But if you *will* encourage public libraries, those robbers of the literary poor, I can do nothing for you. – Yes, I can: go out, buy a decent copy of *T.T.* & paste this letter in it; & sell it to a rare book dealer (Hugh Anson-Cartwright* is a soft touch) for $2 more than you paid.

Samuel Marchbanks.*

To RONALD BRYDEN

[late 1976 or early 1977]

> Ronald Bryden (1927–) had been literary editor of The Spectator *(London), and* theatre critic for the New Statesman *and for* The Observer. *At this point he was visiting professor of drama at the University of Toronto.*

Dear Ron:

Many thanks for the loan of *Trilby*;* I read it with great satisfaction; it supports one of my contentions which my students sometimes think perverse – that extremely effective theatre can exist without any strong literary content. If I had to choose between seeing *Trilby* and seeing yet another company hurl itself upon the thorns of *The Way of the World** I know which I'd take..... As you say, it is a great archetypal situation – the Wizard and his Doll, or the man Who Utterly Dominates and Grabs the Triumph of a Woman. I was astonished to see how jokey and goblin-like Svengali had been made – for Tree,* I suppose; in the book he is much more the demon, but I suppose Tree put that into the acting. My father [Rupert Davies]* saw *Trilby*, but I rather think it was Wilton Lackaye,* and not Tree he saw; he used to tell me of the mystery and terror of the moment when Svengali repeats his own name several times and gets the girl under his spell. This is great Jungian drama. I have several times addressed Jungian societies on Archetypes in the Theatre, and am to talk to the New York Society next October; I shall certainly say a good deal about *Trilby*. Does this aspect of drama interest you at all?

In reply to your question about page 199* in *World of Wonders* and Sir John's adjuration of Eisengrim to do his juggling slowly: several people in my young days in the theatre gave me this advice. One was Edward Carrick,* Gordon Craig's son, when I was a commedia dell'arte figure in *The Taming of the Shrew* (I played five roles, including the Widow!) at the Old Vic; I had some showy stuff to do – not juggling – as I entered by leaping through a window. And EC was emphatic and most helpful about the need to *go slowly* so as not to confuse the audience; the purpose of what I was doing was to enthrall and enchant, not to baffle by whirlwind rapidity. And very true it is; and much harder to do. Another old actor, Frank Moore,* helped me in the same way: few gestures, and take them slowly and hold 'em long. (I put old Frank, who was a dear, in *World of Wonders*.) And Ben Webster* (father of Margaret, and the first Algernon in *Importance*) gave me much advice, all golden, and showed me how Irving did things, and Irving never flashed or bustled – get it clean, and do it deliberately and slowly and *gracefully* because nobody will think you a nobleman, or a hero, or anything else of the first rank if you rush like a common person – deliberation is distinction (I quote Ben). And of course I saw Martin-Harvey many times, who embodied all of this, and I have talked about his style of acting with his old pupil Eric Jones-Evans* (who takes him off a treat) and being able to do things slowly and beautifully was part of it; Eric says this came from Irving..... I should love to talk to you about this some time.

Regards –

Rob.

The watchword is: don't *do* – BE! rather like Yoga.

To COLIN DEVINE

Massey College
University of Toronto
January 31, 1977.

*Colin Devine, a student then living in
Don Mills, Toronto, had written on behalf
of his class, hoping for a resolution of
"several heated arguments" about* Fifth
Business.

[Dear Mr. Devine:]

Thank you for your letter of January 25th. Your questions* are difficult to answer in a brief communication but I will see what I can do.

1) Of course Canadians are different from people of other countries, but not always in obvious ways. Europeans, for instance, very rarely waste any time wondering who they are and what their place in the world is, and yet this is one of the principal preoccupations of Canadians, as any consideration of our literature and drama makes clear. It should be obvious enough that we are a northern people whose culture derives from Europe and whose primary political and economic influence is from the United States. It should be clear, also, that although we have had enormous immigration from a variety of countries the predominating influence here is Anglo-Saxon, though in the case of Canada that should, perhaps, be altered to Anglo-Celtic. These were the people who came first, developed the country and put their mark on it, and it will be a very long time before any other mark is more than superficial. It should be obvious that our immigrants have come here because they want to be like us and to have what we have; our foolish chatter about absorbing the values that they bring with them is part of the want of self-confidence that I spoke of earlier. Of course we shall absorb certain influence from them, but so far no powerful cultural or governmental influence has reached us from our immigrant population.

2) No, I do not think that Canadians lack imagination, though some Canadians do so. Indeed I think that it is dangerous and misleading to talk about Canadians as though they were all cast in one mould. If they have any profound guilt feelings these probably arise from nineteenth century religion and also from something which is very rarely mentioned which is that the majority of Canadian settlers

were, and still are, drawn from the poorer and less well-educated part of the population of their parent country, and that such people are more prone to feelings of guilt than those who are better educated and better placed in the world. Canada has never had an aristocracy, and indeed anything that could be called an "upper class," and consequently has felt the lack of the spirit of adventure and moral experiment that these elements give to a population.

3) So far as I am concerned a Canadian novel is so because it is written by a Canadian. I cannot think of any other definition that has any value.

With good wishes,

Yours sincerely,

[Robertson Davies]

To DOMINI BLYTHE

Windhover
Caledon East
July 9, 1977

> *Domini Blythe (1947–), an English actress, has acted in Canada since 1972.*

Dear Domini:

It is now some time since the first performance of *Miss Julie*,* but it is the first chance I have had to write to tell you how much I enjoyed the whole play and what great satisfaction your performance gave me. It is a favourite play of mine, and perilously difficult for North American actors and audiences, because so often they do not understand what all the fuss is about. If an American girl feels like running off with her father's valet, she does it, and they live unhappily ever after, and that's that. But for a Swedish aristocrat – for Fröken Julie – that's something quite other, and it takes some doing to make it clear what is wrong. But you did it; you made it as clear as Strindberg allows, and you aroused just the right mixture of pity and revulsion; pity, because her state is desperate, and revulsion because every man in the audience knows that to get mixed up with such a girl would be a disastrous experience. I shall remember your performance always, and I do not expect to see a better one. I have seen the play many times (including university murders) but never one in which the principal character was so understandingly realized as yours.

I am writing to Douglas [Rain],* too, for he was admirable and not enough people have said so. There was only one false note in the production for me, and that was the interlude – the interrupted rape. I don't think the director [Eric Steiner]* knows many peasants; they are not like that. And did I spy a pair of white panties on the girl? Since when did a Swedish peasant girl of that era wear such things? Nothing at all, or a fearsome set of flannel trews, would be her lingerie. But that blemish was nothing on a splendid experience.

With great admiration –

Robertson Davies

To HORACE W. DAVENPORT

Massey College
University of Toronto
November 10, 1977

Horace W. Davenport (1912–   ), an
American physiologist, was chairman of
the department of physiology, University
of Michigan, Ann Arbor, from 1956 to
1978 and active as a professor there until
1983. Davies and he had met as graduate
students at Balliol College, Oxford, and
became close friends. His academic
career involved him in a considerable
amount of laboratory-based research in
gastroenterology.

Dear Horace:

We send you huge clouds of sympathy – notoriously a gaseous element – in your affliction. What is so lowering to one's self-esteem as trouble with one's plumbing? Do I divine from your postcard that they did the prostate job as well as the other?* This is something to which we all come in some way or other. My brother [Arthur] – ten years older than I – was in hospital last year because he seemed to have something wrong with his prostate and was spending most of his nights traipsing to and fro to the house of necessity. But in hospital they catheterized him, and then began to shoot water into his bladder, which he obligingly shot out again, until he began to see the funny side of the affair, and broke into song – "Shall we gather at the river"* was his choice; he was roundly rebuked by the young black intern who was doing the work, for his senile frivolity. Subsequently he was dismissed with a few pills, and now sleeps like the babe new-born.

During the last two weeks Brenda and I have undergone a painful experience – the production* of my play *Pontiac and the Green Man*, in which she acted, and which had a very elaborate mounting. The newspapers fell upon it with whips and scorpions, but audiences were large and seemed pleased with what they got. But these public lambastings are hard to bear because, as one grows older, they tend to be from critics whom one regards as Young Squirts, while they regard one as an Old Fogy. But the book – *One Half [of Robertson Davies]* – is going well, and will appear in the U.S. next spring. Thank you for your very kind remarks about it, especially about the chapters on Good and Evil.* This is a theme that haunts me, and the older I grow the more pressing it becomes. How people manage who never attempt to come to terms with it is a never-ending puzzle. I am regarded with mirth by some of the theologues here at the university, because I am supposed to believe in the Devil, whom they have long dismissed as an Ignorant Superstition. But although they are infinitely subtle in their definitions of God (so subtle that He almost fails the test) they still seem to think of the Devil as a medieval bugaboo, without an ounce of subtlety to curse himself with. I don't suppose you run into theologues in your scientific world. Shits, most of them.

And as for academics! Of late I have been asked to assess several publication projects for our Humanities Research Council, which disperses money for publication. Should one laugh or weep? Jung is the new cure-all in Canadian criticism, and every dumb broad who has read a paperback introduction to his work wants to pour all literature into her own Jungian mill, and become rich and famous and awesome and tenured overnight. No wonder Jung shouted at Marie-Louise von Franz* – "Thank God I am Jung, and not a Jungian!" I am getting sick of the Zurich brethren – or rather their two-bit imitators. There is a priest just around the corner from me who is setting up what he calls Jungian Dance Therapy – you just let yourself go loose and dance away your Shadow. Jesus Murphy! I think the good father is on drugs, and wish his Archbishop would wall him up in the wine-cellar of a monastery. Indeed, I have some acquaintance with the Archbp – an eminently practical Irishman – and I might suggest it.

I have a vast program of work ahead of me, and sometimes I quake and grow pale, for it looks as if the Twilight Years, when I ought to be growing roses and sucking my dentures in peace, are going to be passed in back-breaking toil. But I keep hearing my mother's [Florence McKay Davies's]* voice saying "It is better to wear out than rust out." That's what a Calvinist upbringing does to you, and not all my fine Anglican prating* about Good and Evil really makes any difference.

Our very best love to Inge,* and to you, and may you soon be skipping like a lamb among the labs.

Rob.

To HORACE W. DAVENPORT

Massey College
University of Toronto
Sunday, Feb. 5: 1978

Dear Horace:

I should have written to you weeks ago to enquire how things went with your second operation,* but things have been in confusion here, because of 'flu hitting the family, and the College, and the usual uproar of Christmas. Brenda and I have both had the 'flu in various forms, because we don't seem able to shake it, and are at present recovering after a January bout. However, life must go on, so we take the odd day in bed and then crawl around, discharging such duties as cannot be put aside.

I am once again living out a lifelong pattern: people ask me to make speeches,* months before the speeches are to be given, and out of foolish good-nature, or because they back me into some sort of moral corner, I assent, and then in the course of time the dreadful day arrives. Later this week I must go to Calgary, to give tongue at the inauguration of a Faculty of Humane Studies, and return at the weekend only to dash to Montreal to speak again. Shortly afterward a speech for some authors' association must be done, and then I am whisked to Germany to give a couple of special lectures in, I understand, the Black Forest. (I hope this is true as I am very fond of the BF.) Then I come back to more speeches. This is pretty much in consequence of having published a book of speeches [*One Half of Robertson Davies*]; numerous critics said they were awful speeches –

pompous, old-fashioned, patronizing, facetious and everything that is vile – but the dreadful lust for oratory that afflicts the public generally has descended upon me in all its ravaging force, and I am plagued with requests. A friend of mine, Pierre Berton, who is much admired as a public figure, says he deals with this by applying a general rule: he speaks free to Boy Scouts and Worthy Causes, but to all others he says "$3500, please." The strange thing is that large numbers of institutions are beglamoured by this bowelless conduct, and fork over not only the fee, but also give him silver paper-knives, signed portraits of their committees, and additional gifts. I never ask for fees and if I get any I give them to the College Library. But I am going to have to take some strong position soon. I consider getting a card printed which says: "Professor Davies cannot accept invitations to speak as increasing age and infirmity make it impossible." If I did not have a red face and a fixed grin, I might be able to make this work.

I have writing I want to do. A play,* for which a good producing company has asked me, and another novel [*The Rebel Angels*]. Perhaps this summer.....

My retirement impends. According to College statute, I must retire in 1979, June 30. They may ask me to stay on for a while, and I have not yet made up my mind what to say. I like college life and I like teaching, but I am bloody sick of administration, and the endless legalistic haggling of student committees. Also, as I grow older, I suffer from one of the symptoms of approaching senility: I fear poverty. Unless the whole economy falls to ruin, I am not going to be poor (except in spirit) but I cannot shake off this foolish dread. I see myself, in broken boots and a threadbare overcoat, rummaging in garbage cans, while Brenda delivers washing from a child's waggon. Tell me, O man of medicine, is there any pill for this megrim? My children jeer at me; my wife explains the facts, with endless patience: but still I fear the Pinch of Poverty. I have known many people who displayed this unpleasing symptom. My late father [Rupert] avoided it spectacularly; he used to say that he had more money than he knew what to do with. But not me, alas.

I hope you are fit and spry. Do you remember Arthur Spring-Rice Pyper* at Balliol – an Irishman? He told me that once his father encountered a man he knew who had had his prostate removed, and asked him how things went, in consequence. "Aw, sure sorr, I can piss like a horse!" was the reply. Hoping you are the same.

Love from us both to both of you

Rob.

To THE EDITOR OF *THE NEW REPUBLIC**

Massey College
University of Toronto
May 1, 1978

Dear Sir:

In the course of reviewing a book of mine [*One Half of Robertson Davies*] in a recent issue of your publication, in which attention was given to several aspects of Canadian life as it is at present, Joyce Carol Oates* asserts strongly that we Canadians are making ourselves ridiculous in laying claim to a national literature. This may well be so; all manifestations of nationalism are likely to lurch into absurdity. However, it should be said that we have to be more vehement than is strictly prudent in order to persuade the world at large, and some of our own citizens, that we have any literature of any value whatever. It is little more than a century ago that the U.S. was in the same predicament, and English patronage was summed up in Sydney Smith's query,* "Who reads an American Book?" The situation in which Canada finds herself now is not less significant for us than the Civil War* was for you, and we hope to emerge strengthened in several respects, one of which will be the legitimate recognition at home and beyond our shores of whatever worthy literature we possess.

The expression, "Canada's leading man of letters," which Ms. Oates objects to so strongly when applied to myself, pleases me as little as it does her. Not only does it ignore the claims of better men;

it is itself a term somewhat outmoded and comic, belonging to the era of spats and piqué vest-edgings. But when it is used of me by people who mean it kindly, am I to be churlish and snarl? No, but I may be grateful to Ms. Oates, who has done so on my behalf.

About her strictures on my personal character it would be foolish for me to protest. We are not acquainted, and as she says she has read comparatively little of my work it must be assumed she has made her discoveries about me by divination. Critics have often laid claim to this power, and when Ms. Oates portrays me as a garrulous, self-delighted mountebank, and a covert undervaluer of women, I can only hang my head in shame, for when has any man known himself as well as a richly gifted observer knows him?

But when she says that I pay no heed to my fellow-writers in Canada, I must reply that for twenty years before Ms. Oates came to our country I was a weekly book-reviewer of some influence,* and every Canadian book of that period passed through my hands. I applied to these the standards I used in judging other books, and took pride in praising what many of them achieved, as chroniclers of life as it is lived in a country which I do not think Ms. Oates knows as well as she thinks she does.

Desolated as I am by her opinion, I have some hope that Ms. Oates may not have divined the whole truth about me. She confides to your readers that "Davies is said to regret that public floggings and hangings have been discarded." Who says it, I wonder? Whence comes this portrait of Davies, the Hangman's Friend? It is true that I sometimes take extreme views on controversial subjects in order to get the goat of campus sorceresses and others who will believe anything they hear, provided it be ugly enough; I have never been able to resist tormenting people who have no sense of humour.

Considering the character that has been ascribed to me by Ms. Oates it would be disingenuous if I were to subscribe myself "Yours sincerely" or "Yours faithfully," so I am content to remain,

Yours, writhing in deserved ignominy,

Robertson Davies

To ELISABETH SIFTON

Massey College
University of Toronto
July 10, 1978

Dear Elisabeth:

Thank you for the letter saying that *One Half Of [Robertson Davies]* is going pretty well; this somewhat surprises me; I could imagine people in Canada wanting to read it, but in the U.S. – I did not aspire so high. But recently I received a letter from a publicity girl with Penguin saying that I would no doubt have heard that Penguin are bringing it out. I had heard no such thing. Have you? She seemed to know what she was talking about but I would be glad of some certainty.

Is Viking ever looking for ideas? I have one. Why don't you bring out a really *good* edition of Victor Hugo's *Notre Dame de Paris*? Everybody has heard of it, several films have been made of it (all false to the original), the Hunchback is as well known in common speech as Frankenstein (it was his monster, but never mind). So far as I know, there are two translations, both bad. Nelson Classics contains one, which is so bowdlerized as to be a caricature of the original; Everyman contains one, with stupid additional material and awful translators' English of the "Figure to yourself, my reader..." variety. Both are rotten jobs of printing, the plates dating from before the First World War. Why bring the book out now? Well, if you happen not to have read it, it is about a very contemporary theme – a priest in love, frying for a beautiful gypsy girl; his reflections are remarkably contemporary, and he considers deserting the priesthood. The book is on the *Index Expurgatorius*. It is a stunning great archetypal story and melodrama of the high kind – Byron* rather than Boucicault. It wants an understanding, literate, poetical translation, and it wants an Introduction explaining what melodrama really is as compared with what most people think it is. After a handsome edition, a natural for Penguin.*

This thought arises because I am just reading *Notre Dame* for the fourth time because it has a bearing – a very oblique one – on my own new novel [*The Rebel Angels*], which I am working on every day; it also contains a priest (but an Anglican) who loves a gypsy girl (but she happens to be a Ph.D. candidate and rather rich) and he fears to approach her because he thinks he will look silly, as he is 42 and his reversed collar makes him an unchancy suitor. This is only part of the plot which at present looks more complicated than *War and Peace*. But I think it will boil down to one substantial book with romance, melodrama, gypsies, university people, a murder, a love philtre, and a few other makeweights so that I shall not be accused of wanting plot. I am enjoying the work greatly – which as you know means for an author that he is tortured, morose and intolerable to decent society. It is going to take a while in doing, but I calculate to have it in your hands by early spring of 1980, for fall publication (if you do not spurn it from you as it were a menstruous cloth* – one of my favourite Biblical quotes).

Next weekend my wife and I go to Middletown, to Wesleyan Univ., where I shall take part for the third and last time in the Readers–Writers Conference.* It is quite good as such things go, but enough is bloody well enough, and though most of the people are very nice, too many of them are wistful middle-aged people who can indeed write, but not quite well enough to achieve publication. I have ferreted out two in the past two years who were accepted by Curtis Brown,* but it is too painful to have to encourage the others who are in the so-near-and-yet-so-far category.

This goes on too long. Farewell, and warm greetings and please tell Richard Barber* and your nice assistant that I embrace them in the bowels of Christ. (As you see, I have been reading some pretty hefty theology.)

Rob. Davies

To TIMOTHY FINDLEY

Massey College
University of Toronto
July 10, 1978

*Timothy Findley (1930–   ) is a Canadian
novelist, playwright, scriptwriter, and
actor. Davies met him at the Summer
Theatre in Peterborough in the 1950s.*

Dear T. F.

Congratulations on your piece* in the *G&M* on July 8; you said
several things I would greatly like to have said, but I am at least a generation older than you, and among the writers of my age the self-
assurance to speak up in this way was lacking. We thought we were
not as two-bit as the Canadian reviewers did, and we thought Canada
was getting some writing that would one day be a source of pride,
but we didn't quite dare to say so. The reviewers would simply have
jeered, and the public would not have backed us up..... You are quite
right: Canada has the artists, but it has not the critics who should lead
the way in suggesting what is good about them, as well as what is
bad. It is the bland, ignorant patronage that stings; they don't know
good writing from bad, can't distinguish between one individual style
and another, and have no notion of the technical skill that goes into
such a novel as *The Wars*, for example. It is one of the bad jokes of
Canadian life that the critics, who criticise all the arts through the
medium of the art of writing, are themselves such terrible writers.

Result? We turn to the US for criticism that means anything. Our
academic critics do little for us; they are terribly afraid that they might
be caught backing a loser. But last Spring I visited the University of
Freiburg* and was astonished and delighted to meet a Dr. Konrad
Gross who seemed to know more about Canadian writing in both
languages than any Canadian academic I know except Malcolm Ross.*
Duke University now has a large sub-department on Canadian literature and Milwaukee has, as well. Strange that at home we do not
merit serious attention except from graduate students, whose critical
touch is like the caress of a bear – well-meant but deadly..... But this
goes on too long; again, congratulations –

Robertson Davies

To ANGELA FUSCO

Massey College
University of Toronto
August 16, 1978

Angela Fusco (1946–) is a Canadian actress. Davies and Brenda had seen her in campus productions when she was a student at the University of Toronto 1964–68.

Dear Angela:

My wife and I saw *Lady Audley['s Secret]** on Tuesday night and enjoyed it greatly. We were particularly pleased to see you, as it is years since we have done so, and we thought your performance [as Alicia] first-rate.

Why first-rate? Because you preserved an inner truth in your performance which gave it weight and force within the bounds of the burlesque of the old play. This is, of course, the great secret of farce; unless the actors take their situation with the uttermost seriousness the mainspring of the performance is uncoiled. Any suggestion of hinting to the audience – "Pretty funny, don't you think?" – wrecks the pleasure that farce can give. But *Lady Audley* never descended to that sort of thing. It was good-natured and charming in spirit; none of that jeering at grandpa that makes so many burlesques of nineteenth-century plays disagreeable. I will confess that we went with some apprehensions; cruel guyings of melodrama can be painful – but there was no hint of that at Niagara.

Old melodrama seems funny to us now, but for millions of people it once spoke with the voice of truth – because at its root there is a measure of truth, and the unacknowledged dreams of all sorts of people. (Who has not thought how convenient it would be to shove somebody down a well, or set fire to tiresome associates?) *Lady Audley* did not obscure the truth, although it was splendidly funny, and that is art on a high level..... And, I repeat, you had the trick of it superbly, and your glares of hate will long linger in my memory.

Yours sincerely,

Robertson Davies

To JOYCE CAROL OATES

September 7, 1978

[Dear Miss Oates:]

Joyce Carol Oates (1938–) is a prolific American author and professor of English. She had reviewed One Half of Robertson Davies *harshly in* The New Republic, *and Davies had responded vigorously.*

Your birthday card* finally reached me yesterday, and gave me a great chuckle. I hope it means we can now sheathe our daggers; I should like nothing better.

Do you ever get to Toronto on a Friday? On alternate Fridays Massey College has guests at High Table, and we would greatly like to entertain you. We have a variety of guests, as well as the Fellows of the coll., and we are not nearly such bad company as some people (who have not been there) pretend.

If there is any chance of this, I should be delighted to send you a list of possible dates, and you could make your choice.

With cordial good wishes,

[Robertson Davies]

To CORLIES M. SMITH

[Massey College
University of Toronto]
Sept. 7: 1978

Corlies M. Smith (1929–), American, was senior editor at The Viking Press in New York. He had been Davies' editor there from 1970 to 1972.

[Dear Cork:]

Many thanks for sending me the proofs of Daphne Athas's* book *Cora*; I read it with interest and a strong measure of envy, because it is a kind of book I could never write myself, cast in a form that is only possible in our time, and impossible for a writer of my age and background to adopt.

What enviable freedom of expression these young writers enjoy! And how it opens for them avenues of sensibility that have been closed since – since the beginning of time, I imagine. Of course like all gifts it brings traps and problems; being able to say whatever they want to say about sex, they tend to forget that it is not the only, or for many people the primary, preoccupation of life. Indeed in my next novel [*The Rebel Angels*] I hope to take a look at this matter. Since the new science and the new outlook have made sex primarily a *pleasure*, rather than a compulsion and a means of continuing the race, it is sometimes forgotten that there have been innumerable people who either put sex out of their lives, or decided that it would be a minor concern, and who then went on to do extraordinary things. Speaking, doubtless, from the pinnacle of my advanced age [65], I often wonder how the heroines and heroes of modern novels have any energy left for anything else. The heroines, of course, have the best of it; for them sex provides energy, whereas for the heroes it consumes energy, and those long, strenuous nights must make it difficult to cope with the problems of the day. A woman who is not wholly in the mood for intercourse has only to lie still, look ineffable things, and wait till it is over, whereas the man must produce his tablespoonful of library paste or be an object of mockery or, worse, compassion. There is no even-handed justice.

[With good wishes

Yours sincerely,

Rob.]

To THERESA RIORDAN

Massey College
University of Toronto
December 6, 1978

Theresa Riordan (1953–   ), Canadian,
was then in her first undergraduate year at
Simon Fraser University in British
Columbia. Her English professor had
guaranteed an A grade to any student who
suggested plausible symbolic references
for the names Milo Papple and Denyse
Hornick in Fifth Business. *She did not get*
an "A."

Dear Miss Riordan:

I wonder what your professor means when she speaks of "symbolic references" contained in the names of characters in *Fifth Business*. When a writer chooses the names for the characters in a book he is anxious to get them into the same key – to use a musical expression – and when Dickens christens leading characters Chuzzlewit, Pecksniff, and Gamp,* obviously all the other names in the book are going to be equally high-pitched: the names of characters in books by Henry James* tend to be upper-class American, and characters in books by Joseph Conrad* frequently have names which are slightly foreign to the ear of an English-speaking person. The names in *Fifth Business*, which are given to the Canadian characters, and particularly to those in the village of Deptford, are all quite familiar in Canadian ears and there are lots of Papples and Hornicks to be found in any large Canadian telephone directory. It is a wise rule never to assume the existence of a symbol where a meaning is apparent without it. People who disregard this rule are sometimes called "Symbol Simons."

Yours sincerely,

Robertson Davies

To ARNOLD AND LETITIA
EDINBOROUGH

Windhover
Caledon East
[end of December 1978]

*Arnold Edinborough (1922–   ) is an
English-born Canadian editor, publisher,
columnist, lecturer in English literature,
and writer. He and his wife, Letitia
(1923–   ), likewise an English-born
Canadian, had been friends of the
Davieses since the late 1940s.*

Dear Arnold & Letty:

Many thanks for the record of Paul Patterson's* music, to which
we have been listening with great satisfaction. Do you know him –
or of him?.... Hope Christmas went well for you; we had a jolly time,
though now and then I sense an ambiguity of emotion in myself, a
sense of "Out upon Christmas! What's Christmas but a time for
paying bills without money, a time for finding yourself a year older
and not an hour richer, etc." Old Ebenezer* was not wholly without
reason. Though it is not for riches I long, but for repose of soul, which
is apt to elude me when in the presence of my grandchildren. We
drove over to Hamilton on Christmas Day, to have midday dinner
with Rosamond & John [Cunnington] and their four young.* And I
discovered a great psychological truth: one arrives feeling quite spry
and even youthful, but after fifteen minutes with grandchildren one
has been forced into the grandpaternal role; one is, *nolens volens*, an
Old Geezer, falling asleep in front of the fire, trembling at loud
sounds, quavering "Oh my pet, do have a care of Mama's china!" and
whatnot. It takes at least a couple of days, and a lot of spiritual exercise like winking at girls in the street, to get one back to one's proper
sense of Robust Maturity..... The wonder of Christmas was the baby,
Cecilia, who held court and ruled her brothers absolutely; they shriek
with delight when she gives them a smile, and throw up their lunch
at her frown.

So, the Twelve Days pass, like giants in a pantomime. The Ghost
of Christmas Past makes his appearance, and I see myself, a loveable
child, bending happily over a bound volume of *Chums*,* while the
rest of the family whoops at me to Get Outside and Get Some Fresh

Air. Here is the Ghost of Christmas Present; a mad girl hacks the trollibobs off a taxi-driver she has slain,* and sticks them to her snatch with Krazy Glue. (Goodwill toward men.) Please, Mr. Coroner, could she pee through the new appendage? The Ghost of Christmas Yet to Come rises before me; hope springs eternal, and perhaps I may rise above Geezerdom. But these are idle fancies.

Whatever, we send you our love and our hearty good wishes for 1979; the year has an unlikely sound, but it is hard upon us. . . .

Rob & Brenda

PS: I have been reviewing A. L. Rowse's 3 vol *Annotated Shakespeare* for the *G&M*. What a mess! I feel sorry for A.L.R. but really he sits up & begs for condemnation. At it *again* with the Dark Lady!*

To MOIRA WHALON

[January 31, 1979]

Moira Whalon (1924–98), Canadian, was Davies' secretary from 1956 to 1995. She worked for him at the Peterborough Examiner, at Massey College, and, after his retirement from Massey in 1981, on a part-time basis until his death.

Would you please 'phone your friend, Heavenly-Gorgeous the Florist, & order *three* pots of chrysanthemums for Feb. 2ⁿᵈ (Wedding Anniv – 39ᵗʰ!) & could they be varied colours but if poss not that nasty brown?

To ARTHUR LLEWELLYN DAVIES

Massey College
University of Toronto
March 22, 1979

Arthur Llewellyn Davies (1903–96) was Davies' brother. He followed a career at the Kingston Whig-Standard 1926–69, becoming publisher and Chief Executive Officer in 1951 when his father, Rupert, retired. Queen's University, Kingston, Ontario, made him an Honorary Doctor of Laws on June 2. He and his second wife, Jean, spent time in Arizona each winter.

[Dear Arthur:]

I am replying immediately to your letter as I want to get this to you before you leave Arizona. Michael [Davies]* confided to us some time ago that you were going to be offered an honorary degree and we had made up our minds to be present for the occasion. I understand that Michael is combining it with a formal presentation of the room at the Grand Theatre* so it will be an interesting weekend. I am getting the plaque done for the room and I think it will be quite a handsome job.

I should be delighted to lend you Dad's Queen's LL.D. gown which I have, but, with the passing of time, the blue facings have faded to a dismal mauve. There are two things that can be done – we can get Harcourt's to replace the facings with new silk, or you can wear it as it is and make some jokes in your speech about its age and associations and the pride that it gives you to wear it. I recommend the second course, but you may have different ideas; I think it would be interesting to let Convocation know that our family has been associated with Queen's since 1926.

There is no academic cap with the gown and my recollection is that Queen's honorary doctors do not wear them, however, if they do the university registrar will have a variety of caps in the robing room and will fit you with one.

Of course we are very proud that you are getting this degree and I hope you will work hard on your speech, as there will be quite an assemblage of the family there. Jenny and Tom [Surridge] and John and Rosamond [Cunnington] will certainly be there, but Miranda [Davies]* cannot make it. I expect there will be others of the tribe present but I do not know about them just now.

With love to you and Jean,

[Rob.]

To GORDON ROPER

Massey College
University of Toronto
March 29, 1979

Gordon Roper (1911–   ), Canadian, was a professor of English at the University of Toronto 1946–69 and at Trent University in Peterborough 1969–75. He has been a senior fellow at Massey College since 1961. From the 1940s he was an intimate friend and an early astute reader of Davies' novels. He had been gathering material for a book on Davies and his work since 1968.

Dear Gordon:

It is generous of you to hand over to Michael Peterman,* because I know how much the book meant to you, and doubtless means still. Nevertheless, a situation had arisen which could only be solved by heroic measures; I felt long ago that the book had become an obsession with you, and that the obsession was not really with the subject (because what there is to say about me can be said pretty briskly and economically) but with some very deep concern about the scholar who lies so deep within yourself. It would be impertinent for me to try to guess what that is, but I suppose it relates to your deeply held feelings about Canadian literature, for one thing. And for another, I think it has some roots in your discovery that I am not really the man you think I am or would wish me to be. You have known for many years that many writers are two-sided – good father, kind colleague, faithful husband, encourager of the young and modest as the violet

BUT also raging egotists who would boil their grannies down for soup, rob the blind and kick the crutches from under the paraplegic, and paranoid to a degree that even Freud could not stand – and that they combine all this with a toughness that masquerades as wincing sensitivity. You smelled this in me and – kind and truly good man that you are – it pained you, and you didn't want to write about it. But because you are a scholar, and have forsworn the pleasures of hypocrisy when it is a matter of your work, you felt you ought to give just the teeniest hint..... Well, I think Peterman will take that load off your shoulders.

BUT – the book is yours, and I deeply hope and indeed insist that when it appears it will be your book, with all that is generous and necessary in acknowledging Michael's work. I know you, Roper: you will *give away* that book if you are not prevented. Don't you go fer to do it! Michael understands. He is a first-rate fellow and he has your number, and won't put up with any self-sacrifice.

Enough of that. I went to San Francisco in February to talk to their Analytical Psychology Society – a public lecture and a three-day seminar. It went really well. There were over 500 at the lecture, and the seminars were very enjoyable. And what was I talking about? About being a writer, in Jungian terms. Where the stuff comes from, what happens to it, how the unconscious and the conscious must be allowed to kiss and commingle, and then how the conscious has to do the editing. And in addition, what Nabokov* says is the only quality that distinguishes good writing from bad, which he calls *shamanstvo*, a Russian word which means "quality of enchantment," and which cannot really be learned or dissected, because it is different in every writer who has it. I enjoyed doing it, and it was possible with that audience, but I would not want to try it on hearers who have no idea of the Jungian lie of the land. (Last week I was visited by one such, _____, a teacher who seems not to believe in the imagination, is determined that every part of a book or a play *must* in some way be drawn from life, and wholly innocent of what part language plays in literary composition; after she left me I was in despair – is it for these people one writes?) But I certainly would not talk in this way to some of the High School students who have been visiting me recently, and who are prone to begin "What you're trying to say is –" after which comes something that *they* are trying to say, and which would not have occurred to me.

I gather from Moira [Whalon] that you are taking things very quietly. Yes, but the mind never takes things quietly. If I were you I wouldn't take too seriously what the doctors say about not writing. Not now, certainly, but in a year – because you are undoubtedly writing in your head. Doctors don't understand people like us. They think you can turn off a lifetime's preoccupation like a tap. Ho, ho, ho!

Term is winding up, and you know what that means in meetings, committees and the hubbub of the Ivory Tower. But then I shall get away and make a start on my new novel [*The Rebel Angels*], for which I now have notes extending almost to a book in themselves. It is going to be more complex than what I have been doing and I may fall on my rump from a vast height. But the risk is the thrill.

I know Helen* is keeping watch over you – our love to you both –

Rob.

Time, stay thy flight,
   Move ne'er an inch —
Arrested, thou,
      By Robert Finch:
Thy hand, on us
      So grave, so weighty,
Seems thistle-down
      When Robert's eighty.

— with affectionate greetings
from Brenda & Roh.

SECTION

II

he first draft of *The Rebel Angels* occupied Davies from April 13, 1979, to June 30, 1980. As was usual with his novels, he revised this first typed draft by hand; his secretary, Moira Whalon, then typed a fresh copy, and he made revisions on that by hand; finally she made a new fair copy for his publishers, completing it in January 1981. In the ensuing months he answered editorial queries and proofread the final text. Through the fall of 1981 and the spring of 1982, now 68, he endured (and, to a degree, enjoyed) very demanding publicity tours in Canada and the United States.

Davies was immensely productive as an author in these years. He wrote speeches, articles and reviews, made selections and prepared an introduction for *The Penguin Stephen Leacock*, and – a new venture – created a lively libretto for *Dr. Canon's Cure*, an opera for children. He began to have ideas for a new novel even before he finished the first draft of *The Rebel Angels*. He continued to reply to the many readers who sent him letters. And, as always, he would write when something in the newspaper or on television caught his attention. Through translations, his novels now began to be accessible to more and more readers.

On February 2, 1980, he and Brenda celebrated 40 years of an immensely successful marriage. Apart from the colds and bouts of influenza that had always plagued him, Davies' health continued to be good.

His responsibilities as an administrator and teacher came to an end with his retirement from Massey College at the end of June 1981. That month, he and Brenda moved out of the Master's Lodgings into a condominium within walking distance of the College, and Davies took possession of a suite of rooms in the College's northeast corner as his base for work in Toronto. From this point on he and Brenda lived at their country house during the summer, over Christmas, and for four days of every week during the academic year. The remaining three days they lived in their condominium in town, days when Davies met interviewers, worked on one book or another, and, with the help of his secretary, Moira Whalon, dealt with his business correspondence.

↜

TO THE EDITOR OF *THE GLOBE AND MAIL**

[Massey College
University of Toronto]
April 23, 1979

Sir:

In your issue of Monday, April 23, Mr. Scott Symons* graciously names me as the Dowager Duchess of Canadian Literature. But surely Mr. Symons knows that under Canadian Law it is impossible for me to accept a title from any Queen whatever?

Faithfully yours,

[Robertson Davies]

To AN AMERICAN READER

[Massey College
University of Toronto]
May 8, 1979

This reader had written two years running to ask: "Will civilization, as we know it, survive the century?" Davies had also answered the first letter.

[Dear _____:]

In reply to your letter of April 11th, I think the answer to your question must be – civilization will certainly survive, but also certainly not in the form in which we know it. It is essential that civilization should constantly change. If you visit New York within the next few weeks you could see there a superb exhibition representing the civilization that existed in Pompeii in 79 A.D.; it is enviable but it is certainly not civilization as we know it.

Yours sincerely,

[Robertson Davies]

To ELISABETH SIFTON

Massey College
University of Toronto
May 16 '79

Dear Elisabeth:

It was a great pleasure to see you in New York, and I write to thank you for taking Brenda and me to lunch at Le Provencal. We enjoyed it greatly; I am always amused when I see scenes in the movies in which publishers and authors lunch together, and there is a great deal of sharp-edged conversation, getting drunk, and often exchanges of blows; my own experience is that these affairs are among the most

civilized that come my way (though once I was with Alfred Knopf*
when he savaged a waiter, and Salvador Dali,* at the next table, raised
his eyebrows and popped his eyes to such a degree that I feared they
might leave their moorings and bounce about the floor – Alfred was
cross because the man brought some sherry which was not up to his
exacting standards). We returned to Le Provencal the next day, not
because of any barrenness of inspiration but because we could not find
Quo Vadis, which was somewhere nearby, but under wraps.

I write also to thank somebody at Viking – and it may indeed have
been you – who recently sent me a handsome leather-bound copy of
World of Wonders, so now I have all three in gorgeous array.

Little by little I gnaw away at university obligations, and hope that
by next weekend I shall be able to begin seriously on the next book
[*The Rebel Angels*]. I had a queer experience on Monday, at the oral
examination of a Ph.D. candidate: he wrote of *World of Wonders* in
his thesis and made much of the fact that its hero was christened Paul,
and that his life story exactly paralleled that of Saint Paul! I said mildly
that this had not occurred to me: he replied, with an indulgent smile,
that many things appear to the critical reader of a book which have
eluded the attention of the author, and this gave the book "resonance." For me, the resonance of a dull thud.

Our love to you, and also to Richard [Barber].

Rob. Davies

To SIGMUND HOFTUN

Massey College
University of Toronto
August 13, 1979

Sigmund Hoftun (d. 1985) worked for the Norwegian publisher Gyldendal Norsk Forlag in Oslo. Because the firm wanted to present the quotation from Tho. Overskou at the beginning of Fifth Business *in the original Danish, Hoftun had solicited Davies' assistance in locating it in the many-volumed* Den Danske Skueplads.

Dear Mr. Hoftun:

In reply to your enquiry about the quotation from Tho. Overskou's *Den Danske Skueplads* in *Fifth Business* I have a confession to make — it is not from Overskou, because I invented it.

The reason was that I had invented the term Fifth Business,* which worried my publishers here greatly; the English director of Macmillans, Alan Maclean, was particularly concerned, and asked me if I could not find a quotation or definition to support it. I thought this was absurd because surely it is an author's gift to invent — to be what used to be called in English "a maker"; but if they wanted a quotation I would give them one, and I attributed it to Overskou. As a theatre student I knew of his great work, and had been assured by Danish colleagues that it was not read in its entirety by many people. Until now the secret has been complete; the publishers had the quotation they wanted and everybody seemed happy.

Perhaps you could use the story of this mild hoax as publicity for the book. I know it is supposed to be dreadful to fake references, but when people insist on quotations that do not already exist, what is an author to do?

Sincerely yours,

[Robertson Davies]

To J. G. MCCLELLAND

Massey College
University of Toronto
September 10, 1979

Dear Jack:

Thanks for including me among those who received your Preview Edition of Margaret Atwood's *Life Before Man*. I read it with keen professional interest because it is a novel of a type and on a theme quite outside my own range; this subtle anatomization of the relationships and emotions of people between thirty and forty is something I would not dare to attempt, because I see little of it, and what I do see is coloured by the way in which the people involved present themselves to somebody of my age. Consequently it is a matter of importance and revelation when I find it so intimately and feelingly set forth as in Margaret Atwood's novel.

The theme may be outside my range as an author, but I am very well able to appreciate the technical adroitness with which she handles the material, the shifts in time, the changes from character to character, and the presentation of more than one feminine point of view. I was not so much disturbed by this novel as by *Surfacing*, but I was more fully involved – if I am not making a foolish distinction.

An aspect of the novel I thought wholly admirable was its evocation of the city of Toronto. On this continent few cities have a recognizable literary character: New York, Boston, Chicago, San Francisco and New Orleans – that just about sums it up. In Canada there are none, as yet, but Toronto is beginning to figure in the imagination of readers as a city with a distinct literary personality, owing to the work of Morley Callaghan* and a handful of others; *Life Before Man* is a splendid addition to this group of novels, which I think important if we are ever to have a literature in any serious sense. The variety of character, background and outlook is brilliant and, if Toronto has any sense of itself, reassuring.

Congratulations to you and congratulations to Margaret, and also my sincerest thanks.

Yours sincerely,

Rob. Davies

To ELWY YOST

Massey College
University of Toronto
October 29, 1979

Elwy Yost (1925–   ), Canadian, was the host of "Saturday Night at the Movies" on TVOntario from 1974 to 1999. He "loved that letter from Robertson Davies," but was unable to acquire TV rights for the requested films, as he regretfully explained by letter and in person during a chance encounter in the lobby of the Varsity Cinema in Toronto.

Dear Elwy Yost:

My wife and I agree that it would be very ill-natured of us to go on enjoying your Saturday Night at the Movies program without writing to tell you how much pleasure it gives us. We were particularly delighted last Saturday night to see the two horror films, and especially *The Queen of Spades*,* which has long been a favourite with us. I was very sorry to learn from your remarks that Yvonne Mitchell is dead, for she was an actress we both admired greatly, and certainly she was one of the most intelligent members of her profession.

You invite your viewers to make suggestions about films they would like to see on the Saturday night program: may we propose two which are really filmed performances of plays, and both belong to the early days of the talkies. One is *The Guardsman*,* in which Lynn Fontanne and Alfred Lunt appeared, and also Roland Young. It was a marvellous film but too stagey to have wide popularity. The other is *The Man from Blankley's** in which John Barrymore appeared and in which, in my opinion, he gave one of the finest high-comedy performances of his career. It was made before the bottle finally claimed him. This also relied heavily on a late Victorian play by Frederick Anstey and it was a popular vehicle of that greatest of high comedians, Charles Hawtrey, whom Barrymore admired enormously and from whom he said he had copied his own comedy technique.

If it is ever possible to show one or both of these films you can count on at least two delighted viewers. Meanwhile thanks, and all good wishes.

Yours sincerely,

Robertson Davies

To DOUGLAS LOCHHEAD

Massey College
University of Toronto
January 9, 1980

Douglas Lochhead (1922–), Canadian
poet, librarian, bibliographer, professor,
and printer, was the librarian at Massey
College 1963–75. His father, Alan Grant
Lochhead, died January 5. Jean was
Douglas Lochhead's wife.

Dear Douglas:

We were all sorry to read in *The Globe and Mail* of your Father's death. Ninety is a good old age, and I hope he enjoyed it to the end and had a good swift passage. Nonetheless the loss of a father is a heavy blow, whenever it comes; there is a strong strain of Hamlet in us all. I remember losing my own Father and Vincent Massey within a few months of each other, and although Vincent was by no means a father to me, he was a figure of special authority with whom I had worked, and his loss left me bereft. As for my own Father, he was what I suppose many fathers are – authority, but also an embracing geniality and a link with the past, a window through which one glimpsed uncounted ancestors, and I suppose also "a cloud of witnesses."* When my Father died, much of Wales seemed to be taken from me.

I retire in the June of 1981, so I have about 18 months more here. I have done about all I can do, I think, and it is time for a man with some new ideas. There is talk of establishing a Centre for Advanced Studies in this university, and it might have its focus here. I should be very glad if it were so, because it would realize one of my most strongly held ambitions for this place, which the Masseys set going as a college without any college reality – no scholarship and not even (if they had had their way) a library. But I think there is going to be the usual academic dog-fight, with a faction wanting the Mastership to go to some good, safe fellow who "deserves" something, rather than to somebody who can bestow something. We shall see.

Our love and sympathy to you and Jean.

Rob. Davies

PS: I hear Gordon Roper is holding his own, but must be careful.

To ARNOLD AND LETITIA EDINBOROUGH

Massey College
University of Toronto
Feb. 19, Trudeausday,* 1980

Dear Arnold & Tish:

I am late in writing to you to thank you for your delightful speech at our 40th anniversary celebration; it was in your finest manner – elegant, witty and generous, and we were very happy to have such an old friend to call on, for it is a situation that demands grace and fine feeling, qualities so often wanting in – for instance – speeches at weddings. How often I have heard uncles – but enough, the recollections are too dreadful.

I am late, as I think you know, because Brenda and I have been spending a week at Queen's [University], where I was the Brockington

Visitor. This means that I was chained to the chariot-wheel of _____, a man of unbounded energy – especially when it is somebody else's – and extraverted* nature. I gave tongue, chewed the rag and sounded off my big bazoo all day for five days, and ended the week quite hoarse and somewhat depleted in spirit. (On Tuesday talked from 10 a.m. to 11 p.m. including meals!) But on the whole it was great fun, and my affection for Queen's was sustained and increased; I know, I think, what it is that wins and holds enthusiasts like Sarah-Jane [Edinborough];* it is still a comprehensible university, without being a hick college, and its surroundings dispose to learning; Kingston is a beautiful place.

Everything went well, with one or two minor mishaps. I had an unseemly wrangle with some undergraduates who were hog-wild for Canada to open her doors to all U.S. draft-dodgers, and who were convinced that all criminals – especially sex-criminals – are SICK and need love . . . . I got myself into trouble when I said merrily that I had had almost all the childhood diseases, but false compassion had not been one of them; this was in answer to a boy with a mouth like a hen's ovipositor who asked me if I had not been more liberal in my opinions before I GOT SO OLD..... I also had some problems with the Department of Religious Studies when their top man, one _____, informed me that he and all Christians must forever feel GUILT because of the holocaust. When I said that I thought education was no barrier to salvation, a solemn Lutheran (weighing in at about 325 lb) asked me why I thought Christ chose simple men as his disciples. I replied that I supposed he did not have much chance to mix with a better set, and that Christianity had not really got off the ground till the coming of Paul, obviously a university man as he had sat at the feet of Gamaliel.* This attempt at merriment was received without mirth. I was confirmed in my opinion that I do not get on well with the Professionally Good.

(Was interviewed by an undergrad paper & quoted Henrik Ibsen – identified later in print as Henry Gibson.)

The worst experience, however, the Pits, was my visit to the Humanities Society. I had been told they numbered 75–100, but this was obviously in the eye of faith; about 30–35 turned up, all professors and all with the professorial idea that their job was to wrestle the speaker and show themselves his superiors. Questions opened with a Weasel Scot who said: "D'ye *really* know anything aboot this Yoong, or did ye juist mug up eneuch o' his stuff to write that noavel?" I replied winsomely that I had been reading Jung for 30 years, and that *The Manticore* had been kindly received in Zürich, where they were in a position to judge. There followed sundry philosophers, whose questions were in the form of statements – long statements. A French philosopher spoke at some length about Rabelais,* whom I had mentioned as a humanist; did I think Rabelais had been a heretic? I thought he had been a Protestant, at a time when that was about the same as being a Marxist Mole in modern terms. I was seized with unseemly giggles, for I suddenly realised that I was speaking to that widespread body Stephen Leacock* lumped together as the Owls' Club. You remember? Indeed, the president even requested those who had not yet paid their fees to arrange to do so with the secretary, Mr. Somebody, as they left. Leacock said these affairs always ended with the president saying "And if any of you have not yet paid your dollar this year, will you please give it to me or Mr. Sibley as you pass out.".... But in general it was great fun, and the faculty and undergraduates were splendid company, and _____ confided to me that it had always been his opinion that George Herbert Clarke* was an ass, and that the *Quarterly* – called by Clarkey the *KEWkew* – was a fitting reflection of Clarkey's spirit. Queen's – apart from the Owls' Club – does not seem to be as sour as the U of T – but of course I do not know it from inside.

So there you are; that's why I have not written before. Love and all good wishes to you & Tish. Consider yourselves invited to our 80th; we shall try to dig up some better wine.*

Rob.

*Queen's has a lot of wine but I think they make it themselves out of dried apples & Dͬ Ralston's Gripe Water.

To JOHN SMALLBRIDGE

Massey College
University of Toronto
March 27, 1980

John Smallbridge (1928–   ) was a
professor of English at the University of
Western Ontario when he decided to
pursue a doctorate in 1968. Davies
became his thesis supervisor. He laid the
groundwork for the thesis during a
sabbatical year abroad in 1975–76, but
lost momentum when he returned to
teaching and administration, and in the
end decided not to complete it.

Dear John:

What ails you is a distressing psychological complaint called "thesis abdabs" and there is no way of curing it except to press on courageously and dismiss from your mind worries about where the comment on Sturge Moore* ought to be placed; if the shape of your thesis is right – which I expect it is – things of this kind are not of great significance. What you have to do is finish it and get it off your chest.

One of my chief criticisms of the Ph.D. process is that a great many well qualified people, like yourself, work too long on a theme and become obsessed by it. I expect you have dreadful surges of feeling in which you think that what you have written resembles nothing so much as a mud pie. On the basis of what I have seen of your work in the past I know this to be most unlikely. So take a very deep breath and *get it finished*.

I can see you on April 16th, preferably in the morning, but it may be that the afternoon is more suitable for you. You should have seen me long ago: one of the principal jobs of a thesis supervisor is to pump encouragement into the candidate.

With good wishes,

Yours sincerely,

Robertson Davies

To ROBERT FINCH

[May 14, 1980]

> *Robert Finch (1900–95) was a poet, painter, harpsichordist, respected scholar of seventeenth- and eighteenth-century French poetry, and a senior fellow at Massey College 1961–95. This birthday greeting was written on a postcard of Bronzino's* An Allegory of Time *(the painting figures prominently in* What's Bred in the Bone*).*

Time, stay thy flight,
　　Move ne'er an inch –
Arrested, thou,
　　By *Robert Finch*:
Thy hand, on us
　　So grave, so weighty,
Seems thistle-down
　　When *Robert*'s eighty.

– with affectionate greetings
from Brenda & Rob

To ELISABETH SIFTON

Windhover
Caledon East
July 2, 1980

Dear Elisabeth:

On June 30 I finished my novel [*The Rebel Angels*] – or perhaps it would be proper to say the novel finished *me*, for I have never had so much trouble bringing a book to a close. I am a terrible fidget about *form*, and the thing was pitifully ragged and messy. But now it goes to my secretary who will make a clean copy, which I shall then revise extensively, and the final text should reach you for your esteemed consideration early in the New Year – which I gather is necessary if it is to be an autumn book in 1981. But the heavy work is done: I like revising.

The title I propose is *The Rebel Angels*. In one of the Gospels* that did not quite make it into the Bible there is an account of a War in Heaven other than Lucifer's, in which some angels defied God and descended to earth and taught some of God's knowledge to men – but especially to women, with whom they are great favourites. My three principal characters are two university professors, and a girl with whom they are professorially in love; they are her Rebel Angels and teach her a lot, and are somewhat dashed when she deserts them to marry a man of her own age. Half the story is told by the girl, and half by one of the profs, in alternate sections. But as you will understand – the novel being by me – there is a good deal of whoop-de-do, magic, strange goings-on, and even a murder, which is accomplished in a fashion decidedly unusual, and for a reason which, as a publisher, ought to give you a sly smile – he does it to create interest and publicity for a book he has written! Don't tell your publicity department; it might lead to ugly doings in the world of letters. There are also Dirty Bits; not pornographic, just dirty. I hope you will like it. I think it is funny, but not silly-funny. . . .

I hardly know if I ought to mention this, but the principal reason why I found it so hard to finish the novel was because I was already plagued by ideas for a sequel [*What's Bred in the Bone*]. Therefore I had to decide whether to turn off the tap sharply and forever on the last page, or leave a few strings dangling – which is what, in the end, I did. But if there is a sequel it will be a while coming, for in the year before me I have to wind up my twenty years at the College, arrange to move – which assumes proportions as though Louis XIV had to get out of Versailles . . . .

But God's time is best.
Good wishes to all friends at Viking –

Rob. Davies . . . .

To JOHN FRASER

Windhover
Caledon East
December 28, 1981 [1980]

John Fraser (1944–), Canadian journalist
and Beijing correspondent for The Globe
and Mail 1977–79, had recently published
The Chinese: Portrait of a People (1980).
He was editor of Saturday Night from
1987–94 (Davies twice served as its
literary editor) and in 1995 he became the
fourth Master of Massey College.

Dear John:

I have put off writing to you about *The Chinese* until I should have had time to read it and think about it, and now I have done both, which I hope gives colour to my opinions. I am sure you realize that it is not simply an immediate success, but the first big step in what could be a very distinguished career. It is the best kind of reporting, because it is not reporting at all in the customary use of the word; you do not seek incidents and experiences, like the usual "man abroad" – incidents and experiences seek you, and this is because of a special quality in your nature of receptive humanity coupled with good sense and a judgement which is beyond the mere reporter's cynicism (which so often conceals a foolish sentimentality). Jungians have a special term for this matter of encountering what is important and necessary at the right time: they call it "synchronicity" – meaning a kind of falling-together of circumstances. You cannot compel it, but you can be ready for it and worthy of it. You have also a quality as rare as hen's teeth in the journalistic world, and I hope it will not embarrass you if I define it as love; you really and truly do care about people. Such journalists are few.

This is what "style" really means – this *personal* voice – so different from mere "personality."

So what now? I wish you could write about Canada as you have written about China, for what you call institutionalized stupidity is as common here as anywhere, and our present mess* about the constitution, the intransigence of the premiers and the infatuation of the P.M. [Pierre Elliott Trudeau] with that most delusive of will-o'-the-

wisps, a Bill of Rights, is only one evidence of it. The brouhaha at
Stratford,* so shallowly handled in the *G&M*, is another sign of the
same pitiful mutton-headedness and trust in simple-minded concepts.
But I don't suppose the *G&M* would allow any such serious, loving
survey of the country; they preferred the posturings of Scott Symons.*

You will find something, and something will find you and will not
let you go. I know you far too well to adjure you not to be led astray
by the people who will insist that they know how to use your abilities better than you do. I have myself often been cast in the role of
the *idiot savant* by such people, and they are the real enemies, these
well-meaning, stupid advisors. There is only one agency that knows
best for you, and that is not-quite-yourself, but something nearer
yourself than anybody else. And it will tell you what's what. I am
beginning to sound like a fairground gypsy and had better shut up.
But I am sure you know what I mean.

I retire next June 30 – from the university, that's to say. But I have
enough work piled up to keep me going until extreme senility takes
over. . . . including trying to make some sense of the diaries I have
been keeping all my life. Whether this will result in an autobiography or not I can't say, because I regard autobiographies as a pernicious
form of fiction, but something might result, especially from my
Theatre Diaries. . . .

Now, St. Joan, take heed of what your Voices say to you. They may
drive you to the stake but they won't tell you any lies.

I value more than I can tell you the generous letter that came with
the book.

All good wishes for 1981 –

Rob.

To MOIRA WHALON

Windhover
Caledon East
December 28, 1980

Dear Moira:

Many thanks for all your kindnesses, and the gifts at Christmas, especially the *Dictionary of Angels** into which I have been dipping with great satisfaction and frequent loud laughter. I am making a notation in it that it is a gift from you, and that I received it *after* completing *Rebel Angels* so that no know-it-all academic nuisance will be able to say in future that I cribbed from it. A poor author can hardly draw a free breath nowadays.

We had a very jolly Christmas. Rosamond and John [Cunnington] and the children came here for Boxing Day, and as Miranda [Davies] was with us it made more of a family party than we usually have. The children are in great nick, and we scored heavily with Christopher by giving him a *Children's Encyclopaedia of Science* – a new Stoicheff,* that one. Piers is studying the piano, and we gave him a book of songs, which he assures me is well within his grasp, but that may have been pardonable swank. Cecilia, we are agreed, already has the Indian Sign on the three boys, reducing them to pitiful peonage. My God, what an easy time women have in this world! She is the one who knocks balls off the Christmas tree and looks innocent as her father denounces the boys.

Brenda asks me to leave a space on this letter for her, and I shall do so, but not before thanking you again and wishing you every happiness in 1981.

R. D.

NOTE: The picture you put on the angel book of the Angel & the Dog is obviously from the Apocrypha: *Book of Tobit*. Tobit had an angel guardian and a doggy chum, & was thus a good Jungian, in touch with both the divine & the animal aspects of his nature.

To ELISABETH SIFTON

Massey College
University of Toronto
January 12, 1981

Dear Elisabeth:

At last I have read *The White Hotel** which you sent me, I am
ashamed to say, early in November. But I am sure you know how hard
it is to find time to read a book of that sort. It is not that there is no
time – as the clock measures it – but there must be the *right* time or
it is unfair to the author. But I have now read it, and here goes –

I gather that you are enthusiastic about the book, and with reason.
There is so much about it which is admirable and, from another
writer's point of view, enviable. What a capacity for *impersonation*,
which is rarer among novelists than one might suppose. The author's
ability to write a Freudian case-history which might well have come
from the pen of Dr. Freud makes my eyes bulge; I have in my time
read a lot of Freud's work of this kind, and the impersonation is
uncanny. And what a splendid idea – to work over the same material
in several different forms – as poetry (which I did not think half so
bad as the author kept saying it was), as naked fantasy revealed to the
analyst, as the analyst's write-up of the case, as straight biography, as
terrifying history, and finally as a sort of Epilogue After Death –
breath-taking! Great imaginative scope, and splendid control, for
there must have been times when the lure of melodramatic colour
must have been extreme. I cannot guess the author's sex, though I
suspect it is a man; it is usually men who make as much of women's
menstrual functions as in this book, because they are fascinated by
them and rather fear them. The impact of the book is extraordinary,
and I thank you warmly for letting me in on it.

If I were to make a negative criticism, which indeed is not so much
a criticism as a confession of personal prejudice, it is that the control
in the book may be a bit too perfect. I should have liked to be permitted to *like* the chief character more unreservedly. Yet – I am aware

that this would have lessened the sort of impact the author seems determined to make. But I felt a lack of what *Nabokov* calls *shamanstvo** – the enchanter-quality; it is a teeny bit clinical. But obviously the author is not a romantic, like me.

My gobbet of unrestrained romanticism [*The Rebel Angels*] should reach you in February. Meanwhile, thanks and good wishes –

Yours sincerely,

Rob. Davies

To THE EDITOR OF *THE GLOBE AND MAIL**

Massey College
University of Toronto
January 12, 1981

Sir:

I was sorry to read the brief note in your newspaper recording the death, on Christmas Day, of Fred Emney, the comedian, at the age of eighty. But your comment said nothing about the fact that Emney toured in Canada with The Dumbells* during the late 'twenties and early 'thirties, and was a great favourite in Canada.

He was a wonderfully funny man, huge in bulk, grave and courteous in manner, and usually dressed in tweeds that could hardly be believed, they were so extraordinary. His monocle and cigar were marks of his indefeasible Britishness, as were also his upper-class speech and reserved manner. There hung about him at all times an air of astonishment that he should find himself in the company of tear-away comics like Pat Rafferty and Red Newman, but he was far too polite to say so. Astonishment and incomprehension were the tools of his trade as a comedian.

He played the piano splendidly – better, in my opinion, than Chico Marx* – seeming to hit the notes by inadvertence, rather than intention. It is not easy to play the piano absent-mindedly, and at ferocious speed.

He gave us enormous pleasure, and I should not like to think that no word of appreciation was offered about his Canadian appearances.

Yours faithfully,

Robertson Davies

To THE EDITOR OF *CHIRON*

Massey College
University of Toronto
February 11, 1981

Chiron *was the newsletter of the Analytical Psychology Society of Toronto. Davies and his daughter Rosamond were members.*

[Sir:]

I was greatly struck by the letter in your February issue from Rosamond Cunnington, a writer unknown to me personally, but with whom I am in strong agreement in her suggestion that our Prime Minister, Mr. Trudeau, is an astonishing exemplification of the *puer aeternus* archetype. I have thought for some time that Canada's political soul calls loudly for Jungian examination because the application of even the barest principles of that cast of thought to some of our actions in the past yields astonishing illumination. Ms. Cunnington speaks of Canada as having "a negative mother complex of daemonic proportions." I am sure that she is right and it takes no Zurich wizard to identify that mother as Great Britain, whose calm and almost unaware acceptance of our loyalty since 1776 is extremely irksome. We were, after all, the Good Daughter who remained faithful to Mother when the Naughty Daughter* ran off to paddle her own canoe. Is it too much to see in the extreme protestations of loyalty to the British crown, which are sometimes heard in Canada, an over-protest which seeks to quiet a deep sense of grievance? It is not enough to say that Canada at the moment stands at a cross-roads; it is important that we should not do the usual Canadian thing and try to go in all four directions at once.

In only one thing am I slightly in disagreement with Ms. Cunnington and that is in her suggestion that the late Mackenzie King* was also a *puer aeternus*. A recent reading of Rix Weaver's fascinating book, *The Old Wise Woman*,* convinced me that it was in this category that Mr. King belonged and never more so than during the 1939–45 war when he urged this country to "put on the whole armour of God"* and immediately reduced the proof strength of alcoholic liquors sold in Canada – a national weakness which has never been made good.

Yours sincerely,

Robertson Davies

To HORACE W. DAVENPORT

Massey College
University of Toronto
Feb. 26, 1981

Dear Horace:

I have been neglecting you shamefully – two or three communications from you and not a peep out of me. Excuses, as usual. (1) I ruptured myself* quite extensively last November, coughing, if you can believe such a thing, and in January had to go into hospital to have it put right. Went very well – excellent surgeon, nice hospital, good healing and all that – but was rather more of a knock than I had been led to believe. But I am much better now, and ready for all the hauling and lugging that goes with our move in June. (2) I have completed and sent off my latest novel [*The Rebel Angels*], and the response from the publishers has been encouraging, but it took a lot of doing and has left me tired. The scientific passages in it will no doubt have you helpless with mirth, but I done my best, and what can man do more? But now, at last, I am able to write. Brenda has gone off to Australia for three weeks, to settle up some family business and to see her sister [Maisie Drysdale]* & her sister's husband [Sir Russell Drysdale], who . . . [is very ill]. Poor man, he is a distinguished painter and a great talker . . . . But a big exhibition of his stuff is planned in Melbourne, and B. will be there for the opening.

This business of retiring puts a lot of extra work on me, getting things ready to hand over to my successor, and in addition a lot of university groups think it would be just wonderful if I would come and talk to them about what I have been doing for the past 20 years, and I cannot refuse them all. Universities like to get the last drop out of the lemon before throwing it away. But they are giving me an honorary degree next autumn, which they do not do for many of their former faculty, so I regard it as a great honour; the only trouble is, if they have read the novel before Convocation they may strangle me with the hood. I mean it to be a celebration of whatever is great in universities, but I am somewhat chilled when my agent [Perry H. Knowlton]* says from New York: "My God, Robby, that must be a crazy place you have up there." And when I insist to Brenda that it is a great paean to the learned life she goes off into fits and rolls on the floor. What have I done?

We have our plans made for retirement: we keep the place in the country, and have taken a little pad in Toronto, as we expect to be here for part of each week. Also, I expect to have a room in this college to write in, as I have several jobs to do, including some work on a theatre history of Canada,* and I must have a place where I can have a writer's necessary mess. But moving is going to be a monstrous job of planning, to get everything headed in the right direction. Movers have tendered on the job, and their quotations are awesome, chiefly because we have so many books, and we can't waltz cartons of books all over the landscape at the prices they regard as their due.

Mysterious things are going on in the college, & rumour reaches me that when I totter off into senility, something will probably be NAMED after me. Not, I hope, a scholarship. I never knew anybody yet who held a scholarship named after some bygone worthy who had the slightest idea who said worthy had been.

I shall not be sorry to step down. I have done all I can do here, and what they need now is a man who can collect some money – a task at which I have been a total failure. I think the incoming man [J. N. Patterson Hume]* has some ideas, and may God attend his footsteps. I want to spend the coming years, whatever they may be, writing, and thinking of things to write that I shall decide not to write. I might write a very short history of the founding and early days of this college, not for publication but to repose in the college library. It was a story with some hilarious moments, and it should not be wholly lost.

When Brenda is away one of the big problems is meals; at weekends I am alone in this house, and always at dinner; I eat in the college Hall a good deal but sometimes I feel I cannot talk to anybody under any consideration, and I lurk morosely in my own quarters, eating peanut butter sandwiches and drinking instant coffee. Any skill I ever had at cooking has vanished with the years.

Very best love to you & Inge – I do hope she is much better* –

Rob.

To SHEILA KIERAN

Massey College
University of Toronto
April 6, 1981

Dear Miss Kieran:

Sheila Kieran (1930–), Canadian freelance magazine writer, was preparing an article for Homemaker's *magazine at the time about the popularity of Harlequin romances (published January–February 1983). She knew Davies a little, having interviewed him twice on other matters.*

At the moment I am very busy with matters relating to the end of the university term and it would be difficult for me to arrange to see you personally; however, here are some comments on the matter you raise in your letter of March 30th.

I do not find the success of Harlequin books particularly surprising because I think that a very great number of people are perpetually hungry for *narrative* and although they are not quite like the people of an earlier day who delighted in hearing the same story over and over again in precisely the same form, they do, nevertheless, like stories which embody fantasies which feed their imagination and in some measure give meaning to their lives; of these the Cinderella fantasy is certainly one of the most powerful.

I agree with you that in spite of the strong move towards a different place in society for women which is going on at present, there are very great numbers of women who do not wish to be liberated in the sense of being cut off from the age-old relationship between male and female, which is protective on the one hand and supportive on the other. Women and men both want to be loved and only a few of them like to make hard and fast deals in this relationship. In the main I think that they get what they want and that what may not appear to be romantic fulfilment to an outsider is more or less satisfactory to an insider.

Furthermore, great numbers of people, male and female, have a strong feeling of Regret For Lost Youth and through romantic stories they recall and amplify their own romances. There is nothing in the world wrong with this and narrative art has ministered to this desire for ages.

I do not think that it makes the least difference that the Harlequin books are undistinguished from a literary point of view. People who like narrative need not have an exacting literary taste any more than people who like music need have a highly trained or sophisticated musical taste. It is half-baked intellectualism which insists that nothing is satisfying in the theatre or in narrative or in music which is not of the currently fashionable top class.

I repeat that I do not see anything new or anything reprehensible with the taste which leans towards Harlequin books. In an earlier day the story-teller, or *shanachie*, at the fireside satisfied the taste for narrative. In our day, when everybody can read, the Harlequin does the same thing and it is dangerous to condemn stories as junk which satisfy the deep hunger of millions of people. These books are not literary art, but a great deal of what is acclaimed as literary art in our time offers no comfort or fulfilment to anybody. From time to time some academic authority proclaims that the novel is dead and this may be true of what he considers to be a novel, but narrative is undying because the appetite for it is never completely satisfied.

With good wishes,

Yours sincerely,

Robertson Davies

To DAVID GARDNER

August 17, 1981

David Gardner (1928–   ), Canadian actor, was writing his doctoral dissertation under Davies' supervision. They had been friends since the late 1940s and early 1950s when Gardner acted in several of Davies' plays and once performed under his direction.

Dear David:

Here is your chapter, complete with notes. I am at a loss what to say to you about it. As a portion of a thesis it is much too long and diffuse: as a portion of a book it would be excellent. All the vagarious chasing-of-rabbits is great fun and you always make it, in the end, add something to your theme. I compliment you on the charm and directness of your writing; I know how hard it is to get a lot of widely varied material to pull together to make a single pattern. But I keep wondering: What will some crabby External Examiner make of this?

I have not made any suggestions as to how to shorten it, with one exception respecting pp. 75–9, simply because I do not know how it could be done without drastic rewriting, and because I would hate to see anything go. But I think you could do some helpful surgery by cutting a word here, a line there, and now and then compressing a paragraph; however, this is the most vexatious and time-taking sort of work and I do not demand it, I just hint at it.

My problem is that I *like* what you have done; it is like one of those 17th century chaps – Burton or Aubrey* – who are so breathlessly interested in everything they couldn't bear to leave anything out. That is the kind of scholarship I like, and I think the public would like it, too. So why not take a flyer at it, with perhaps some trimming, and say somewhere early that you have been diffuse because otherwise you can't make your points?

Regards

Rob.

To IAN ALEXANDER

Massey College
University of Toronto
August 19, 1981

Ian Alexander (1950–　), Canadian, had been a junior fellow at Massey College and a student in one of Davies' courses. At this point he was a self-employed broadcasting consultant in Vancouver, British Columbia.

Dear Ian:

Since Jean-Claude Parrot* (Whom God Preserve!) has at last graciously acceded to the resumption of rational communication for a time, I have been able to receive your letter of August 7. It was most kind, and I do not know how to thank you for it without becoming maudlin, as retired persons do so often and so regrettably. I have had a number of letters from people – all men, by the way – who say that their time at Massey was significant for them, and that is my assurance that the College was indeed successful in attaining the mark set for it by its Founders. It was such a nebulous idea – clear enough to Vincent Massey and his son Lionel,* and to me, but extremely hard to put into words – to set a place going where young people could shake off some of the odium of being "students" in the bad sense, and see themselves as scholars and as people. Some of our people never understood, but many did so, and you were one of them, and reason to hope that there will be many more.

I am so glad to hear that your work is going well and satisfying you. I always had slightly cold feet when I advised a Ph.D. student to get out of that grind, but I did so on several occasions and the results have always been good. Canada is still a country where great importance is attached to labels, but the Ph.D. is not hard currency; some are all that the degree should imply, but too many are narrow blockheads who know little outside their speciality. Increasingly the University world reminds me of the medieval church – a scattering of saints, a few hundred worthy men, and thousands of scaredy-cats who couldn't face the world and sought protection in Mother Church or the Alma Mater. And, by the way, it is astonishing to look at the history of the Renaissance and see just how little of the new learning and the new world emerged from the universities. It was the men of quality outside who did the serious work. . . .

Every good wish

Rob. Davies

To ELISABETH SIFTON

Massey College
University of Toronto
August 25, 1981

Dear Elisabeth:

I have not replied to your letter of July 2 which, because of our pestilent mail strike, did not reach me until July 30, as I knew you were on holiday, and I was in the throes – and what throes! – of moving. The banditti who undertook the job, and who have the brass neck to advertise themselves as The Friendly Movers, made quite a hash of it, gouging a large hole in a 350-years-old Flemish tapestry, losing the pedals off my piano and otherwise disporting themselves in a manner to shame the Vandals. But it is almost all done with now, and I am trying to distribute a large number of books – I never count, for fear of what I may discover – between two houses, one a condominium (have you heard about the Newfoundland woman who gave up the Pill because her husband had acquired a condominium?) in Toronto, and our house in the country which has, providentially, a bookstacks in the basement. So, on September 1, I shall officially and with immense ceremony, set out on my Fourth Career (actor, editor and professor hitherto) as a Writer. I have lots of projects in hand, including a sequel, or linked novel, following *Rebel Angels*. This book [*What's Bred in the Bone*] forces itself into my mind when I am lugging furniture, or pulling weeds, and I have some hopes of it. I often read, with amazement, of people who suffer from Writer's Block; I might enjoy a wee Block, just to have time to catch my breath. If it did not take me so long to write a book I might be as productive as Joyce Carol Oates (whom God preserve!).

I received the rough of Viking's design for the novel jacket, and like it very much. I like the Macmillan one, too, though it is perhaps somewhat *muted* in its suggestion of what lies within. However, it is a fine photograph. Sometimes I yearn for a really awful jacket – nudes and full frontal sex and what not – but your splendid fiend sticking out his tongue comes very near. I hanker to be a great success in the porn shops, but long ago I realized that pornography and a sense of humour are mutually exclusive. I think often of the girl who described her work at the Windmill in London as "you have to be able to stand naked on the stage without bustin' out laughin'." That girl must have been fun to know.

My Retirement was a great success and I was treated with the greatest kindness and generosity by all concerned. Best of all was a party* the University gave in the Great Hall at Hart House, where 350 friends sat down to a really good dinner accompanied by wine not positively disgusting – a great feat in this Canada of ours – which was followed by a Masque composed in my honour, made up of bits from my writings, acted by former students who are now professional actors, and with splendid music, specially composed. The culmination was a scene inspired by the elements of magic in my work, with a wizard and superb big shiny serpents who belched forth vapour (these contrived by a young man who wanted to marry my eldest daughter, but was refused, but who does not hold it against me). Best of all, there were very generous tributes to Brenda, who has always stood by me in my various academic goings-on, but who is sometimes overlooked. The students of Massey College gave me as a parting gift *Little Dorrit** in the original monthly parts – a really imaginative and stunning gift. And the College staff gave me a lectern-bookcase, in which I can store my *Oxford English Dictionary*.* If this is what Retirement means, I shall do it every year.

But enough of this boasting. Thank you for *Memoirs of an Anti-Semite** which arrived last week and which I look forward to reading..... What else? Ah, yes; we are going for a brief jaunt abroad in October, to Vienna, Budapest and Prague, to see pictures and opera, and shall return home by way of London, where our eldest daughter [Miranda] has just qualified as a Jungian shrink, and is sowing doubt and dismay among the neurotics of that ancient city – chiefly its children. Actually, I think she will be very good, as she has boundless patience and a lot of good, plain horse-sense which, as Dr. Jung pointed out, is one of the principal requirements. I have not yet told Macmillans that this will keep me out of the country just as *Rebel Angels* appears; they want me to do things. But I am sure anything significant can wait till I am back in Canada, refreshed by a huge dollop of Foreign Culture.

Love from us both & respectful salaams to your Judge [Charles P. Sifton]* –

Rob.

To DEREK HOLMAN

[Fall, 1981] ·

Derek Holman (1931–   ), English-born organist, choir conductor, composer, and teacher, had collaborated with Davies on several occasions. This note was appended to a draft of Dr. Canon's Cure, the children's opera for which Davies was writing the libretto and Holman the music. The opera was first performed in May 1982.

Dear Wolfgang Amadeus:

How will this do, for the first part of our *jeu d'esprit*? Everything is, of course, subject to criticism and revision, as I make no claim to knowing what words singers can sing with ease, or where you intend to lay stress which may obligate changes in vowel sounds, etc. It may be also that you think Dr. Canon is too irreverent about the Great Masters, for whom I know that you feel an awe amounting to neurosis; that can be tempered. Just one word: I will gladly make changes at your suggestion, but I think we should beware of busybodies with special notions of their own, who wish to interfere.

Ever thy —

Lorenzo (da P.)

P.S.: I hear Salieri* is quite unwell. Naughty!

L.

To A WOMAN IN MANITOBA

[Massey College
University of Toronto]
October 13, 1981

This woman read "Benefactor" (an excerpt from The Rebel Angels) *in the September issue of* Saturday Night *and wrote to reprove Davies for presenting "Barn Yard pornography," which "stinks of syphilis" and is written "in terms of degradation, lies, sacrilegious slander and filth."*

[Dear Miss _____:]

Many many heartfelt thanks for your letter of September 25. Though it filled me with shame and remorse, I was grateful for the Christian impulse which moved you to stretch out a hand to me in my wretchedness. You say "We become that with which we busy our mind." Too true! Alas, too true! I recall that as a boy the school chaplain said to my class, "If you tell dirty jokes you will grow to look like a dirty joke!" This has been my hapless destiny..... Would you do me a favour? Will you send me a photograph of yourself, so that I may behold a countenance suffused with Christian love, and perhaps even yet repent?

[Robertson Davies]

To RONALD EWING

Massey College
University of Toronto
Oct. 13, 1981

Ronald Ewing was an M.A. student at McGill University in Montreal. He had written Davies several times and had come to Toronto to talk with him about the source and nature of evil in the Deptford trilogy (the subject of his thesis).

[Dear Mr. Ewing:]

I beg you to believe that I am sincere when I say that I really do not know how to answer your questions in a manner that will satisfy you, for you seem to be in search of some certainty that I am in no position to provide. I am a novelist, not a philosopher, or a Jungian analyst, and what I write in my novels is primarily fiction, and must be examined as fiction – that is to say, not trivial or irresponsible utterance, but certainly not a guide to good conduct or a final answer to problems of the uttermost difficulty. I think you have misunderstood what Liliane Frey-Rohn says;* knowledge of the Personal Shadow is necessary for responsible action and a lessening of moral darkness in the world, but it does not *guarantee* it. Jung's attitude appears to me to be that Ultimate Good and Ultimate Evil are beyond human comprehension or control; the best we can do is to put the best of our carefully adjusted selves at the service of what appears to us, under given circumstances, to be Good – but we must never make the mistake of thinking we have some final answer to what Goodness may be..... Certainly Boy Staunton* never attempted to come to terms with himself, and his final recognition of the unsatisfactory [nature] of his life was partial, or he would not have done as he did. As for David, what he will do is whatever the individual reader thinks he will do. The book is fiction, meant to engage the imagination of the reader, not a guide to conduct.

Sincerely,

[Robertson Davies]

To LEON EDEL

Massey College
University of Toronto
Thanksgiving (Canadian Style)
1981

Leon Edel (1907–) is an American editor, critic, academic, and author of a celebrated biography of Henry James. Davies met Edel in New York on May 21, 1980, when Davies was inducted as an Honorary Member into the American Academy and Institute of Arts and Letters.

Dear Dr. Edel:

Your letter of September 15 has just reached me; how kind of you to take notice of my mischievous introduction of Henry James into my review of the book by John Irving.* It was irresistible, however, because there are people who cry up Irving as a writer of significance, and when the Wash. *Post* asked me to review his book I read *all* his novels in order to prepare myself, and I could find little in him. Rough stuff aplenty (woman bites off lover's penis) and pages of adolescent honing after the unattainable; but of psychological insight or subtlety, of sensitivity to the nuance of language, of any perception of the insubstantiality of passion, there was not one crumb. And as I was at the same time reading your splendid evocation of all these qualities in James I could not help but wonder what HJ would have made of such an innocent, but not pure, spirit as Irving..... In my original review I quoted some of the heroine's language; she habitually addressed the brother with whom she had an incestuous affair as "asshole," and consequently she was strapped for a term to describe the man who raped her, and was reduced to "rat's asshole"; I wanted to illustrate the poverty of language into which the uncontrolled use of intensives may lead a writer. But the *Post* could not print this in its chaste pages, so they asked me to tone it down..... Irving is simply not a *grown-up* writer and if he grows old in the trade, as James did, he is bound to come a cropper in the next few years. The great leap for writers comes in their forties: they either gain new energy, or go to pot. But who am I to be telling *you* this?

The notion that you have been reading my books and liking them fills me with pride, for as a Canadian writer I have had quite a struggle to persuade my countrymen that I am rather more than a pedantic joker; indeed it was not until I received kind attention in the U.S. that this judgement came to be questioned. One of the queerest moments of my life was when an influential Canadian reviewer, who had knocked *Fifth Business*, came to see me and said (I quote his very words), "I don't get this; the book didn't go very well up here, and I didn't like it, but now they're praising it in the States. What's wrong?" A foolish sense of courtesy forbade me to tell him what I thought was wrong..... So glad you liked *Manticore*; there have been many books which describe Freudian analyses, but I know of no other that describes a Jungian analysis, and I was deeply fearful that I would put my foot in it, for I have never undergone one of those barnacle-scraping experiences, and knew of it only through reading. So I was greatly pleased when some of my Jungian friends in Zurich liked it very much. The method appealed to me as a way of telling a great deal about several people (especially David's awful father) in a newish way..... Greatly pleased too that you liked the gypsy's advice about fortune telling in *World of Wonders*; I love fortune-tellers, and if I had my way there would be a good one on every campus.

I hope you will not think me intrusive if I send you a copy of my new novel, *The Rebel Angels*, for it also has some gypsy stuff in it. It will not appear in the U.S. until next year, so I am sending you a copy of the Canadian edition which is just out and is being, I am delighted to say, received with great kindness here. Perhaps the university atmosphere will amuse you.

My wife and I remember meeting you and Mrs. Edel in New York at the Academy affair, which was a great thrill for us, if bewildering, as it seemed that we had wandered into a filming of *The Oxford Companion to American Literature*. I hope it will not be long before we may meet again under, as you say, less distracting circumstances.

With thanks & good wishes –

Robertson Davies

To GORDON ROPER

Oaklands
Toronto
November 29, 1981

Dear Gordon:

   This business of retirement will be the death of me. I don't think
I have ever worked so hard in my life, and everything is complicated
by the fact that I have no machinery of work – no single place where
everything is concentrated, no full-time secretary, no defence against
that instrument of Satan, the telephone, and an army of people who
are certain that as I now have nothing to do I am free to address their
god-damned gang of detrimentals in every part of the continent, or
give a course in "Creative Writing" – that most deceitful of all impos-
tures on weak minds – or read their MSS, which stupid publishers
won't accept. I think seriously of shaving off my beard, dying my
white hair red, and going off to join a Gypsy band under an assumed
name – how does Petulengro, the Horse-Breaker, sound to you?
   Writing does *not* grow easier with the years, and reading reviews
of one's book does *not* become less painful, and doing all the chat-
tering and head-nodding and cap-touching that passes under the
name of Publicity does *not* become more agreeable. This afternoon I
take flight to the West, to do a city-a-day tour, reading, being interviewed, talking to audiences and glad-handing, because my publisher
[Douglas Gibson]* thinks it will help to sell the book, and it would
be absurd pretension to pretend that I don't want to sell it. I am a
tradesman, an entertainer, and I must take on the jobs that have to be
done. To behave otherwise is Arty and silly. But I won't pretend I like
this part of it.
   Therefore, to get to the important matter, you will realize that your
letter was balm to my mind and spirit, because you know your stuff
and you know me, and I value your opinion very greatly. I was
delighted that you thought the *writing* was better: if only I could live
long enough and keep my wits, I might at last write really well. I toiled

over *Rebel Angels*, trying to keep in check my tendency to over-write, and to do things that please me but spoil the shape of the book. This is what some reviewers have said – it is wordy and chases too many rabbits – but I feel strongly that if you choose to write about a university, you must try to convey the sort of talk and the feeling that make a university an important and indeed a great place: I did not write one of those tedious books that treats a university as a stage for farce, full of silly professors and dewy students, but as a great conserver and fosterer of the intellectual life, and some discerning readers – you, Claude Bissell* and Hugh MacLennan* – have said I managed it, and this is the best of my reward. It is not an easy book, though I hope it reads easily, and it will take time for it to be seen for what it is. So my heartfelt thanks, my dear old friend, for your encouragement.

About Judith Grant* – she frightens me, as I suppose a biographer frightens anybody who has not the vanity of a peacock and the hide of a rhinoceros. She wants to know so *much*, and I don't know what to tell her and what to reserve. She wants to see those letters I wrote from Oxford to a girl [Eleanor Sweezey]* with whom I was, at that time, very much in love. But who that is not a ruffian and a thick-skin, shows love-letters? The experience was sufficiently painful, without now dredging it up and offering it to readers who have no right to know, and wouldn't understand. Judith is a first-rate person, but she has the voracious appetite of a scholar; she would, without being in the least aware of it, grind my bones to make her bread. My ideal of a biographer is Parson Weems,* who wrote about Washington with all the innocence of ignorance. I won't strip in public – except insofar as a writer of fiction does so, which is painful enough – and I shrink in terror from being stripped by somebody else. What do you advise? She has seen the letters I wrote to you* when you were ill, and you certainly know that I did not write them with one eye cocked toward a biographer. If I had done so, they would have been very different, and not I am sure so welcome to you as I wished them to be. What am I to say about my family – the matrix from which everything I am and have written arises – the rhizome from which a few blossoms peep upward in the form of novels and plays? But whatever I may have undergone or felt, I am not going to present them as minor characters in a drama of which I am the leading player; they too had their troubles and dead or alive they have their rights. Nothing they did was done in malice, but in the hurly-burly of daily living, in which one stumbles from hour to hour under burdens that are nobody else's affair. What do you advise?

I am being loaded with honours I do not deserve. I am not a fitting person to have a library named after me;* what was denied to men in comparison with whom I am a zero should not happen to me. I greatly value the honour from the University of Toronto,* for I did what I could while I worked there, but that is another thing..... I remember the dismay of Vincent Massey, after whom a High School was named, and who thereafter saw headlines in the sports pages which read "Vincent Massey Lambastes Sacred Heart"! But all this moaning is wearisome, I know.

Brenda and I are trying to get a new sort of life going, and perhaps after Christmas things will be a little more manageable. Must close now, for I must go and bathe (sacred ritual bath before flinging myself upon Winnipeg, Edmonton, Calgary and Vancouver and Victoria) and pack my case (what does one take, will the weather be warm or cold, how many clean shirts, how much indigestion medicine can I cram in?) and go to Malton*..... Be kind to yourself. I know that Helen is kind to you in the highest degree, but you must co-operate, you know. And be assured that your letter will lighten my way.

Our love to you both –

Rob.

P.S. To complicate matters I am making notes for the next book of this romance [*What's Bred in the Bone*], & my Unconscious seethes & bubbles & won't let me alone. Well, at least I haven't got Writers' Block, that Constipation of the Invention!

To ALTIE KARPER

Massey College
University of Toronto
January 6, 1982

*Altie Karper (1956–   ), American, was
Elisabeth Sifton's editorial assistant at The
Viking Press in New York from 1979–83
– "a remarkably warm-hearted and quick-
witted woman" possessed of "perfect
manners, a delicious smile, and a fantas-
tically elegant waist" (to quote E.S.).*

Dear Altie:

I have just received your letter of December 21st about the signed
sheets [of *The Rebel Angels*] for Kroch and Brentano* in Chicago and
am sending them off. It was kind of you to enclose a prepaid mailing
bag, but it is quite impossible to use it as Canada, being a country
separate from the U.S.A., and indeed a monarchy, insists on the use
of its own stamps. You have, therefore, flung away $1.39 in U.S. cur-
rency and you had better keep this from Mrs. Sifton or she will stop
it out of your wages at the end of the week.

With good wishes for 1982,

Yours sincerely,

Rob.

Dear Judith:

Many thanks for the splendid
Christmas cake,which is now all gone,
down the red lanes of guests,children,
grandchildren and of course ourselves.
A fine effort.You redeem the academic
world from the charge of being insensitive
to the sensualities....Before Christmas
I was knocked down by a car in the
dark,which was rather too near to
concluding our joint effort for my
taste.Consequently I spent the merry
season rather under the weather with
aches and pains;the dr. told my wife
that I was not to be babied,but she
wisely did not heed him, and I am now
in pretty fair nick, though stiff and
grumpy.He said I would have what he
nastily called 'geriatric depression' for
about five or six weeks;this is the
new name for the mulligrubs.But I only
have it for about half an hour each day.
However we are staying in the country until
next week,and I am trying to get on with
the book,which is excellent therapy.
...Every good wish to you and John and
the boys for 1984,upon which Orwell
has attempted to put a literary hex.
Heed him not.....

Rob.

Windhover
January 2
1984

SECTION

III

FEBRUARY 1982–JULY 1984 – *WHAT'S BRED IN THE BONE* PLANNED AND WRITTEN

uring 1982, the year he turned 69, Davies made notes of ideas which he used in both *What's Bred in the Bone* and *The Lyre of Orpheus*, deciding which strands of plot belonged to *What's Bred* only that July. The following February or early March, he began to write the first draft, completing it on August 9, 1984.

In 1982, too, he prepared the eighteen Massey College ghost stories for publication as *High Spirits*, made final additions to the libretto for *Dr. Canon's Cure*, wrote the lectures which were published as *The Mirror of Nature* and completed an account of the history of theatre in Ontario.

It was at this time that I began to gather materials for my biography of Davies. Between April 1982 and May 1984, he met with me to discuss his life 44 times (the experience prompted him to introduce a biographer into *What's Bred in the Bone* and *The Lyre of Orpheus*). And in the fall of 1982, Davies was interviewed at length about Kingston, the Ontario city where he lived from 1925 to 1935, from the age of 13 to 22, for the BBC television series called "Writers and Places."

From 1983 on, the roughly annual trips that he and Brenda took to London to see theatre, visit their daughter Miranda, and keep in touch with publishers were made pleasanter by the acquisition of a time-shared flat on Pont Street near Harrods. There were trips to Bavaria and Austria in 1983 and 1984. Apart from colds, Davies' general health continued to be good. By 1983, however, the cataract that had been developing in his right eye caused him enough trouble that he had to wear glasses with one darkened lens until the cataract was removed in 1986. His worsening eyesight was probably a factor in December 1983 when he stepped in front of a moving car on Avenue Road in Toronto and was knocked down, luckily without any serious consequences.

To ELISABETH SIFTON

Windhover
Caledon East
February 6, 1982

Dear Elisabeth:

Delightful to hear from you. Don't feel obliged to reply to my letters; I am seized from time to time with a zeal for correspondence of the personal kind – I have far too much of the cautious, impersonal kind – and I write when often I haven't much to write about and am simply in the grip of a need to chat a bit.

Probably you have seen the piece* by Jean Strouse in *Newsweek*. Very kind and generous, I thought. Long years ago, when Brenda and I worked at the Old Vic, the Secretary to the Governors of that institution was a lady named Miss Evelyn Williams; she later became Secretary to the British Council and a woman of great influence, which she used very intelligently. But in the Vic days she had a passionate crush on the Director, Tyrone Guthrie,* whom she called Lamb. When one of his productions was favourably reviewed – critics heaping Pelléas on Mélisande* in their ecstatic commendation – Miss W. would say, consideringly, "Yes, I thought they were *fair* to Lamb."

This has become a saying in our family, and Brenda and I agreed that Jean Strouse had indeed been fair to Lamb.

As for Kenneth Galbraith,* he has sent me a copy of his article for the *Times,* and he is even fairer to Lamb, declaring Lamb to be not merely one of the best writers of the time but of this century. A Puritan upbringing forbids me to believe this, but I am glad to have it said, and by a man with a loud voice. He tells me the *Times* thinks his piece more a book review than an article, so they are going to use it in the Book Section, and cut it quite a bit; I hope they don't cut the really juicy bits, like the above.* Better in the Book Section, I think, as it is so widely read and, Douglas Gibson assures me, the Bible of the booksellers' trade.

Meanwhile, I toil on. Have to get the Ghost Stories [and several other things] ready . . . .

But beneath this work there is a perpetual nagging inward reverie about my next novel [*What's Bred in the Bone* and *The Lyre of Orpheus*] and it really has me up a tree, for I want to combine three narratives: (1) the childhood of Francis Cornish, explaining what it was that made him a notable connoisseur and collector, despite a Philistine and loveless childhood, and (2) what happens in the marriage of Maria and Arthur Cornish, which runs into some stiffish problems, including a tough illness for Arthur and the complications involved in his determination to be an active arts patron in the world of the theatre, and (3) complications about the publication of Parlabane's horrible novel, arising from the appearance of a terrible fellow who asserts that he is Parlabane's son. Getting these threads together into something that makes sense is gnawing at my vitals like the fox chewing on the Spartan boy.*

What the novel is really about is Heredity. How much do we get from our forbears, and why is it so unlikely and improbable in its effects? Heredity is a discredited notion at present, but I agree with the late Alfred Tennyson* that it is a fearful problem that occurs in everybody's life whether they recognize it or not. As you see, this lures me dangerously close to what Jean Strouse mildly faults me for – dealing with systems and ideas rather than people. Unfortunately nobody can be of much help with these literary miseries. Theme One is the most attractive and threatens to swamp the others; Theme Two must pursue the theme Jean Strouse emphasizes – the dominating place of friendship in a marriage that expects to last. (I sense that Jean Strouse had had some tough experiences with loving but unfriendly people, for she kept coming back to this theme in our talks, and talking of it with enthusiasm.) Theme Three is easier – Son of Parlabane, without his father's brains but with all his exploitative, ugly greedy spirit. And so the inner wrangle goes on, and on, until I long for a rest from it. As it stands at present the novel sounds like one of the really great Literary Turkeys of all time. . . .

Must shut up. Once again, this requires no answer. You must be accustomed to neurasthenic letters from authors. Incidentally, a background to the new novel includes a look at what psychiatry meant in remote places before the Freudian epiphany. Pretty grisly.

Good wishes to all, including Altie [Karper],

Rob.

PS: Why do you always address me as "Mr. Davies"? I near the age when I half expect to be called Gaffer.

To THE HONOURABLE FRANCIS FOX

Francis Fox (1939–   ), Canadian, was a Liberal member of parliament from 1972–84 and Minister of Communications from 1980–84.

Massey College
University of Toronto
March 2, 1982

[Dear Mr. Minister:]

As a Canadian author, I write to you to support the proposal that has been made to you by the Canada Council, respecting the programme called Payment for Public Use, which would in some measure recompense Canadian writers for the use of their books in Canadian lending libraries.

The justice of such a programme seems to me to be beyond question, for, as every Canadian writer knows, his books are circulated by Canadian libraries to a large public, and for this use of his literary property neither he nor his publisher receives any payment. In some libraries new books are lent on a system that requires the reader to pay a *per diem* charge, from which the library receives all the benefit. I have on several occasions referred to this system, publicly, as a form of sanctified theft, for the self-righteousness of the libraries when the system is brought into question is both comic and infuriating.

The Payment for Public Use proposal would give the strongest public evidence of national support for literature – an art which presents special difficulties to benefactors or government patrons because it does not, like music, theatre or the visual arts, involve the originators in obvious and easily calculable personal expenditure. But Canada's authors, like Canada's other artists, give the country that kind of substance in our own eyes and in the eyes of the world, which is one of the assurances of civilization. The author works alone, he exploits no resource but his own talent, the return from his work is rarely comparable to that of other professional people, but it is always possible that his work may give a lustre to the whole of Canada that will endure for many generations and reach beyond our borders. The recognition proposed is modest, but it would be an assurance that the nation values its literary men and women.

I am, yours most sincerely, Mr. Minister,

[Robertson Davies]

To THOMAS R. HARRIS

Massey College
University of Toronto
March 11, 1982

Thomas R. Harris (1948–   ), Canadian,
has been a teacher of English and drama
at Sackville High School, Lower Sackville,
Nova Scotia since 1974.

Dear Mr Harris:

How your students ever got the idea that the names of Dunstan Ramsay's girlfriends* relate to the Trinity I cannot imagine; don't they learn any Latin? Are there no Catholics in the class? Here are the derivations:

AGNES DAY – from *Agnus Dei, qui tollis peccata mundi* – a Latin prayer (O Lamb of God, who takest upon Thee the sins of the whole world...)

GLORIA MUNDY – from *Sic transit gloria mundi*, not a phrase of religious origin, meaning simply "Thus pass the glories of this world"

LIBBY DOE – most certainly not religious, and equally obviously derived from "libido" meaning drive, or energy, not necessarily sexual; they could have checked this in any dictionary

So Dunstan's girls were Agnes, the Sufferer – a type well known to all men; Gloria, the Good Time Girl, and Libby, the energetic go-getter. He does not give their real names because he is a gentleman of an old-fashioned kind who would never mention by name a woman with whom he had had a sexual affair. No, I am most decidedly NOT taking "an oblique shot at conventional Christianity," though I am often amused and exasperated by people like your students who, as conventional Christians, are always ready to see offence in anything they have not understood. Tell 'em so from me.

Sincerely yours,

Robertson Davies

To PHILIP JOHN STEAD

Massey College
University of Toronto
March 17, 1982

Philip John Stead (1916–),
Yorkshireman and friend of Davies' since
their Oxford days, was dean of academic
studies at the Police Staff College,
Bramshill, in England, and later, of
graduate studies at the John Jay College of
Criminal Justice, New York. He retired in
1982 to Hyannis. In 1938–39 he had
shared a flat in Leith Mansions on
Grantully Road, Maida Vale, London,
with Davies and Alan Hay. For part of that
period, Davies was assistant stage
manager for Traitor's Gate at the Duke of
York's Theatre. Hay, who helped finance
the production, lost his fortune when the
play ran only two months.

Thanks for your splendid letter; I hope this catches you before you depart for Hyannis, though not before you flit to the Old Sod to have your likeness struck.*

What adventures you have had! I should not, all those years ago, have guessed that you might become an expert on police methods, though you were always interested in criminals and their curious doings. It was you who told me about the trade in "favourite tankards of Haigh the Vampire"* that was conducted by the pub where he hung out in London..... Yes, I well remember us watching the escape artist beneath the Irving statue;* I also saw a street Punch and Judy with you, on an occasion when you gave the showman a piece of your mind for diverging from tradition. Indeed, you bulk substantially in my recollections; I still cherish tales of your extraordinary Uncle Bingham, who used to poke into people's cupboards and comment "No stillborn bairns in there!" And your aunt, who was obliged to be careful about what she ate, but could "take cream" and most of any sweet that was going. You regaled us with these tales at Leith Mansions, when Hay was the third. Poor old Hay; have you seen anything of him? I last beheld him a few years ago when I was in London and wretched with 'flu, but Brenda persuaded me that a visit to a Somerset Maugham* play that was being revived – *Lady Frederick*, I think – would cheer me; first figure to appear, carrying a tray, was our old pal and boyhood chum, looking precisely the same; he was also Stage Manager of the show. I confess I was yellow; I should have gone round to extend the manly grasp and hash over old times, but I did not; I felt rotten, and seeing him in such a very minor situation made me feel worse. (He was the butler: no lines but Yes, Madam & No, madam. It was at the Duke of York's where *Traitor's Gate* burst upon an unfeeling world.)

I retired last June 30, and I know what you mean about the problem of lugging books from one dwelling to another. And yet it is so stupid ever to get rid of a book, for it is certain to be the one you want desperately within a month.

You ask about my progeny: all grown and at large. Eldest daughter [Miranda Davies] a Jungian analyst in London, specializing in work with disturbed children: 2nd [Jennifer] lives with her husband [Thomas Surridge] in Ottawa, where he does something very complex with computers* for the Solicitor-General and she is becoming an expert on embroidery, like her Ma; 3rd [Rosamond], married to a doctor [John Cunnington], and bringing up four children – 3m. 1f. as French's catalogue says – she is moving toward being a writer. We live part of the time in Toronto, and a substantial part of each week in the country away from the telephone.

Rebel Angels has been doing well in the U.S., which has always been very kind to me. When you get your Hyannis house in shape for additions to the bookshelves, let me know, and I shall send you a copy; it has a murder in it of which I am rather proud. "Where does an apparently quiet academic like you find all this violence?" my doctor

[Jaroslav M. J. Polak]* asks me: poor innocent, where do any of us find our violence.

All good wishes to you and Judith,* in which Brenda joins me.....

Rob.

To JACQUES BERGER

Massey College
University of Toronto
April 6, 1982

Jacques Berger (1934–95) was an American microbiologist, a professor of zoology at the University of Toronto, and a senior fellow at Massey College from 1973–95.

[Dear Jacques:]

I am sorry to have been so long in acknowledging your kind note of March 10th and the clipping* that it enclosed. I am keenly interested in this question of owls attacking human beings because I want to use such an incident in a novel [*What's Bred in the Bone*] on which I am at work at the moment. I shall keep the clipping, if I may, and if you can tell me anything further about the owls that did serious damage to women's heads I should be very greatly obliged. I am going to be at High Table on April 16th and hope that I may have a chance to see you then.

With good wishes,

Yours sincerely,

[Rob.]

To DEREK HOLMAN

Windhover
Caledon East
April 19, 1982

Dear Derek:

Here is the additional stuff [for *Dr. Canon's Cure*]. I hope it fits; I have sung it over and over in my rich baritone and it fits *for me*, but you have the more sensitive ear. Anyhow, it can be tinkered until it *does* fit, so call me if you need me..... It occurred to me, from the music, that you were working to a bigger climax in the Operatic Chorus's wedding piece than the words as they are at present really support, so I have tried to be a little more expansive in this:

Plot and passion –
Execution – yes, and revolution!
Nations crumbling –
Popes and monarchs sadly stumbling!
Are of small concern
When Love demands its turn.   or "his" if it sings better
The World and Rome may –
All the world may –
BURN, may BURN!

I have written the words on your score (included) to show how I think they fit. But as I say –
Glad you are enlarging the Canary Aria. I like it and hope it will prove funny in the way I like best – the affectionately satirical. I have tried this in my own coloratura, and it works, but if you don't like it –

When I contemplate my lover's tender suit,
    Or my fragile wits desert me for a season,
I'm invariably accompanied by the flute,

> And together we make trills of love or reason.
> For the silver flute's the coloratura's friend –
>   Bless its hemi-demi-quavered bright staccato!
> Sane or dotty it's my partner to the end;
>   I'd be lost without its brilliant obbligato!

And that brings me to a point which I think important. The fun of the opera-within-the-opera will be greatly enhanced if there is applause for the big numbers. How can it be encouraged? My experience is that audiences of kids respond to humour as if a match were thrown into a bale of wet wool. Could we hint to the director that some form of clap-trap be devised – Rhingiaro and Dispettosa applauding perhaps – though applause onstage tends to quell it among the audience – or some cunning device. I should love to see Columbine taking her bow, kissing her hand to the auditors, large-souledly bringing forth the Flute for a hand, and all the rich crappola of operatic courtesy. We might even resort to the vaudeville trick of getting the Chorus to encourage applause by gestures. But applause we *must* have if the right atmosphere is to be created.

As I told you by 'phone, I think that _____, dear soul, has a somewhat sugared attitude toward children, who are, in my experience, cheerfully derisive creatures, but keen to get in on any fun that is going. So we must do all we can to ensure that the *satiric* mode of the op-in-op is understood and enjoyed..... I presume that Dr. Canon conducts – or appears to conduct – the op-in-op, and at some point he should be shaken hands with by somebody – it always delights me when the hand-shaking goes on, as if the shakers had never seen or heard or abused one another until the moment of performance. Perhaps we could have a word with the director if he has not already twigged this – which, as an experienced man I expect he has.

I shall attend a few rehearsals – but don't want to seem to *butt in*, as is my unseemly wont. Brenda will come too, and she restrains me when she can, which isn't always.

I have gone over the score as well as I can with my ten thumbs – no Ubukata,* I assure you – and congratulate you heartily. *Very* funny and also musically adroit and learned and wholly delightful. The bit where the singers play instrumentally* ought to bring down the house while charming them – the best sort of theatrical effect. But we must keep all suggestions of Disney at bay for, as we have agreed, children are immensely more intelligent than sentimentalists are inclined to admit.

Enclosed is the Synopsis for the programme, and hope it encourages the right sort of atmosphere.

Rob.

To JOYCE BEDFORD

Massey College
University of Toronto
April 29, 1982

Joyce Bedford (1928–   ), Canadian librarian, had complained in an amusing letter that she had to "thumb wrestle" the pages of The Rebel Angels *apart so that she could pursue the story.*

Dear Miss Bedford:

It was good of you to write to me about the pleasure that my books have given you, and quite agree with you that *The Rebel Angels* is not an easy book to read because of the way in which it is put together. I am sending your letter to the publishers and I am sure that they will be interested in your comment, but would be unable to produce a more easily manageable book without increasing the cost to a figure that would seem ridiculous for a novel. Doubtless you are aware that the costs of printing and binding books have increased very greatly in the past few years and the technology by which books can now be produced at anything like a reasonable figure is such that the book is not always a pleasant physical object. I do not know what the technical problems are though I suspect that it is now impossible to have books stitched as they once were and so the backs have to be set in some sort of composition. You say that some English books are better produced in this respect, but I have received books from England within the last few years which open with an ominous crack unless one handles them with extraordinary care.

The only solution that I can suggest sounds so egotistical that I am ashamed to put it forward, but it is a fact that if you read and re-read *The Rebel Angels* several times you will find it will open more easily every time. An alternative is to allow your cat to keep the book in its basket for a few weeks and the warmth of the cat will so soften the binding that the book will be more manageable.

With thanks and good wishes,

Yours sincerely,

Robertson Davies

To LEON EDEL

Massey College
University of Toronto
[shortly before July 29, 1982]

Dear Leon Edel:

I have been far too long in acknowledging the copy of *Stuff of Sleep and Dreams* you asked your publishers to send me, and my excuse has no originality whatever – I have been so busy with things which managed to be imperative without being really important that a lot of correspondence has been neglected. But also, I did not *gobble* the book; I found it so much to my taste that I wanted to spin it out, and did.

Let me say at once that I admired the book greatly, and its attitude of psychological examination and explication without the know-it-allness that mars the work of lesser folk than yourself, is one that has been of keen interest to me for at least forty years. My admiration is partly that of one who would like to be able to do something in that line himself, and partly that of an author who fears such investigation of his own work.

Why "fears"? Well – you put the heart across me with some of your comments on writers who had heralded their own imminent demise in books they wrote in which you had discerned the Black Angel, lurking. I am at present laying the foundations – a process for me of careful note-making, collecting of relevant references, and even making files of newspaper clippings – for a new novel [*What's Bred in the Bone*]. The subject is the difficulties of a man who has been commissioned to write the biography of someone he knew (Francis Cornish, the art collector and benefactor in *The Rebel Angels*) and who can gather heaps of facts but knows the facts don't tell the true story. "Only the Recording Angel has the real story," says he (and as he is the clergyman in TRA, Simon Darcourt, the Recording Angel is more real to him than it might be to someone else) and then I proceed to tell the life of Francis Cornish as the Recording Angel knew it. But – superstitious wretch that I am – I thought: all this stuff about angels, about the ultimate record, about a judgement not of this world – are you heralding your own death, my boy? Will you topple from your chair as you type the last words? Don't tempt Fate.

With the passing of time I have been able to still these fears – almost – but you see how profound your influence is.

I thought the first part splendid, and it recalled to me the sense of emancipation I experienced when first I encountered Freud. It seemed as though he had made real so many things that had been wispily present in my own mind, but which I did not dare to trust. Later I found even more to enlarge my life in the Jungian heresy, and I sometimes wonder how much of that is personal disposition, reaching far into one's background. The deeply Viennese, and in certain respects the profoundly Jewish, cast of Freud's mind commands my respect but not my immediate assent or final loyalty: as a Northerner and a Celt* I am more at home with Jung, not because I think he has Truth by the tail, with a downhill pull, but because whatever he has of truth speaks to me in a tongue I can understand more readily than that of Freud. More sentimental, somebody might say. But also not so over-whelmingly egotistical; Freud so often seems to be persuading people to look inward, who have never looked anywhere else, and who might profitably take a peep at the world outside themselves. But perhaps I am talking like a YMCA secretary.

Anyhow, I mustn't get into the lecturing vein, but hasten to thank you again for a book that has given me much pleasure and enlightenment, and to which I shall surely turn again and again.

Robertson Davies

PS: A woman [Judith Skelton Grant] is writing a biography of *me*: no way of stopping her. But it gives me the trembles. I have made her read your *Literary Biography* & she admires it hugely.

To DAVID GARDNER

Davies returned part of the final typescript of Gardner's Ph.D. thesis with this note.

[on or just before August 19, 1982]

Dear David:

Yes, this is all hunky-dory. The only thing – a trifle, but it is trifles that betray us – is your derivation of "carnival" from *carne vale*, which is dog-Latin, though reasonable Italian. See the big *Oxford English Dictionary*. Don't change it in the typescript but be ready with an answer if you need one.

R.D.

To ELISABETH SIFTON

Massey College
University of Toronto
[October 1982]

Dear Elisabeth:

. . . Now here I am at the end of my paper and ought to desist,
but I have an odd adventure to relate. For some months – about a
year – I have been receiving very kind and praising and humble letters
from John Irving, author of *The World According to Garp* and *Hotel New
Hampshire* – fan letters,* no less. He says I am his ideal among living
writers. Well, well; I am totally unaccustomed to this sort of approach
from anyone, let alone immensely successful and popular novelists.
Recently he came to Toronto to give a reading, and wrote to ask if
he could take me to lunch. I replied, as a boy educated at Upper
Canada College* (the Eton of the North) ought to do, that I couldn't
think of it, and he must allow me to take *him* to lunch. I nominated
the York Club, the second-stuffiest club in Toronto, and told Brenda
to get herself a Big Mac somewhere as We Authors were going to
have a heavy session. So, prompt to the hour, Irving arrived, splendidly dressed, but to my astonishment wearing running-shoes,* which
I gather are all the thing now among the younger fashionables though
in my young days we were assured that they "drew your eyes" and
caused the feet to give forth a powerful fragrance, like a hot motor
tyre. But what really surprised me was that he had a lady in tow, who
was introduced simply as Rusty,* but who after a while emerged as
Mrs. Guinzburg-as-was, the ex-wife of the former head of Viking . . . .
She proved to be a nice and funny lady, and Irving was delightful, and
we had a high old time. Brenda – who might just as well have eaten
with us, and not been banished – turned up later and we all got on
like a house on fire, if I may coin a phrase. The York Club astonished
Irving and Rusty, as I do not think such funeral parlours come their
way often – though it is really a very nice club, though on the quiet
and formal side. But there it is, you see – literary high-jinks in

Toronto, of all places! Irving is very modest; I asked him if the *Garp* film was doing well. He said not.... But here I am again at the bottom of the paper and this time ENOUGH must positively be E*N*O*U*G*H!

Rob.

PS: I am making a short movie* in Kingston next month for the BBC *Authors and Places* series. Should be fun.

To GORDON AND HELEN ROPER

Windhover
Caledon East
January 10, 1983

Dear Friends:

Christmas has come and gone, and Brenda and I are recovering our faculties and our strength. We had Brenda's sister Maisie [Drysdale] here from Australia, and Miranda from England, which does not seem like a crowd when you think of Christmas at Dingley Dell,* but at D.D. they had a crowd of servants and the inexhaustible Dickensian *verve* to carry them through. Whereas here we had only Brenda (Ol' Black Mammy) and me (Old Black Joe) to do all the cooking, serving, heaving and lugging. Guests make a feint of helping, and doubtless are convinced that they do help, but there are things no guest can do, which have to be done..... But we spent a good deal of time in Toronto, and our friends came forward nobly to entertain, and that was splendid, except that my digestion was driven to the uttermost extreme of endurance, for from Tuesday to Friday of the week between Christmas and New Year, we ate lunch and dinner at a different house every day, and all the hosts extended themselves on the seasonable goodies and the festive booze. Reviving the Good Old-Fashioned Christmas is a delightful ideal, but I wish the Good, Old-Fashioned Gizzard could be revived with it.

My sister-in-law is immensely popular, for she is a very amusing talker, loves company, and being Lady Drysdale she strikes awe into the bosoms of those who are impressed by such gauds – not strong republicans like ourselves. But on the other hand she smokes not three, but 3½ packs of cigs a day .... Her great enthusiasms are painting and literature; she has been married to two of Australia's foremost painters* and is now a "resource-person" for students of that subject. But her literary taste was formed in the 'thirties and 'forties, and has stuck there, so that she is impatient of later developments, particularly in the realm of sensibility – she has never forgiven Waugh for writing *Brideshead*.* But I suddenly realize that anything I write to you may end up in some damned "archive" somewhere, and I must watch my step. Not your fault, I know, but the ghouls and resurrectionmen are on the march.

Chief among them La Grant, whom I am beginning to like, but whom I do not really trust – not because she is a designing crook, but because she is a modern researcher, and they have no bowels of compassion, nor were they trained in any school of scrupulosity. I recently let her read a diary of mine, and was astonished to find that she had Xeroxed a part of it! So that she could return it to me, of course, but what happens to the Xerox? As a matter of fact, I don't care passionately about such things and I shall take care she doesn't get her mitts on anything really explosive, but I wonder what her book will be like? Her deep desire, I know, is to knock Elspeth Cameron* into a cocked hat; EC's book about Hugh MacLennan fills her with rage – as well it might – and she wants to outdo it. Well, good luck to her. I do wish, however, that I could be left in peace till I have shuffled off this mortal coil* and completed my work. I feel like a turnip that is being dug up half-grown to see how it is getting along. Or, worse still, like an author whose later work is considered to be so ineffective that it need not be considered. I hope I have a surprise or two in store for La Grant.

Now Shhhhh! both of you. Absolute and unbroken Shhhhhhhhhh! I am beginning work on my next novel [*What's Bred in the Bone*], and it is to be the life of Francis Cornish, who appears at the beginning of *Rebel Angels*: a great collector of paintings, works of art, MSS and caricatures, and musical MSS as much as anything. Francis is dead in RA; but in this book he is recorded from childhood, and the influences that made him a great art-collector are carefully examined. But – the person who has been enjoined to write his life is Simon Darcourt, who is doing it for the trust that Arthur and Maria Cornish have set up to advance various sorts of artistic work; Simon complains piteously that he can find out all about the externals of Francis's life, but the really important things have vanished and can never be recovered; the book tells what Simon can never hope to know – the curious details that go to make a great connoisseur, which might equally well have made him a miser, a pawn-broker or a pervert.

You see? What La Grant is doing to me has brought sharply to my attention things I know have been influential in my life of which no record exists, or can possibly exist, and which I would not dream of telling her. If I am being biographed, I might as well watch the process with an author's eye.

I have been reading the recently published correspondence between Bernard Shaw and Lord Alfred Douglas,* and it is fascinating. Rather too much Douglas to the amount of Shaw, but that was because Douglas was a compulsive letter-writer, and also a whiner who thought GBS was not doing right by him; it seems to me GBS treated him with extraordinary generosity. Doubtless it is in the Trent Library, and I recommend it. Some of the best letters were written when Shaw was 88. Now *there* was a writer who refused to lie down and die to oblige the critics. But then, he wasn't a Canadian. We are a biddable people.

Don't move from the country* till you absolutely have to. Life in the country is salutary; without this place I should be in an asylum.

Love from both of us –

Rob.

To MORLEY CALLAGHAN

Massey College
University of Toronto
Feb. 22, 1983

Morley Callaghan (1903–90), Canadian, is
one of Canada's best-known writers of
novels and short stories.

Dear Morley:

After Barry's call to me in London I had hopes of being with you
for your eightieth birthday celebrations,* but as he may have told you,
I had 'flu then, and have returned to Toronto with it in an even more
miserable form. I do not want to be the skeleton at your feast, whoop-
ing and coughing and sneezing like some afflicted creature in a bad
Biblical film, and my doctor [Jaroslav M. J. Polak] is against it. But I
cannot let the day go by without greeting you.

When I first began to be aware that there was any Canadian writing
by living authors, you were in the first flush of your reputation, and
I remember you as an inspiration and a flag-bearer for all Canadian
writers. Since then you have always been at the head of the procession, and your high sense of the dignity of authorship and your refusal
to be patronized or made a social figure by people who do not give
a damn about literature but are strong for some generalized uplift
which they call "culture," has helped many of us to stand out for
reality and firmness of purpose in our work, however varied it may
be in approach. You have fought strongly and bravely for the establishment of an indigenous literature and so long as it lasts your name
will be held in honour. Though I cannot be with you in the suffering
flesh, I am with you in the spirit at your birthday celebration, wishing
you long life and health, and thanking you sincerely not only for what
you have done, but for what you have been.

Brenda joins me in every good wish to you and Lorette on this occasion and in the future.

Robertson Davies

To ELISABETH SIFTON

Massey College
University of Toronto
April 11, 1983

Dear Elisabeth:

Thank you for the long article* on my novels by Timothy Norris in *In Print* which Katy Brooks* sent to me on March 29, and which our decrepit mail service has delivered today. I have read it with great care, and am pleased to have come off so lightly in an article written by someone who seems to be trying hard to be a hostile critic. It arrives as I am getting deep into my next novel *What's Bred in the Bone*, and makes me think seriously about what I have been writing in its early pages.

I know it is a mistake to be too much influenced by criticism. As Thornton Wilder* wisely said, if you pay too much attention to critics, they will get into your head and write your next book – and then where will you be? Norris seems displeased because my books are sometimes ingenious in plot, and make a display of varied knowledge; too many people write me saying how much they like precisely those things for me to be much worried by *that*. But I sense what he is about: I have had so much praise recently – some of it decidedly uncritical and of a kind to make me blush – that he has decided to knock a few corners off me, and that is fair enough. Woe unto me when all men praise me! as T. S. Eliot makes the Archbishop say.*

But the criticism which I feel I must take seriously is in the end of the article. "Davies has yet to move us to tears," he says. True, some of my readers would disagree, but I have never really pulled out the *vox humana* and the *vox celeste* stops, and I am wondering if perhaps I may not do so. Norris calls for "the pleasing vice of honest senti-ment," which is a choice of words that warns me that if I became too free with sentiment this man would be quick to jump on me. He says he wants to be "gripped by great emotion." Obviously he does not regard mirth as an emotion, because I know I have made quite a few people laugh a lot, and that is not the easiest thing to do. But if he wants tears, how about a few tears?

What's Bred In The Bone could become pretty tearful, in places, for it draws upon experience of my own which was not comic, particularly in the childhood episodes. I am rather leery of this, for I do not want to tear myself to bits writing it, but the pull is toward tears. The theme is of a man whose childhood is marked by neglect, but not the obvious neglect of poverty, but the equally distressing neglect that can go with wealth. The book makes frequent reference to a popular Victorian picture called "Love Locked Out,"* and that is in part the motto of the narrator's – no, the hero's – youth, and it makes him into a tough, sardonic crook – though not a crook that anybody can accuse unless they want to bring down quite a piece of the elaborate fabric of the international art trade. He offers love to two or three people during his lifetime and gets stung every time – last of all by a young man who uses him as a ladder for his own ambition. Not funny. Could be tearful, if tears are what's wanted.

Like a few tears, Elisabeth? I can switch on the sprinkler any time. I should value your opinion.

Unfortunately, for people who think as Norris does, the plot tends to be ingenious. Has to be, if I am to link it with *Rebel Angels* and the book that follows this one [*The Lyre of Orpheus*], and I want to do that. But I can minimize the ingenuity, instead of exploiting it, as I have done before. There is less than the usual deployment of curious information, though there is some of that and it can't be avoided. My wife thinks highly of what I have done; says it moves very rapidly, but there must be a few tricky bits or it wouldn't be a book by me. I love mystification, as Norris says, reprovingly, but I can hold back a bit.

A lot of readers seem to look to me to make them laugh, and I confess I love to do that. But – how about a few tears? Blub, blub: snuffle snuffle. I've got 'em, if anybody really wants 'em.

I should greatly value your opinion. I know you are terribly busy, but some reflections on this subject, which is very important to me, would make an immense difference to

Your faithful slave,

Rob.

To ARNOLD EDINBOROUGH

The Canadian Society for Italic Handwriting*
June 15, 1983

Dear Arnold:

Like water, fiction cannot rise above its source, and it is not in the power of Morris West* to draw a picture of C. G. Jung. What he has done, in my opinion, is to clothe a rather conventional tale of the wild Hungarian beauty who beats the whey out of her lovers but yearns for salvation with a very thin layer of ill-perceived historical reconstruction. He makes free with Jung, his wife and Toni Wolff* in a way that makes my hair curl. The real story of that odd *ménage à trois* has not yet been told, and Jung's heirs sit tightly on the evidence; but I have known people who knew them all, and several who were analysed by Jung and also by Toni Wolff, and they tell a much soberer tale than West. Jung's methods were not Freudian – no couch, often worked in the garden, sometimes scolded (but did not swear at) his patients, but was in the main a v. professional Swiss doctor. Toni Wolff was described to me as the ultimate in upper-class Swiss demeanour (one analysand told me she never saw Toni's back touch the back of her chair) and she lived in great respectability with her Mum, and was on the whole rather like a super-intelligent governess. All this sobbing, roaring and creaming the jeans West describes exists nowhere but in his superheated, lower-class R.C. imagination. I read the novel carefully; West has a compelling narrative gift, but in my view he uses it irresponsibly; to drag in a great man to deck out his Harlequin tale is in my view inadmissible and unprofessional.

A fine tribute to Toni Wolff* appears in *Jung & the Story of Our Time* by Laurens van der Post who knew her well. Emma Jung also declared her "gratitude" to T. W.

This would not concern me greatly if it were not something of a trend in modern fiction. Have you seen Anthony Burgess'* *End of the World News*. He introduces Freud and Jung as characters, and exploits Freud's agony in placing the terrible prosthesis he had to wear because of his cancerous jaw, and paints a strange portrait of Ernest Jones* – who was an odd man as any super-intelligent man is likely to be, but not a freak. And, like West, Burgess carries on a good deal about anti-Semitism. West, however, is mischievous in this respect, for he says Jung was anti-Semitic, which a mass of evidence shows he wasn't. But one of his pupils told me Jung wasn't prepared to take nonsense from Jews in analysis, because it clouded the issues – no attributing things to Jewish blood or anti-Jewish prejudice which in fact came from other sources – and this didn't sit well with some Jewish patients. But just how anti-Semitic and anti-Freudian he was appears in this: when the Nazis invaded Austria, Jung offered the money and the means to take Freud and his family to England or to Switzerland, as they chose, and Freud refused, because he wouldn't accept help from a man he regarded as a renegade, and was bitter about Jung's birth-Calvinism. Doesn't sound much like anti-Semitism, does it? When Hitler quashed psychoanalysis in Germany-dominated Europe, it was Jung who kept the ship afloat, which he could do because he was Aryan, even by the demanding standards of Drs. Hitler, Himmler, Goering and other experts..... But I grow tedious. Many thanks for letting me see the book.

Rob.

To JANET FRANKLAND, and
Students of Grade 13 Canadian
Literature Class

*Janet Frankland was then a grade 13
student. She had written to Davies on
behalf of her class at R. H. King Collegiate
Institute, Scarborough, Ontario.*

Massey College
University of Toronto
June 21, 1983

[Dear Miss Frankland and Grade XIII Students:]

I was interested to receive your letter of June 6th about *The Rebel Angels* and glad that some of you enjoyed it. However, there are some matters that you bring up in it which I would like to pursue further. The first was that several of your members thought that the book was above the average reader's comprehension because of its vocabulary. May I suggest to you, as gently as possible, that the book was written for average readers, and that a Grade XIII class in a collegiate institute cannot quite claim to have reached that status. You hope some day to be average readers but that is not your status at present.

You may think this is hard, but consider these matters: you say that you felt that Ozias Froats was a lampoon of a professor doing fairly useless research, but being paid to do so. If you had read the book with the care that the average reader would bring to it you would see that one of the principal points of the book was that Froats' research, which was not understood by anybody but himself, eventually produced remarkable results and that the theme of the discovery of great value in what is rejected and despised is one of the main themes of the novel. I wonder if you finished the book. If so, you could not have missed the fact that Ozias Froats is about to receive the Nobel Prize for science. The Nobel committee does not give its prize to fakes.

You may have found that the professors' conversations dragged for you, but I have had many letters from average readers who liked them very much. As for Maria, when you arrive at the university you will probably meet a number of girls like her and you should – particularly the boys – prepare yourself for this experience. You may say that you have never met anybody like her but I presume you study some of the plays of Shakespeare and I do not expect that you have met anybody like the heroines of those plays either. It is not an author's object to give a photographic reproduction of reality.

This also answers your final question: none of the characters in the book are portraits of living people. Fiction may be portrait painting but if it is any good it is not photography. The purpose of the book was to suggest that universities are great and fascinating places and I hope that some of you will find it so when you attend university next year.

With good wishes, I am

Yours sincerely,

[Robertson Davies]

To MARGARET ATWOOD

Windhover
Caledon East
June 30, 1983

> Margaret Atwood (1939–   ) is a best-selling, internationally respected, influential Canadian poet, novelist, and critic.

Dear Margaret:

Congratulations on your speech at Convocation, which I have just read in the *University of Toronto Bulletin.** The graduating class must have enjoyed it hugely..... I am a veteran of many Convocations and may claim to be an expert on Convocation addresses. In my experience the worst ones come from scientists; they lovingly rehearse their careers from their first poisoned rabbit or nasty smell right up to the present day, leaving out nothing. But some of the humanities people can give them a close run; I have heard monstrous exordiums from theologians, and the worse they are the poorer is their sense of when to shut up and sit down. Yours was exemplary – funny, witty (not the same thing) and with one piece of really good advice,* which is all any speech will bear.

Interested that you quoted from Oscar Wilde. He has haunted me all my university days; grad students love him, and some of them are subsumed in his persona, and queen about the place, making cracks in class which can only be described as Wilde-and-Ditchwater. I have a high regard for him, but stop several hundred yards this side idolatry. Did you know that his first lover, literary executor, and most faithful friend was a Canadian? Yes, Robert Ross,* one of the Baldwin family. Ross was a man of true dignity and decency, and was very good to Constance Wilde and the children, so far as their beastly uncles would permit. To me the saddest remark in the whole silly mess was Ross's "If Oscar had stayed with me none of this would have happened." But Oscar was doom-eager,* as our ancestors said, and was hogwild for martyrdom – martyrdom, the ultimate in sensational publicity. I sigh when I hear him brought forward in evidence by the fiercely political gays of our time..... But it delights me that Canada had a good big finger in that scandalous pie; it decreases our image as a nation of stick-in-the-muds.

Didn't mean to carry on like this. Congratulations again.

Rob. Davies

To ELEANOR SWEEZEY

Massey College
University of Toronto
August 8, 1983

*Eleanor Anne Sweezey (1915–   ),
Canadian medical illustrator, worked for
Queen Mary Veterans Hospital in
Montreal from 1945–75 and for the
neurosurgeon Wilder Penfield. She and
Davies dated (and he fell in love with
her) while both were students at Queen's
University.*

Dear Eleanor:

I shall be in Montreal on Monday, September 19, to attend an affair
at McGill, and I wonder if it would be possible for you to have lunch
with me that day, probably at the Ritz, which is where the university
is putting me. If you can – and I hope you can – will you let me
know, so I can warn them to kill the fatted hamburger for two?

We have not met for* – I cannot really say how long – and I am
sharply reminded that this month I shall be seventy, and ought not to
lose time seeing old friends. Not that Time's winged chariot* is
absolutely roaring in my ear, but I have been, for five years, officially
and by government reckoning, an Old Geezer. Are you, too, old? I
bet you are not. I always think of you as about twenty.

But if you can come to lunch, be prepared to see me sore stricken
in years – white-haired, stout and apt to shout "What?" at people
who mumble when they talk.

All good wishes.....

Robertson Davies

To DOMINI BLYTHE

Windhover
Caledon East
August 29, 1983

Dear Miss B.

Congratulations and warm admiration for your Margery
Pinchwife;* my wife and I agreed it was quite the best we have ever
seen.

So what have you seen,* sez you? Well, to begin, the first modern
revival of the play that Sydney Carroll did in London in 1934, in
which Lesley Wareing as Margery was quite obliterated by Athene
Seyler as Lady Fidget. Then the Old Vic production in 1936, in which
Ruth Gordon played Margery, but was (in the director, Tyrone
Guthrie's words) "acted right off the stage and out into the alley"
by Edith Evans as Lady F. Ruth G. was too cunning, too foxy, too
knowing, for the part. Then in 1959, Julie Harris's undistinguished
venture in New York, in which nobody shone; a common grayness
silvered all.* Then the Stratford production in which Helen Burns
was very good as Margery, but the teeniest bit too much the simpleton, the witling. Where you scored heavily was in making Margery
an innocent, rather than a fool – a good-hearted determined, sensible girl. It was sensible of the director to make the relationship
between Pinchwife and Margery not all disagreeable; he shows some
affection, and she some compliance. This is so much better than the
usual cat-and-dog affair between a brute and a scheming yokel.

The play has great charm; how much better it plays than it reads!
It needs the players to bring humanity and softness to the essentially
nasty story. One would never think, to see Restoration drama, how
many loving couples there were even among the aristocracy, whose
letters to one another are of a touching tenderness. But the wit
redeems everything, and we know we are watching a make-believe
rather than any society that ever existed anywhere.

So – once again we are greatly in your debt for a very fine performance, and as we have seen all the important productions of the
play since it rejoined the repertoire (the Victorians simply couldn't
endure it) I hope that gives you some satisfaction.

Sincerely

Robertson Davies

To KENNETH HART GREEN

Massey College
University of Toronto
Sept. 7: 1983

| | Kenneth Hart Green lived in Brookline, Massachusetts, when he wrote to Davies. |

Dear Mᴿ Green:

The question of Morality and Art that you raise in your letter of
August 25 is a very large one and I am not convinced that I can say
anything that is more than merely tentative about it. But I have given
the matter a great deal of consideration, and without being in any
sense dogmatic, I offer you a few ideas that I have formed.

Art is necessarily moral, in that it is comment on life, but it is most
successful when it is moral by indirection. This is particularly true of
literature. When it sets out to be overtly and dogmatically moral – as
in *The Pilgrim's Progress** – the result may be splendid and often
moving narrative, but one is always aware that the writer is not
writing in freedom, and that his chains are those of dogma. Art is
creation, and art cannot function at its highest when it is in the
service of anything but itself. You speak of Tolstoy: in *War & Peace*
and *Anna Karenina* he wrote as a great, and free artist, describing
life as it appeared to him; when he became resolutely moral, and
wrote to better mankind, his work was of a markedly inferior level.
Dostoevsky,* who never wrote to prove a moral point, was a great
moralist without intending to be so. So also Zola and Flaubert*: *Nana*

and *Madame Bovary* are highly moral works, but that is not their primary purpose. Such books are moral because they exemplify great moral truths, such as God is not mocked,* and The dog shall return again to his vomit and the sow that was washed to her wallowing in the mire:* but they do not set out to prove these things – rather, the moral precept is inherent in the convincing stories they tell. A great novel – indeed many great novels – may show that As a man soweth, that shall he also reap,* because it is an observable truth about life. But if he writes simply to prove that, he ceases to be an artist and becomes a preacher – which is what happened to Tolstoy.

It has been the fashion since the end of the First World War to decry moralism in art, and many artists have taken the fullest advantage of the freedom they enjoy to depict aspects of life which are trivial and squalid. But a novel which seems to deal with trivialities may be at root deeply moral: *vide* Evelyn Waugh. And squalor may, on inspection, prove to be the harvest of an unreflecting, determinedly foolish mode of life. Squalor is fashionable in books for the intelligentsia; it is not so popular with simpler readers.

To prove my point: examine the Detective Novel, which is unfailingly popular. It is simply and resolutely moral. An offence against justice and humanity is committed, usually a murder. The murderer is tracked down by a man who may assume a variety of guises – the Great Intellect (Sherlock Holmes), the apparently foppish aesthete (Lord Peter Wimsey), the Tough Guy (Sam Spade) or the simple priest (Father Brown). But whatever the disguise, he is undoubtedly that figure common in medieval drama, Divine Correction, who hounds down the wrongdoer and brings him to justice. The Spy Novel runs on much the same tracks; the traitor must be found, and punished. This is simple morality, and it is what millions of readers ask for. Morality is the basis of order, and the human heart hungers for order.

In my own books morality is certainly discernible, because I am a Canadian and write about Canadians, who like to think of themselves as free from the bonds of religion, but religion and morality are not the same thing. Religion is the poetry of faith, and not all people are open to poetry. But morality is the structure of society, and however we may tinker with society we have to have some general notions of what society will tolerate and what it must reject if it is to survive. The roots of morality I believe to be archetypal, and the archetypes are not readily comprehended, and sometimes function with what looks like caprice and ambiguity, but they always tend toward a pattern which is at the depth of human life.

That's enough for the present. If you want to write again, please do so.

Robertson Davies

PS: We are at the end of a millennium & such times throw up great moral tumult, followed by a reconsideration. Consider what happened in the years 900–1000 A.D. Consider what was the moral climate at the time of the birth of Christ.

To ANDREW DAVIS

Massey College
University of Toronto
October 14, 1983

Andrew Davis (1944–   ), English, was the conductor of the Toronto Symphony Orchestra from 1975–88. He has been musical director of the Glyndebourne Festival Opera since 1988 and chief conductor of the BBC Symphony Orchestra since 1989.

[Maestro:]

On October 12th I returned from Germany, where I heard some admirable music, and on the 13th I attended the TSO concert and had the immense satisfaction of feeling that, within my lifetime, the Toronto Symphony had grown from something not much better than a scratch town band to an orchestra which does not surpass the best, but which can stand comparison with the best. A great part of this is owing to your great abilities as a trainer and conductor, and I know that I speak for all my musical friends when I say how deeply grateful we are to you. A fine orchestra is one of the things one expects in a fine city, and the TSO under your direction gives lustre to Toronto.

My own experience goes back 55 years, when, as a schoolboy at

Upper Canada College, I was one of the group that went regularly to the five o'clock concerts, when the conductor was Luigi von Kunits.* He was not a musician of great capacity, but he made an orchestra of a sort out of a rabble of pit musicians from the movie houses. They appeared in all sorts of outfits – Blachford, the concertmaster always in morning coat, but declining from that to detrimentals in running-shoes; when a bass clarinet was needed a canon from St. James's played it, presenting an oddly Trollopian* figure in his clerical collar. von Kunits had a regrettable habit of combing his abundant hair, worn in a Viennese fruzz, in public.

Some of the playing was truly awful. The Third Act Introduction from *Lohengrin** brought out the worst in the musicians, and the sound of the brass section was like giants tearing up huge rolls of linoleum. Sir Ernest MacMillan* did much to refine the orchestra and give it musical coherence, though for some reason they always played painfully loudly under his baton. Subsequent conductors have built on what he did, and you have brought the TSO to the pitch which gives me so much pride in its quality that I am prompted to write this.

On Thursday night my mind wandered over many memories of things that have altered, or more often not altered, in 55 years. The concertmaster still acknowledges the applause that greets his entrance with a glare of fearful malignance at the audience. The orchestra still clambers to its feet when asked by you to take a bow as if they were pondering whether such exertion was really part of their contractual duty. In the back row of the violins a young man still waves and grimaces at his friends in the audience. They still practise all their hardest passages at full blast for half an hour before the concert begins, making the hellish racket common to orchestras all over the world. (If actors shouted, hawked, spat and strutted in full view before the play began, what an outcry there would be!) But as time passes Stanley Solomon's* entry has ceased to be diffident, has become the assured pace of the successful Don Juan, and has now become positively processional. Such reflections are part of the pleasures of age.

But the concert that followed – ! No doubt you have your reservations, but the applause of the audience must have assured you that we were truly and gratefully pleased.

That brings me to one difficult matter, which I must discuss before I conclude this letter – already too long. The orchestra, the musicians, you yourself, are obviously in the best of artistic health. But the organization, and especially the public relations of the TSO, seems to me to be going off its head. My wife and I subscribed as usual last Spring, and got our usual tickets (G 18 and 20) which are neither the best nor the worst in the house. But during the summer I had a call from a young woman with an unusually charming voice who said, as I remember, that the organization was anxious to provide better seats for those who wanted them, and would I like to sit in one of the sugar scoops,* which are supposed to be acoustically the best in Roy Thomson Hall. Wooed by this invisible seductress, I said I would indeed like that, and sent off the required money – something like $190. – to the address given me. Nothing more was heard till I opened my mail on returning from abroad, and found a letter from somebody called _____, of Direct Results Marketing, explaining in complex and opaque detail that it had all been a mirage, and no sugar scoop seats would be forthcoming. Accompanying this letter (in which it was obvious that poor _____ was eating a heaping plateful of crow) was another over a facsimile of your signature, urging me to give, give, give to the TSO or only God knows what horrors may result.

This is simply crazy. Every arts organization in Toronto is at the same game, shrieking doom if more money is not forthcoming from the people who are already giving, and have been giving for decades. The impression this makes on me – and on many others, for we talk about such things in the secret bunkers where we donors hide from the PR people – is that the boards and committees of these organizations, including the TSO, are consumed with inordinate greed, a disease more dreadful in corporate persons than even AIDS. Is it beyond the wit of man to devise a program of money-collecting which is convincing, courteous and congruous with the high artistic standards of the TSO or whatever other cause is being served? I will do a great deal for the TSO as an orchestra, but I'm damned if I will be bullied and panicked by the PR people who too plainly know nothing, and care nothing for Art, and have no conception of the dignity which should be accorded to artists and to those who understand and support them.

With every good wish for your continued success, I am

Yours sincerely,

[Robertson Davies]

To ELEANOR SWEEZEY

Massey College
University of Toronto
December 7, 1983

Dear Eleanor:

Judith Grant has just told me that Maggie [Eleanor's sister, Margaret Mitchell Sweezey]* has died, and I hasten to write to you, though I have no idea what I can say. From your last letter it is clear that you will be neither surprised or dismayed, after the inexcusably priestly way in which the medicos ignored your wishes and brought her back to life when she had died once already. I believe that there is a psychologically right time to die, and such meddlesome interference is contrary to every psychological decency. The time of death is decided upon and acted upon at a level of being which is well below consciousness, but is not for that reason to be flouted. But such attention to the dictates of the psyche is well beyond the comprehension of all but a few rare doctors. Scientifically they have come a long way, but psychologically they are kin to the priest-physicians of ancient Egypt. No, that is wrong; the priest-physicians appear to have had some fear of the gods, and modern doctors have no god but the Canadian Medical Association.

My recollections of Maggie go back to an occasion long ago when I visited your Mother [Harriet Mitchell Watson Sweezey]* to arrange about that terrible performance of [*The Importance of Being*] *Earnest* we did at Pineledge at the following New Year. She was a vivid figure, full of energy and mirth and she thought I was the funniest thing she had ever encountered – which may well have been true, for I was a solemn young man. But as time passed and that house-party developed because we were snowed in – or thought we were – I saw that from time to time she hid herself and burst into unaccountable tears. And it is thus I remember her – elation and depression alternating. I noted this in a diary I was keeping at the time.

So poor Maggie's tale is told, and you are the one who must have sympathy and assurance. Such partings, however we may think we are ready for them, are always a blow, and the blow may be deferred. Is there any chance that you can get away, and have a holiday, and get things straight after the long strain of Maggie's illness?

Thoughts of the death of someone near inevitably make us think of our own death, and the task is to think of it in the right way – not as something imminent but as an ending, a rounding-off, an exit from the scene. I have seen this countless times, and especially in my brother [Arthur] who was convinced when his first wife died that he would follow in no time at all. Not so. You are not old – not *that* kind of old – and much may await you now that you no longer have to look after Maggie, who must have needed a lot of care and patience as time passed. You will think me mad, but I am not – merely Jungian in my thinking – and I am sure that in some cases the dead are jealous of the living, and the living feel the chill of that jealousy. A pupil of Dr. Jung's told me* that when her extremely dominating father died, Jung insisted that she give the keys of her car to him, so that she could not drive it for forty days or so after the father's death. He did not develop the theme, but merely said that she should not do dangerous or risky things for a while. SO – take the best possible care of yourself, be gentle with yourself, and get away if you can. Then you can take up a life which is directed in quite another way.

What an odd letter to be writing on such an occasion! Yesterday I had to write one in a very conventional strain to the widow of a very good friend, and perhaps this is reaction against that. But I mean what

I say. YOU are the most important person in your life, and you deserve every consideration you can give yourself.

All good wishes – try to have a *merry* Christmas –

Rob.

To JUDITH SKELTON GRANT

Windhover
Caledon East
January 2, 1984

Dear Judith:

Many thanks for the splendid Christmas cake, which is now all gone, down the red lanes of guests, children, grandchildren and of course ourselves. A fine effort. You redeem the academic world from the charge of being insensitive to the sensualities..... Before Christmas I was knocked down by a car in the dark, which was rather too near to concluding our joint effort for my taste. Consequently I spent the merry season rather under the weather with aches and pains; the dr. [Jaroslav M. J. Polak] told my wife that I was not to be babied, but she wisely did not heed him, and I am now in pretty fair nick, though stiff and grumpy. He said I would have what he nastily called "geriatric depression" for about five or six weeks; this is the new name for the mulligrubs. But I only have it for about half an hour each day. However we are staying in the country until next week, and I am trying to get on with the book [*What's Bred in the Bone*], which is excellent therapy..... Every good wish to you and John and the boys for 1984, upon which Orwell* has attempted to put a literary hex. Heed him not.....

Rob.

To PHILIP JOHN STEAD

Massey College
University of Toronto
April 24, 1984

Dear John:

I have had you much in mind since your last letter came, and would
have replied at once, had that not coincided with getting the 'flu, or
as my Mother grandiosely called it The Spanish Influenza. Have been
rather out of commission with this megrim; I am subject to such ail-
ments, having a family disposition toward all coughs, colds, oppres-
sions of the chest, rot of the bronnikkles, imposthumes and indeed
anything that springs from, or tends toward Snot. I recall at Oxford
you dropped in on me one day and found me under a towel inhal-
ing steam from Friar's Balsam, and were much diverted by this treatment, which you termed Jonsonian.* Ah, my friend, you should see
me now! Volpone was as nothing to me. But enough on this melancholy theme.

Your suggestion that I might be a candidate for the Royal Society
of Literature delights me. I have always had a high regard for it
without knowing anything about it, except that some obviously
worthy people like yourself possess it. What must I do? Submit a cv
or what?

Have been working hard to complete a novel [What's Bred in the
Bone], which moves slowly, but so far surely. But it is on a theme
where I have to tread gently – the world of painting; I know little
about it and have to check every step lest I should tread in a cow-pat
and be exposed as a charlatan. It is not really about painting but about
the relative nature of truth and deceit in matters of art, but painting
is the excuse. And in addition I have been under the kindly, remorse-
less interrogation of Judith Grant, who draws forth my soul, eats it
and asks for more – and bloodier. You met her. Indeed, she said she
had a most agreeable time with you and Judith, who is, she tells me,
a painter,* which I had not known.

Judith Grant brought me the article about Surtees,* which I read with great pleasure. I have always admired Surtees without really being a devotee. Such refreshing common sense from a Victorian writer – but really I suppose he never emerged mentally from the Regency. I have just been reading a book about the marriages of a number of Victorian literary figures by a woman called Phyllis Rose,* of Wesleyan University – called *Parallel Lives*. Flawed by a strong feminist bias, but not bad. What extraordinary didoes the Victorians got up to, and so long as they *talked* in highly moral terms nobody blew the whistle on them.

Speaking of blowing the whistle, how are your works on police practice and police biography going? I have a copy of your early *Lacenaire*,* which I thought excellent; are you following the same path? You have never told me what your opinion was of police training in the US; I should have thought markedly different from the UK. Certainly my encounters with the fuzz in the States – always as an unoffending foreigner – have not been reassuring. Their manners lack that sweet repose that marks the caste of the London cop – who may, of course, be an appalling crook, but *talks* sweetly.

Must now plunge into a mass of correspondence far less interesting than this. For the present, then, adieu and all good wishes to you and Judith.

Rob.

To HERBERT WHITTAKER

C. G. JUNG FOUNDATION*
of the Analytical Psychology
Society of Ontario
Toronto, Ontario
May 7, 1984

Herbert Whittaker (1910–), Canadian, was drama critic for The Globe and Mail *in Toronto from 1949–1975. He had been a friend of the Davieses since the late 1940s when they were involved in amateur and summer stock theatre.*

Dear Herbert:

You put the question: The Theatre, whither? The answer must be, I think, almost anywhere, but always side by side with mankind as one of his most delightful companions in all his tribulations.

The Theatre is a wonderful creature, ever-renewing, like Spring. Sometimes people – usually Broadway people, who do not know her as well as they imagine they do, refer to her as The Old Lady, but she is not old. Of course she makes such johnny-come-latelies as the lyric, the novel and the philosophical essay seem like babies, because she is as old as Prophecy and the Epic, with which she has a strong kinship. But that is not to be old; that is merely to be greater and wiser. She is wonderfully wise and generous, and large-minded enough to be proud of her bastards, the film and television, even though they are still somewhat embarrassing in their attempts to find their feet.

If she has a fault, it is that she is too obliging. She is ready to listen to anybody who seems to need her help. If professors woo her with leaden seriousness, she puts on her horn-rimmed spectacles and her flat shoes and flatters them. If sour-bellied playwrights want to use her as a tin horn through which to squall their grievances against society, she dirties her fingernails and coarsens her voice – even abjures her mighty gift of eloquence – to give the poor fellows a hearing. But she can shrug off such lendings with a laugh, and become once again the lover of all accomplishment, whether of the great tragedian, the elegant comedian, or the baggy-pants clown.

So – whither? Wherever we push her, for she is infinitely oblig-ing. But always, when we have said our fashionable say (for she is the Mirror of Nature,* and reflects us in whatever guise we choose to wear) she becomes her real self, which is the Essence of Nature and to her lovers she shows an ever-loving, ever-beguiling face.

Wonderful to see you at lunch

Rob.

* 3 *

After supper we played games--best
of all The Game--where people acted
out words,or phrases given to them
by the opposing team.We specialized
in book titles, and the most difficult
was The Bobbsy Twins At Atlantic City
which is a facer, undoubtedly,but
Scott Young (his son Neil, the rock
singer, was present as a lad) guessed
it brilliantly in under fifteen seconds.
The funniest one I remember was
Lady Chatterley's Lover which my
mother-in-law had to act out, and
I would not have dreamed she had in
her what emerged....We always concluded
the evening with some rounds of a game
I invented called Homicidal Maniac.We
had an old Victorian house--Tom Symonds
lives in it now--with lots of nooks
and crannies and backstairs;everybody
drew a lot, and the one with the Black
Spot on it was the Maniac who,unknown
and unrecognized,crept around the totally
darkened house and choked anyone who
could be found;the victim was supposed
to give a blood-curdling scream, and sink
to the floor.It was only when the
Maniac was challeneged that he or
she had to give up.When all the children had been reduced to hysteria
the lights were restored, everybody
had another drink, and it was mid-
night.I sometimes yearn at Christmas
for just one more round of Homicidal
Maniac....We shall be alone this Christmas;
all our children are away, and our
grandchildren will be skiing.But I
do not suppose we shall sit, tear-
sodden, a couple of pitiful Old Age
Pensioners,snuffling about Old
Times.Indeed, I think we may be glad
to rest from the exertions leading
up to Christmas, which get more exacting

SECTION
IV

August 1984–December 1986 – *What's Bred in the Bone* revised and published; "keel laid" for *The Lyre of Orpheus*

avies, now 71, had completed the revisions of *What's Bred in the Bone* by December 1984 and the book went to his publishers the following February. Between November 1984 and April 1985, he gathered the three Marchbanks books into a single volume. *What's Bred* and *The Papers of Samuel Marchbanks* both appeared in Canada that October. Throughout this period, ideas were flooding up for *The Lyre of Orpheus.*

When Davies was not intensely involved in the actual writing of a novel, he enjoyed lecturing and writing short pieces. In 1984 and 1985, he accepted many invitations to give speeches and to write reviews. In 1985 there were publicity tours for the new books, excursions he found both exhilarating and tiring. And 1986, a year for which he had accepted several commitments that were likely to be interesting, proved to be exhausting as events unfolded. In January, he participated in the International PEN (Poets, Playwrights, Editors, Essayists, and Novelists) meetings in New York, catching the attention of New York journalists with his august appearance and wry contributions. In June, he had a successful cataract operation. In August he spent a week at the Banff Centre School of Fine Arts in Alberta as the winner of its National Award and as writer in residence. That fall, while on a seventeen-day publicity tour of Scandinavia, he learned that he had been short-listed for the Nobel Prize for literature. Before he reached England, where he expected to have a month's vacation, he had also learned that he was short-listed for the prestigious Booker Prize. He relished the recognition, and it made an appreciable difference to the sales of his books. But it turned his much-needed vacation into a welter of interviews and book-signing sessions, and culminated in a double disappointment when he won neither prize.

He and Brenda continued to see a great deal of theatre, to attend the Canadian Opera Company's offerings, to enjoy their Toronto Symphony Orchestra subscription series, and to see their wide circle of friends. In fall 1985 they took a trip to Florence and Rome.

But Davies' colds and episodes of influenza and bronchitis were becoming more tenacious.

To JOSEF SKVORECKY

Massey College
University of Toronto
August 27, 1984

Josef Skvorecky (1924–), Czech novelist and editor, came to Canada in 1969. He was a professor of English at the University of Toronto from 1971–90.

Dear Professor Skvorecky:

I have just finished reading *The Engineer of Human Souls*, and write to congratulate you on your achievement. I gather that the book is being well received in the States, but I have read some sharp criticism of it here, and it is about this I am concerned, for it suggests that the critics have read the book with one eye closed. Certainly it is satiric and sometimes dismissive about things that are Canadian, but not to the same degree that it is critical of the Czechoslovakia of your youth; nor is anything you say about the stupidity of Canadian youth more severe than what is said about the foolish idealists, clumsy patriots and downright scoundrels of your native land.

Canadians are extremely sensitive about any criticism of themselves, and as a Canadian I am deeply concerned about such things. This sensitivity springs, I think, from a nagging self-doubt; we know in our hearts that we are not the sort of people we pretend to be. This was not always so: I think this trouble dates from 1945, when Canada discovered a new awareness of itself, but mistook what that awareness meant. We set out then on the psychological folly of trying to be like the U.S., in its extreme psychological *extraversion* and we failed because Canada is, and has always been, an *introverted* country, as Norway, Sweden and – yes – Russia are introverted. We see the world differently, and experience the world differently, from our great noisy neighbour, and nothing will make us like the U.S. Trying to be so is our present mania and stupidity. Anything that threatens our neurosis is bound to draw sharp rebuke, and that is what your book has done.

As for Canadian youth, I understand and sympathize, for trying to teach them anything is like talking to people behind thick glass. For many years* I taught English drama at the U of T, and perhaps my greatest difficulty was in trying to persuade them that tragedy is rooted in reality. Just before you were born, I would say, the Imam of Yemen* came to his throne and immediately murdered his five brothers, for fear they should prove rivals. In my lifetime, I would say, American troops in Italy put one of America's greatest poets [Ezra Pound]* in an iron cage and hung him up in the principal square in Pisa, for people to throw filth at him and jeer at him – because he had offended against their ideal of loyalty. You live in a time when Josef Stalin, one of the greatest tyrants in all history, is still a dreadful memory. Why do you think the horrors in these tragedies are "exaggerated for effect"? And because they had no real understanding of tragedy, their sense of comedy was shallow and limited. But with an educational system like ours, which virtually ignores history, what can one expect?

I must say, however, that I did have some excellent students. And I envy you the number of beautiful girls who seem to have appeared in your classes; mine were almost clinically free from beauty..... But I am committing an unpardonable sin in assuming that your novel is autobiographical; we both know that all novels are inventions, and that all novels are autobiographical at the same time.

I write to you because we rarely met during my time at the University. But all my life I have been writing, trying in one way and another to rouse Canadians to some recognition of the truth about their own nature. They are *not* Americans; history and climate forbid it. But Oh, how despairingly they try to be what they are not!

Again with congratulations and warm greetings,

Robertson Davies

To PHILIP JOHN STEAD

Windhover
Caledon East
September 16, 1984

Dear John:

I have just received a letter from the Royal Society of Literature, informing me that I am virtually a Fellow, pending the receipt of fifteen nicker, which I have dispatched with glee. I have you to thank for this, and thank you I do most sincerely, for I have always admired the Soc. and am delighted to be on its roster. It was good of you to think of me, and take the trouble to see this matter through. Hugh MacLennan* is the only other FRSL in Canada, so I am in excellent company, and marked off from the Monstrous Regiment of Women who are attempting to take over the scribbling trade in this country.

I have been finishing up the novel [*What's Bred in the Bone*], and doing final revisions, which I always find a fearful business, and at least once every quarter hour I think I should rewrite the whole thing, so jejune, repetitive and generally nugatory does it seem. But I have been distracted by the visit of the Pope, who has monopolized the TV and is being received everywhere by rapturous crowds, shrieking "We love you, John Paul!". Yesterday he celebrated an open-air Mass quite near here, to a gathering of just under 500,000, and never has such a baking of Risen Lord been consumed at one time within these borders. Brenda and I watch the TV transfixed, for he wows the crowds, and speaks splendidly, saying things that ought to be said in this dollar-dominated dump. His visit also makes clear something that everybody has known, but has not quite swallowed, which is that since the War Canada has become a predominantly Cattholic counttry (damn! tthe "t" on tthis machine has taken it into its bloody head tto stick.....) and I must continue by hand – and is also predominantly non-Anglo-Celtic-Saxon in origin, being composed of what are called "ethnics." Next week H. M. the Queen turns up. Will the ethnics turn out and cheer? It is more than likely they will.

Again, many thanks for all your efforts and our best to Judith –

Rob.

To HORACE W. DAVENPORT

Massey College
University of Toronto
[after November 18, 1984]

Dear Horace:

Many thanks for your letter and the photographs. Do you, as I do, look with astonishment at every picture of yourself? I don't feel that I look at all like what I obviously do look like..... Yes, I meant the copy of the Gilman* for you, and I am glad you liked it. And I am interested in your speculation about how many of my hearers took "Death, thou shalt die,"* as you say 90% of them must have been atheists. I knew that, and did it on purpose, because I like to jolt atheists, a group of marked instability.

In my experience, which includes some very good scientists, atheists are people who have rejected the Faith They Learned At Mother's Knee, and have never considered that such a faith was the intellectual equivalent of The Three Bears. They never think that religion might be a poetic approach to some important questions, and that of all poetry, only about a third is good poetry. They have believed that salvation is free – which would make it the only thing in a complex world which is not achieved by a serious struggle – and they have very sensibly rejected such an idea as nonsense. Christianity is very much to blame for this; the notion that salvation is free and may be attained by the idlest, the dullest, the stupidest is understandably very popular with persons who may be so described. Christianity was very harsh toward the Gnostics, who suggested that maybe salvation called for some intelligence and the rigorous exercise thereof. And the idea of the Pale Galilean – the Sanctified Wimp – has appealed to the inadequate everywhere. Whatever Christ may have been in historic reality – and I suspect that he was the lucky one of a score of wandering prophets teaching a roughly similar faith – he cannot have been an ineffective boob. Christ as a poetic ideal, as a paradigm of the fully-realized soul, is quite another matter and hasn't much to do with the carpenter's son. . . .* Persuasion, for its splendid ritual and its music which, as Aldous Huxley* said, grace what one really believes with style. But what I really believe – it is a continuing quest toward an ever-fleeing goal. What I cannot put up with is the brash certainties of the atheists, who reject all poetry, all beauty, all humility and decent dubiety, and who are so often desolated when something happens to them that cannot be healed with their astringent medicine. They are a pompous, humourless, self-honouring lot, and I like to disconcert them whenever I can. God knows I do not want to save them; that is the work of another kind of idiot. But perhaps now and then I may make them wonder if they really do know all the answers..... So I quote Donne to them, hoping that for an instant the chilly laboratory walls of their minds may be darkened by a fine seventeenth century shadow.

Regards

Rob. . . .

To GORDON AND HELEN ROPER

Massey College
University of Toronto
[December 1984]

Dear Gordon & Helen:

Very good to hear from you, but sorry for both of you about your trouble with your eyes.* I am not too bad; one cataract, and except that I see ghosts and cars that aren't there I am not too badly off. But poor Moira [Whalon] has great difficulties, and I never cease to admire the courage with which she faces them. Which of you typed the letter? Whatever the answer I write to you both, as this letter must be shared.

You say you are in doubt as to what criticism is all about. Oh, my dear man, I know what you mean! Recently I have been astonished and disturbed by two "explanations" of *Fifth Business*. The first,* by an American whom I had always regarded as more than usually sane, is that the whole Deptford Trilogy is parodic of the life and death of Christopher Marlowe, who, as you recall, was murdered at Deptford. The ingenuity with which he works this out gives me the shakes; how can any book stand up against such determined lunacy? The second comes from some fellow at Brock University, who has published a "paper" on *Fifth Business*;* the big secret is that there never *was* any stone in the snowball; Ramsay simply pretended there was to *get* Boy Staunton, and he palmed off on him an old piece of stone that his father had used as a paperweight; the whole trilogy is a study in *spite*. One of the things that astonishes me is that these critics are aware that the whole book is an extended letter to the Headmaster, but it never occurs to them that the Headmaster might be anyone other than the chief executive of Colborne College. They never think that Ramsay writes it on what he thinks may well be his death-bed. Luckily the books have readers who are not academics, and who just ‛treat them as novels, and write me very welcome and encouraging letters about them. . . .

I have been working very hard, and am deeply tired, and am under orders – Brenda's orders – to take a six months break from demanding tasks. I have finished *What's Bred In The Bone* and am at that stage where I cannot tell if it is passable or the worst botch ever put together and called a novel. . . .

There is to be still one more volume [*The Lyre of Orpheus*], exploring the marriage of Maria and Arthur, and although I have a vague notion of how it will go it is still shadowy and because of fatigue I dare not press it.

Increasingly I am torn between the Inner and the Outer Man. The Inner wants to keep quiet and think and write. The Outer keeps saying "Yes, but how about accepting this invitation to speak, or read or do some other thing which is rather fun, but an awful waste of time for a writer." The Outer gets his way, quite often. This autumn I went to Washington and did a reading at the Library of Congress. It went very well and they treated me royally. Then I went to New York University,* where I found to my dismay that they were using me (without having said anything to me about it) as a means of begging for money to set up a Chair of Canadian Lit. Their standard of hospitality was certainly not that of the Lib. of Congress; I spoke in a very strange room where the light on the lectern was broken, so that, for seventy minutes, I had to hold it aloft over my MS, like the Statue of Liberty. My pleadings for a glass of water fell on deaf ears. I shall not go there again. Later I read at the National Library in Ottawa. They paid me $200 and paid for my hotel room, but not for my meals or transportation (taxis, not air), so I emerged rather in the hole. I don't really mind, but I do wish things one does for patriotic reasons did not so often turn out to be done on the cheap. Why don't they say, We have no money, but will you come for love? Love goes a long way. This summer* I went to Vienna to take part in a conference on Canadian Lit, and they had no money, but their kindness and hospitality was truly splendid and I would go again like a shot. It was wonderful to sit at dinner beside a Czech professor who quoted Canadian poetry – especially that of Douglas LePan* – as if he really loved it. (37 European universities now offer courses in Can. Lit.!) . . .

Brenda and I are well – pretty well, that's to say – we have both had wretched bouts of 'flu, Brenda much worse than I and as she is so seldom ill I was very worried about her. As a lifetime hypochondriac I can take my own illnesses in my stride as part of a life-style, but when the really strong and indispensable partner is in bed, pale and weak, life becomes very dark.

This letter seems to go on and on, and I still have not said anything about Mike Peterman. You like him. Moira likes him. I do not really know him, but it seems to me that his critical method is truly academic – which is to say that at all costs the critic must Know Best about Everything. It is thus that academic reputations are made. So let it be, as the Masons say at funerals.

Again, love and Season's Greetings from us both.

Rob.

PS: My agent [Perry H. Knowlton] recently told me that I am now to be read in 10 languages, and am coming out next spring in South America. I can't help boasting a little. I never expected any such thing. After all, it is not as if I were Farley Mowat, and wrote engagingly about animals – *that's* what really travels. But I have never known any animals.

To HORACE W. DAVENPORT

Windhover
Caledon East
February 3, 1985

Dear Horace:

I cannot remember whether I said anything in my last letter about your pilgrimage* to Stratford this summer; of course we shall be delighted to see you. Stratford has been going through a bad patch;

inevitable in anything that has gone on so long. The director [John Hirsch]* who is now leaving, to be replaced by John Neville,* was a Hungarian Jew, enormously talented but with a passion for intrigue which is very disturbing to everybody associated with the venture. He also had a way of interpreting Shakespeare in a half-assed Marxian manner – all aristocrats and rulers are necessarily bad, all lower class characters are worthy and witty, all lovers are frying to hop into the sack or else have intercourse in plain view, all churchmen and religious associations must be shown up as an imposture on the peepul, etc. Very unShakespearean, for Old Bill was a snob, orthodox and a royalist, and had a turn for the more poetic forms of romance – and audiences are happy to follow him in these directions, whatever their views outside the theatre. But John Neville should be an improvement; he has distinction of taste and a very pretty hand at putting a show together. So we shall hope for better things.

I have had a brief and disappointing passage with Stratford this past year: they wanted to do a show for about five actors and two musicians that would be made up of passages from my books, linked by some integument I undertook to supply. But the project has been messed about, and there has been whining about money, and doubts about whether there would be any audience for it, and all the depressing aspects thoroughly explored, so as I did not initiate the scheme, and am not prepared at my time of life to be treated like an amateur, I have closed the matter, and will do nothing for Stratford again. It has always been bad luck for me; long years ago Tyrone Guthrie asked me to do a version of *Bartholomew Fair** for them, which they subsequently decided not to use, and I had to threaten suit to get my fee – which was $300! They simply do not understand living authors; I recall years ago when they were about to do *Cyrano de Bergerac** they thought it would be unnecessary to pay royalties; when I pointed out that Rostand had two sisters still living, a very rich industrialist on the Board had the brass neck to say – "Oh, maybe they wouldn't hear, and we could get away with it!" I gave him a short lecture on the nature of literary property.

Brenda and I were in London for Christmas, and enjoyed it greatly. A niece of ours [Kathryn Davies Bray]* – my brother Fred's daughter

– and her husband and three girls were staying with Miranda, and we linked forces and had a very good time. We took them all to a real English pantomime – *Sleeping Beauty** – and the kids thought we had lost our minds when we hissed the Fairy Carabosse, and obediently looked under our seats for the lost kitten when the clown told us to, and all of that. But next day we took them to *Starlight Express,** which is the big musical hit, by the author of *Cats* and they loved that. It was the loudest show I have ever been at, Brenda and I stuffed our ears with Kleenex and then put our fingers in, and it was *still* loud! The plot will blow your mind: the whole theatre had been filled with steel runways, so that one seemed to be sitting in a structure of Meccano, and on the runways the actors whizzed up and down on roller skates, pretending to be trains: the plot was that nasty Diesel and horrible Electric despised poor humble Steam. You will need little further prompting in plot when I tell you that Diesel was very vain and all the girls loved him, and Electric was a homosexual and all the boys thought him desirable, but poor Steam was – A N★E★G★R★O!!!!! Furthermore, he was religious and prayed to his Daddy in the Assembling Yard Beyond the Sky for help, and his Daddy assured him loudly that There's Light At The End of the Tunnel. So of course in the show-down, Steam won. And this horse-shit which makes my old 19th century melodramas look like Goethe's *Faust,** is wowing hundreds of thousands of people, and had our great-nieces sagging on the ropes at its intellectual splendour and moral greatness. Like the fellow says,* there's nothing new under the sun.

Unless, of course, it is new varieties of 'flu, which is one of the Devil's staples. Brenda and I came home with what is called here Ninety Day 'Flu, though we seem to be almost over it in about forty days of hoiking, spewing, snorting and deep depression. I think that for the first time I felt really old, crawling around like a tortoise, spilling things and whining. Brenda, who is very rarely ill, scared me by retiring to bed, absolutely beat. But There's Light At The End Of The Tunnel, as Ol' Daddy Steam says and we are practically on our feet.

I have completed my new novel [*What's Bred in the Bone*], and as usual think it awful. But it must go to the publishers very soon, after which it is on the lap of the gods – who may open their knees any time. I am also revising, annotating and jazzing up all three Marchbanks books, which are to come out this autumn in a single vol [as *The Papers of Samuel Marchbanks*]. You shall have one as soon as they are ready. I have had fun editing and annotating, in real academic style – correcting the author, throwing doubt on his memory and veracity, and generally trampling him beneath my feet, like a real academic editor. The book will include an Introduction which is in effect a Life of Marchbanks. All of this makes a lot of work, and I am getting tired. Brenda says I must take six months off this summer during which I write *nothing*, and I think she is right.

I was greatly pleased by the news about your book.* Don't allow doubts to nag you; it will take time to find its place, but when it does thousands will call you blessed. You have joined the great line of Aubrey and Anthony à Wood,* though you write better than they do, and where should we be without them? In such matters one must have faith; the work is good and *no good thing is ever lost*. I believe that most firmly, even if it does make me sound rather like Daddy Steam. But great institutions are built upon the memorializing and recovery of just such historians as yourself and in the future they will have cause to say "Davenport has shown..." in the historical as well as in the scientific range of your work.

All the best to you both from us.....

Rob.

PS: Yesterday we celebrated our 45th wedding anniversary! Astounding!

To MIRANDA DAVIES

Windhover
Caledon East
[February 1985]

> *Miranda Davies (1940–   ), the Davieses'*
> *eldest daughter, who is a Jungian analyst,*
> *was practising at the time in London,*
> *England. She has strong musical interests:*
> *earlier she had studied at the Opera*
> *School at the University of Toronto and*
> *pursued a singing career.*

Dear Miranda:

Sunday morning, and snow falling gently over the splendid Brueghel* landscape outside my study window. So – what to do? Write to Panda, of course. . . . Last Sunday – a week ago today – we rushed to Toronto in a snowstorm because I had been called upon to pinch-hit for Lotfi Mansouri,* talking to the Opera Association about *Faust;** he had an unexpected rehearsal. It went very well and there was a good audience despite the bad day. I did my best, concealing as far as I could my opinion that *Faust* is a laughable piece, and only a Frenchman could have picked such nonsense out of Goethe. But it is an enduring old nonsense, like *Il Trovatore** and for the same reason; it goes right to the jugular, and wows us as *Capriccio* and *Die ægyptis-che Helena** don't – not really, vastly superior works of art that they are. After the talk we (just ourselves, not the riff-raff of the Assoc.) were allowed to watch some of the rehearsal, which was a great pleasure, as we both love the *preparation* of a production. Mansouri is solving the problem of the intimacy of the opera and the huge stage at O'Keefe by having quite a small raised revolving stage in the middle, for Faust's study, Margaret's bedroom and other intimate bits, around which crowds and the Kermesse can surge. He is restoring the Walpurgis ballet in Act Five, though not all of it, because as he hissed to us "Some of the passages are – please excuse the expression – a little bit *kitsch.*" Isn't it funny what expressions people want one to excuse?

Faust is being done in romantic 19th century dress. . . .

Now I must go and see how your Mum is getting on; she is making orange-ginger marmalade, having prepared her own ginger from the root. Ever see ginger in raw form? The roots look like a Chinese woman's bound foot, all writhing and twisted, but foot-like. Beats bought ginger every way. Oh, we eat high on the hog at Windhover, let me tell you!

Love from us both,

Daddy. . . .

To ROBERT FULFORD

Windhover
Caledon East
Feb 25, 1985

Robert Fulford (1932–　) is a Canadian editor, essayist, and critic. His "Notebook" (Saturday Night, March 1985) begins with a description of Mrs. Ramsay's neighbourly helpfulness during Paul Dempster's premature birth and difficult first six months.

Dear Robert Fulford:

I was greatly complimented that you should have made use of *Fifth Business* in your article on public charity, and the withering of private charity. What I wrote in that book was rooted in personal experience; when I was a very small boy my brother Fred suffered a kidney injury, and part of his treatment was that he had to be dipped in a bath of warm water every three hours; of course there were no nurses, no hospital or service of any kind in our village (Thamesville) but a local grocer organized a roster of local men who turned up throughout the day and night, dipped him and left after consuming a gallon or so of coffee, and kept it up without a miss for two weeks! That was kindness, just as it was when my Father was quarantined in the house with smallpox, and the wood-man dumped our wood in the road for fear of infection: but the Presbyterian minister and one of his elders wrestled it back to the woodpile, for my Mother and my brothers were forbidden to step off the front porch. There was no obnoxious charity about it; these were just the things people did for one another, and my mother was a great dasher about with blankets and soup, and once hauled an old man who had tried to commit suicide out of a well – quite a struggle for he was fat and a tight fit.

But as you observe, that has gone, and we don't seem to be able to pay to replace it. As a Jungian I am aware of the shadow that is cast by everything, and I am sadly aware that the Poor and Needy have to be helped, but also that the more you help people who are disposed by destiny or psychology to be Poor and Needy the more they are going to want, and the pitiful whine of destitution rises to an imperious snarl. "Ye have the poor always with you"* said Christ (who so far as we know never gave a shekel to anybody out of his own purse) and nothing – not the most inclusive program of public benefit – will assuage their need, for much of their poverty is psychological and beyond anything money can help.

When I retired my wife and I decided that we would strike off our list of gifts all charities except two for which we have a special, personal feeling, and would give whatever we had to give to the arts, which are our chief interest. But it is not easy to resist the clamour and craving of the appeals for this, that and the other that crowd our mailbox – very costly printing-jobs, a lot of them – every day – literally every day for some monster must sell lists of possible donors to the charity-collectors.

But I am raving..... All good wishes –

Rob. Davies

To THE EDITOR OF *THE GLOBE AND MAIL**

The Oaklands
Toronto
March 7, 1985.

Sir:

Many Prime Ministers before Mr. Mulroney* have made piece-meal changes in the Senate's powers, always to reduce them. Is the time not ripe for a radical reform of the Upper House, in a totally different direction?

May I propose Senate reform under three heads:

(1) That the Senate be given not less work and less power than at present, but more work and more power, to lift some of the burden from the Commons;

(2) that Senate seats be apportioned among the provinces on a basis of population;

(3) that Senate seats be achieved by competitive examination, to be repeated after seven years of tenure.

If this were done, the way would be opened for reform of the Commons. Each party would, as now, nominate its candidate in each riding, but the seats would be achieved by competitive examination rather than simple voting. The examination would comprise required papers in governmental theory, economics, general knowledge and an examination in the use of one of our two official languages; one further examination might be chosen by the candidate from a group of other subjects relevant to government. The examinations would be of a Civil Service character, rather than academically weighted.

The advantages of such a system would be:

First, it would assure an alert and reasonably well informed Parliament, both Senate and Commons.

Second, it would substantially reduce the now heavy cost of general elections.

Third, it would eliminate the show-biz-popularity-contest element which has so greatly increased during the past forty years in political life that it has deformed the democratic process. When it is widely acknowledged, and even boasted of, that a fine television presence may assure a man the Presidency of the United States, other qualifications taking second place, the need for reform and a return to seriousness is plain to be seen.

If Canada moved in this direction, it would gain immense international prestige as the first country in the modern world to put qualities of informed intelligence foremost when choosing its rulers. Would other countries dare to lag behind?

I do not suggest that the examinations be designed for experts, or predominantly people of scholarly mind, but only that they should assure an informed competence in important matters.

Yours faithfully,

Robertson Davies

To GORDON AND HELEN ROPER

Windhover
Caledon East
March 9, 1985

Dear Gordon & Helen:

. . . So the book* is finished? And it must be trimmed by 60 pages? Simple: cut all the rhapsodical descriptions of my idyllic childhood, of the Don Juan period, of the wanderings on foot through Asia Minor. Just get down to the FLAWS – that's what students want to hear about. Last Wednesday night as I sat, thinking no evil, listening to the program about Bach, the phone rang and it was a girl of fifteen from Alberta; her class had deputed her to call me and ask why Dunstan Ramsay [in *Fifth Business*] was interested in saints. It seemed such a dumb thing to be interested in. "What Church do you and your friends go to?" I asked. "Lutheran Reformed," she said – or something of the sort – Lutheran anyhow. "And you don't take much account of saints?" said I. "None at all" said she. On this promising basis we began a conversation, which I do not think convinced her of anything – not even that I was not, personally, Dunstan Ramsay, because, as she explained, they knew I was a prof, and so was Ramsay, kind of. But what I tried to get over to her was that what she and her friends had experienced of life might not be the whole thing, and that adventure of the spirit was possible. She wasn't interested in the spirit, and I had to repeat the word several times. But she ended up by saying they liked the book, so perhaps sometime later they will get something out of it..... I could write a Twayne book for such students myself.

The novel [*What's Bred in the Bone*] is finished and is in the hands of the publishers. And the Marchbanks book [*The Papers of Samuel Marchbanks*] is finished, and goes to the publishers next week. I feel bereft; what do I do now? . . .

As you will judge from the tone of this letter I am a little low in spirits. *I have nothing to do.* This is a terrible state of affairs for somebody who is used to being busy. Brenda says I should enjoy myself. But the horrible truth is that I enjoy myself when I am working; the usual pursuits of the Retired Senior Citizen fill me with despair. No, no – not carpet bowling! Please, no excursions to Toronto Island, pushing the wheelchairs of the Less Fortunate! No I *won't* try finger painting and *have fun with colour*! Give me my typewriter and my dictionary, and just let me suffer!

Moira [Whalon] goes into hospital on March 18 for a critical operation,* and I don't think her doctor would undertake it if he were not virtually certain that it will work. But of course it is worrying. For so many years she has prided herself on a special kind of perfectionism, and this eye trouble hits her in the most sensitive place..... Delighted to hear that Helen's operations have been so successful; I am sure she embraces the role of Milton's Daughter* with all the kindness of heart that has characterized her entire life.

For the present, that is it. Gloomy, I'm afraid, but one has one's gloomy post-parturition spells.

All good wishes

Rob.

To HORACE W. DAVENPORT

Massey College
University of Toronto
April 2ⁿᵈ, 1985

Dear Horace:

I have read the Apology of a Second-Class Man* with great inter- est and total approval; so has Brenda and concurs in my views. Yes, I quite understand that it is not false modesty; one must know oneself and it is a mark of inferiority to lay claim to what is not properly one's own in terms of achievement and distinction. I am very much aware of this in my own life and work: I do not think I could claim to be second-class for if first-class takes in the truly great, and the second-class the top-notchers like Conrad, Henry James, Trollope and the like, I would be lucky to make it into the third division. But as I sometimes said to my students, who were apt to be dismissive about anybody who was not manifestly in the first-class – "You have no conception of the labour, talent, courage and sheer persistence required to get yourself classed at all." In declaring yourself Second-Class you measure yourself against the highest, and that cannot be done unless you are of some stature approximating to theirs.

I was impressed by what you said about the part luck played in your career. Brenda says that people make their luck, and I do not quite say that, but say something else that is at the root of my new novel *What's Bred In The Bone*. It is Something Else that makes you close by when one professor asks another if he knows of anybody that wants a job. I hope you will like this novel; I knew you had reservations about the last one [*The Rebel Angels*], because of the figure of Ozy Froats who built his kingdom on a foundation of shit. But as you well know, Ozy was simply a metaphor for one of my main themes: that which is despised and overlooked may contain some great secret. And to my great delight a medical friend of mine tells me that somebody in the States has been working very much along Ozy's lines – though not preparing slides that look like moss-agate – and has found out a lot about lung troubles – which is what Osler* was saying in 1900.

You scientists have one extraordinary advantage over those of us on the other side of the fence: your achievement is in some degree measurable, and at least you know the best or the worst and can face it. With the writer, or any other artist, the returns are never all in, and the older you grow the more you are aware of the enviable reputations that have sunk without trace.

I have finished the novel, and the publishers like it very much; indeed the editor at Viking [Elisabeth Sifton] thinks it is my best work. I am just now getting Marchbanks [*The Papers of Samuel Marchbanks*] ready for the press, adding copious notes and cutting out a lot of the merely silly stuff. Silliness is the rheumatoid arthritis of the humorist's trade.

So – thanks for the Apology, which is what it was in the true sense of the word. Did you know that the verdict on Colley Cibber* is much more generous than it used to be? He had remarkable qualities and obvious defects, but his comedies stand up astonishingly well – below but not out of sight of the work of the later Goldsmith and Sheridan.*

We look forward as always to seeing you in the summer. I believe Brenda has written to Inge. We both send our love to both of you –

and a Happy Easter –

Rob.

To ELISABETH SIFTON

Massey College
University of Toronto
June 13, 1985

Dear Elisabeth:

May I ask you to do a favour for me? Would you get in touch with the designer of the jackets for my books – Bascove* is the name I believe, and she signs her work "B" – and tell her how strongly appreciative I am of what she has done; it seems to me that she catches the spirit of the books in a very individual style, and suggests what is inside (without being illustrative) in a way that would certainly take my eye if I were in a bookshop. And she does it with great style and distinction. I feel that her contribution to the books is substantial and I don't suppose designers of covers get thanked very often by authors. Penguin has just sent me the Salterton novels in the new jackets by B and they are absolutely first-rate. Tell her I drink her health.

Macmillan are prancing along with *What's Bred....* I am glad you all decided that the full title is preferable to *Bred In...*, which I never really liked, but agreed to. I am as nervous as a kitten (a Persian kitten) about the book; I fear that the angels will get on the nerves of some of the reviewers, at least. I don't want to fall into the category of horribly *twee* authors..... I am patiently making notes for the next novel, though it will be quite a while in preparation; I have some hopes of it. I should like to write a really *good* novel before I wind up.

Rob.

To FATHER H. GREENWOOD

Massey College
University of Toronto
June 19, 1985

*Hilary Greenwood (1929–   ), English, is
a member of the Society of the Sacred
Mission, a small Anglican religious order.
In 1985 he was Prior of a small house and
rector of the church of St. John's Longsight
in Manchester. He got to know John
Pearson in the early 1950s when, as a
novice in the S.S.M. headquarters at
Kelham, he shared a room with him.*

[Dear Father Greenwood:]

I was delighted to receive your letter of June 4th about *The Rebel
Angels*. You are correct in every detail. Parlabane was founded upon
my old friend John Pearson.* I had known him when we were school-
boys and from then until the end of his life, and as a young man he
seemed to possess enviable promise; however, drink and drugs and a
sort of underground life involving a great deal of rough homosexu-
ality ruined him completely. A number of us tried to keep him afloat
in Canada but it was hopeless and in the end he blew his head off,
and, characteristically, he chose to do so on Hallowe'en.

I am interested that the Society of the Sacred Mission put up some
money to get John to Canada for I was only one of three or four
Canadian friends from whom he extracted sums for that very purpose.
He was, I fear, a dreadful crook, but he had been a most engaging
person in the early part of his life. Incidentally he was the only man
I ever knew who got himself thrown out of the Canadian Navy.

When he died I discovered he had appointed me, rather grandiosely, his literary executor and had left me a mass of rather peculiar material, including his university thesis and the typescript of a
very long novel which he had wanted me to get published. With the
best will in the world this would have been impossible for it was not
a novel but a long philosophical harangue in which he settled scores
with everybody with whom he had crossed swords during his
unhappy life. There were times when I felt rather a stinker to make

use of John in a novel of my own, but while he was alive I paid for that privilege in good hard cash, and also I think he would have enjoyed the joke for it was his sense of humour that made him endurable during his last years.

With many thanks for your letter, and in the hope that if you have any further recollections of John you might send them to me, I am

Yours sincerely,

[Robertson Davies]

To CELINA CARDIM
CAVALCANTE

Celina Cardim Cavalcante, Brazilian, is one of several translators who sought and received Davies' assistance.

Massey College
University of Toronto
July 2, 1985

[Dear Celina Cardim Cavalcante:]

Many thanks for your letter of May 29th which has just reached me. I am delighted that you have translated *Fifth Business* into Portuguese and I can understand that you would have met with some difficulties, as there are expressions in it which are peculiar to Canada, and especially to the province of Ontario, which is a very old English settlement.

Now a Calithumpian parade* would be very familiar to you if you saw it as it is a sort of Carnival parade in which people wear grotesque costumes and often great heads made of papier mâché. It used to be customary when a very dignified parade had been organized to have it followed by the Calithumpians, as a sort of counterbalance to the solemnity of what had gone before. In a village like Deptford it would have been very simple in nature but would undoubtedly give immense pleasure.

I look forward to seeing your Portuguese version of the book when it is in print.

With good wishes, I am

Yours sincerely,

[Robertson Davies]

To HERBERT WHITTAKER

Windhover
Caledon East
August 19, 1985

Dear Herbie:

What jolly lives you critics lead! London this week, then off to Bayreuth, then to Venice to recover from the fatigues of entertaining three irresistible mistresses — ! Contrast the doglike existence of the author, tied to a mass of proofs and hounded by publishers [Douglas Gibson] who assure him that if his hero is 17 in 1917 he cannot be 27 in 1932. But this ritual whine of heavy involvement is simply to explain why I have been so long replying to your letter of July 23.

All sorts of reports come in about Grant [Macdonald]* and I am glad you have actually seen him. My nephew Michael [Davies], a friend and one of Grant's guardians, says he is "a vegetable," and others report he does not know them; one lady says she has had to stop visiting him because he insists on kissing her and the cancerous smell of his bad lip is more than she can bear; you represent him as somewhat remote but by no means out of reach. I have duly reported what you said to Clair Stewart* who is, as you know, an old friend and another of those who keep an eye on Grant's affairs — so far as one can, for he has no will, and no real lawyer, though Ben Cunningham* does what he can. At least the pictures are in the care of the Queen's gallery, though they have no title to them – but they can't be pinched.

I can't get to Kingston before November, but when I am there I hope to get to Grant, though I rather dread it, and I admire the courage with which you faced it. Though a long-time friend, I have always found him likely to become very thorny and distant without notice. At various times I tried to lend him money. Nothing doing. Once, when he was really in deep financial trouble, my father tried to give him a wholly sinecure job on the *Whig*, just to keep him eating – wouldn't hear of it – smelled charity. He was for years kept wretchedly poor by his father, who was dotty, and thought *he* was keeping Grant, and spent money on new heating-systems for the house, and other costly follies. The old man was convinced that I was a contemporary of his, a friend from Edinburgh days – this cloak of ancientry has always enwrapped me. I never liked the father – a sanctimonious old boob – but Grant's affection for him and his uncomplaining care for him was very touching. His mother, whom he hated, was in the asylum at Kingston, and was another drain on an already anaemic purse. A sad life, which seemed to emerge very clearly in his latest pictures, in which an eccentric old man (a self-portrait) appeared among joyous young people. Poor Grant had most of the miseries life has up its sleeve, including painful betrayals by young men he tried to befriend and in whom, of course, he sought the love that was not to be found elsewhere. Or I must qualify that: do you remember a Toronto journalist called _____? She had the hots for Grant in the biggest way, but he wasn't having any. Wise of him, I think, but there it is. Anyway, bless you for going to see him. (Do I sound like Nathan Cohen,* who was always blessing everybody; his last words to me, by phone, were "Bless you, muh bhoy, bless you" – I had provided him with the source of a quotation he could easily have found for himself, but Nathan had a strongly executive spirit.) . . .

Love, in which Brenda enthusiastically joins –

Rob.

To WILLIAM J. KEITH

Massey College
University of Toronto
Sept. 10, 1985

*William J. Keith (1934–   ), literary
critic and professor of English at the
University of Toronto from 1966–95,
published an article about Davies in the
Spring 1985 issue of the* Journal of
Canadian Studies *which argues that the
"playful confusing of the real and the
fabricated is an important part of his art
and provides interesting links with the
work of such post-modernist writers as
Jorge Luis Borges."*

Dear Bill:

I found your letter of Sept. 4 and the reprint from the Journal
waiting for me when I came to the College today, and I read it with
the greatest pleasure – indeed, I rolled about with laughter – thinking what a clever chap you are to probe a portion of my work that
has not, to my knowledge, been written about before..... Of course
I love to set traps and puzzles and mingle fact with invention because
so many of my readers seem to be astonishingly literal-minded. The
worst are school children – often not children but great lumps of 17
– who get me on the 'phone and demand "What was the trouble
between you and your Mother?" and "When was it you travelled with
a circus?" and "Where in Toronto can I find some Gypsies?" The
worst was the boy who demanded: "I need some help with these-
here Jungian archeotypes." But there are adults – some of them in the
academic world – who seem to have no notion whatever of what
Imagination might be, or that it might slop over into the world of
Fact, creating something different and delicious, as when one's cup of
coffee slops over and wets one's Dad's cookie, making a very nice,
tasty mess..... I was complimented out of my mind by the implied likeness with Borges,* but I must protest that although I admire Nabokov
– clever as a wagon-load of monkeys – I am repelled by his cruel,
atheistical mind; I do not write anything to *hurt* anybody, and I think
he does..... But people miss things: Robt. G. Lawrence* twigged that

Sir John Tresize [in *World of Wonders*] was Martin-Harvey (scarcely a Sherlock Holmesian deduction) but he utterly missed the portrait of JMH's wife "Lady Nell," which was drawn from life; she was a misunderstood, large-hearted woman, fated to blindness..... Now, as to Tho. Overskou and *Den Danske Skueplads** – I have several times been urged to give the exact reference for that quotation; but it is out of the question, for the book is in several volumes and most sketchily indexed, and besides I have never seen it. But when Macmillans in England were considering publishing the book their director, one [Alan] Maclean (and incidentally brother to traitor [Donald] Maclean)* fussed and fidgeted and urged me to provide some reference for the title, which bothered him. A definition, perhaps? A reference to some authoritative work on the theatre? Well, under the circumstances, *Den Danske Skueplads* was the obvious source, just the sort of thing Overskou would include. Since then doubt has been sown in my mind by Lise-Lone Marker,* herself a Dane and a theatre historian, who tells me "Overskou never wrote anything so unambiguous." So – who knows where the truth lies? Doubtless some toilsome scholar will some day turn up the passage in Overskou, and certainly I shall be infinitely obliged to him..... The next volume, following *The Rebel Angels* [*What's Bred in the Bone*], appears this October, and I shall ask the publishers to send you a copy. Comes out in England and US as well. As you divine, it is also about fakes – layers upon layers of fakes including one important non-fake which is, by the time it reaches the world, a fake. It includes some discussion of fakery, which is very shadowy ground, as you indicate. But I am now just getting to work on the third in this group, which is about a fake which is now [not] a fake, because it does not set out to deceive – but unless it deceives on a very important critical level, it is a failure..... Why do I do it? To attempt to explain would be wasted time; all I can say is that I am a true child of Mercurius, god of writers, crooks and fakers, having been born at a time, astrologers* tell me, when his power was at its highest in the heavens. And that says it all, or nothing, according to where you stand..... Once again, thanks for your most generous and perceptive article, which has filled me with pride. I thank you especially for saying that I deserve to be considered at a highly sophisticated critical level. I get so sick of being considered simply as A Humorist – which in Canada means a Village Idiot who manages to keep out of jail.

All good wishes

Rob Davies

PS: A collected, annotated Marchbanks [*The Papers of Samuel Marchbanks*] appears shortly – another fake.

To MORDECAI RICHLER

Massey College
University of Toronto
Sept. 12, 1985

Mordecai Richler (1931–   ) is an important Canadian novelist and controversial journalist. His novel The Apprenticeship of Duddy Kravitz *(1959) established him as a major writer. He and Davies met only a couple of times.*

Dear Mordecai:

I have been meaning to write to you for several months, but have not done so because I was not sure that you would welcome a letter from one who has been emphatically taped as a member of The Establishment – which for a variety of reasons is something I cannot help, though I do not glory in it. But I wanted to congratulate you on your essay on Karsh,* which only recently came my way. In my opinion, you have the ineffable Yousuf dead to rights. I have twice been photographed by him, not of course as a Face of Destiny,* but as a Face of Canada, and both experiences were painful. Mr. Karsh arrives with his camera, and a fixed idea of who and what his sitter is: I am filed in his mind as a Humorist, and as he has little sense of humour he is certain that a humorist is quite simply a funnyman, and it was our struggle – he for and I fiercely against – this image that eventually wore me down. He wanted, he insisted, to get a picture of a really funny man. Unwisely I gave way to a sudden disastrous impulse and said: "You mean like this?" and hammed a funny man, leering and tapping my nose with my forefinger. Like a shot he pressed the bulb, and my joke – so gross that I thought even he would see it – is now perpetuated, not only in his book but in a huge photograph hanging in the National Library. I begged the . . . Lady who is now our National Librarian [Marianne Florence Scott]* to take it down. She smiled demurely and shook her blue curls: Karsh is Karsh and it is not for any author to say him nay.

But I am emboldened to write to you now because yesterday there arrived on my desk Volume 6 of *Canadian Writers and Their Works*, in which you and I both have our noses roughly wiped by a couple of critics, Mills and McSweeney,* neither of whom is known to me. Each has decided, after long and minute analysis, that we have both *disappointed* these great and good men: I am prolix and shallow and cannot carry a novel through without making a mess: you have been going downhill ever since *Duddy Kravitz* and though there is time for you to recover yourself you had better look sharp. I am sententious: you are obscene, but, curiously, not obscene enough. Our popularity is inexplicable save on the grounds that the public cannot rise above "mid-cult" works, whatever that term may mean. I assume that both men are academics; they appear under the umbrella of the ineffable George Woodcock,* known to the irreverent as Old Timberdick. For years I have been telling audiences that a novelist is the descendant of the medieval story-teller who sat down on his mat in the bazaar and cried: "Give me a copper coin and I will tell you a golden tale." The academic critic, I think, settles on his mat on the campus and cries "Give me tenure, and I will knock a book."

My wife and I were angry recently when we saw, on The Journal, some film about the opening of your film *Joshua Then and Now*: hardly had we time to register what was happening than some over-eager wretch employed by the CBC was on the screen telling us why it had disappointed him, in illiterate but damaging terms. How quick Canada is with the knife! We hope to get to see it for ourselves next week.

These critics – I do not know what you make of them but I am foolishly open to destructive criticism and my digestion, sleep and – far the worst – my self-confidence is shattered by these assaults. I picture myself reeling, in deepening senility, from botch to botch, as Beckmessers* with their score boards and their clicking pencils mark me down..... I salute you from the slough to which they have banished us. ⁄

But be of good cheer, there is always hope. Before the end I may manage a tolerable rewrite of *The Three Bears*. You have longer –

Rob. Davies

To JANE GOLDENBERG

Massey College
University of Toronto
September 24, 1985

Jane Goldenberg, then resident in Washington, D.C., had read the Deptford Trilogy and The Rebel Angels, *and had heard Davies speak at the Library of Congress. She wrote to enquire: "Do you think marriage too mundane for a marvelous life?"*

[Dear M͟s͟ Goldenberg:]

Thank you for your letter of July 25th which has been forwarded to me from Viking Press and just reached me this morning. To reply at once to your question as to whether marriage is too mundane for a marvellous life I find myself somewhat puzzled as to what you mean. A marvellous life is extremely difficult to attain and is usually the result of luck rather than planning, but certainly I do not think that marriage is in any way hostile to a very good life, and I speak as one who has been married to the same woman for forty-five years and have never felt an instant's regret. Of course I am aware that many people have ill fortune with their marriages and frequently I think that this is the result of bad judgement. There is a persistent idea that a marriage must be the continuation of a romance, when a minute's reflection shows that it can be nothing of the kind. It must be an association of people of similar or complimentary tastes who enter it with a firm resolve to make it work. Very often I think of the couple in *The Way of the World*,* the woman of whom said when agreeing to marry, "Let us be as strange as if we had been married a great while, and as well bred as if we were not married at all." In what I have been able to observe more marriages are ruined by a vulgarly proprietorial attitude and a want of genuine respect between the partners than have ever been ruined by cruelty or unfaithfulness.

With good wishes, I am

Yours sincerely,

[Robertson Davies]

To JOHN J. ESPEY

Oaklands
Toronto
January 24 [1986]

John J. Espey (1913–), an American who was born and raised in China, became a professor of English at UCLA. He and Davies were friends at Oxford from 1935–38, and the two corresponded sporadically over the years.

Dear John:

How delightful to encounter you in New York, and how unexpected! I was, as I believe I said, in flight from the PEN* conference people who were in occupation of the St. Moritz Hotel, along the Park, and of whose company I could get enough. The whole PEN experience was enlightening, for I had never previously attended one of their corroborees and quickly found out that although a lot of heavyweights attended, the people I would most have liked to meet did not. The reason was clear: the energy of the conference was political, and oppressed countries and aggrieved writers held the floor. Aggrieved women strove to hold the floor and sometimes succeeded. But the climate of grievance is not one in which I blossom, and although I do what I can for Amnesty International, a full week of protest and denunciation of the USSR, South Africa, and the Male Sex is more than I can stand. Much of the tone of the conference sprang from the personality of Norman Mailer:* I don't know if you admire him – I don't read his books which are in a *genre* I avoid – but his dominating and sometimes tyrannical spirit pervaded the affair, and much of the women's shrieking was provoked by his crushing manner of conducting meetings. He had much right on his side, of course: the women wanted equal time on all panels, but they made no move to do equal work in organizing them. And, as Nadine Gordimer* said, literature is not an "equal opportunity employer" and as equality of talent is easier to assert than to prove, the women suffered. It must be said, however, that some of the representatives of their sex were not impressive: one panelist was an elderly, frowsy, hole-in-the-gray-sweater Jewess who chewed gum not only while listening, but while addressing the meeting, and was so illiterate – or I suppose she thought herself as "of the people" – as to be almost incomprehensible to a Canadian, so what must she have been to a Yugoslav however well versed in the mandarin dialect of our tongue? Furthermore, the "rubrics" we were called upon to discuss were so vague and so jejune – sub High School quality, some of them – that the talk was inevitably vague and often silly. A strange week. When I spoke my cry was "Back to your ivory towers!" and I got a good deal of support.

I reckon it to be 48 years since last we talked. God! . . . we must not lose each other again. I remember you at Oxford very often, and always with affection. Your rooms at Merton, Percy Scholes, the on-going stories about "The Myth," Elias Cabot,* your hilarious assumption of Chinese demeanour – great stuff and much cherished.

Rob.

To N. C. LANDOLT

> *N. C. Landolt, an appreciative reader of*
> *Davies' books, lived in New York State.*

Massey College
University of Toronto
February 4, 1986

[Dear Miss Landolt:]

Many thanks for your very kind gift of ginger snaps which arrived safely and which I have consumed with the greatest pleasure. This is one of the most sincere fan letters that I have ever received and I was delighted with it.

Yours sincerely,

[Robertson Davies]

To LIZ

> *"Liz" was an assistant in the publicity*
> *department at Viking Penguin in New*
> *York.*

Massey College
University of Toronto
February 17, 1986

Dear Liz:

Thanks for sending me the letter and the reviews [of *What's Bred in the Bone*] on Feb. 4. The Washington one was certainly a stinker. But I think you are wrong in attributing it to the *Post*; the *Post* reviewed the book very generously before Christmas, and printed a large and flattering caricature of me as Prospero.* Couldn't have been more kind. The review you send, by James S. Oppenheim* (may he be stricken very grievously in his organs of generation and become a mockery to all his female friends!) seems to come from something called *The Washington Book Review*, of which I know nothing. I hope its circulation is not more than five − all relatives of the editor..... I consoled myself by re-reading the very flattering review in *The New Yorker* of Jan. 27. On the whole the reviews have been wonderful and it is nice to be on the best-seller list even fleetingly. The book comes out in England shortly and we shall see what we shall see; England is not fond of Canadian writers, or indeed of Canadians. The German publishers have already taken the book, as they have done well with the Deptford Trilogy. So *The Washington Book Review* (may it burn down while Oppenheim is contracting AIDS in the stockroom) must just be endured, as part of the whips and scorns of time.*

All good wishes, & my best to Elis. Sifton –

Robertson Davies

To JUDITH SKELTON GRANT

Windhover
Caledon East
April 7, 1986

Dear Judith:

When you asked to see my notes for *The Rebel Angels* and *What's Bred in the Bone* I agreed, but since then I have been looking over those notes, and a very strong feeling which I dare not ignore comes over me that I should not let them out of my hands. There are three reasons. First, the two novels are so linked with the one on which I am now working [*The Lyre of Orpheus*] and which will complete this trilogy that I need the notes for checking and reference, because they contain matter important for the third book, on which I am now hard at work. That is the *least* of the reasons. The second is that the notes contain references to people and incidents that are clear to me but which might be misunderstood even by so perceptive a reader as yourself – references to living people, real incidents and matter which could be construed as libellous. Like every novelist I protest that my characters and incidents are without any relation to real people or happenings, and like every novelist I know that this is true only in the sense that real people and incidents are the spark of something which is changed totally in quality when it appears as fiction, but which can be misunderstood if the fictional process is somehow overlooked. Such revelations could give pain, and I do not want that to happen even in the consideration of so judicious a reader as yourself. Like most novelists I know a great deal about people whom I know only slightly, because of gossip or indiscreet revelation from other sources; such material is suitable for fiction but it is troublesome if it becomes confused with reality. That is the *second* reason and a good one. But the third reason is the real one: I am, I suppose, superstitious, which I interpret as meaning "heedful of omens" and I feel in the deepest marrow of my bones that to open the workshop, or the butcher's shop, before all the work is done there – to admit even a guest like yourself to the kitchen – is unlucky in the most profound sense.

I do not of course associate you with this, but while I was thinking about your request I looked through the book of criticism of *The Deptford Trilogy* brought out by the Univ. of Victoria.* So much of what was said there attributed to me ideas and attitudes that never entered my mind. Ah, but you will say, it is the art of the critic to make clear what the writer has not himself grasped. Perhaps – a very big perhaps – when the critic is also an artist, but like most writers I am dubious of the concept of the writer as an *idiot savant*, or a patient in the analyst's consulting-room. Two papers in that collection made me wary. One, about *The Manticore*, explained with wondrous precision where I learned about the Bear Cult, and precisely how I had located the Bear Cave; the only trouble was that I had never read or heard of any of the books cited and had picked up the idea from a brief reference in Joseph Campbell* upon which I built an imaginary structure. But for the critic imagination was not enough; there *must* have been *research*, and here was the research neatly sorted out, reducing the imaginative structure to drudging scholarship. The other one was about the Martin-Harvey tours, full of more or less accurate information, but with no imaginative appreciation whatever of the plays, or the players, or what they really meant to the people who saw them. The effect on me was diminishing; I do not work like that and when it is suggested to students – who will believe anything rather than trust their eyes when they read a novel – that this is how I work I am desolated.

My books are works of imagination. Every time one appears I receive letters explaining to me that I have made mistakes about this, that and the other, as though historical accuracy were my principal aim. Of course I try not to make mistakes in matters of fact, but if I were a better historian I would be a lesser novelist. The imagination is a cauldron, not a filing cabinet. But in most of the criticism of my work I read I find that imagination is the quality that appeals least to the majority of critics. To compare small things with great, I would infinitely rather have *Twelfth Night*, in which Illyria has a seacoast, than Hakluyt's *Voyages*.* Imagination is all I have to work with; take it from me, and I am rotten meat for any critic with a pocket-knife.

Imagination is in short supply in Canada. Whenever I meet with students I invariably hear the question: "Where do you get your ideas from?" and whenever I read criticism I know that many of the critics will be hog-wild for *research* and consider imagination a rather sneaky trick. It is the NOTHING BUT attitude toward literary art..... Admittedly I try, like a good conjuror, to persuade my readers, for as long as they read, that I am offering them reality. I bring in Sir Wilfrid Laurier and King George V* as front-men for illusion. But in the end the illusion is the best I have to offer.

None of these hard words applies to you, but – Samson should have stayed away from the barbershop.* So, with apologies – no notes.*

Robertson Davies

P.S.: please feel at liberty to use any or all of the above letter in the book, if you want to.

*This, if it should come to the eye of certain critics, will undoubtedly give rise to a really terrific paper – *Davies' Castration Complex:*

the Vagina Dentata or Kleinian Bad Breast in Three Trilogies*. It will be a triumph of imaginative criticism.

To HORACE W. DAVENPORT

Windhover
Caledon East
April 20, 1986

Dear Horace:

I have now had a chance to read *Doctor Dock** and I compliment you sincerely on it because you have achieved a fine portrait of a remarkable man – a remarkable man who reminds me in many ways of another remarkable man, namely yourself, in that he brings a humane and essentially common-sense attitude to work that attracts many people who are essentially anti-humane and elevate the complex and the high-flown above the simple and – to a special sort of mind – obvious. So Hooray for Davenport, yet again, and I hope the book has the distribution and the understanding it merits..... Another thing that gave me great pleasure was the essential Yankee-ness of the book – I mean the direct, characteristic and often elegant use of language, as I recall it among my mother's old American cousins;* they spoke an enviable, easy, racy but never low or illiterate English that seems now to be gone. E.g., pages 166 and 168, where Dock is talking about the man who ate so many bananas:* could ultra-scientific gobbledegook do it better, or indeed as well? You have written something that is rather more than medical history; it is a portrait of the best medicine of an age, when the local Doctor was one of the learned men in any community, and probably the local atheist – which so often meant not atheist at all but simply a rebel against a peanut conception of God..... So – once again I congratulate you, and thank you, you astonishing man!.... Your note about "whomever"* roused my sympathy. I have given up writing for almost all magazines because they employ these semi-literate, obsessed pinheads who have no understanding or feeling for language, and usually know nothing beyond the stupid "style-book" compiled by someone no better informed than themselves. I suppose you have read Jacques Barzun's fine attack* on them? To attempt to tell Barzun how to write demands the temerity of ignorance, but that is what they would be full of, if they were not already full of Doctor Dock's banana shit.....We look forward to seeing you. Our love to Inge.....

Rob.

To ROBERTSON DAVIES
DAVENPORT

Windhover
Caledon East
August 7, 1986

> Robertson Davies Davenport (1955–) is an American physician and associate professor of pathology at the University of Michigan, Ann Arbor. He is Horace Davenport's second son and was Davies' godson.

Dear Rob:

It was very good of you to write to me in detail about possible causes of impotence, and because you have been so kind I venture to put a more definite question: would mumps do it, and how does mumps affect an adult male, and would it leave him impotent or merely sterile? I ask because in my next novel [*The Lyre of Orpheus*] – successor to *What's Bred* – there is a case of disputed paternity; if the hero's wife does not know that he is infertile, could it not create a doubt as to who had fathered her child? I want to be sure to get the scientific part right, because there are always people who write to authors if they make any sort of technical mistake. So – does mumps leave a man impotent, i.e. incapable of an erection, or merely sterile – no pollywogs? If you can find time to fill me in on this, and any relevant details about mumps in adults, I should be deeply obliged.

We were delighted to see your father and Inge, as always, but I was saddened by Horace's growing dejection; he has always had a tendency toward melancholy, but now he seems to be almost despondent. Yet from my point of view his life has been one of great achievement, and high honours. He has had some bad times, but who hasn't? And I keep assuring him that his work on medical history – or the history of medical education – is of great importance, and if that is not recognized now, it certainly will be in the future. He is simply ahead of his time – though that is a discouraging thing to be, certainly. . . .

It was wonderful to hear from Horace about your success, and the assiduity with which you pursue your forensic work.* Like Sir Bernard Spilsbury,* who has always fascinated me, though I expect you have a wider ambition than can be contained in that sort of work. But – speaking as an author – what a window upon a world that is usually hidden! The criminal mind, the murderer's mind – dark and astonishing. We had a honey of a case here in Toronto about three years ago:* girl who dressed herself as a boy courted another girl and wanted to marry her: father smelled a rat and told him to go away, as he was not a man. So: the man-girl went home, called a taxi and when it came asked the taxi-man (middle-aged, father of a family) to come upstairs and carry a suitcase that was too heavy for her; when he came, she stabbed him to death, cut off his privates and attached them to herself with Krazy Glue; went to her girl's father, exposed the result and said, See, I *am* a man. Now locked up, of course. To me the truly macabre touch, the touch that would never occur to any novelist under the rank of Dostoevsky, is the Krazy Glue; it gives the whole thing an extra chill. Ordinary glue would not have been the same.

You raise an interesting point about how one can identify the artist from his work. Only experts can do it with any degree of certainty, for a great painter has an individuality of style that lends itself to convincing imitation. But as a great expert [Kenneth Garlick]* of the painting of Sir Thomas Lawrence said to me about a non-Lawrence with which he had been confronted: "When everything else was considered, it simply didn't *say* Lawrence to me." I suppose it is an intuition that comes from long acquaintance and a strong affinity with the artist.

Again, many thanks for your letter, and every good wish to you and
Nancy.....

Rob. Davies

P.S. Yesterday we went to the Shaw Festival and saw the whole of
*Back to Methuselah** in an afternoon and an evening. Stupendous, but
a knockout: we have felt groggy all day.

To GORDON AND HELEN ROPER

Massey College
University of Toronto
September 2, 1986

Dear Gordon & Helen:

Your very kind letter of August 28 catches me on the hop, for I
am just in the final stages of getting away on the Scandinavian jaunt.
If, as you say, you cannot see it, I have double cause to be grateful,
for it is not simply legible, but very decorative, as your writing has
always been. When I was in the hospital for my implant* I had a tiny
taste of what it would be like to have no sight, and your philosophical acceptance of that deprivation, like so many other aspects of your
character, humbles me.

Glad to know the book* is to appear at last, after so many vicissi-
tudes. My feeling about [Michael] Peterman, with whom I had only
one talk about the book, was that he belonged to the class of academic who regards authors as candidates for marks, and himself as a
stern examiner. I found nothing in him of appreciation of literature
as an art – only a man who applies a system he has learned from others
like himself, and which is certainly not "bred in the bone." Nor did
we appear to live in the same world; what is precious to me had no
meaning for him, or appeared contemptible. My next book [*The Lyre*

of Orpheus] will puzzle him a good deal, I think, if, having finished his academic task on my work, he troubles to read it.

That book is now ready to be written. You know my method, Watson – I make notes, and fuss and fume over a book for a couple of years, until at last it is ready. This is why I do not have the many re-writes and re-castings that plague so many authors; I revise twice, and that is it. The hardest work is done before I begin at the typewriter. This book will complete the present trilogy. I look forward to getting at it because the theme appeals to me greatly: I am getting back to the world of the theatre – this time, opera – not simply because I know quite a bit about it and love it, but because it seems to me to be in such a real sense, a mirror of nature.* All the *Rebel Angels* characters will be in it – those who are still alive – and the reader will find out what finally becomes of Uncle Frank's money, and of Uncle Frank's dubious pictures.

Like the other two, it will be a story for those who like a story, and something beyond that for readers who care to see it. There will be one or two surprises, which the critics probably will not like – they get so cross because I will *not* play by their rules – and you may be sure a copy will speed to you as soon as there are any copies, which won't be for a while.

Judith Grant presses on. I have come to have a high regard for her, both as a person and a biographer. I shall probably not like her book, but who *does* like a biography of himself? But that doesn't matter; it will be a view of me and my work rooted in sincere and sympathetic scholarship, and that is what it's all about. I am being urged by a publisher* to write my memoirs. I *may* do a book, but it won't be an autobiography . . . .

We are off to Denmark, Norway, Sweden and Finland and are looking forward to it with keen pleasure, though I expect it will be hard work. I shall give readings and speak, and hope I shall have a chance to say a few kind things about Canada, for I feel we socialist-monarchies should know one another better; we share the myth and the clear vision – though at the moment, under the rule of Mulroney, our vision seems to be rather clouded. That tax on books from the U.S.A.! That Canada should impose a tax on literacy!

After Scandinavia we go to England for a spell and I shall do some publicity work there. My books don't do well in England, in spite of good reviews and that grieves me, for although I have no illusions about Mother Britain I should like to be better known to the land from which all our literature stems. Have you looked at the latest edition of *The Oxford Companion to English Literature* edited by Margaret Drabble?* Not much of a book, I fear, for she has dropped a lot of the significant English authors of the second rank (if one thinks in terms of ranks) and includes some oddities. Paul Harvey's remains the better book.

No more for the moment. If I see a nice troll in Norway, would you like it for your island?*

Love to you both from both of us

Rob.

To MARGARET LAURENCE

Windhover
Caledon East
November 3, 1986

> Margaret Laurence (1926–87) was a
> highly regarded Canadian novelist. Davies
> knew her from the year she spent at the
> University of Toronto as writer-in-
> residence when she had an office at
> Massey College.

Dear Margaret:

Peggy Atwood tells me* that you are unwell, and that letters help to pass the time – so here goes. I have hesitated to write to you for some time past, as I heard that you wanted to be quiet, had abandoned many of your former occupations at Trent, and I hoped you might be contemplating a book – because your long silence has been a deprivation we cannot easily endure. Of course I knew also that the foamings and raving of the Moral Majority* had been a nuisance to you; I know the obstreperous morality of the Peterborough district very well, having contended with it for twenty years as an editor, and it is of an especially grubby, pig-ignorant variety. Why, I so often ask myself, does Christ's teaching appeal so strongly to people of narrow and malignant nature, who use it for their own ends? I am not an enthusiastic Christian myself: it is a Mediterranean faith, rooted in the harshness of the desert, dismissive of women, and totally lacking in humour. But Christ deserves better followers than he gets among the Canadian evangelistic sects.

My life has been rather a scramble these last few months, for publishers seem suddenly to have discovered PUBLICITY, and they are certain that the best and simplest way to get it is to squeeze it out of the bodies of their authors. The public readily assents; the craze to *see* authors rages like a fire, though anybody with any sense knows that authors are in the main an unsightly lot, given to dandruff and rough table-manners. But one can only stand out against this craze to a certain extent, and I have been a kind of travelling show for some months. Brenda and I have just returned from eight weeks abroad, jaunting through the four Scandinavian countries where I talked and read and was interviewed to spread the news of Canadian literature, and to try to persuade our Scandinavian friends that we are *not* an acquiescent dependency of the U.S. I must say they were wonderfully hospitable and kind, and welcomed the message. In fact I think we are more like them than any other group of countries anywhere. Climate, the pink rock and the ragged pines, the minatory climate that gives you a taste of everything every year, and a somewhat morose attitude toward life which can melt into wonderful geniality – and above all a desire to get on with our own affairs and have done with the ugly rivalries of the U.S. and the U.S.S.R. – serve to unite us. I am delighted that my books are popular there. I cannot think of any other groups of peoples whom I wish to please more. Your name is well known and greatly respected there; you speak to them in a voice they can understand. As you know, the educated class – a large one – reads English readily.

What I said to them was that while the Americans had had their national character formed by strong-willed Puritans and some aristocrats of the Washington-Jefferson order, we had made a people out of a sad group of losers – exiled Scots and Irish, and the Loyalists that were driven north in the ugly behaviour after the Revolution. And out of those losers we have made a people who know they must survive or perish – and we have done better than just survive. And in doing so we have formed a national spirit of endurance wedded to a rather sardonic spirit, and our climate has formed us in a way that Texans and Californians cannot understand without taking more pains than they usually do. We are a people without territorial ambitions, aching for a world at peace – or as much peace as this troubled planet can manage. But I am making a speech. Sorry.

We came back by way of England and saw a lot of old friends and made some new ones. I was greatly pleased to meet a few people* I had not seen since Oxford days, and delighted that life had used them, on the whole, well – though they had known rough times, as who does not. Some have made lives in the theatre, which was where Brenda and I had hoped to work. As I look back, however, I think we may have been lucky in not being bound to that chancy, knockabout life, where so much depends on luck, and success may mean repeating the same words in the same play for months on end. But the theatre people know immediately if they have pleased their audiences: we writers have to wait for months and often for years before any echo comes in response to the signals we have sent out. The hullabaloo of PUBLICITY does not really count. It is dismaying when some eager pseudo-fan tells you of his enthusiasm for a book he attributes to you but which was really written by somebody else.

Do you get lunatic letters? Of course you do. All authors do. I had one last week from a woman in B.C. giving me the devil because in my last novel I had not introduced some juicy incest between a father and his daughter which was – this profound psychologist said – implicit in every word I wrote about them. People who think incest is simply a matter of sexual involvement on the most obvious level ought not to read anything but The Three Bears (where of course the messy involvement of Baby Bear with Mama Bear is clear, and Goldilocks is simply an intruder in a family tragedy). "Who's been sleeping in whose bed?" is the cry of much modern fiction, and I am sick of it. Come to think of it, I suppose Mama Bear was driven to her child-abuse by the cruel neglect of Father Bear, who was having it off with Mother Goose, or maybe the Old Woman Who Lived in a Shoe – that Single Parent of nursery fame.

Brenda and I send you our love – no mere form of words, I assure you – and our belief in your great courage. I shall write again but I do not, I emphasize, expect replies. Do you know the old medieval medical advice? –

Use three physicians still:
First Doctor Quiet,
Then Doctor Merryman
And Doctor Diet.

If I may presume on a long friendship, I shall appoint myself Doctor Merryman.

Rob. Davies

To HORACE W. DAVENPORT

Windhover
Caledon East
November 22 [1986]

Dear Horace:

Many thanks for the piece from *Nature*.* As I grow older the whole notion of belief grows more important to me, and I am grieved to find what awful company it sometimes puts me in. As I explain, when I am asked, I am a religious man, but that does not mean that I am a card-carrying Christian and certainly not a member of any sect or coven of zealots. I think that the Christian business is beginning to ravel out – has indeed been doing so for over a century – having made an astonishing change in a great part of mankind. But an Oriental faith, hitched to a lot of Mediterranean hierarchical and sacerdotal organization, embraced and changed by people of all sorts and degrees of intelligence, and now face to face with the demand of women to be treated as people, cannot survive in its present form. It has shoe-horned a little mercy into the savagery of mankind, and somewhat mitigated the ghastly egotism which blasts all civilizations. I have no reason to believe that there was a single hospital in Rome, for instance, when Christ walked the earth, and the lot of the wretched was about as bad as anything can be. Nevertheless, civilizations have existed before Christ – great ones, too – and some very remarkable people lived and said their say without benefit of Christian morality.

For myself the figure of Christ was made hateful to me when I was a child; the simpleton, the patsy, the Bearded Lady, the big-eyed snoop who watched your every move – and nothing that I have learned since has made the image more attractive, for the reports we have of him are full of contradictions. He was, I suppose, a Jewish nationalist agitator and a prophet of great charisma. But the Son of God? He very perceptively said that we may all claim to be that, and failed to add that most of us are disgraces to the family.

No, I suppose I am somebody who cannot live without a belief in a power beyond what man can compass, and that attempts to make God in one's own image are folly, as are notions that God disposes the universe with an eye to one's personal convenience. Philosophy cannot capture God, nor can Science winkle him out of his vastness, and as for humble faith, it is too often the refuge of boobs and a stick with which they beat people who do not agree with them.

I once had a blazing row with the chaplain of Massey College, in which he accused me of being a Gnostic, which he thought was a horrible accusation. But so far as I can discover the Gnostics were people who thought that being intelligent and acting accordingly had something to do with salvation – so of course they were heretics, because the notion that intelligence makes any difference in religion has always been hateful to the Church. The Protestant Reformation, said C. G. Jung,* took man's soul out of the care of the Church and gave it into his own keeping – thereby striking the Church a blow from which it has never really recovered.

But this is becoming tedious. All the best to you and Inge. I must write when I can and tell you about our adventures in Scandinavia. But now I must scamper to New York for some nonsense or other.*

Rob.

To MARGARET LAURENCE

from ROBERTSON DAVIES

December 18, 1986

Dear Margaret:

Sorry to write to you on this paper which looks rather pompous – but I have no other at hand. Believe it or not this is a hold-over from my business days, when it was thought I ought to have paper of this sort. At least I avoided the foolishness of "From the desk of;" which is popular in some circles, but none I frequent. This is meant as a Christmas letter, and should have been written much earlier, but both Brenda and I have been miserable with 'flu. . . .

At this time of year Brenda and I think often of the Peterborough district, because we used to direct and put on a Nativity Play* at a little church called St. George's run by a delightful man called Father Moore.* It was done on a shoestring; the costumes were all made from oddments, but we touched them up with gold paint, and on head-dresses we stuck jewels, which were made from glass alleys stuck into sealing wax. We lit the whole thing with candles (very dangerous, but we trusted in the Lord) and it really had a splendidly mysterious, rich look, and Father Moore took care that it reeked of incense. We used a very old play – the Coventry Nativity – and had some excellent early music provided by a choir accompanied by recorders, and if I may say so, it was pretty good and drew great crowds. But alas, as the years passed the actors lost their simplicity, and began to think them-selves grand, and what had been an act of worship became a show, and so we had to let it drop. Nevertheless, there were some good moments when it was at its best.

We used to have Christmas parties,* too; all generations. The party began at five o'clock, and first of all the children of the guests gave some sort of entertainment, usually a puppet show. One year, I recall, it was Dr. Faustus, and the old story was strangely interspersed with satirical bits about their school teachers. Then a huge supper, the great offering of which was Amethyst Tarts – tiny pastry shells with grape jelly in them. After supper we played games – best of all The Game – where people acted out words, or phrases given to them by the opposing team. We specialized in book titles, and the most difficult was *The Bobbsey Twins at Atlantic City* which is a facer, undoubtedly, but Scott Young* (his son Neil, the rock singer, was present as a lad) guessed it brilliantly in under fifteen seconds. The funniest one I remember was *Lady Chatterley's Lover* which my mother-in-law [Muriel Ethel Newbold]* had to act out, and I would not have dreamed she had in her what emerged.

We always concluded the evening with some rounds of a game I invented called Homicidal Maniac. We had an old Victorian house – Tom Symons* lives in it now – with lots of nooks and crannies and backstairs; everybody drew a lot, and the one with the Black Spot on it was the Maniac who, unknown and unrecognized, crept around the totally darkened house and choked anyone who could be found; the victim was supposed to give a blood-curdling scream, and sink to the floor. It was only when the Maniac was challenged that he or she had to give up. When all the children had been reduced to hysteria the lights were restored, everybody had another drink, and it was midnight. I sometimes yearn at Christmas for just one more round of Homicidal Maniac.

We shall be alone this Christmas; all our children are away, and our grandchildren will be skiing. But I do not suppose we shall sit, tear-sodden, a couple of pitiful Old Age Pensioners, snuffling about Old Times. Indeed, I think we may be glad to rest from the exertions leading up to Christmas, which get more exacting every year. What Christmas really needs is re-discovery, and some simplification. I suppose it is foolish to long for the simplicity of the Christmas I remember as a very small boy, at my Grandfather Davies' house;* it was mostly musical, being a Welsh family; everybody sang – my Father sang *The Holy City* and my Aunts Mary and Elsie sang weepy songs about lost children, and my Auntie Bess (whose voice had been TRAINED) sang fashionable ballads, and Uncle John Robertson sang *The Mistletoe Bough* and scared me out of my wits, and Grandfather sang *Nazareth* in a voice like the north wind roaring through the forest.

But perhaps some new simplicity could be found.

But now I must stop and Brenda and I send you from the bottom of our hearts good wishes and love for the great season.

Rob.

Dear Devlin:

I address you thus from old custom because as boys at U.C.C. nobody was admitted to the ignominy of a Christian name — just a surname & an initial. I don't suppose you recall that at Christmas 1930 you gave me a book called _A Christmas Book_, compiled by D.B. Wyndham Lewis and G.C. Heseltine. It has been with me for 58 years and has been an invaluable companion. I have not only read with delight in its pages but have culled from it X⁹ mas readings & verses which musical friends set for X⁹ mas parties & Gaudy Nights at Massey College. Of how many books & how many gifts can one say that they have been companions for a lifetime? Thanks, & thanks again. — I hope this book may give you some pleasure.

Davies

October 7
1988

SECTION
V

avies (now 73) began writing *The Lyre of Orpheus* on January 1, 1987, and a year later it was ready for his publishers. It appeared in Canada and Britain in September and in the United States in December. Publicity tours occupied several weeks in May and June in Scotland and England, much of the fall in Canada and England, and another two weeks, early in 1989, in the United States. Davies began making notes for *Murther & Walking Spirits* in June 1988, before *Lyre* was published.

Through these two years Davies also wrote a few articles, reviews, and introductions to books, and gave a number of speeches. There were other distractions too – the week-long Wheatland Conference on Literature in Washington in April 1987, and, also in 1987, the promise (never fulfilled) of a television mini-series of *What's Bred in the Bone*.

His recurrent bronchitis, asthma, colds, and periods of influenza prompted a visit to a respirologist in 1987. He was told to stop smoking, an injunction he obeyed with regret, for he had enjoyed the couple of small cigars he smoked most days. In February 1988, Brenda prevailed on him to take a trip to Arizona to give his chest a respite from the Canadian winter.

To YOUSUF KARSH

Massey College
University of Toronto
January 13, 1987

Yousuf Karsh (1908–   ) is a Canadian photographer (born in Armenian Turkey). He is known internationally for his portraits of famous personalities.

Dear Mr· Karsh:

I am extremely grateful to you for the portrait which you sent me with your letter of January 8th and I am greatly honoured that you are including it in the group of pictures that you are giving to the Rideau Club.* To be in such company is flattering indeed but I am sure you felt that there should be some Canadians in the group. I am pleased that you should have thought of me.

I am glad that you liked what I said about Margaret Laurence;* she was a writer whom I admired greatly because of her splendid sincerity. In the world of writing, as in all the arts, even admirable people sometimes deviate from the kind of behaviour one would hope for from them. I knew Margaret for many years and in all that time she never did anything that was not perfectly sincere and actuated by the highest principles. I was particularly impressed by this when she came to the University of Toronto as writer-in-residence during which time she stayed at Massey College. Her dealing with students was exemplary because, although she was unfailingly kind, she was never anything but honest in talking to young people who wanted to write and sometimes this meant telling them that they had no apparent talent. She never shrank from doing that and I think that in future those young people will understand how privileged they were to be given even unwelcome advice by a person of such admirable honesty, both as an artist and as a person.

Certainly when next my wife and I are coming to Ottawa we will

write to you beforehand and would be delighted to see you and renew
our long friendship.

Yours sincerely,

Robertson Davies

To MIRANDA DAVIES

Feb. 22: Sun. [1987]

Dearest Miranda:

O thou jewel in the heart of the lotus! When I opened the package
of tapes I almost swooned away, for I had never dreamed of hearing
*Undine** in this world! So far as I know, there is no recording. I listened with greedy ears, and was astonished by what Hoffmann does;
sensitive orchestration, good use of the wood-winds (not doubling
with the strings as so often with composers of that time) and occasional affectionate Mozartian hints. He seems to me to have everything an opera composer could have at that time, except a really great
gift of melody. But then, the great melodists like Schumann &
Schubert* flopped in opera as they lacked dramatic feeling – which
H. abundantly has.

Could you confirm by letter what you say about his use of the two
male voices in the overture – I want to mention that in my book [*The
Lyre of Orpheus*],* for I have never heard of anyone doing it – not
even Wagner.

Do you know anything about Hoffmann? A fine critic, understood
Beethoven before anybody else, was influential on Schumann and
Weber,* and Wagner refers to him repeatedly as an influence, intellectual and musical. I am enjoying writing the book, and want to do
justice to Hoffmann if I can. There is a book about him by Murray
Schafer* which is quite good, but like a real musician Schafer plays
down H. as a composer; the old trade-union jealousy of somebody

who is not a composer and nothing else. How people hate to admit that a man might be good at more than one thing! And of course H's great claim to fame is as a writer, where he was one of the earliest and most innovative of the Romantics.

But to return to your superb gift – it makes it possible for me to write with intimacy and certainty about H's music, which otherwise I knew only in a few examples – just snippets – given in Schafer's book, which illustrate his weaknesses rather than his strengths. It would not surprise me if H had a new life as a composer – certainly with *Undine* – as the modern musical world is so much more sympathetic and understanding of that pre-Wagner, post-Mozart music, and may want to explore beyond Donizetti and Bellini* (both contemps of H.) who were melodists, but not great at orchestration or character depiction.

By the way, do you know an opera called *Der Vampyr* by Marschner?* He came a wee bit after H. and in my view was not so good, but *Der Vampyr* is a very accomplished piece of work all the same and there is a good recording, so if you get a chance, have a hearken to it.

We are off to New York on Monday. I detest New York, and hate the interruption in my work, but needs must. Am going to harangue the Jungians about folk-song, after the BIG DOINGS.* We shall send you news..... Again, warmest thanks.....

The Aged P.*

To **MICHAEL F. ROBINSON**

Massey College
University of Toronto
March 3, 1987

Michael F. Robinson, an English dealer and appraiser in the fine arts and a reader of Davies' novels, was then in business in New York City.

[Dear Mr. Robinson:]

Thank you for your letter of February 10th with the copy of your earlier letter which must have gone astray. The references to "J. B." in *What's Bred in the Bone* did, indeed, refer to Burgon Bickersteth.*

During his long stay in Canada he wrote regularly to his mother, who preserved all his letters, in which he offered interesting and sometimes "insider" comments on Canadian affairs. He was also in frequent correspondence with the Secretary to the British Cabinet and with the Foreign Office, to which he supplied information of a confidential kind which they requested. Burgon's letters were left by him to Massey College and are now in our library. When some years have passed they should prove of substantial interest to historians.

With good wishes,

Yours sincerely,

[Robertson Davies]

To THE EDITOR OF *THE GLOBE AND MAIL**

Massey College
University of Toronto
[between March 4 and April 8, 1987]

[Sir:]

Thomas M. Paikeday, in his letter of March 4,* quotes the *Oxford English Dictionary* (vol. 3 of the *Supplement*) in support of the use of "momentarily" to mean "at any moment," and I must concede a lexicographical victory to him.

But dictionaries exist to record usage and pronunciation, not to dictate it. One is permitted individual taste in one's use of language and I do not like to see a word taking on unnecessary and confusing meanings. As Mr. Paikeday says, it is bad form to quote from one's own works in support of an opinion and that is why I offer the following comment from my old friend, Samuel Marchbanks:

"I had a wrangle today with a man who said that there was no such thing as grammar, and that 'the living speech' was good speech. He talked about 'Everyman's grammar' – meaning anything anybody cares to say – as the only guide to usage. Humph! I wouldn't particularly like to trust myself to Everyman's medicine or Everyman's ideas about the law. Why should I accept Everyman's grammar?'"*

[Yours faithfully,]

Robertson Davies

To JUDITA PAMFIL

Massey College
University of Toronto
March 31, 1987

Judita Pamfil, once a Romanian art curator, had come to Canada several years earlier and become a teacher of French. She yearned to meet Canadians who relish art, literature, and philosophy, and found one such in the writer of What's Bred in the Bone.

[Dear Miss Pamfil:]

I read your letter of March 22nd with great interest and felt strong sympathy for you. I wish that I could give you more helpful advice than I have at my disposal but all that I can say in reply to what you have written, and all that I can offer to mitigate your disillusion with Canada is that you must do what all new Canadians have to do, and that is to grit your teeth and endure many things until you find that it is unmistakably your home. What I think you forget is that Canada was made by people like yourself who came from elsewhere and brought all the skills or strengths or cultural ambitions that they had with them and gave them to the new country as generously as they could. What you must understand is that we need you and depend on you and that however difficult it may be to make your point of view clear to the people you meet, you have, at least, the freedom to do so and, although you may meet with many rebuffs and a great deal of neglect, nobody is going to put you in prison for thinking differently from somebody else. The lot of the immigrant is never an easy one, as I know very well from the experience of my own family, but in the end you will find that the new country grows very dear to you – very possibly as a result of the difficulty that you have had in associating yourself with it. Even if it makes you unpopular you must speak your mind because that is the greatest privilege the new country has to give you.

Yours sincerely,

[Robertson Davies]

To THE HONOURABLE FLORA
MACDONALD

Massey College
University of Toronto
March 31, 1987

*Flora MacDonald (1926–   ), Canadian
politician, Progressive Conservative
member of parliament from 1972–88, was
Minister of Communications from
1986–88.*

[Dear Madam Minister:]

I was greatly pleased to receive a cheque for $4,000. under the new Public Lending Right legislation. As with all Canadian authors, I was extremely pleased when that legislation was passed because it asserts the property right of an author in his work, which is something that public libraries have long refused to recognize. Public libraries, like all benefactors of society, have also a shadow side and their cynical exploitation of living authors is part of it.

As an author who has enjoyed a substantial degree of success I cannot, with a good conscience, accept this money simply as an addition to my income, and I thought that you would like to know that I am using some of it to support a lectureship at Queen's University which is being founded as a memorial to the late Margaret Laurence, and a part of it to go to The Canadian Writers' Foundation, which has for so many years done admirable work in assisting Canadian writers who have had bad luck.

It was kind of you to write to me about the National Arts Club award which I received in New York. I am sure that I do not have to tell you that Canadian writers are doing a very great deal to give Canada a good reputation in the rest of the world and the recognition of Canada as a country from which good writing may be expected is extremely gratifying. What some admirable films are doing for Australia, books of no less excellent quality are doing for Canada.

. With congratulations on the legislation, and personal good wishes, I am

Yours sincerely,

[Robertson Davies]

To ELISABETH SIFTON

Windhover
Caledon East
April 20, 1987

Dear Elisabeth:

It is kind of you to send me the first vol. of the life of Robert Graves:* I have always admired him, and read even his crankiest books with pleasure. There is much in *The White Goddess* to prime the pump of inspiration, even if a great deal of it is moonshine; his most remarkable characteristic, in my view, was to pretend that his wildest flights of fancy were merest common sense, and that the great accretion of Greek myth was to be read rather like a comic strip. The way he was neglected in Britain after he went to Majorca is a shame to them; after Yeats* died I do not think they had a better poet. So – after a preliminary dip, I put the book on the heap that is to be read, when my present Old Man of the Sea* is off my back. I mean, of course, the novel [*The Lyre of Orpheus*], at which I toil like a swimmer who feels himself about to sink beneath the waves at any moment.

Like all my novels, it began with quite a simple idea, but as I work on it a mass of complexities assert themselves, and I have to struggle to keep from being overwhelmed by extraneous detail. A recent professorial criticism* of *What's Bred In The Bone* was very severe with me for my attraction toward arcane lore and weirdo belief: no use explaining that to me the arcane lore isn't really arcane at all, and makes wonderful sense, and that almost all belief is strange, if you catch it with the light falling on it in a certain way. I wish professorial critics, who write so badly themselves, would give me credit for a minimum of wits, and stop elevating their dull selves as the standard by which all belief and understanding should be measured!

When I was last in New York I made a grave mistake: talking on the McNeill–Lehrer Hour I said innocently that I expected that the year 2000 – give or take a century – would see a great new development in religion. Since then I have been deluged with rubbish from nuts of all kinds, who send me their awful writings, and implore me to find publishers for them. If only I could learn to keep my mouth shut, and realize that nobody – absolutely NOBODY – who is listening to me on the air has any brains at all.

To return to the novel: I don't like the title *The Platter of Plenty* and I wonder if *The Secret Sympathy* would do? It fits the book and is not so alliteratively displeasing as the other.

Now I must conclude this letter because (a) I know from experience what a bore long letters are, and (b) because I must get back to that damned novel, which obsesses me.

On Wednesday next I go to Washington to a Great Monster Rally of Literary Folk, financed by the Wheatland people (Gettys) and enriched and made glorious by that great and good man Lord Weidenfeld.* I am not sure why I am going, but I can't resist a whiff of what will be – judging by the agenda I have received – in Shelley's phrase* "pinnacled dim in the intense inane." Authors should stay at home. Over the void, I greet you –

Rob.

To MIRANDA DAVIES

Windhover
Caledon East
[May 1987]

Darling Miranda:

I am immensely obliged to you for the BBC material about
Hoffmann;* your Mum was reminded of Elsa [Larking]* when we
worked out the patience and care you had taken to elicit an answer
from the broadcasters; Elsa had the patience of Job and in the end
always got what she was after.

Delighted to have the assurance that in the overture to *Undine* the
scene of the two male voices had originally been introduced; I had
been trying to trace that, by getting the score of *Undine* from the
Library at the Edward Johnson building* – but there the overture runs
straight through. So you have helped me to establish a point that is
of considerable significance in my novel [*The Lyre of Orpheus*].* The
score of *Undine*, by the way, fills three large volumes of a Collected
Hoffmann got out in Germany; extraordinary as it seems, all his music
has been collected and published and there is even some hint that
he may be recognized as a composer, though a minor one. Wouldn't he
have been pleased! That was what he always wanted. But he died at
46 – of the pox, though there were complications, one of which was
champagne – when he was getting into his stride. And that is the
foundation of my story: he leaves an uncompleted opera, which hints
at much of what Wagner was later to take from him, and what Weber
saw in *Undine* – and in the book the opera is completed and presented
on the stage – at the Avon in Stratford, in fact. Is it a success? Who
can say? The ordinary critics have to wait until the musicologists
tell them whether it is good or not; without some past record to
help them, they are quite unable to form an opinion of a hitherto
unknown nineteenth century work; none of their clichés fit! But that
is only one of the complications; it is, as they say, a multi-textured
work. But it is a fact that poor old Hoffmann has always suffered under

Berlioz' sneer* that he was merely a literary man, and all Wagner's and Weber's praise and Beethoven's appreciation goes for naught. Strange how a *negative* opinion is always so highly valued.

Read the offprint of your commentary* on the analytical paper with great interest, and having read it once, read it again with care to take note of the writing. Now, my dear, you really must recognize that you *can* write, and that it is a strong string to your bow. This piece was exemplary – all the scholarly stuff was incorporated but without screeching of gears or clumsiness, the criticism was politely and kindly expressed (this is golden and marks the fine writer from the status-seeking dub) and you had managed to give it a personal and *feminine* quality without either grabbing attention or declining into Pretty Pussy nonsense like _____. I am sure much of your future lies in this sort of literary exposition of the work you are engaged in; most analysts (including Fordham)* write stuffily and clumsily, and what is wanted is somebody who can say it all, and say it right, without clubbing the reader into insensibility. The fact that so much of what is written is presented in translation is a problem. But I am sure you are on a very fine upward path.

Your *proud*

Daddy

You have found your *style* – and a very good and individual style it is!

To DOUGLAS GIBSON

Windhover
Caledon East
May 29, 1987

*Douglas Gibson (1943–), a Scot who
came to Canada in 1967, was editorial
director and later publisher at Macmillan
of Canada from 1974–86 and Davies'
editor there through that period. At the
time this letter was written he was
publisher of Douglas Gibson Books, an
imprint at McClelland & Stewart, and no
longer Davies' editor.*

Dear Douglas:

If my recollection serves me rightly I wrote to thank you for
Margaret Drabble's book [*The Radiant Way*], which I had not at that
time read. Since then I have read it, and I am sure you must be proud
to have published such a book, which is a remarkable reflection of
our times in the U.K. The shadow of Mrs. Thatcher is strong in it,
as is also the somewhat naive revolt against her by people who want
"freedom" but would not much like paying the price it would cost if
Labour got back in – freedom to be struck against, and exploited by
a cynical labour group, and held to ransom by the entrepreneurs and
the so-called "workers." (How on earth have they promoted that
usage, which suggests that people like you and me do not really work
– just trifle our lives away at the Ritz.) I am no Thatcherite, but at
present I do not see any other salvation for Britain; her Philistine contempt for the arts and for education gags me, but she seems to be able
to salvage the currency, and that is a great thing.

But enough of that: I thought the book was a fine thermometer
of its time, and consequently the temperature was not always comfortable. It was also very feminist, in a sensible and irresistible way. I
was, during April, in Washington for a meeting of writers called The
Wheatland Conference on Literature, financed by the Gettys; unlike
most literary conferences I have attended, it made sense, was intelligently small – about fifty people – and had a firm program for discussion. Everybody had a chance to speak. There I met Margaret
Drabble with her husband Michael Holroyd,* whom I had already

met. No question about who leads the band in *that* marriage. Now I shall tell you a story about Holroyd I heard from a very good source in London last autumn: the day before he was about to be married he confided this fact to his mistress; she made a scene; he was astonished; "But I thought you would be delighted to be on the periphery of my happiness!" said he. There's a complexity of sensibility for you! I liked him but he seems utterly subsumed in his book on Shaw, which has been ten years in the making; I think he likes leaving all the decision-making to Miss D. I liked Miss D. too, but somewhat feared her, for she had absolutely not one scrap of humour about her, and in conversation one had to be careful not to make jokes, or one would be greeted with a look of incomprehension – and I respect her too much to insult her by explaining a joke. Talked a bit about the *Oxford Companion*, a queer compilation in which rather too many contemporaries appear and too many oldies have been dropped. But God forbid that I should ever have to make such choices!

We must get together and exchange gossip. But at present I am over my head in my latest novel [*The Lyre of Orpheus*], which completes the trilogy begun with *Angels* and *What's Bred*; it is a complex book but I must not make it too complex or ride my hobbies too hard – a fault for which some grave Western critics* have been scolding me recently. I am also the subject of a Twayne book by one Michael Peterman of Trent University; he is down on me for all the old things – élitist, given to big words, sloppy construction, too fond of improbable (unPetermanlike) characters, can't draw women, and flawed, flawed, flawed. All written in the kind of Quaker Oats prose* one expects of a Peterborough academic. But I suppose I am an old lion and the asses want to skin me and hee-haw in my shrunken skin.

I hope life goes well with you and that your wife is restored to full health.

For the moment, farewell –

Rob.

To JUDITH SKELTON GRANT

Windhover
Caledon East
May 29: 1987

Dear Judith:

　After we talked on Thursday morning I thought a good deal about
those letters to Eleanor [Sweezey]* which she has kept, and which
you have seen, and which you described to me as "abject" and marked
by a running-downhill depression. I cannot recall what they said,
except the general hopeless theme, but the *feeling* is intense, and I have
to be careful not to evoke it too carelessly, for fear that it may overcome me, even now. For it was, as you perceptively said, an archetypal feeling; I was in the grip of an archetype which I suppose might
be called the Quest for the Ideal Love, which is one aspect of another
very great archetype relating to femininity altogether. Thousands of
men undergo it, but as I was a young man of very romantic disposition – romantic in the true sense of placing primary importance on
personal feeling, and not simply disposed to love affairs – and it had
me in a strong, choking grip. But what I write to tell you is that a
recognition of that feeling revisited me many years later – perhaps
forty years later – when I was teaching a graduate course in Resto-
ation Drama at Massey Coll. Of course I had to take note of the work
of Thomas Otway,* who had always been a favourite of mine, but in
order to talk about him to a seminar group I had to look at him again
and anew. Speaking of the intensity of passion that makes *Venice
Preserv'd* a great and undeservedly neglected play, I directed my students to the love letters that Otway wrote to Elizabeth Barry, which
are quite the most tortured love letters I have ever read. I said to my
students: Tell me truthfully, and I shall respect your confidence, how
many men here have felt something of the passion that speaks in these
letters? Always a majority, and sometimes all the men, admitted that
they had done so. Then I said: How many of the women here would
wish to be the recipients of letters like these, even from a great poet

and dramatist? Only rarely would a girl or two say that she would have liked that.

My letters were in the Otway strain, but not in Otway's poetic eloquence; there was something about that affair with Eleanor that completely quenched and set at naught my literary quality – not that I could have matched Otway, in any case, but I might have whined less. (No, probably not; Otway whines; we all whine when tortured.) But I think the tenor of my letters was Otway's, when he says "Think and be generous," as he addresses "My Tyrant!" How I wish I had said: "...I cannot bear the Thought of being made a *Property*, either of another Man's *Good Fortune*, or the *Vanity* of a *Woman* that designs nothing but to *plague* me." But I wrote miserably, which is something I now very much regret. What vanity! But I suppose the poor girl found me a great nuisance; she was not to blame for being the peg upon which an archetypal possession chose to hang itself.

Make any use of this letter you please. And thanks for bringing all this back so poignantly.

Rob. . . .

To BIRGITTA HEYMAN

Massey College
University of Toronto
June 10, 1987

Birgitta Rydbeck Heyman (1919–   ) is a Swedish speech therapist. In 1938–39 when Davies fell in love with her, she was a student in the Old Vic's theatre school in London. After she got in touch (though they did not meet) during Davies' Scandinavian tour in 1986, he began a new correspondence with her which lasted until his death.

Dear Birgitta:

I have been much too long in replying to your letter of April 13, but since it came I have read it many times. The reason for the delay is that I have been trying to make up my mind what to say about the

enquiries sent to you by Dr. Judith Skelton Grant, who is writing a
book about me; she has been urging me to write to you to say that
I agree to your giving her copies of my letters to you, and I really
think that those letters are between you and me, and are of no
concern to anybody else. Tell her anything you like, but I do not think
she needs to read our letters. Because, you see, I have your letters, too,
and would not dream of letting her see them. There is nothing that
we need be ashamed or secretive about, but the letters are *private*, and
were not written for strangers to read forty years later. What I have
done is to give her a copy of some verses I wrote to you on your
birthday; they were meant humorously, and if she wants to use them
I do not mind, if you don't. But letters are a different matter. She is
a nice woman, very honourable, and I think she will write quite a
good book, but like all biographers she is very curious, and there is
a point beyond which curiosity should not go.

I am deeply interested in your account of your family. You have had
a very full experience of life, and you write about it like a wise woman.
I do hope very much that all goes well with your daughter Agneta
[Engdahl] and the baby – but what anxiety it must give you! I was
interested too in your son Anders* and his enthusiasm for the "working
classes." Why are they called that, I wonder, as if the rest of us did not
work. I have worked very hard all my life, and I bet you have done so
too. My own feeling about the so-called working class was strongly
influenced by my twenty years as a newspaper publisher, during which
I had to keep peace with three different labour unions; the men who
worked for me were mostly very good fellows, but they were very
easily persuaded by their leaders that I, and all the management staff,
were in a conspiracy against them, and they could always be persuaded
to threaten a strike if they could not have everything they asked for.
I was glad to get away from that, though when I became part of the
university I found that students were just the same – if they could not
have their own way in everything they felt that there was a terrible
plot to rob them of their rights. I suppose this is the experience of
everyone who has the job of directing some sort of business or institution, and has to think of the future as well as the present, and who
has to find the money for all the changes and improvements that the

workers or the students demand. I suppose I sound like a very old man, but I wish to God that sometimes they would stop talking about their rights and give some thought to their duties.

Did I tell you that Sweden is very often in my mind, and for a strange reason. My Swedish publishers [Wahlström & Widstrand] told me that for the last two years I have been on the short list of nominees for the Nobel Prize in Literature. This is an honour that had never entered my head, but this year some Canadian literary groups are nominating me again in strong terms, and though I do not expect anything to come of it, I cannot help thinking about it now and then. However, I shall *not* be chosen, because the Swedish Academy seems to have a strongly political bias, and makes its award to writers in countries where free expression of opinion is suppressed, and being a writer is dangerous – and certainly that is not Canada. Also, Canada is an *unfashionable* country, if you understand me; we have no glamour. . . .

But it is foolish to bother one's head about prizes. The strangest people get them, and I have had a fair share of them. So I am working as hard as I can on my next novel [*The Lyre of Orpheus*], which may be my last. I tend to write stories that take three books to complete, and I do not like the idea of setting out on another six or eight years of work. I might write a book about my life, which will certainly not be like the one Dr. Grant is planning. I might call it *My Three Fathers* – for I had three. First, my own Father, a wonderful man, an imaginative, humorous, tyrannical, energetic, loving, hating, unpredictable Welshman, to whom I owe a very great deal. Second, Tony Guthrie, who used to tell me that he was my Father In Art – which he wasn't, but he was an inspiring, marvellously imaginative, but also treacherous and untrustworthy man, who finally became very jealous of me, because I was a successful writer and that was what he wanted to be, and had no way of achieving it. Third, the man who founded this college, the late Vincent Massey, a diplomat, scholar, benefactor of education, and also a very queer and often cruel man – but I learned a great deal from him, not least how to get along with rich people (who are a very special and peculiar group, as you know). Of the three my own Father was best of the bunch, though he was so mercurial one never knew quite what he might do next. I think it would make an odd and amusing book.

Do please write again when you feel like it. Your letters are very refreshing. Brenda sends you her very best good wishes; summer has come and I only see her after nightfall, as she spends all her time standing upside down in the garden.

Love —

Rob.

To HARRY M. FURNISS

Massey College
University of Toronto
August 5, 1987

Harry M. Furniss (1920–   ), Canadian journalist and public relations consultant, is the grandson of Harry Furniss (1854–1925), English caricaturist for Punch, *humorist, and author of* How to Draw in Pen and Ink, *which figures in* What's Bred in the Bone. *Furniss was curious to know where Davies had found this book, as it had long been out of print.*

Dear Mr. Furniss:

I was delighted to receive your letter of June 26th which was forwarded to me by the Penguin people and therefore took rather a long time to arrive. I have always been an admirer of your grandfather and when I was a small boy I used to recognize his drawings in bound volumes of *The Illustrated London News*. I am glad also to have a copy of his two-volume autobiography* which is very lively reading.

The copy of *How to Draw in Pen and Ink* which I read as a boy was given to my brother, Arthur,* as a prize for a poster that he had designed for some charity when he was in high school. I read it, not because I particularly wanted to draw, but because it was such a lively and amusing book. My brother still has it and I have never quite summoned up the courage to steal it. I remember being greatly impressed by the ingenuity he showed in getting a special texture into some of his drawings by shading the flesh with inky thumb-prints.

I do not know whether your grandfather really drew Lewis Waller* but I think it very likely as he did innumerable theatrical drawings and caricatures. I have no example of your grandfather's work and would be delighted to have one. If it were at all possible I would like to have one of his drawings of one of the actors whom he caricatured with such penetrating but kindly wit. I feel, however, that it would be an imposture to ask for it as a gift and, therefore, let me make this suggestion: If you have any drawing by your grandfather of Henry Irving I would be delighted to obtain it at a price set by you, as I am a great enthusiast for Irving's work and have, for many years, collected material relating to it.

Once again, my warmest thanks for your letter. These are the things which bring a special satisfaction to an author.

Yours sincerely,

Robertson Davies

To JOHN MCGREEVY

Massey College
University of Toronto
September 29, Michaelmas
1987

John McGreevy (1942–   ) is a Canadian director of Irish origin, and a producer and writer of films and documentaries for television. He directed the 1983 BBC "Writers and Places" film about Davies and Kingston, and the PEN '86 television documentary which Davies narrated. He was developing a script for a BBC and CBC television mini-series of What's Bred in the Bone.

Dear John:

I enclose the letter you asked for, as a sort of general approval. This one is for your eye alone, and that of William Humble.* I begin by repeating the general approval of the public letter. Now let me go on to some details.

The first, and probably the most important, is that in your proposed treatment the character of Arthur Cornish appears as unsympathetic – a rather pompous, know-it-all fellow who wants to push the story of his uncle's life into a mould congenial to his personal needs. This is not Arthur as he appears in *What's Bred In The Bone*, nor in the earlier book, *The Rebel Angels*, in which he is rather a nice fellow, with a sense of humour, who manages to win a marvellous girl for his wife. I am working now (and am on the last quarter of) a novel [*The Lyre of Orpheus*] of which Arthur is the hero, who falls into the pattern of myth, and lives out, in modern terms, some of the myth of King Arthur of Britain. If your TV piece appears as it is shaped here, it will quarrel dreadfully with my latest Arthur, who is a hero indeed.

There is a solution which I put forward somewhat tentatively, because I sense that both you & Mr. Humble have thought of it and rejected it. But hear me out: when I was writing *W.B.B.* I struggled for a long time to find a way of telling the story as *economically* as possible, and the solution I found was the use of The Lesser Zadkiel (The Recording Angel) and The Daimon Maimas (Francis's personal guardian spirit). I was afraid the publishers and the public would dislike them, but quite the contrary: they liked them very much and I have not heard a squeak from anyone who thought them too spooky or whimsical. So – could you use them instead of having so much argy-bargy between Arthur and Darcourt?

I know this gets into realms which TV has shunned, except in the awful stuff of sci-fi programs like *Dr. Who*. TV seems deathly afraid of whatever might hint at an unseen world (note that I do not say a religious or "afterlife" world) and the result has been a kind of Masterpiece Theatre vise in which all serious TV drama is locked; admirable in its way, but it is by no means the only way. Could Canadian TV make a giant leap into a realm hitherto unknown in the medium – an extension of comment and feeling which would show everybody – the Australians, for instance – that we are not such a nation of turnips as they assume. In your treatment you introduce the name of Jung several times, and I wish you wouldn't. In drama, I am convinced, the way to use Jung is not to talk about him, but to *live* him and *act* him and *show* him as a force which is powerful, but not defined with a name. The Ingmar Bergman touch, in fact. The Angels would do the trick. (Darcourt's task is to write Francis's life: he yearns for the Angels & what they could reveal.)

It could be visually strong: the Angel of Biography, heavily robed and rather a sweet old party, and the Guardian Angel, naked as a jaybird, a hermaphrodite, and tough as old boots. By using them you could eliminate pages of the sort of thing your Arthur and Darcourt go in for.

I put this forward tentatively, of course. You are the professionals. But I think what worked in the book would work on TV, and it would be something nobody else has done. Spirits, as used in so much drama and film, are treated in a cute fashion, and are given smart-ass things to say. Take them seriously – not religiously or spookily, but seriously – and they might work like a dream. Yes indeed, like a dream.

That's Comment Number One. Here is number two. You have somewhat altered the story to suggest that Francis's lifelong yearning and desire is for his Mother. It works, and your final shot of the man and his aged Ma melting into the Cupid and Venus of Bronzino* is marvellous. But I beg you to be careful with it, if you are set on it, because it would be a pity to reduce Francis to another two-bit Oedipus, who has become altogether too familiar in drama and film. In the novel, when Francis dies, he descends into the Realm of the Mothers and I quite agree that would be hard to do on TV (though Goethe did it onstage).* But I think it is a little too simple to make Mary-Jim the mainspring and explanation of his life. Real men don't eat quiche, and real men get their mothers into focus as a usual thing. . . .

So there. Congratulations. I look forward to seeing what comes next. I am delighted with the truly Canadian flavour you have kept; I am sure viewers elsewhere will respond to that. When you want to talk, you know where to find me.

All the best

Rob.

To JOHN JULIUS NORWICH

Windhover
Caledon East
December 18, 1987

*John Julius Norwich (1929–   ) is an
English writer and maker of documentary
films on history and architecture. Norwich
discovered Davies' novels in 1986, wrote
Davies a fan letter, and sent him a set of
his "Christmas Crackers," pamphlets of
poems and literary extracts he distributes
to friends. Davies replied with a verse of a
hymn that he found amusing.*

Dear John Julius:

I have put off – and put off and put off – replying to your letter of
November 19 because I wanted time to write to you in a *considering*
manner, and to thank you adequately for including The Bowel
Hymn* in the latest *Cracker*. Your printers really did screw things up.
But that is the way of modern printers. I have been reminded recently
– because of a broadcast about ghost stories* I am doing – that in
1848 Dickens wrote *A Christmas Carol* in late October and early
November, and it was in the shops in lots of time for Christmas, set
without an error, finely bound, and including splendid hand-coloured
plates, and sold 6,000 copies. My publishers now tell me that it takes
about ten months from the receipt of a typescript to the appearance
of the book in the shops – and that is if the book is "slotted" properly into their scheme. Because they want to get my new novel *The
Lyre of Orpheus* in the shops next September, they want the typescript as early as possible in January, and so I have had to hustle my
stumps and get it done. I have finished it – I am what Shakes calls
"a gasping, new-deliver'd mother"* – and my secretary [Moira
Whalon] says that if she spends most of Christmas Day banging the
machine, all will be well.

The way in which publishers are behaving astonishes me and somewhat abashes me; I am not accustomed to their caresses. But for
various reasons there is competition for this book, and at my age,
and after what Dr. Johnson* calls "the life of a retired and uncourtly
scholar," I feel like the secretary in one of those movies where the

boss takes off her glasses and exclaims – "But Miss Eggdrop – you're beautiful!" The passage of time has robbed me of some resilience of spirit, and I am no longer able to respond to such approaches with youthful zeal; I know what I am, and it is a sobering recognition. I had mentioned to Felicity [Bryan]* that this would probably be my last novel. She passed it on to Peter Mayer,* who wrote to me urging me to put away such thoughts; he has just completed arrangements with Graham Greene* for his latest novel, and it seems that G.G. has several more in prospect. As G.G. is a full ten years older than I, I must not entertain any such absurd notions. Away with melancholy! On with the motley! Back to the cotton-field, Uncle Tom! It is flattering, but having just finished a book I can think of nothing but Death and the Conqueror Worm.* However, things may perk up a bit when Christmas is over. Yesterday I had a long lunch with my lawyer [Richard Winter],* who has been looking into my royalty situation with his tax-expert, and it appears that the illusion of the Canadian Government that I am their principal source of revenue must continue undisturbed. I cannot hide a kopek. Perhaps I should take to the gaming-tables; it seems that money won on games of chance is not taxable. But I was brought up a Presbyterian and cannot gamble. My dear Father once, when he was a small boy, cut school and went to the races; he was discovered and his father lectured him and beat him, and his mother wept, and of the two punishments it was the latter that washed gambling out of the Davies tribe for several generations. So it seems that not less than 40% of what I get – the lawyer says mournfully it will be about 48% – will be scooped up by the grim wolf with privy paw* who runs our tax department..... But these miseries are all too familiar to you, I am sure. I would like to put by a trifle for my posterity, but it looks as though Brenda would have to take in washing when I join the Choir Invisible.* We are laying in soap while it remains at present prices.

I hear that the MSS of your work on Venice* has been auctioned in aid of PEN. This reflects the greatest credit on your generosity and humane feeling. I have been doing a little in that direction. I was one of a panel* which recently discussed before an audience what might be done to wipe terrorism and torture from the face of the globe. I

am afraid I was a disappointment, because I said that although much
might be done to get writers out of jail and the torture chamber, I
thought that any notion of ridding the world of tyranny was a rosy
dream. It is astonishing how idealistic nice people are. The man who
heads these things in Canada – a very fine chap named Israel
Halperin* – told me that unlike myself he does not believe in the
reality of Evil, or God, or the Devil. Lucky Izzy! Only a man so
deluded could throw himself into the fray with the enthusiasm he
possesses. But I spent many years in the university trying to persuade
my wide-eyed students that slavery was still a reality in about half the
world and that torture, as evinced in tragedy – which was what we
were studying – was still a popular indoor sport. In Canada these
things seem improbable to the young, though our police are still said
to use harsh methods of persuasion when they get a chance.

But this was meant to be a Christmas letter, not a wail from an
exhausted writer. . . . Tomorrow Brenda and I take our younger
grandchildren to see *H.M.S. Pinafore*, and I look forward to it; next
week we take our older grandchildren to a film of their choice, adver-
tised as "Adult Theme, frank language and scenes of nudity which
may offend Some." I look forward to that, too; scenes of nudity and
offensive language grow more and more acceptable to my senile taste.
I wish you and all your circle a wonderful Christmas and a marvellous New Year..... We come to the Old Land next summer and will
be in London in early June. I hope we can meet and re-greet.

Rob.

To JOHN LETTS

Massey College
University of Toronto
January 6, 1988

John C. B. Letts (1929–) is the founder and chairman of the Trollope Society in London, England. Davies was familiar with his name from the period when he was joint chairman of the Folio Society (1971–87).

Dear Mr Letts:

Yes, indeed I should like to become a Foundation Member of the Trollope Society and enclose a money order for £70.

I am interested in the proposal that the Society should produce, in so far as possible, a complete edition of Trollope. I most sincerely hope that you will succeed in this aim for I have seen two ventures of this kind collapse, one made by the faint-hearted Oxford University Press and one by the late Alfred Knopf, who produced three or four very handsome Trollope volumes at a time when there was no enthusiasm for them in the United States. May you be more successful.

May I detain you for a personal anecdote? I possess what I think is as near to being a complete edition of Trollope as has ever appeared. It is in 99 volumes and they are the Tauchnitz editions* which have been very handsomely bound in half Morocco (blue), titles stamped in gold, and the binder was Bayntun.* I came by it when I was living in the Ontario city of Peterborough. A local man died who, as he was an avid reader of books, had a reputation for eccentricity, and his executor found himself confronted with the problem of disposing of a considerable library. The executor was a lawyer of almost impenetrable illiteracy and before the auction he asked me if I would like to look at the library to see if there was anything in it I would like to buy. My eye fell immediately on the handsome Trollope and I enquired of him what he wanted for it, expecting a price that might be staggering. Instead he looked at me with a crafty leer and said, "Would you think 10 cents a copy would be too much?" As a crafty collector I displayed no emotion, but said, grudgingly, "Yes, I guess that would be all right," and for $9.90, Canadian, I secured the edition of Trollope which drives my book-collecting friends out of their minds with envy. As well as being handsomely bound the books are nicely printed on very good paper.

I wish your society every success and I may add to you personally that, over the years, I have had great pleasure from the publications of the Folio Society.* John Saumarez Smith,* who is a member of your committee, is a valued friend of mine.

Yours sincerely,

[Robertson Davies] . . . .

To TSIPORA LIOR

Massey College
University of Toronto
January 19, 1988

Tsipora Lior (1940–　) is a Canadian translator and editor. She had relished five of Davies' novels, only to be "stunned to come across" what she saw as "gratuitous stereotypes of the Jew" in Tempest-Tost on pages 137 and 207–10.

Dear Mʳˢ· Lior:

Thank you for your very kind references to my books, but I am at a loss to understand the latter part of your letter of January 13th, for you seem to have misunderstood my book [Tempest-Tost], and found offence where none exists or was ever meant. To say that Humphrey Cobbler looked like a Jew was to establish him as a man from the West Country of the U.K., where that type is common, and of Celtic origin. My own father belonged to it. Nor is there any suggestion that the man who bought the rare books at the auction "cheated" anyone; he simply used his head and his professional expertise, and the incident is included as yet another instance of the provinciality of the people of Salterton. The incident is, indeed, based on a recollection of the late Dr. A. S. W. Rosenbach,* the king of New York book dealers, who often visited Canada on vacations, and found many fine things here which nobody in Canada valued.

You overlook the fact that Humphrey Cobbler is by far the most attractive character in *Tempest-Tost*. You will find another very positive portrait of a Jew in *A Mixture of Frailties*.

You are, of course, quite right to protest against anti-Semitism, but permit me to warn you against the danger of falling over the edge into hyper-Semitism, and seeing offence where there is none. If you do that, your indignation against novelists will have to include* Isaac Bashevis Singer, Saul Bellow, Budd Schulberg, Norman Mailer and my friend Mordecai Richler, all of whom write in a spirit that would never enter my head.

Yours sincerely,

Robertson Davies

To JOHN SAUMAREZ SMITH

Massey College
University of Toronto
February 23, 1988

John Saumarez Smith (1943–   ), English, is manager and one of the directors of G. Heywood Hill Ltd., sellers of old and new books, in London. Davies began to order books from Heywood Hill in 1982 or 1983.

Dear John:

Thank you for your note about the Trollope Society. I would be delighted to write an introduction to one of the volumes but I cannot, at the moment, think of a special one that I might ask for. For many years I have been interested in Trollope's women – his young women that is to say – who so frequently have no career open to them but marriage but who fight like tigers against entirely suitable young men who would like to open that career to them. There is a queer kind of Victorian perversity about this which I suppose gave great pleasure to Trollope's young readers. And certainly if the girl said yes the first time she was asked it would be hard to fill 700 to 900 pages of a novel. In fact, in *The Belton Estate*, it is the readiness of the heroine to accept her suitor that puts the whole romance on the rocks.

I received your February list of new publications and I would be very glad if you would send me the *Letters of Max Beerbohm 1892–1956*, edited by Rupert Hart-Davis, when it is possible.

With good wishes,

Yours sincerely,

Rob. Davies

To PATRICIA KENNEDY

Windhover
Caledon East
Good Friday, 1988

Patricia Kennedy (1946–   ), Canadian, was managing editor at Macmillan of Canada. She had coordinated the editorial queries raised by Davies' American, English, and Canadian publishers.

Dear Miss Kennedy:

Herewith the typescript of *The Lyre of Orpheus* and my replies to the queries and corrections of the copy-editor. I have tried to be as accommodating as possible, but there are one or two proposals to which I cannot agree, because I think of the book as something *heard*, rather than scanned, and questions of nuance are important to me as they are not in a manuscript solely for perusal.

I hope these changes will bring the typescript up to scratch, but I am not wholly confident of it. In *What's Bred in the Bone** I wrote of Bonnie Prince Charlie as the son of King James II, though I ken fine he was his *grandson*. The copy-editors all missed it, including Douglas Gibson, a Scot, and since then Scotsmen have been writing to me in every modulation of sorrow and anger. As James Agate sadly remarked,* there is no such thing as a book without error, and as Shakespeare said* before him –

> At copy-editor's mistakes, they say
> Jove laughs.
>
> (R.&J. II:2)

Two points: I must stress that neither Planché* nor Hoffmann wrote 1988 English and I have not made them do so; I have introduced a few early nineteenth century usages that the discerning will catch, and others will *feel* as something not wholly modern. As for people who do not know what Christ's First Miracle* was, I pause on this holy day to drop a tear for them. I deal with the Swanee Whistle* in my notes. As for Calvinistic Methodists, whoever doubts their existence may find it well set out in *The Oxford Dictionary of the Christian Church*; it dates from 1743, as an offshoot of the C of E and nearly two years before the establishment of Wesleyanism, and though like all sects it is on the wane, it still has a quarter of a million adherents. The note you conveyed to me, by the way, is wrong in supposing that Calvinism and Methodism are mutually exclusive. Hundreds of my forbears were of this sect (many also were Wesleyans) and Welsh grandmothers need no instruction in how to suck doctrinal eggs.

Robertson Davies

To BIRGITTA HEYMAN

Windhover
Caledon East
[April 1988]

Dear Birgitta:

. . . I am fascinated to hear that you are helping in your daughter's bookshop.* That is exactly right for you. St. Birgitta, as I am sure you know, was a great scholar and there are lots of pictures of her with books and manuscripts. . . .

I was delighted to read about how you used to meet Pär Lagerkvist* when you were skiing. The only book of his I have read is *Barabbas*, which was unquestionably the work of a master. What I liked so much was that you said he skied "slowly and with great gravity." I'll bet he did. Those great European writers took themselves very seriously, and the public took them seriously, too. I remember the enormous reverence that was shown toward Thomas Mann.* Of course I am no Lagerkvist or Mann, but sometimes I see young people whizzing past me and realize that I am walking "Slowly and with great gravity." But I never meet anyone who shows any sign of curtseying.

Thank you so much for the tape of Frej Lindqvist;* I am very glad to have it because I remember having a splendid talk with him on September 23, 1986, (my diary tells me) at the offices of Wahlström & Widstrand and I see that I wrote "...inspires confidence, is sensitive and is said to be a better Salieri in *Amadeus* than Paul Scofield."* I wish I had known that he was a friend of yours. I met several journalists on that day, some of them extraordinarily good, and a few very solemn, especially Eva Weide, who writes for a lot of provincial papers and asked questions like "What is the underlying theme of all your books? What do they *teach*?" I could only say that they didn't really *teach* anything but were simply pictures of life as it appears to me – comic, tragic and endlessly fascinating. I also had quite a long time with Sonja Bergvall,* who translates my books, a tiny very deaf lady who asked a lot of questions that I could not answer; the publishers told me I was to "charm" her, but I am not sure that I was successful.

Did I tell you that we had a marvellous day in Uppsala and met some charming people at the University: what astonished us was that in a place of so much history and many treasures what really seemed to interest the professors was that Ingmar Bergman had filmed *Fanny and Alexander* there, and they showed us all the places where that had been done. We went to a very good restaurant and had a fine dinner, and had a wonderful debate with the professors as to which country was the most boring – Canada or Sweden? They insisted that Sweden, with its longer history, was undoubtedly the winner, but Brenda and

I insisted that in Canada we *worked harder* at being boring and enjoyed great worldwide success. It was one of the most delightful evenings I have ever spent, and the professors were certainly among the least boring people I have met – witty and merry. We all got a bit drunk. A woman from my publishers, an anti-smoking fanatic called Mrs. Märta-Stina Danielsson, nagged another of the publishers, named Söderberg* because he smoked a pipe: "Do you do it to get a high?" she asked. "No, I do it to avoid a low," he said, which was a fine Swedish answer. . . .

Rob. . . .

To ROBERT FINCH

June 27, 1988

Dear Robert:

Some notes about the college bells: they were founded (if that is the right term) in Kitchener, so they are Canadian bells; regrettably, the Kitchener people are not first-rate and the bells lack the clarity of timbre of Dutch or English bells, but the cost of importing bells would have been horrendous, and the college was already in trouble with trouble-makers in the university and the Legislature because the bricks used in the building were not Canadian. (There were no Canadian bricks of comparable quality or range of colour, but objectors do not care about such things.)

I was given the job – what a lot of odd jobs I was given – of naming the bell and preparing an inscription for it. I chose the name Sancta Catharina, & fudged up the inscription from two or three very ancient ones, thus:

Vivos voco: mortuos plango
Excito lentos: paco cruentos.

– which I hope means "I call the living, I mourn the dead, I rouse the sluggards, I quiet the angry (literally, the bloodthirsty)" – but you can make a more elegant rendition.

There were two bells, and the smaller was to hang in the dining hall, but it proved too big and noisy and was transferred to the tower, from which it could be controlled by a button in Hall. But engineers stole it* quite early, as they stole everything else they could get their wretched hands on. I put a Welsh curse on that bell, and whoever has it now probably has AIDS as well, or perhaps merely the deafness I suggested to The Powers.

The bell was first rung on August 21, 1963, by the then Archbishop of Canterbury, Dr. Ramsey,* who visited the coll. with his wife. This was the Archbishop who also sent a letter which is in the college files (if anybody ever looks in them, which I doubt) saying that though our Chapel performed its services in the Anglican rite, anybody who presented himself seriously wishing Communion should certainly have it. (This was because one of our first Junior Fellows, named _____, made a fuss that non-Anglicans were horning in on our Anglican magic; I trumped him with the Archbishop, and subsequently with the Bishop of Toronto, Bishop Wilkinson,* who fully concurred. _____ was the son of an Anglican parson, and rather a wee pill.)

The first of the tollings of the bell for the dead was, alas, for Lionel Massey. It has tolled for many others, since, including many Senior Fellows, and Vincent and Raymond Massey. I shall jog Ann [Saddlemyer]'s* mind about this; Pat Hume neglected the custom, as he did not take much heed of ceremonial observances. Some strokes of St. Catharina – 9 for a man & 6 (O, Shame!) for a woman, is surely owing to a member of our community? But if not 6 for a woman, how do you indicate the sex of the departed one?

Rob.

To DAMA BELL

Windhover
Caledon East
July 15: 1988

Dama Frances Lumley Bell (1906–   ),
Canadian architect, was a member of the
Stratford Festival's Board of Governors for
ten years. Her husband, Alfred Mumford
Bell (1909–88), was a Canadian chemical
engineer and general manager of Sealed
Power Corporation, which made piston
rings in Stratford, Ontario. He was vice
president and then president of the
Festival's Board during its crucial first four
years, 1953–57. Davies was on the Board
from 1953–71. (His letter is reproduced
exactly as he typed it.)

Dear Dama:

A story is told about Alf which I have always thought of and
retold often, for it seems to me to be wonderfully Canadian: somebody – it may have been Tony [Guthrie] but the story is told of Tanya
[Moiseiwitsch] and Robin Phillips* – said to Alf, "How does an engineer become so much involved with an arts festival?" To which Alf
replied: "I first got the idea at Hart House, from a man named Burgon
Bickersteth." This is wonderful because it includes so much that is
Canadian – the great influence of the university, the influence of
Burgon, the great inspirer of young men, the realization of the dream
the Masseys had when Hart House was built that it would be a place
from which fine things would emerge, and the first-class quality of
the man who had learned so much at the university apart from his
professional studies. Alf was truly a splendid Canadian: apparently
reserved and cautious, but splendidly on fire within, and firmly convinced that nothing that was not first-rate was good enough. The
flawed piston-ring and the flawed artist – he had no time for either.

People will have told you how greatly he was missed on July 13,
when the people who had been at the First Night were assembled;
his name was on everybody's lips. But not sadly, not regretfully, but
with gratitude and thanks for what he was and what he had meant to

us all. We remembered the good sense, the calming voice when meetings began to be competitive or silly, but we also remembered the inner fire, the conviction that nothing but the best would do. He would not have been overjoyed by the performance of *Richard III*; of the four productions of that play at Stratford this was by far the least, wanting sadly in distinction, understanding and sureness of touch. The Festival wants re-animation. It is silly to call for a return to Tony's values, but of course Tony's values were the qualities which have always made great theatre – vigorous dedication and distinction of taste, in the face of all the outcry about "box office" and a people's theatre. The only theatre fit for the people is the finest that can be achieved; the public will always respond to the first-rate and the energetic.

It is impertinent of me to offer you advice, for you are one of the strongest characters I know. But here is advice, anyway: let your grief have its way, and it will pass in time. To repress grief is to do violence to something very important in life. You and Alf have been, and still are, one of the great unions that gives one faith in that much-besieged institution, marriage; such unions are not really dissolved by death, though the immediate blow is grievous. But the riches of a great marriage are not bankrupted by a parting which can never truly be a final parting.

All your feinds feel for you, and with you (Why did I write "finds"? That is the kind of error Tony would have loved.) But friends can be fiends, sometimes, and I have always cherished a death notice in a Welsh paper that an old friend of mine had in her scrapbook, and which concluded "Fiends will gather at the church." Forgive this seeming frivolity, but Alf dearly loved a joke, and we must not forget that, even now.

It goes without saying that Brenda endorses everything I have said, and we are together in sending you love and tenderness.

Rob.

To JOHN JULIUS NORWICH

Windhover
Caledon East
October 7, 1988

Dear John Julius:

Brenda and I are at home, picking up the fragments of our lives after our lightning descent upon London.* The highlight of the expedition was undoubtedly dinner with you and Mollie* on September 27, and we thank you again most heartily. I hope your time in Venice was pleasant and productive.

Knowing your fondness for oddities, let me beguile you with this one from the Memoir of the Rev. Richard Harris Barham that precedes the Third Series of the *Ingoldsby Legends*;* you may know it, and if so I apologize, but it is one of my favourite anecdotes of the Regency Theatre:

"Cannon (the Rev. Edward Cannon, one of the priests of the Royal household) told a story of a manager at a country theatre, who, having given out the play of 'Douglas' found the entertainment nearly put to a stop, by the arrest of 'Young Norval' as he was entering the theatre. In this dilemma, no other performer of the company being able to take the part, he dressed up a tall, gawky lad who snuffed the candles, in a plaid and philabeg, and pushing him on the stage, advanced himself to the footlights, with the book in his hand, and addressed the audience with, 'Ladies and Gentlemen –

This young gentleman's name is Norval. On the Grampian hills
His father feeds his flock, a frugal swain
Whose constant care was to increase his store,
And keep his only son (this young gentleman) at home.
For this young gentleman had heard' &c.

And so on through the whole of the play, much to the delectation of the audience."

The authority for this anecdote, said Cannon, was a celebrated singer who told it to Cannon as having been herself at the representation.

Barham is one of my bees-in-the-bonnet. The *Legends* are an extraordinary manifestation of the mirth and disdain that the Anglo-Catholic movement provoked, and I still find them funny, while deploring such John Bullishness in a man who was himself a Cardinal of St. Paul's. (Does St. Paul's still have Cardinals? I never hear of them.) Years ago Edmund Wilson* wrote a splendid piece in *The New Yorker* about Barham, which he later reprinted in *The Devils and Canon Barham* (Farrar Straus Giroux, 1987). I wrote to Wilson to declare my own enthusiasm, and he wrote to me that the only other person he knew who shared our interest was the Bishop of Texas! But I still think a fine study of the *Legends* as a byway of social history will one day emerge, but not, I hope, from some sweating doctoral student who will miss all the fun and toil over the dates.

Once again, it was a great delight to see you both, and I hope the time is not too far off when we can requite your splendid hospitality.

Rob.

To EDWARD WADE DEVLIN

October 7, 1988

*Edward Wade Devlin (1911–   ),
Canadian editor, radio announcer, and
producer, was Davies' roommate at Upper
Canada College in 1928–29. This note is
inscribed in the copy of* The Lyre of
Orpheus *that Davies sent to him.*

Dear Devlin:

I address you thus from old custom because as boys at U.C.C. nobody ever admitted to the ignominy of a Christian name – just a surname & an initial. I don't suppose you recall that at Christmas 1930 you gave me a book called *A Christmas Book*, compiled by D. B. Wyndham Lewis and G. C. Heseltine. It has been with me for 58 years and has been an invaluable companion. I have not only read with delight in its pages but have culled from it X⁵mas readings & verses which musical friends set for X⁵mas parties & Gaudy Nights at

Massey College. Of how many books & how many gifts can one say that they have been companions for a lifetime? Thanks, & thanks again. – I hope this book may give you some pleasure.

Davies

To RUTH M. DANYS

Massey College
University of Toronto
October 11, 1988

Ruth M. Danys (1946–), Lithuanian-born Canadian freelance journalist, was researching her privately published book Where to Live? Older People's Housing Options and Experiences *(1990). It included a chapter titled "Special Homes for Writers and Actors."*

Dear Mˢ· Danys:

Thank you for your letter of August 4th which was received by Penguin on August 9th but did not reach me here until October 11th. In reply to your question, I would be doubtful if a home for elderly writers would be a good idea. Writers are an extremely contentious group and old age does not make them any more peaceful. I think that they are better spread around among the rest of the population.

Yours sincerely,

Robertson Davies

To JEFFREY SEROY

Massey College
University of Toronto
November 10, 1988

Jeffrey Seroy (1953–), American, was
publicity director of the Oxford University
Press in New York. In anticipation of the
publication of The Oxford English
Dictionary, Second Edition *in April 1989,*
he had invited Davies and several other
writers "to describe his feelings about the
OED, *how it served him, where he kept it,*
and so forth."

[Dear M*r.* Seroy:]

Thank you for your letter of September 13th and the volume 2 of
the Second Edition of the *OED* which accompanied it. I have had a
great deal of pleasure in examining it, and the Introduction which
you also sent.

You ask for my response to the new edition. I have none except
admiration and delight, which is, of course, wholly uncritical and for
your purpose worthless. But I have been a lover of dictionaries all my
life. I have a collection of them, including Johnson's, but of those I
have met with, the *OED* is the unchallenged sovereign.

I was brought up on dictionaries. My grandfather [Walter Davies]
always had one at hand on the dining-table, and my parents followed
him in that custom; mispronunciations and misuses of words were
strongly forbidden, and were somewhat uncharitably jeered at when
people outside the family (parsons, teachers and the like, who were
supposed to know better) showed ignorance. It was a tyranny of
words, but I would not for the world have grown up without it.

My Canadian school (Upper Canada College) adopted the *OED*
as its guide, and every boy had to have his own copy of the *Concise*;
for spelling and pronunciation no other standard was permitted. I
used to read my *Concise* when I should have been doing other work,
and indeed all my life I have been a reader of the *OED* in one or
another of its forms. When I was a journalist – an editor – I made
the *Shorter OED* the standard for my paper, and when later I became

an academic I bound my students to it which, as some of them were Americans, they accepted with varying grace.

It was a great day for me – a birthday – when my wife gave me the full *OED*, with the *Supplement* and the further supplementary volumes; these, with Partridge's* *Dictionary of Slang and Unconventional English* have been laid under tribute every day of my life since. When I was a boy I knew a professor who never travelled without packing first of all his bulky Liddell and Scott* (just in case he wished to verify something while away from home), and I have often wished I could cart the full *OED* about with me, which of course I can't.

So now a second edition is in progress, is it? I doubt very much if I shall acquire it, but I shall certainly examine it when it comes into our college library. One must, at some time of life, admit one is becoming a fossil, and I suppose I shall remain a First Edition man.

I am greatly pleased, however, that you are using the International Phonetic Alphabet; Murray's method* was very good for its time, but the IPA is immensely superior, especially for foreign users. Luckily for me, I grew up with the IPA, for at my school French and German were taught with its aid, and we had to learn to write the symbols quickly and correctly.

So there it is, you see. I wish you well in your great venture, and as you pass me by, still rooting and fossicking in the First Edition, you must not imagine that I am unaware of the benefit you are conferring ·on the whole literate world. There has never been such a Dictionary, such a world of words, such a treasure-house for the scholar, and the mere magpie of learning. What pretensions it is possible to set up, by merely scanning the quotations that illustrate a few hundred of the words! What an incomparable book for a desert island, or a lighthouse! Is it blasphemous to cry: "Not *Dominus illuminatio mea*, but *OED illuminatio mea*"?

Yours sincerely,

[Robertson Davies]

To HERBERT WHITTAKER

Windhover
Caledon East
November 21, ELECTION DAY! 1988

Dear Herbert:

I have just been digging out my SIN number, which is demanded by the latest government assault on the pitiful earnings of the peasantry. Do you remember a song current in our youth* –

My SIN
     Was loving you –
     Not wisely but too well:
Your SIN
     Was letting me,
     And getting me in your spell:
Our SIN
     Was following
     A love that could not be:
Now my SIN
     Is wanting you –
     Though you've forgotten me!

It is nothing, of course, without the music, which should be sung in a simpering, eunuchoid manner. I am thinking of making a tape of this piece and sending it to our great leader. But which great leader? This is the morning of the day of decision. Will it be Brian [Mulroney], God bless his ould Oirish hairt, or Jolly Jack the Hangman [John Napier Turner]?* I bide the event.

It was good of you to send those clippings. I have seen Barnacle's name* often, but have no deeper knowledge of him. He is a great man for the wisecrack which is so useful to the reviewer, as it reduces the author and makes the reader laugh. Reviews of *Lyre* have been mixed, ranging from frenzied ecstasy in the London *Times* to piss and vinegar from the ineffable John Metcalf.* But the book is selling like hotcakes, and if I may judge from the people I meet on the publicity tour, to many who will be puzzled by it. The publicity tour – it still goes on. . . .

Rob.

⚓WINDHOVER⚓

RR1 CALEDON EAST ONT LON 1E0

Dear Mordecai:

Three cheers - bi-lingual, of course-
for you splendid piece in the <u>New
Yorker</u>! Of course idiots are declaring that you wrote it with your pen
dipped in gall and tabasco,but I
have talked to many who are delighted
that at last somebody has poured some
cold water,instead of gasoline,om
this national bonfire.Your factual
analysis of the situation was masterly
and I find it hard to believe that
the intelligent Quebecois have not
weighed the alarming cost of setting
up a separate state.But factual
analysis,valuable as it is,does not
always wow the reader as does your
brilliant style,never outrageous,but
genially acerbic and putting the
theme in a psychological, rather than
a solely political,light....I have
been saying for a long time that this
is our Civil War, and it is a psychological civil war, which is something
we must learn to fight intelligently,
and not like enraged schoolchildren.
...You have done us all a great service,
and those who are cheering for you
are numerous and alert.

More power to you -

Rob. Davies

SECTION
VI

JANUARY 1989–SEPTEMBER 1991 – *MURTHER & WALKING SPIRITS* PLANNED,
WRITTEN AND PUBLISHED

avies was 76 when he began to write the first draft of *Murther
& Walking Spirits* on November 20, 1989. He completed it the
following December, and the typescript went to his publishers
in February 1991. The book appeared that fall.

This was an immensely productive, rewarding, and exhausting period.
In November 1989, Davies was interviewed at length on camera by the
filmmaker Harry Rasky for the television film *The Magic Season of
Robertson Davies*. In the early months of 1990, he interrupted the writing
of *Murther* to write the libretto for the oratorio *Jezebel: The Golden Tale
of Naboth and His Vineyard, and of King Ahab and His Wicked Queen*
for which Derek Holman was to compose the music. In addition, he took
on a stunning number of book introductions, speeches, and articles.
Many – like the Tanner Lectures at Yale – were signal honours, but they
took a great deal of time and effort, including the travel and interviews
and entertainments that had to be coped with. The most taxing of these
commitments was the Göteborg Book Fair in Sweden in September 1989

where he was to give a speech on "Jung and the Writer" and publicize translations of his books for his Swedish publishers. He managed to give the speech, but the cold he had been fighting worsened into bronchial pneumonia and such racking asthma attacks that Brenda feared that he might die. He was weeks in recovering.

There were many great satisfactions in this period. Davies took huge pleasure in the honorary degrees awarded to him by Trinity College, Dublin, in 1990 and by Oxford in 1991. Always intensely responsive to music, he (and Brenda) now enjoyed several special musical treats: the 1989 International Choral Festival in Toronto, the St. Louis Opera Festival in 1989 and again in 1990, the operas of The Ring in Bayreuth in 1990, and the operas and concerts that were part of the celebrations for Mozart in Vienna in 1991. And on February 2, 1990, they celebrated their 50th wedding anniversary with a splendid dinner for sixty-three guests at the York Club in Toronto.

To JOHN J. ESPEY

Windhover
Caledon East
Easter Monday, March 27, 1989

Dear John:

I seem to be spending Easter Monday writing to the members of the Long Christmas Dinner Society;* Willie, and Horace, and now you. And how better could I be occupied? I have been a while getting to it because I have been somewhat under the weather. Not bed-ridden, but troubled by post-flu depression and my old enemy asthma, with consequent *taedium vitae* and a snarling, rancorous spirit, with which Brenda copes philosophically. Perverse wretch that I am, I find that nothing relieves an asthmatic bout like a large pipe of tobacco; this gives my doctor [Christopher J. Allen]* fits, but he is younger than I am and can be bullied.

Nor has Dame Nature done anything for the old and infirm. After a mild winter we have had hellish snow and rain, which brings floods. Twice our driveway has had to be pumped out (at $40 an hour) as it was under 18 inches of icy slop; once in darkness, we were in the mess before we knew what was happening, so that the car foundered, and we had to wade for 200 yards in water to our knees. And this in darkness, so it was no picnic and we were in constant fear of falling, and getting drenched all over. The car requires $750 spent on it to get it on the road again, and the insurance company shakes its hoary locks and doesn't quite see its way to do much about it as their prophets had not foreseen anything of the kind. Years ago my brother [Arthur], who knows about money, told me that insurance was money thrown away, but I was too craven to heed him; I have always been a victim of superstition, a realm in which insurance ranks high.

At last I have finished that damnable publicity tour. With brief periods of surcease, it has gone on since last September, and for a man of my years and temperament it is much too much. Thirty years ago I might have welcomed such attention, but now I long for the chimney corner and a good book written by somebody else. Did I ever tell you that owing to your example and recommendation (you gave me *Swann's Way*) I have taken great delight in Proust? A wonderful man; no Norman Mailer nonsense about wanting to save the world. I have recently been pestered by people who want me to say something inflammatory about Salman Rushdie. I could, if I had the courage, say something really inflammatory: that he was trailing his coat and asking for trouble. His book [*The Satanic Verses*] contains some disobliging remarks (fantasy of sexual intercourse with H.M.* The Archbishop of Canterbury is going after Rushdie with a bow and arrow.) about the Queen, which I consider cheek from anybody and especially so from one upon whom the British Raj lavished all its treasures – but I am getting to be a Tory crank.

Thanks for your excerpts from your memoir.* Sorry you had such a bad time with Ridley;* he was, I fear, a fraud, but an amusing fraud and his last days were dreadful – writhen with arthritis – probably all that sherry striking inward. (I liked Ridley: I love a mountebank.) But it is awful to have an important part of one's career in the hands of such a messer. As a teacher, I found myself torn between deep compassion for graduate students and exasperation with many of them who were suffering from desperate literary tunnel vision and often got mired in Retrospective Influences – the influence of James Joyce on Shakespeare, of Henry James on Fielding,* etc. But enough.

As for Bryson,* I never really liked him and was snubbed by him very severely when I sent some books of mine to the Balliol Library, of which he was in charge. You must understand, said he, that we cannot find room for *everything* written by Balliol men. He preferred economic papers written by Jacobus De Wett* and other serious-minded chaps. He was in the highest degree, the most *wooden* man I have ever encountered. Many people have wooden heads, but JB was wood clear through – *lignum vitae.*

It was a refreshment to see you again* and have a chance to talk, however briefly, to your wife – is she? It doesn't matter. Don't let's lose touch.

Rob.

To HORACE W. DAVENPORT

Massey College
University of Toronto
April 3, 1989

Dear Horace: /

I write to you knowing full well how ineffective anything I can say must be. I did not know Tom:* met him only once as a little boy, the merriest and liveliest of the two. To my surprise he wrote to me once or twice during recent years, and we exchanged Christmas greetings. So I can say nothing of him. But to you, my dear old friend, I send only what is true under such circumstances – love and sympathy, and the hope that you will be able to find your feet as soon as possible after this heavy blow. I know that the loss of an eldest son can be devastating, for it happened to my Father.* It was in part the feeling that Nature had reversed reasonable expectation and that somebody had vanished whom one had always counted on as a survivor of oneself, and that a lifetime of hopes and fears and expectations had been whisked away in some unaccountable error. All one can offer are the clichés of condolence; but one remembers that they have become clichés because they are also inescapable truths. May you find comfort in Inge, and in Rob, and when enough time has passed, in the remembrance of what Tom was in your life. But I know very well that only those who have sons can truly enter into the feelings of those who have lost sons.

May I make a suggestion, hoping it is not an impertinence? Write it down: write what you feel. It is sometimes a wonderful help in misery.

Our very special love to you both

Rob.

To ELISABETH SIFTON

Windhover
Caledon East
April 14, 1989

Dear Elisabeth:

Thanks for your letter of last week; I thought the *Paris Review* piece* was good, though one always wishes one had said better things, and said them better..... I seem to be in hot water now about an article of mine which appeared in *Harper's*;* it was boiled down (by them) from a speech I gave in Edinburgh last spring, and which was reprinted in the *TLS*; but *Harper's* titled it *Selling Canada's Soul* and emphasized everything that was in it about Canada's Free Trade pact with the U.S. Many readers interpreted it as being anti-American (which God knows it was not) and I have had a lot of letters, some of which suggest that I get a one-way ticket to Moscow, and others which tell me that Canada allows itself to be protected from its enemies by Uncle Sam, and ought to be grateful and not find fault. As my point was that Canada was not aware of any enemies, and rather liked its present form of government, there had obviously been serious misunderstandings, and I was astonished that *Harper's* circulated to so many blockheads. My speech was, in fact, about writing, and was called *Literature In A Country Without A Mythology*. Ah, well.

This past while – since September the first – has been devoted rather more than two-thirds to publicity for *Lyre of Orpheus*, and Brenda and I have gone from coast to coast in Canada, then to England, then in Ontario to every trapper's hut and Inuit igloo, then to the U.S., West and East (doesn't anybody read in the middle?) after which we escaped to Bermuda, where it was rather cold. . . .

How do you fare in your life *chez* Knopf?* Bloomingly, I hope. The publishing world in Toronto seems to be in chaos. The leading literary agent has decided to become a publisher and does not seem to understand that this might create some conflict of interest. The two heads of Macmillan – the president and the chief editor – have left to become agents. My agency work appears to have been taken over by a woman who is only in Toronto one week a month . . . . Things fall apart, the centre cannot hold.* The good old days when one knew whom one would face when one went into a publisher's office appear to have gone forever..... Well do I remember my first encounter with a publisher, old Mr. Dent* at Dent's in London; silvery-haired, courtly of manner, never seen except against a background of polished walnut. Rather an old rogue, it proved; he sold my book to a US publisher without consulting me, having assumed that I had been killed in World War II; he always wore a length of Liberty silk as a cravat, drawn elegantly through a ring of beaten silver which he had made himself, for he was a weekend silversmith. I stood in awe of him and worshipped him because he was actually going to put something of mine [*Shakespeare's Boy Actors*] between covers. . . .

Love from us both –

Rob.

To BRONWYN DRAINIE

Massey College
University of Toronto
May 23, 1989

Bronwyn Drainie (1945–) is a Canadian writer, journalist, and radio and television broadcaster.

Dear Bronwyn Drainie:

This is a personal letter, *not intended for publication*, to congratulate you, first of all, on your appointment as national arts columnist at the *Globe & Mail*; I have very much enjoyed your work so far, and expect that I shall continue to do so. But at this moment I want to congratulate you on a passage in your review of *Ritual Slaughter** in the issue of May 20, in which you ask why a novel so lacking in merit was supported by the Canada Council, the Ontario Arts Council and the Ministry for Multiculturalism and Citizenship? It is time somebody asked a few such questions, for the importunity of grant-seekers – some of whom have almost professional status – I know of one man who has had twelve grants from the Canada Council alone – is beyond all bounds. Every writer whose name has gained any acceptance is besieged by requests from grant seekers for recommendations to all the granting bodies, more often than not by people unknown to him, who want a few words of praise based on a brief description of the work that will be undertaken if money is forthcoming. Such eagerness is understandable, but what baffles explanation is the readiness of the granting bodies to fork out, apparently to anyone and everyone. Surely some stricter standards can be applied? It now appears that anyone who has once had a grant is justified in feeling aggrieved if he does not get something at every subsequent application. I try myself to be as discriminating as I can when faced with requests for recommendations and support, but it has often been made very clear to me that any refusal is rooted in a spirit which hates youth, or fears competition, or laughs at the ambition of the beginner. The Canada Council people seem to fall for this sort of thing, inexplicably in the light of the responsibility placed on them.

Of course the position of the writer in Canada, and everywhere else, is not a happy one, when he is trying to establish his reputation, but the wholesale encouragement of obvious ineptitude hardly seems the way to improve it. I know no solution, but surely there must be a better way, and perhaps you have some ideas which I assure you your readers would be happy to consider.

On another subject, I am sure you are aware of the cut in the Public Lending Right payments to Canadian authors. The average is now something like $500 a writer, with plenty below this figure. What particularly got my goat was the sanctimonious letter which accompanied this news, explaining in effect – though not in these words – that in these times of stringency, when every effort is being made to reduce public expenditure, such frills as PLR must expect to feel the chill. In the name of God, how much money is saved by this pennymite reduction, which can only be explained as an evidence of the malignance of the bureaucracy – including those overpraised functionaries, the librarians – against the originators of what one likes to think of as a form of art?

With appreciation & good wishes,

Robertson Davies

(forgive my typing – secretary ill)

To WILLIAM J. KEITH

Massey College
University of Toronto
June 21, 1989

Dear Bill:

Thank you for the offprint of your article* on the Cornish trilogy from the *Journal of Canadian Studies*. You continue to be by long odds the most perceptive and generous critic of my work, and I cannot tell you what deep pleasure it gives me to read what you say, because you are more aware than anyone else who writes about me as to just what sort of creature I am, and what I am attempting in my books. It always seems to me that what I am doing is as clear as day, but astonishing numbers of readers and critics seem to miss it. The readers are so often people who want what they call "a good read" or "a funny book" and look no further than an ingenious narrative and an easy style. My deeply held notion that Comedy is just as revelatory as Tragedy, and is far less egotistic, is not for them; if it's funny it is necessarily "light." The critics are so convinced that I am "old-fashioned" that they cannot see beyond the fashion of my literary hat. They are themselves the lilies of a day, and have not much concern with the broad stream of Time and our small place in it. So, as the hart panteth for the water brooks,* I pant for your reviews.

When I wrote *Lyre [of Orpheus]* I knew I was doing something very dangerous in re-working some old themes of mine – the patrons, the protégée, the charismatic artist and so on. But years ago I was impressed by some remarks of J. B. Priestley's,* who said that he wished writers had the liberty of painters to work over a subject time and time again, until they had done all they could with it. Picasso may paint as many Harlequins as he pleases, but woe betide the novelist who re-works a plot. But I wanted to go over that ground again, with some new ideas and a creative genius (Schnak) instead of a fine interpretive artist (Monica).* I appear to have got away with it, but chiefly because so many reviewers have short memories.

You are entirely right about my preoccupation with the problems of art and time – as also the painful sense in every artist of any weight that his reach so far exceeds his grasp.* I can never get it "quite right." But I intend to have one more try and I am at work now on a book which I hope will do something about Time, but will not be quite so much concerned with Art..... I have for at least forty years been puzzling over the link that Thomas Mann explored in so many ways between the artist and the crook. Both are deceivers, undercutters of conventional morality and accepted ways of life. His four *Joseph* books are the finest exploration of that notion that I know; Joseph is *such* a thumping crook and egocentric genius, and what extraordinary emotions he generates in everyone around him, even when they cannot resist his superficial charm. And Mann wrote a wonderful comic variation on that theme in *Felix Krull* – O *felix* indeed, O happy rascal! But the artist cannot help it: however conventional he may be in his way of life, however submissive to his time and place, he exults in inadmissible desires and observations! Great numbers of artists, and many writers among them, are not greatly aware of this groundbass in their natures, but it is always there. Contrary to popular belief, many of them are not possessed of unusual self-knowledge – except deep down below, from which it wells up in their work.

This September I go to Göteborg, to the Book Fair, where I have been asked to speak on *Jung and the Writer** and in what I shall say I hope to dig as deeply as I can into the sources of imagination. It cannot be explained, but I think it can be approached a little more plainly than is usually done. Long ago, in *The Road to Xanadu* (Livingston Lowes) a splendid adventure was begun but it was Freudian in attitude, and as I have repeatedly said, I think Jung is the better guide toward that sort of investigation, simply because he is not so doctrinaire; he allows his reader or his pupil a necessary leeway. There is not really a *Road* but there is a plain full of quagmires over which one may attempt a little journey..... Then back to the new book [*Murther & Walking Spirits*].

One of the disadvantages of growing old is that critics are determined that one must be running downhill. It may be so, but there is much to be observed from the bottom of the hill..... Again, my warmest and most appreciative thanks, and compliments, by the way, on the limpidity of your style. So many critics are awful writers!

Every good wish –

Rob. Davies

To WILLIAM L. SACHSE

Windhover
Caledon East
July 17, 1989

> *William L. Sachse (1912–   ), American*
> *professor of history, was one of Davies'*
> *circle of friends at Oxford from 1935–37.*

Dear Willie:

By this time you must think me (a) dead or (b) the rudest, most ungrateful ruffian in the whole world. In fact I am neither, but simply a confused creature, who has somehow mislaid your letter in the chaos of three desks. I was delighted to hear from you, and placed your letter in a safe and obvious place, saying "Must write to Willie at once," after which a procession of duties and demands supervened, pushing your letter down and down until – where is it now? I *must* find it for the only address I have for you is, I fear, long out of date – Mount Carmel, Conn. – and I recall that you have moved to the coast, and are now a beach-comber.

My life is too full of incident for an aging creature, who longs to sit in the sun, contemplatively sipping sherry and reminiscing to anybody who can be persuaded to listen – *The Ancient Landlubber,** in fact:

> It is an Ancient Landlubber
>   And he stoppeth one of three;
> "By thy long grey beard and glittering eye,
>   Why the hell do you pester me?"

But no; nothing of the sort. For no reason except that I am – my wife tells me – pathetically good-natured I get trapped into doing things – making speeches, mostly – and writing Introductions to books – that eat up my time and involve me in a lot of running about and even flying – which I hate. Not all of it is painful. During June Toronto mounted a huge Choral Festival,* with 4,000 people from all over the world, singing every sort of choral music from Tibetan temple chants to the most advanced modern stuff; there was never less than two concerts every night and some of them – Bach's B. Minor [Mass] by a German choir conducted by Helmuth Rilling* of Stuttgart (magnificent) and Verdi's Requiem sung the best I have ever heard it – absolutely transporting. I remember your enthusiasm for music – were you not an organist? – and thought of you. This and a lot of other things have kept me on the hop.

I met John [Espey] in the Spring when we were in L.A. (an awful city) and we talked of the Long Christmas Dinner Society, and you and Horace [Davenport] and laughed a great deal, thinking of Elias Cabot, and those extended luncheons. Have you heard that Horace has had a rotten blow – the sudden death of his son Tom, of a long-standing heart trouble but he died almost instantly – poor H. is very sad. But he has found a new career as a medical historian, and he sends me macabre articles* about how Frenchmen in the 19th century studied bowel gas by opening the bodies of men who had been guillotined; it seems to have stunk of brandy, with which they had fortified themselves before the dreadful chop. Apparently the medical profession loves this sort of thing, and Horace writes it with fine style and a measure of wry wit. He is dropping in on us early in August, on his way home from the Stratford Shakespeare Festival – which is excellent this year. His health is not good; legs giving up,* but he continues to drive without difficulty. Have you met his 2nd wife, Inge? We like her very much. German and partly Jewish, and a great strength to H. But Horace is determined that in some unspecified way he failed Tom and also his first wife, Virginia,* and he grieves a great deal. I am the ear into which he pours his grief, and I try to be as helpful as one can, but that isn't much. And you remember that Horace had a strong talent for grief.

When last I heard from you, you had yourself found a congenial retirement task and I hope it goes well. Was it place-names?* You would like it here for we have some beauties which originated in the minds of homesick surveyors – Albion, Caledon, Asphodel and the like. They sit strangely on the Canadian landscape but are much more to my taste than Moose's Gut, Wolf's Cave and Bear's Grease and Indian names meaning all sorts of strange things. Our aboriginal people insist that these are part of what they call Our Heritage. Not *my* heritage, dammit, and now and then I long for Wales. My youngest daughter Rosamond [Cunnington] has just had her children in Wales for a holiday, where they saw their great-great-great-grandfather's* portrait in the Town Hall in Welshpool; he was the first Nonconformist and the first Liberal ever to be mayor of a Welsh borough. Apparently it grabbed them strongly, for which I give thanks. . . .

Now I must write to Horace, to congratulate him on his latest and excellent paper on how to carve up a beheaded criminal – which must have been somebody's idea of fun. And I must write to John who has sent me his latest book of verse & prose [*The Nine Lives of Algernon*], which is all about cats. I love cats but they think nothing of me, so we have never been able to keep one; they run away. Brenda has no touch with cats, though her mother was a great cat-lover, and in her house one had almost to sit on the floor, because every good chair was the property of some resentful pussy..... Are you an animal man? Is Nancy* a great friend of the cat & the dog? Blessed are they who can get into the confidence of our Dumb Chums – but I am not of their number.

But I am rambling – the disease of age. Do write again and I promise to be more prompt in my reply..... Our very best to you both.

Rob.

To HORACE W. DAVENPORT

[late October 1989]

Dear Horace:

You must immediately revise your estimate of the readership of your first chapter on *Gastrointestinal physiology*,* which you confined to the proof-reader; *I* have read it from end to end, not always with total comprehension but with more than you might suppose, and I send you my compliments. The style is admirable and clear, the vocabulary choice, and the occasional flashes of wit which you allow yourself are *very* choice. I am awed by your extraordinary industry. Those 558 references! Don't come here next summer and moan that you are washed up and can't lift a feather. You are a giant, an *avatismus*. Dogs, Trojans, niggers* and other notoriously industrious types pale into insignificance beside you. Bravo! Well done!

Some of the experiments make me blink. All those ingested balloons! All that subjection of students, who had either to do as they were told or else seek some non-medical employment. Those troops of dogs, skulks of cats, and lesser creatures, even getting down to ferrets! And the cast of characters! What more do you know of "young Soma Weiss"* (p. 81) presumably a Swiss but how did he come by that extraordinary name? Could he have been the love-child of old Semmel Weiss,* of whose unhappy career every schoolchild knows?

Your chapter is a cabinet of marvels to me because as you are well aware I have all my life been much troubled by my tripes, as was my father before me. We knew damned well what ailed us,* but being children of our time we sought the aid of the medical profession, and suffered for our folly. Sometimes I used to wonder if I had not eaten more barium meals than Christmas dinners. For a time I was in the hands of a man* who liked to dig into my arsehole with a tiny scoop, to secure what he called "a bolus of stool," which he then tested with litmus. It was always acid, as I could have told him, for at the very thought of him my whole digestive tract turned sour. But he was a real doctor, and the idea that the mind might have some influence on the body was repugnant to him.

We have been home from abroad for about two weeks. Our jaunt* was not quite as pleasurable as we had hoped for I arrived in Göteborg feeling unwell, but managed to get through the work set down for me, and deliver my address ["Jung and the Writer"], which was a sell-out and very well received. But then I became quite ill and was lugged off to the hospital. It was a weekend, and the senior medical staff were absent, but a charming young woman assured me that I had asthma (which I had told her beforehand) and also – this was not known to me – I had a pneumonia spot on one lung. I was then turned loose to savour the delights of being ill in a hotel, with no doctors available until Monday. I became delirious, and Brenda appealed for help to the Canadian Embassy, who worked with exemplary speed. We were whisked away to Stockholm by car (400 miles or more, as you will recall) and put to bed in the ambassador's residence, a most luxurious place to be sick in, I assure you. A first-rate doctor [Dr. Olsson] appeared, who was himself an asthmatic, and he prescribed 300 crowns' worth of drugs – a whole apothecary's shop – and there I stayed for a week, getting better, but not feeling very chirpy. It appears that I had something called viral pneumonia.

When at last I could travel we flew to London, and shacked up with my daughter [Miranda]. But London is no place for asthmatics; the weather was humid and the stench of the motor exhaust was so awful that once I had to pause in the street – I was attempting a brief walk – and lean against the wall, feeling ghastly. As soon as possible we got out of London and down into Wiltshire, and spent a week getting good air, quiet and restorative country walks.

As you can imagine, this was hard on Brenda and we were both pretty badly used up when we went to London, and took things very quietly at our share-flat for a couple of weeks. . . .

All good wishes –

Rob   Oh! a postscript

P.S. Your passages on the rectum, anus, sphincters, etc. turned my mind to a subject much in the news these days, and of curious interest – i.e. sodomy. This is an aberration I do not understand, though years ago I had a friend [John Pearson] – the model for John Parlabane in *Rebel Angels* – who was much given to it and carried on ecstatically about its pleasures. To my astonishment I see it now recommended as a diversion for married couples, provided (as these articles invariably say) "that both partners are squeaky clean." (Can you imagine the delayed union while both partners achieve the required degree of squeakiness?) This seems to me to be mischievous nonsense, and I was supported in this opinion by a doctor friend of mine who had had to deal with some problems arising therefrom, who said in good round terms that the moralists who condemn sodomy as *contra naturam* were absolutely right on biological if not on ethical grounds, as the tissues involved are of quite the wrong kind and very open to injury, with consequent infection. Why am I telling you all this, as they say in the bad TV shows? You know it better than I. Because I have long thought that sodomy, now touted as "an alternative life-style" is indeed a neurotic game, springing not from sexual feeling but from an infantile desire to mess with shit (as all children do). The details of sodomy are repellent to the ordinary mind and difficult to relate to any tender feeling, which normal sexuality clearly is not. This notion has lingered in my mind since Oxford days, when my studies of Restoration Drama led me to a rather obscure poem called *A Satyr on the Players,** resurrected by that old rogue Montague Summers. A passage in this savage and cruel piece runs:

> You Smockfac'd Lads, Secure your Gentle Bums
> For full of Lust and Fury see he comes!
> 'Tis Bugger Nokes, whose unwieldy Tool
> Weeps to be buryed in his Foreman's Stool;
> Unnatural Sinner, Lecher without Sense
> To leave kind Cunts, to dive in Excrements.

(Nokes – James Nokes (?–1696) – was an actor who specialized in women's roles – old women – and was one of the last of the hold-overs from the earlier days when all female roles were played by boys or men. From his excellence in this kind of work he was known as Nurse Nokes.)

I think it cannot be long before this sort of squeaky clean fun will be condemned, not by the Puritans, but by the medical profession, and will pass into the hands of the psychiatrists.

Rob.

To RICHARD DAVIS

Windhover

Caledon East

December 27, 1989

Richard Davis (1948–), a Canadian family physician, is a collector of Daviesiana (manuscripts, editions, ephemera, articles by and about Davies).

Dear Dᵣ Davis:

How kind of you to send me those books for Christmas!* *Anomalies and Curiosities*, as you have rightly divined, is very much in my line. I suppose it is rather disgusting, but I have always been fascinated by human oddities, and although I am truly sorry for them I am astonished at the things that can go wrong with the human body, and the miseries that the victims can endure. A writer, of course, is by nature curious, and to really know what happens when a sword-swallower does the apparently impossible (page 624) is very satisfying. Thank you very much.

Your choice of *Recollections of Death* must have been intuitive, for at the moment I am embarking on a new novel [*Murther & Walking Spirits*], to which that book is strongly relevant. Medical friends of mine have talked to me from time to time about such phenomena, and I have long been acquainted with C. G. Jung's description* of his apparent leaving of the body during a heart attack (he didn't want to return, and was annoyed when he was resuscitated) but this is the latest word on the subject. And because I am, as I have said, starting a new book, your kindness emboldens me to ask you some technical questions which only a medical man can answer. It would help me greatly if you could drop me a line about these things:

(1) Could a man who was struck from in front, on the head, with a weighted cudgel, be killed instantly? Where on the head would it be necessary to strike him?

(2) Is it always necessary to have an inquest in a case of murder? How long after the murder does it take place? Do the police release the body for burial before the inquest, or must they keep it until afterward?

I want to be sure to get my details right, for readers are quick to notice any mistake. I am not writing a murder mystery, but my book begins with a murder, and I don't want to say anything stupid.

Again, thanks for your kindness, and I wish you and yours a very happy and prosperous New Year.

Robertson Davies

To THE EDITOR OF THE GLOBE AND MAIL*

Massey College
University of Toronto
[on or soon after Feb. 1, 1990]

[Sir:]

The Ontario Court of Appeal has rejected the provincial regulation which compels school boards to provide prayers as part of their daily program. The same court has declared that the study of a single religion is unconstitutional and contrary to the rights of pupils who are supposedly adherents of other faiths ("Public-school Religion Programs Likely To Halt In Wake Of Ruling" – Feb. 1).

The court has said, however, that the study of religions in the plural is legal. I go further and say that it is eminently desirable.

Why should we not – I say "we" because the schools are our schools and not the property of the government or any local board – institute as soon as possible an obligatory study of world religions?

It is not as if this were something new. Sixty years ago, when I was a boy at Upper Canada College, the senior classes studied comparative religions from an excellent book called This Believing World (Macmillan, New York 1928) by Lewis Browne. Animism, Jainism, Confucianism, Zoroastrianism, Buddhism, Mohammedanism, Judaism and Christianity were all described and considered objectively. We knew that Dr. Browne was a Jewish rabbi and as such, although he gave Christianity a very fair consideration, he did not plump for it above the others. As I recall, only Animism was thought to be primitive, though in our ecological, Greenpeace world it seems to be staging a comeback.

Surely what worked well in a private school 60 years ago is not unthinkable in public schools today.

What is unthinkable is that our schools, which are so often and so sanctimoniously trumpeted as fitting our young people for life, should wholly reject religion, which has shaped our history since the dawn of human life and which is an inextricable element in our thought and history. And if religion, why not some elementary instruction in the history and principal problems of philosophy? We are short-changing our children grievously if we offer them nothing really serious or nutritious for the mind.

If it should be objected that such instruction lies beyond the abilities of teachers as they are at present, it is time to change the teachers. If better teachers cost more money, pay them out of the school taxes of millions of people who, like me, have not had a child in school in 35 years but who are mulcted for the school tax and are being offered religious and ethical illiterates as our reward. Sensible religious and ethical instruction might be expensive, but nothing is so expensive as playing the fool with something so important as education.

[Faithfully yours,]

Robertson Davies

To BIRGITTA HEYMAN

Windhover
Caledon East
February 12, 1990

Dearest Birgitta:

What a splendid anniversary card!* How wonderful of you to have
found and included so much stuff from the past. That awful picture
of me, in *The Shrew,** with Freddie Bennett and the man who played
Sly, whose name eludes me. All I remember about him is that he was
absent at one matinee and I played Sly in his place, and enjoyed it
hugely. The card brought back wonderful memories and gave us
immense pleasure.

Memories of Freddie Bennett, for instance. He was a very fine
person, though not a particularly good actor, and he was a true friend
of the Guthries. When Tony died it was Freddie who went to Ireland*
and took charge of all the business that inevitably followed, and he
was angelic to Judy.* But she was much too unhappy to notice, I believe.
I don't know how much you know about all that. In their later years
Tony and Judy were not very happy together, for she smoked so much
she was quite ill, and also began to grow deaf – which Tony hated,
and he was not kind to her about it. Also, she drank quite heavily.
Tony had a dreadful fear of old age, and sometimes when Brenda and
I met him he would talk about it in a most painful manner; he saw
it as nothing but decay and foolishness. He was, indeed, what the
Jungian psychologists call a *puer aeternus* – an eternal youth, and that
is a cruel fate, for such people grow old like the rest of us, and protest
against it stupidly. He did something which shocked Freddie profoundly, when he was settling up the estate: he had left the whole of
his considerable property in Ireland – house and land – to the Irish
government, to be turned into a home for needy artists – *and he had
not told Judy anything about it!* Consequently she found herself with
just about nothing and not even a house under her feet. All she said
was "I think he might have told me." Freddie was able to make a deal

with the government to leave Judy undisturbed for the rest of her life – which was not very long; the government people were very decent about it. But Tony was a devil in some ways, and as he grew older he became very incalculable. He was not at all pleased when I began to achieve some success in the world; he wanted all his friends to be subordinates. We valued him and Judy enormously, but as time passed it became more and more difficult.

But that is enough about that. I hope everything goes well with you. We are very busy, and I have more work than I can manage, which is foolish, but I never seem to be able to say No. I have begun a new book [*Murther & Walking Spirits*], which is difficult, but they are all difficult. Writing never seems to get any easier, however much one does. This book is going to be – in a veiled way – about my forbears (they were too humble to be called *ancestors*) and why they came to Canada. I shall have to walk carefully, because I have regiments of relations, who will be after me with clubs if they think I have not dealt reverently with the past. But the fact is that the past of my family was not reverent at all, but peculiar and scandalous, as the true story of most families is. Some of my forbears were absolute demons and one of them at least was suspected of murder. His wife became dotty – Alzheimer's, I suppose, though it was not called that then – and he coaxed her out to the side of the road and then ran over to the other side and tempted her with a box of chocolates, of which she was very fond. "Come Annie. Come on, Annie, and have a chocolate," this old devil cried and of course poor dotty Annie ran out into the road, was hit by a car, and that was that! Not a spectacular murder, and he was never charged, but what God will say to him at the Day of Judgement I can hardly wait to hear. Lots of lively stuff for a book; just the simple lives of simple people, and full of the devil.

Our anniversary party was a great success. We had 63 guests to dinner at our Club;* the oldest [Robert Finch] was ninety (and looked and behaved like sixty) and the youngest was our granddaughter Cecilia, who is eleven. All our grandsons were there, and looked very fine in their dress clothes. It was a fine gathering of friends, and I wish you could have been with us, but we thought of you because your wonderful card arrived *on the very day*, which was brilliant timing. I shall send you some pictures as soon as we get them made; you might like to see the children. Only our daughter Miranda, who lives and works in London, was not present; really too far to come, and leave all her patients, but we talked to her by telephone. Did I tell you she had produced her first book? About child analysis. She is now working on another.* Writing is the family trade; she is the fourth generation in it. We were worried about her during the terrible storms in Europe, but she had no trouble as she was able to stay indoors; it was the people in the streets who had a hard time.

I shall write again soon, when we get the photographs. Meanwhile, what is your news?

Love and warm thanks from us both –

Rob.

To MORDECAI RICHLER

Windhover
Caledon East
February 12, 1990

Dear Mordecai:

Belated, but none the less sincere, congratulations on *Solomon Gursky*. I have read it with great pleasure and satisfaction, and so has my wife, and we meet people everywhere who share our enthusiasm. In my opinion, it is the best thing you have done, but opinions vary on that, and in time the academic critics will have their say, and weigh and inspect in their accustomed fat-headed manner.

I looked at it, of course, not simply as a reader but as another novelist and I was impressed by:

(a) The big scene. One gets so tired of novels that all seem to take place indoors, with a small cast of characters, and in which nobody shows vital quality above the level of a branch bank manager.

(b) Extraordinary energy and sweep of the writing. This too is uncommon, and especially so in Canada. You pelt along at a cracking pace, as if you did not think you could possibly crowd in all you have to tell – and of course this whips the reader along with it, breathless and spellbound.

(c) Individuality of voice. There is not a paragraph which fails to belong to the book so strongly that it could be transferred to anywhere else. Individuality of vocabulary. Individuality of attitude, which cloaks a great pity in a hilarious acerbity. This is the great achievement: to make what is sad, or macabre, or repellent, splendidly funny without diminishing its true character.

Altogether a brilliant performance – and I do not mean "brilliant" in the sense of flashy or meretricious. In the world of CanLit today it is gigantic, and of course far beyond the puny grasp of the CanLit coterie. The Gov-Gen's Award people diminish themselves by snubbing it. That award has lost most of its clout and will soon sink to the level of the Leacock Medal. Awards are, of course, a lot of crap, but they awe the simple.

Again, congratulations & good wishes

Rob. Davies

To JEFF SCHAIRE

Massey College
University of Toronto
April 10, 1990

Jeff Schaire was editor of the New York-based magazine Art & Antiques. *The article proposed in his letter to Schaire was never written.*

[Dear Mr Schaire:]

Thank you for your letter of April 4th accompanying the April issue of *Art and Antiques*. I assure you that I am extremely happy to get it and that I have not forgotten that I promised a long time ago to contribute to the magazine. Indeed I have an idea which I would

like to put before you. For many years I have been a collector of theatrical prints which generally appear in the form of engravings, but
for about thirty years at the beginning of the nineteenth century they
appeared in a very popular form that were indeed engravings, but on
quite a humble scale. The pictures were of popular actors in their most
famous roles. These engravings could be bought for a penny and were
generally sold to children who coloured them. These were the engravings which were meant in the expression "Penny plain Tuppence
coloured." There was a further extension of this venture when it was
possible to buy a selection from over 1500 tinsel decorations – span-
gles, swords, feathers, daggers and so forth. These could be fastened
to the coloured engravings and from the delicacy with which some
of this work is done I suspect it was done not by children but by their
governesses as a nursery amusement.

I have been collecting these things since I was 18 and I am astonished to find that things which I bought for ten shillings or a pound
at that time are now being offered at from £80 to £100, and possibly
more if the subject is a popular one. People who kept them generally
had them framed in curly maple frames, which are very characteristic
of this work.

Would you be interested in a shortish piece about these things,
with illustrations from my own collection if you could not secure
them elsewhere? They are very entertaining popular art and I may say
with some satisfaction that the collection in the Victoria and Albert
Museum is not as good as mine.

I could not do this in a twinkling but I could get it done, if you
are interested, after a while.

Yours sincerely,

[Robertson Davies]

To HORACE W. DAVENPORT

Windhover
Caledon East
June 29, 1990

Dear Horace:

We are here for the summer now, and a cold wet summer it has
been during June. I am pegging away at my book [*Murther & Walking
Spirits*], which moves slowly, because it is in part historical, which is
new ground for me, and demands a lot of attention to detail; however
careful I am, there is always some smarty-boots who writes to me
after every book, pointing out some stupid mistake I should have
avoided, so getting into the historical field adds a new terror to
authorship. I have some hopes of finishing before the end of the year,
but it is impossible to predict with accuracy.

Have you seen [John] Espey's most recent book?* More reminiscences of his childhood in China, very well done, and obviously
rooted in a sense of guilt toward his parents.

We are winding up now to get away next Tuesday for a brief visit
to Ireland, where I am getting an honorary degree from Trinity
Coll. Dublin, and am filled with glee to be even so faintly associated with the college of Congreve and Goldsmith, and of course
you-know-who and even that old grouch Swift.* We shall make a
short by-trip to Cork, which I have always wanted to see because of
that poem* about –

The Bells of Shandon,
    That sound so grand on
The mighty waters
    Of the River Lee –

which used to be read to me by my Mother.

What's up with you? We shall be very sorry to miss you this year,
but I think you will like Stratford very much. We thought *Macbeth*

excellent – the best we have ever seen in a long experience of
Macbeths. (I am sure you remember that awful *Macbeth* in Oxford.)*
And there is a very good *As You Like It*, very funny because the action
has been cast in New France, and the show is full of maple leaves,
the banished court are *coureurs de bois*, and their simple forest fare is
the biggest spread you ever saw of game and fish and fruit. This is all
done with taste – never nudging – and it works extremely well. The
Congreve, *Love For Love*, was rather heavy, but one of the modern
plays, *Home*,* was absolutely first-rate, and deeply pathetic. Do you
know it? About some people in a mental hospital who are not so mad
as to be confined, but who for one reason or another cannot be
outside. One would not think this funny, but in part it is.

Did you see the broadcast of *The Ring** from the Met.? We saw the
first three, but for *Götterdämmerung* our TV went on the fritz, and we
missed it. What we saw we liked, but were not ecstatic. The thing
about Wagner that gets me down is that he is so mercilessly *slow*.
Wotan sings: then twenty bars of loud music: Brünnhilde replies. It
is as though they were all retarded but had extraordinary submerged
passions. Furthermore, old Dick feels that he must recapitulate the
plot in every opera, for those who came in late, one presumes. Last
Tuesday we saw *Der Rosenkavalier** here, and the rapidity of the pace
was a joy. I am not so bold as to blaspheme against the Divine Dick,
but he certainly had a Teutonic sense of the unimportance of time.

I near the end of the page. Shall I send you a shamrock from the
Emerald Isle? The Department of Agriculture probably forbids such
antics. Best to you both.....

Rob. . . .

To DR. JOHN O. STUBBS

Massey College
University of Toronto
December 11, 1990

John O. Stubbs (1943–   ), a professor of history, was President and Vice-Chancellor of Trent University from 1987–93. He had met Davies on a couple of occasions.

Dear Dᴿ Stubbs:

Thank you for your letter of December 4th. I have given it serious thought and, because you had the courtesy to write to me personally, I feel that I should make a personal reply and explain my situation. I fear that I cannot undertake to contribute to Trent University in the circumstances that you have outlined for, although I have a high regard for Trent and played some small part in securing a university in Peterborough, I am an honorary graduate of 22 universities, of which Trent is one, and every one of them appeals to me for money at least twice every year. They also have continuing schemes of contribution and most of them feel, as you do, that $10,000. over five years would be a proper donation from me. I am not happy about refusing these suggestions but I have obligations to two universities of which I am a graduate, and also to Massey College, of which I was Master for twenty years. These are educational obligations only, but my wife and I have long-standing obligations to several institutions related to the Arts, of which the Canadian Opera Company, the Toronto Symphony, the Shaw Festival and the Stratford Festival are the principals. Apart from this there are certain charities whose appeals we simply cannot refuse, although when I retired we resolved that we would stop giving to charity and give only to the Arts groups with whom our strongest sympathy lies.

In addition to these obligations we receive innumerable appeals from Public Television, groups who wish to fund scholarships in somebody's name and an extraordinary range of benevolent groups whose cries are deafening. Under these circumstances, as you will see, we can only give to a selection of recipients.

In conclusion let me assure you that I have every sympathy with you in the task in which you are engaged. It has become the horrible

custom of educational institutions to invite scholars to be at their
head and then demand that the scholar spend a tremendous amount
of his time as a money raiser. I had a taste of this at Massey College
and it was the most difficult of the tasks I faced, as I have no talent
in that direction whatever.

I have answered you at some length because, although I am sure
that you could duplicate my story 100 times over, I felt that it was
owing to you to make a personal explanation of why I cannot accede
to your request.

Yours sincerely,

Robertson Davies

To BIRGITTA HEYMAN

Massey College
University of Toronto
December 18, 1990

Dear Birgitta:

I was delighted to get your November letter, and as usual have been
putting off replying until the Right Moment – so that it is now almost
Christmas and it must be now or you will think I have forgotten you
– which I most certainly have not. First of all, it is splendid news that
your eye operation* has been such a success. I know that feeling of
seeing the world anew; two years ago I had my right eye operated on
for cataract, and it is now better than it ever has been in my life. But
the left eye is now pretty hopeless and next Spring I must have it
done, and then I hope I shall have eyes like a hawk. But as you say,
growing old is no fun: I become extremely irritated with myself
because I cannot do things I want to do – climb ladders to fetch books
from high shelves, run for buses, carry wood in from the pile for the
fireplace without puffing, and all that sort of thing. Brenda is amazing;

she still plays tennis twice a week, and is considered pretty good. But women always seem to last longer than men: I suspect that it is because they don't eat as much. . . .

Later in the summer we went to Bayreuth* for the Festival and had a wonderful time. The operas were splendid musically, though rather gloomy to the eye because the director had decided that it should all be done as if a nuclear holocaust had exterminated most of the human race, and that was the Twilight of the Gods. This meant, of course, that all Wagner's wonderful stuff about nature, and birdsong and the surge of life did not really fit into the terrible settings, which looked like factories. But directors have to have their way, whatever nonsense comes of it. We did not stay in a hotel but in a guest-house, and were treated very kindly by the owners, who seemed to think that we ate twelve times a day. Extraordinary to have to dress up in evening clothes at three in the afternoon, but that's the way it was. The music was magnificent – Georg Solti* conducting. And of course the theatre was jammed as full as it would go for every performance. All sorts of odd people in the audience, including a young American who was, I think, not quite right in his head, because he wore a tee-shirt with "I Have Survived The Ring" on it; I suppose he wanted people to look at him, but nobody did. The only thing I dislike about such jaunts is the air-travel. We have to cross the Atlantic twice in 1991, but we are not going to any of the uproars in Vienna in honour of Mozart.* Frankly, admiring his genius, there are times when I have had enough of Mozart.

How wonderful that you are going to Uruguay and Argentina!* How does it work? Do you teach the lawyers how to do their work in intervals between sight-seeing, or how? And do you have to be very stern with them, and insist that they behave with proper dignity and decorum? I cannot imagine you as a governess, correcting their speech and making them wash their hands before sitting down to meals. I am sure it is all much more entertaining than that. But how? I have told people here about your work with lawyers, and they say they wish you would do some work on our Canadian lawyers, some of whom are almost like savages and appear in court in the most horrible old gowns and dirty white ties and bands. It is not unknown for a judge to tell a lawyer that he will not listen to him until he dresses himself properly. Of course they have to wear robes – but what robes! The judges are very gorgeous and have blue sashes and bits of scarlet all over them – but they have a servant who takes care of their things and it is very funny to see that each judge's chambers contains a full-length mirror in which he can make sure he looks gorgeous enough to go into court. This is one of the ways in which we differ from the Americans, who appear in court so that you can't tell the lawyers from the criminals.

Interesting to hear about your sister* who is writing a family history. That can be desperately hard work. My father did it, and almost went mad trying to track down dates and details. His book* is not easy to read because he was determined to get in every scrap of information he could discover, and it makes for a slow narrative. Also, he would not print anything that was the least discreditable about any member of the family, and that meant that all the best stuff had to be omitted. When I argued with him about it he would explain that it was utterly impossible to say such things about your own kinsfolk. I don't see why. If they were crooked, or stupid, why not say so?

I discover by looking in my diary that I began my present novel [*Murther & Walking Spirits*] on December 27, 1989; I am just finishing it now. It has been very hard work, as I told you, because it is based in the history of my family, and although it is a good deal fiction-alized, the basic facts are true, and the whole thing is, in my opinion, truer to the reality of what happened than a strictly historical book would be. But it was not easy to write about my Mother, whom I now realize I never understood very well, or knew very well. She was an unusual woman, strongly imaginative and very good at business, but her life never gave her a chance to use either of her gifts to their fullest extent. My Father could not have endured a rival in business matters. He was a remarkable man, who made a fortune from nothing, possessed a strongly romantic temperament, and saw the world very much according to his own ideas. It was exciting, but not easy, to be his son. My Mother was very much a creature of North America, for her ancestors came to the new World in the seventeenth century from Holland, and she never cared for the United Kingdom, which my

Father regarded as the Earthly Paradise. This made for great tension between them, and their three sons felt it strongly. A psychiatrist* once told me that it was much to my credit that I had survived such powerful parents, reasonably sane! . . .

I repeat, and emphasize: it is marvellous to get your letters. They are a fresh breath from a far-off land for which I have come to have a strong affection. So – a very merry Christmas to you and all your family, and a splendid and adventurous New Year. I have not forgotten that it was at this season of the year, in 1939, that I first met you at the Old Vic, and that meeting was part – a large part – of the romance of that extraordinary production* of *A Midsummer Night's Dream*. You were an Amazon; too tall to be a fairy. Do you remember how the fairies flew and _____ – who must have been the fattest fairy in all Fairyland – bashed into a side-wing, and almost brought about an unseemly death in Fairyland? How delightful it all was!

Love!

Rob . . . .

To HARRY RASKY

Oaklands
Toronto
January 9, 1991

Harry Rasky (1928–   ) is a Canadian film and television producer, director, and writer. His The Magic Season of Robertson Davies *premiered on CBC-TV on December 27, 1990.*

Dear Harry:

From what I hear, *The Magic Season [of Robertson Davies]* was very well received, and many people spoke particularly about the prominence you had given to the Caledon countryside, and had made its beauty a part of the work. I was myself especially pleased that when some words of mine were read, the background was a maple leaf, with its veins and fabric and colour showing, almost as if it were the interior of a mind – which I took as high compliment. Indeed, I thought the whole film had a quality of poetry about it which you had evoked by simple means, but which spoke of a Canada that few people seem to see, but which I should like to think is akin to me, for I speak of a Canada that is real, but overlooked.

Such films inevitably present difficulties, because they are serious in intent, and not just pretty things and vapid compliments. To get really deep into somebody's personal truth would create a film that most viewers would find alienating or incomprehensible. The truth about anybody – and especially a writer or other artist – is so complex and often so banal, or so ugly, that it cannot be conveyed in a work that is for the most popular of mediums. And thank God for it! The truth about me would not please anybody – beginning with myself. But what you showed, with great art and perception, was what the public wants to believe about me, and what it can understand about me, and you gave it a style and a physical beauty which was a compliment to me as well as to the viewers.

I was delighted with the variety you were able to bring to the film. The scenes of a bygone Ontario, the old photographs, the excerpts from my plays (acted better than I have ever seen them on the stage) kept the piece from ever being static visually; there was no suggestion of the Talking Head.

Of course the trolls got after you. It is a compliment in its way. The trolls are jealous because they cannot do what you can do, or see what you can see. Canadian journalism is, at a conservative estimate, twenty-five years behind the times, and is staffed by nonentities. Anybody in Canada who *does anything well*, is a mark for the trolls.

I hope you are able to spread the film widely abroad; it is handsome enough to interest viewers from Greenland's icy mountains to India's coral strand,* and with it goes not just my reputation but yours.

Making the film was a delightful experience. Brenda and I did not know what to expect, and were fearful, but it could not have been pleasanter. Our very best to you and your staff –

Rob.

To ROBERT FINCH

Massey College
University of Toronto
January 10, 1991

Dear Robert:

I was delighted by your story of the lady who thumbed through
*The Satanic Verses** and complained that they were not in verse! It is
such nugacities that give flavour to life. Here is one that may amuse
you –

Oh Christmas Eve I found myself at eleven o'clock in the morning
at the corner of Yonge and Bloor Streets, and my ear was teased by
music which seemed somehow familiar, but which eluded recognition. A young black man in a pink skiing suit was playing a steel drum
– one of those contraptions which, struck at different points, give out
different notes. But what was he playing? I listened for a while and
finally it came to me that this was Beethoven's *Für Elise*! Not one note
truly in tune with any other, and the rhythm all askew – but *Für Elise*
sure enough. Why? Recollections of long-ago piano lessons? A soul
above street musicianship? I have a weakness for street musicians, and
for a giddy moment I thought of giving him a dollar. But no – the
assault upon Beethoven was too grievous and I fled.

All good wishes for 1991

Rob.

To HORACE W. DAVENPORT

Windhover
Caledon East
February 8, 1991

Dear Horace:

. . . I don't think I have written to you since we returned from
Bayreuth; that was really an adventure. I have known Wagner in scraps,
but *The Ring* in full was a stunning experience. I have not become a
card-carrying Wagnerian; I do not rank him with Shakespeare or insist
that his psychological insight is superior to Freud and Jung or that his
kind of opera has rendered all other kinds derisory. But he is a great
man, and his world is a startling world. A world, by the way, utterly
unlit by one scrap of what I consider to be humour. (Yes, I know all
about Beckmesser, and think him a pretty mild joke.) This is significant to me at present because I have undertaken to give the Hesse
Lecture at the Aldeburgh Festival* in June, and I am going to talk
about *Opera and Humour*; my pitch will be that music accommodates
humour only sparingly, because music cannot manage irony, which is
the mode of much humour in drama, and which words accommodate superbly, but which music – slow and imprecise – can't manage.
I shall have to define humour, and I rather look forward to that, and
shall do so in Jungian terms – that humour is implicit in the tendency
of all things to run into their opposites if pushed unreasonably
(Heraclitus)* and the strong emotions that opera can accommodate
do not admit of the double-mindedness of all real observation of life.
(My God, what a sentence; I don't really understand it myself, but I
shall.) But Bernard Shaw, helpless with mirth at his mother's funeral,
shows the idea at work. To do this job at all, not to speak of success-
fully, will keep me busy for some months to come.

I go to Yale in a couple of weeks to give two lectures on Reading
and Writing,* and I have worked hard on them and tried to pare away
nonsense. Result, I shall advise reading a few books several times and
reading them slowly and lovingly. Of writing I shall say: everybody

writes, but that is not what Shakespeare and Shaw did, and no amount of Creative Writing Courses will produce talent where it has not existed before, and if it has existed before, Creative Writing Courses may be left to wistful aspirants, because to a real writer the only Creative Writing Course is life itself and its goes on for 24 hours a day. As I grow old I get sick of the bullshit that insists that everybody has an immense amount of Creativity which must be unleashed by striking off the fetters of technique. People who can write, do, and those who can't should shut up. This is sour but I am oppressed by the amount of crap that comes over my desk about how tough it is to be a woman, or gay, or a lesbian or a Red Indian, and that every peewee minority has a "right" to a literature of its own.

From the things you send me – which l greatly appreciate – I sense that your reputation as a medical historian waxes mightily, and that delights me. You have always had two strings to your bow and it is marvellous that the other string is now getting a lively plucking.

Give our best wishes and love to Inge and Rob and be assured of our warmth of feeling toward you all. We survivors find new riches in one another as people fall away beside us.

Rob.

The new book is called: MURTHER & Walking Spirits – a quotation from Samuel Butler (1613–80).*

To DOUGLAS GIBSON

Windhover
Caledon East
Lady Day,* March 25, 1991

Dear Douglas:

Douglas Gibson, by now publisher at McClelland & Stewart, was Davies' editor in Canada again, since Davies had moved to M&S in 1990.

Herewith the typescript of *Murther and Walking Spirits* which now embodies many of your suggestions and alterations. Not all, for I thought some of them needless, and some inadvisable, because I sense that your notion of the novel is different from mine; you have edited always for a rigorous clarity, and I feel that a certain fuzziness is essential to the nature of the book which is, after all, about a man whose perceptions are not those of ourselves. This is also a part of the reliance on a film presentation of the narrator's past, for film presents itself to us as photographic – and the camera cannot lie – but is in fact extremely selective and often downright duplicitous in what it offers; Christine [Pevitt]* asked that this be given a clearer statement, and I have re-written the last two pages of Chapter One to meet this criticism, and they are in the script now.

Kicking and screaming as I wrote, I have shoehorned another generation into the Gage-Vermuelen family, to meet your objection that everybody lived too long; I did not feel when I was writing that a statistical realism was needed, but you do, and now you've got it, though it creates a lump in the narrative that I do not like. I agree with Christine, however, that a family tree would be a mistake; it encourages people to think of the book as one of those sweating family narratives – *The Hoogows of Dogmess: A Saga* – which it is not. Strip aside all my mists, and you kill the book.

Because I have incorporated all the changes directly on the pages, the typescript is not as tidy as I – or Moira Whalon, who takes great pride in such things – could wish. But I think it is clear, and if you or anybody concerned finds my writing difficult, I can explain by phone. Here and there, my comments on your criticisms are a little saucy – a protest against a too-literal reading. Do not take it personally.

I have altered a couple of chapter headings.

I welcome enquiries, protests, loud screams, or whatever.

Rob. Davies

To HORACE W. DAVENPORT

Windhover
Caledon East
April 29 [1991]

BUT TO RESOOM – as Artemus Ward says.....*

It is good of you to send me reprints of your papers in *Gastro-enterology International*: I read them with partial comprehension, and wonder at the arcane world in which you tread like a giant. I reflect, humbly, that nothing would ever have made me into a scientist, or even a lab sweeper; inconsequence would have intruded every hour, to my destruction. But I wish I could think like that; indeed, I wish I could think, for never in my life have I enjoyed five unbroken minutes of anything that could be called true ratiocination. "Maggoty-headed" is the term the Elizabethans would have applied to me: a scatterbrain. But, as even the blind pig sometimes finds an acorn, I have been able to make something out of the mess (what Yeats calls "the foul rag-and-bone shop")* that is my mind.

I have been particularly concerned with your piece about Rudolf Heidenhain, and whether he was or was not a "vitalist."* Reading your masterly summary of the dispute I am moved to wonder, as I have wondered a thousand times, how any scientist of quality can do what he does without some sense that he is a marvel at least partly inexplicable by any means that lie within his specialized knowledge. He is a thinker, but can he think, as he works, without any intrusions from outside – is his wife unfaithful? has the cat really run away or simply gone on a walkabout? what's for dinner? how a good yoke of bullocks [would sell?] at Stamford Fair? etc. Practitioners of yoga tell us that they can achieve "one-pointedness" in their thought, or con-templation, and continue it for quite long periods, but they never seem to bring anything back from these journeys that we greatly wish to hear – unlike the scientist. The flow of thought, as Joyce reminds us, is extremely various but not without some eventual point. Is the scientist never disturbed by the variety of his thoughts and emotions and physical feelings as he works? And can he attribute this variety simply to physical and chemical forces?

I suppose scientists are deeply concerned that they should not get into any situation that suggests the existence of a God, but so far as I have followed them, their notion of a God is rather crude. In fact, they propose an absurd God, and then throw him away because he is absurd. But what if he is not absurd? What if he embraces and moves them, as he moves the milkmaid, the financier, the rapist, the poet and the cretin? It appears to me that scientists cannot conceive of a God who has no purpose comprehensible and friendly to mankind, but who is getting on with some other job of which mankind is a complex but not perhaps a major part? Considering how short a time man has inhabited the earth, and how long it took him to get down out of the trees (insofar as he has) God seems to have been busy for quite a while without caring much about us, although he seems unable to make us anything less than marvellous and unceasingly various (within limits).

This is, I fear, blather, but blather is all I can manage on such subjects. I cannot follow the theologians, who are as determined to comprehend God as the scientists are to steer clear of him – and the God they comprehend is as various as they are themselves – one for the Archbishop of Canterbury and one for Billy Graham.

You had better destroy this letter. If it should fall into hands other than your own it will unquestionably be used to prove me an idiot – which is not wholly true. A simpleton, perhaps, but when I look at the people who are determined not to be simple I do not repine. My next novel [*Murther & Walking Spirits*] – of which I wrote earlier – is an attempt to make a little sense of this question, but fiction is not really the right medium, and I am no poet. But the gist of the novel is that anybody at all, *who has achieved some measure of self-awareness*, is engaged in the Hero-Struggle, and however uneventful or quiet his life may appear to be to the outward view, it is all he can endure of testing and turmoil. It is not to have climbed Everest that matters: it is to have seen the Everest in oneself.

I suppose I am talking like a vitalist. But in my profession I don't have to worry too much, though it invites the scorn of the most modern, and post-modern, and deconstructionist of my contemporaries.

Rob.

Epigraph:
"Printers finde by experience that one Murther is worth two Monsters, and at least three walking Spirits. For the Consequence of Murther is hanging, with which the Rabble is wonderfully delighted. But where Murthers and walking Spirits meet, there is no other Narrative can come near it."
    SAMUEL BUTLER (1612—1680)
    the one who wrote *Hudibras*

To HORACE W. DAVENPORT

Windhover
Caledon East
May 22, 1991

Dear Horace:

Many thanks for yours of May 3. I am very grateful for your concern about my health,* and when you speak of affection, I assure you it is warmly reciprocated; we are getting to be the survivors of our generation, and old friendships are very dear.

Have you had [John] Espey's book *Two Schools of Thought*? You figure in it prominently, also the Long Christmas Dinner Society and much else from Oxford days. I thought John's tone somewhat bitter, which saddened me; but I saw little of him during his third year and I gather that he had some disappointments. He seems to have disliked Ridley, which I am sorry to learn, because Ridley was very kind to me, and his eccentricities did not really trouble me. I do not think he was a scholar of the first rank in the Shakespeare world, but I have met quite a few since who were in that category and I really liked Ridley better, and his guidance of my thesis was all it should have been. Scholarship, as I don't need to tell you, is poor stuff when allied to a peewee man, and my life has been studded with scholarly peewees. I think Oxford seems very different to a Rhodes Scholar from what it is to someone like myself, who came from a good, but obscure university, where the teaching was old-fashioned and narrow. My Shakespeare professor [George Herbert Clarke] at Queen's had one scholarly god – Gervinus,* who died in 1871 and had taken rather a poor view of the extravagances of the Bard. So Oxford was an immense opening-out and I have always been grateful, and do not yearn for UCLA, which seems to be John's spiritual home. I don't know whether I told you or not, but Balliol has elected me an Honorary Fellow,* which is generous, for I am in the category of Balliol's writers, and not its Empire builders and economists and other serious-minded chaps. But what really astonishes me is that on June 19 next I am to receive an honorary D.Litt. at Encaenia,* and this has nothing to do with Balliol, having been promoted by some people at St. Catherine's and St. John's and Christ Church; I am enormously pleased, as well I might be, for a scholar I have never been, and I gather that I am getting it as a writer. Like Mark Twain, I shall wear my gown in private life, and even in the rain.

Brenda and I go to Vienna on Friday next, to spend a couple of weeks and take part in some of the celebrations of the work of the Divine Moistheart – five operas, some concerts and what not. Then to England, where I am giving a lecture at Aldeburgh, in connection with the opera festival, and later doing a reading from my new book [*Murther & Walking Spirits*] in London, at the Royal Festival Hall. . . .

I read your medical history papers with fascination. In my new novel you will find imbedded, like a gem in honey, your fascinating story* about the French scientists who chopped up a couple of fellows who had been guillotined, and sniffed the brandy they had drunk before going up the fatal steps. What a picture! The covered wagon jolting away over the cobbles from the place of execution, and the sawbones, with their sleeves tucked up, digging into the bodies, probably still warm: only Frenchmen could do it like that.

Will send you a card from Abroad, of some unsuitable design, if I can find one.....

Love from us both

Rob.

To RICHARD DAVIS

Windhover
Caledon East
August 30, 1991

Dear Rick:

How very kind of you to remember my birthday! I enjoyed the day greatly, but wish the number it celebrated had not been quite so high..... We heard Evgeny Kissin* when we were in Vienna on June 6 last. He is enormously talented and great hopes are held out for him. But we also heard Alfred Brendel* a few days earlier, and the contrast was very interesting. Kissin – a prodigy of technique, daunted by nothing, stupefying in his virtuosity – but when he played Romantic music of Chopin* or Schubert he had nothing to bring to it except what he had learned from his teachers. Brendel, on the other hand, plays superbly but one is never aware of technique; everything is in what he brings to the music, and what he finds in it – a life's experience and a sense of beauty and pathos that is deeply moving. After his concert the Vienna musical association made him an honorary member, and when he was presented with his scroll, the young man who did so, knelt and kissed his hand. It sounds melodramatic and rather absurd, but I assure you it wasn't; it was a proper tribute to a great artist..... Will Kissin ever be a Brendel? Only a lifetime in art can make him so – if he is wise and lucky. You will probably see the result. I won't, so you must watch on my behalf..... Again, thanks and all good wishes.

Robertson Davies

To MORDECAI RICHLER

Windhover
Caledon East
Sept. 26, 1991

Dear Mordecai:

   Three cheers – bilingual, of course – for your splendid piece in the *New Yorker*!* Of course idiots are declaring that you wrote it with your pen dipped in gall and tabasco, but I have talked to many who are delighted that at last somebody has poured some cold water, instead of gasoline, on this national bonfire. Your factual analysis of the situation was masterly and I find it hard to believe that the intelligent Québécois have not weighed the alarming cost of setting up a separate state. But factual analysis, valuable as it is, does not always wow the reader as does your brilliant style, never outrageous, but genially acerbic and putting the theme in a psychological, rather than a solely political light..... I have been saying for a long time that this is our Civil War,* and it is a psychological civil war, which is something we must learn to fight intelligently, and not like enraged schoolchildren..... You have done us all a great service, and those who are cheering for you are numerous and alert.

More power to you –

Rob. Davies

MASSEY COLLEGE
in the University of Toronto

Dear Greg:

You are a merciless man and God will
punish you in the next world. Have you any idea
how much time it takes to sign 150 copies of
anything, to say nothing of numbering them?
I do not know how much time it will be but it
will be quite a while and when the things are
ready I will let you know.

Of course the Government is cutting
the grant to Harbourfront; it is their well
understood policy to quench every artistic
venture in this province, hoping to achieve
that end before they are defeated in the next
election.

With good wishes--though I don't know
why considering your unbearable cruelty toward
me, I am

Yours sincerely,

Rob.

Mr. Greg Gatenby
Artistic Director
Harbourfront Reading Series
410 Queens Quay West: Suite 100
Toronto, Ontario
M5V 2Z3

June 22, 1993.

SECTION

VII

y the fall of 1991 (when he was 78), Davies was noting down ideas for *The Cunning Man*. He began writing the first draft on December 31, 1992, and completed it on December 10, 1993.

His willingness to take on minor writing projects continued unabated, be it a scenario for an Irish academic periodical, a piece for the *New York Times*, a film version of *Fifth Business*, an article for the Canadian Opera Company's souvenir program, a speech for the Stratford Festival or for the Pierpont Morgan Library in New York or for his old college in Oxford. He continued to respond – often whimsically – to the many letters from readers and inquirers after his opinion, and to write to old friends.

Until his retirement from Massey College in 1981 he had walked a great deal, gaining much-needed exercise that way. But in the years since then he had walked less and less. In the early months of 1992, at Brenda's urging, he reintroduced a little exercise into his life by using a stationary bicycle for 20 minutes a day. Later that year, in October, a second successful cataract operation gave him a sense of well-being. But the schedule of work he continued to impose on himself was taking its toll: in

December and again the following January, he experienced attacks of angina. Tests revealed some degeneration of the heart.

In this period, to his delight, he had two important successes on the stage. Elliott Hayes' adaptation of *World of Wonders* drew full houses at the Stratford Festival in 1992. And in June 1993 the oratorio *Jezebel*, for which he had written the libretto, was greeted with enthusiasm at its first performance in Toronto.

To LISA ROSENBAUM

October 29, 1991

> *Lisa Rosenbaum (1936–) is a French literary translator resident in Paris. She had sought Davies' assistance with several knotty points in* What's Bred in the Bone.

Dear Mlle. Rosenbaum:

Thank you for your letter of October 15th. Here are the answers to your enquiries:

p. 31 [Penguin 36]: *one of the great Fox beauties*; the lady who became Countess of Powis at the time of the story, had been Charlotte Lane Fox, one of three sisters who were the most beautiful debutantes of their season in London.

p. 85 [Penguin 102]: [*chiel o' pairts;*] this is an expression common in Scottish Vernacular speech and it means a young person (*chiel*=child) of unusual abilities (*pairts*=parts).

p. 215 [Penguin 259]: "*Marry come up, m'dirty cousin*": this is certainly a tricky one. The whole phrase is a quotation from an old play, which I cannot identify, which became a catchword among people of a literary bent. "*Marry*" is an oath, meaning Mary the Virgin; "*Marry come up*" is an exclamation of disapproval or incredulity, as one might say, "Hold on, there!", or "Wait a minute!". *M' dirty cousin* means someone akin to oneself, but not regarded as an equal or a credit to the family. I use it to show that Francis Cornish did not like Ismay's over-familiar behaviour.

p. 387 [Penguin 467]: ["*Helter-skelter, hang sorrow, care kill'd a cat, up-tails all, and a louse for the hangman*":] the quotation is from Ben Jonson's play, *Every Man In His Humour* Act 1, scene 3. It is just an explanation of high spirits — carefree — To Hell with everything!

p. 306 [Penguin 368]: [*I'm wearin' awa', Jean/Like snow-wreaths in thaw, Jean/I'm wearin' awa'/In the land o' the veal*. What was the original word substituted by "*veal*"?] the word is "leal," and it means "loyal" in Scottish Vernacular speech. What Francis says is a parody of the well-known Scots song which begins —

I'm wearin' awa' Jean,
 Like snow-drifts in thaw, Jean,
I'm wearin' away
 To the Land o' the Leal

Meaning, I am approaching death, and will go to the Land of the Leal — meaning those who were loyal to the Stuart cause when the Hanoverians came to the throne of Britain..... Francis is making fun as so many North American visitors do, of the insistence on veal in the Bavarian diet.

Sorry to be so troublesome. I hope you are well and that the translation will shortly appear in print. My friends who understand French intimately tell me your translations are brilliant.

With all good wishes,

Yours sincerely,

Robertson Davies

To DAVID WILLIAMS

Massey College
University of Toronto
November 26, 1991

*David Williams (1958–   ), Canadian
mental-health worker and drug and
alcohol counsellor, is the volunteer Death
Penalty Abolition Co-ordinator for
Amnesty International Canadian Section
(English Speaking).*

Dear Mr. Williams:

Thank you for your letter about your campaign to find a world-wide abolition of the death penalty. I cannot consent to lend my name to such a movement because I cannot see any likelihood that it will ever achieve its end, nor am I convinced that abolition of the death penalty is an entirely good thing. It seems to me to be unjust to maintain a number of people who have offended against society in the most serious way possible while millions of unoffending people are living in conditions infinitely worse than those in our prisons.

If your campaign sought to ensure that the death penalty would be applied in a humane manner I would certainly support it. For very dark and unworthy reasons, however, mankind has always chosen to get rid of its criminals in inefficient, cruel and humiliating ways.

With good wishes,

Yours sincerely,

Robertson Davies

To ELISABETH SIFTON

Windhover
Caledon East
December 2, 1991

Dear Elisabeth:

Thank you so much for sending me *Crime & Punishment* and *The Brothers Karamazov** in your new translations. I read the Russians many years ago, as a young man, and have re-read them to some extent ever since, because I had a strong feeling that they *must* be better than they seemed – for to me they always seemed to be written in a fog. The translations I know best are those of Constance Garnett – whom Nabokov despises and condemns in his usual snotty manner – and Magarshack,* who may be a fine Russian scholar but who has not much sense of English style. Tolstoy seems to come better out of translation than Dostoevsky, probably because he is less rhapsodic and given to whimwhams than D. I was much impressed by Nabokov's opinion of Dostoevsky,* in his insistence that the books are shot through with "poshlust" but I always take a Nabokov opinion with plenty of salt. But now that I have grown old and am no longer hypnotized by Dostoevsky's ravings about guilt and his belief in the spiritual grandeur of whores, I see what Nab is on about; these *are* the novels of a man with a screw loose – not an epileptic, particularly, but a man obsessed with gambling, and a child-raper – apparently driven by some kinky compulsion..... Nevertheless, one cannot *not* read him, and I have always been intrigued by his assertion that he learnt much from Dickens.* What can it have been? His humour is, I suppose, Russian, and an old friend of mine – a genuine Russian count, George Ignatieff (Michael's father)* told me once that the Russians had *no* sense of humour in the English understanding of the word, whatever, and that their fun was chiefly an elaborate facetiousness. The Russians I have met are tremendous smilers and gigglers, but not really any funnier than Germans. My favourite line* in Russian literature is Vershinin's in *The Three Sisters* – "Let us philosophize for a while." Thus do they dignify their chance musings.

I welcome your translations, which I have been comparing with those I have, chiefly Magarshack's. Pevear and Volokhonsky* win hands down for literacy of English; one has not that uneasy sense of being talked to by a foreigner. And I like the Notes very much; one cannot really understand the books without such help and this is tactful, never nudging. Of course the translator of Dostoevsky has a terrible problem: Russian *is* very foreign to us; Russian attitudes, especially those of a past time, are strange indeed; and – perhaps most troublesome of all – a translation must have the quality of a foreign book without simply being bad English. (Like the translations of Dumas I read as a boy, which were full of "Figure to yourself, my old one" "It gives me furiously to think" "A thousand thunders – name of a pipe!" and kindred inanities.) It seems to me (and certainly my opinion is not very weighty) that Pevear-Volokhonsky are the best at this puzzle that I have encountered.

We come to N.Y. early in January to give tongue;* perhaps we could have lunch together?

Rob.

To CLAUDIA SADOWAY | *Claudia Sadoway was an appreciative*
                             | *reader of Davies' novels.*

Massey College
University of Toronto
December 3, 1991

Dear M⁵̇ Sadoway:

Thank you for your letter about my most recent book [*Murther & Walking Spirits*]. I note your concern as an employee of the Edmonton Public Library about the fact that I have twice in the book used the word mischievious, on pages 170 and 206. I assure you that these are not spelling errors, as you suggest, but repetition of the speech of a man who would naturally use that form. You tell me that you cannot help correcting people who use this mistaken form of speech and I am sure that you have little time for people who say "I et my dinner" or for people who say, "I had as lief go as not," but I assure you that these are direct descendants of eighteenth-century cultivated speech, and I am rather pleased to find these fossils existing still among people who have not suffered the tortures of "education."

I am sure that this will make you think that I am a very peculiar char-ACter (another eighteenth-century pronunciation which still persists with a few people), but that is the way authors are.

Yours mischievlously,

Robertson Davies

To ANN SADDLEMYER

Massey College
University of Toronto
December 12, 1991

Ann Saddlemyer (1932–), Canadian, was a professor of English and drama at the University of Toronto from 1971–95, senior fellow at Massey College from 1975–88, and its third master from 1988–95. She was a colleague and friend.

Dear Ann:

Here's a pretty kettle of fish! You, upon whom we had all relied so confidently as a Tower of Strength, suddenly brought low by a horrid illness!* Something must be done.

But what? Well, I have a number of friends who – many of them long years ago – have been stopped momentarily by your malady, and they are all in good order and doing interesting things. They simply refused to be Got Down. Indeed, I may offer myself as an example: when I was about thirty-five or so I became unwell, and was diagnosed by the medicos as having Hodgkin's Disease.* They painted a gloomy picture, with the sad smiles doctors conjure up so affectingly. I was for the High Jump. But I wouldn't have it. This was not bravery; my upper lip was in a dreadful state of liquidity. It was sheer necessity. I had a wife and children and a lot of things I wanted to do, and I simply couldn't oblige the doctors. To put it bluntly, Death was beyond my means. So what follows?

I took my own advice – and it is advice I have given to several friends who, like yourself, have had this particular kind of Nasty Knock. Of course, it wasn't really my own advice: it was some advice I had discovered years before in a translation of the counsel offered in the great medical treatise of the School of Salerne:

Use three Physicians still –
First, Doctor Quiet,
Next, Doctor Merryman,
And Doctor Diet.

I could not wholly escape the doctors; they gave me ray treatment for a year, and when I showed signs of recovery covered their tracks by saying that I must have been the victim of a mis-diagnosis. Nonsense! They had never heard of the medieval advice I have set down here. And which I now offer you. If I can be of any assistance – I have made a slight reputation as Doctor Merryman – say the word, and I'll get out my cap and bells and do my best, probably by correspondence.

With love and Christmas greetings.

Rob.

To ANN SADDLEMYER

Windhover
Caledon East
Boxing Day & The Feast of Stephen [1991]

Dear Ann:

Here I am again: Dr. Merryman, making a house call. We both send you our love and greetings for the New Year; may you see the end of all your present troubles long before the season comes round again.

On Sunday last I went to church at St. Mary Magdalene. Do you know it? It is the highest of the High Church Anglican establishments in Toronto and I have been going there at intervals since I was a schoolboy, for the splendour and magnificence of its services are a great lift to the spirits in our sometimes quotidian manner of life. This time I was delighted to find that the present Rector is an old Massey Fellow; Harold Nahabedian,* and as you divine from his name, an Armenian who has become an Anglican priest; he gave me a most friendly welcome. (How these Massey men do get around!) The church has changed greatly since my first acquaintance with it; a lot of the tinselly stuff which was High Anglican style in the early '30s has been removed, and it is now simple, clean and deeply refreshing. Why I am going on about all this is that when the Prayers for the Sick were said during Mass, I thought especially and affectionately of you, as I am sure that many of your friends have done at this season.

One of the striking things about St. Mary Mag. is the large number of black people in their congregation; like me, I suppose they like their religion with a bit of style and splendour. Why should God always be served in a cold-potatoes mode?

The week before Christmas Brenda and I gave ourselves a treat; since September we have been very much on the go, because of my latest book [Murther & Walking Spirits], and we wanted a change. So we went to New York to see the première of the first new opera the Metropolitan has mounted since 25 years. The director, Colin Graham,* is a friend of ours and he invited us to see the dress rehearsal and the opening. We were glad of the dress rehearsal, because it is an extremely complicated work, and confusing at first encounter. Title: The Ghosts of Versailles; composer John Corigliano.* The plot is of a complexity that I think dangerous in opera: the period is just after the French Revolution, and Marie Antoinette has not fully accepted her trial and execution, and her lifelong lover, Beaumarchais* (yes, the playwright) sets to work to lay her ghost by getting her to die properly. He does this by invoking all his characters from Le Nozze di Figaro and The Barber of Seville and a few from a play of his unknown to me, La Mère coupable, and they all horse around, sometimes as theatre characters and sometimes as real people; Mozart is wittily quoted in the score, as is Rossini, and there is comedy and melodrama in perplexing juxtaposition. A cast of seventy appears, headed by two Canadians:* Teresa Stratas (Marie Antoinette) and Gino Quilico (Figaro) and a lot of other astonishing and wonderful people. Colin's production was a marvel of ingenuity applied to a very recalcitrant text. The music was exciting, but did not leave much impression on the – on whatever absorbs music apart from the brain, which is a poor critic. Indeed, I am reluctantly compelled to say that it put me in mind of the old Welsh proverb – "The Devil shearing a sheep: much cry and little wool."

But it was a thrill to see a Met opening, and we sat grandly in a box – which I do not recommend for one sees much better from the body of the house. But I thought that something was demanded of our situation, so I waved at people in opposite boxes (whom I did not know from Adam) and even kissed my hand to a few pretty ladies, to give the impression that I was a grandee, much involved in opera society. My notions of opera house behaviour are strictly derived from the nineteenth century.

Having thus disported ourselves grandly, we have retired to the country for a couple of weeks. We need a rest from the activities of the past few months, during which the publishers have kept my nose to the grindstone working on behalf of my latest book. Writing books is easy work: publicizing them is ditch-digger's work, and rather igno-minious. Like Shakespeare* –

Alas! I have gone here and there
And made myself a motley to the view –

and I am bloody sick of it. However, as soon as the holiday season is over I must go again to New York, Washington and Boston and be a motley and a reader-to-the-kiddies for a while longer. After that, back to Toronto, to have an operation on my left eye: nothing tremendous, just the removal of a cataract, but it is time-taking to get the eye back to work again, and I won't be able to do much for a bit.

And so, dear friend, Dr. Merryman takes farewell of you for a

while, urging you to keep your spirits up for, as the Good Book says:*
"A merry heart doeth good like a medicine, But a broken spirit drieth
the bones."

Love and repeated good wishes for '92

Rob.

To ELLIOTT HAYES

Massey College
University of Toronto
March 11, 1992

Dear Elliott:

*Elliott Hayes (1956–94) was a Canadian
playwright and literary manager at the
Stratford Festival in Stratford, Ontario. He
had adapted Davies' novel* World of
Wonders *for the stage, and the play was
being prepared for performance from
May 16 to August 9.*

It was a delight to attend the rehearsal on Monday, and Brenda and
I were immensely refreshed by it. Inevitably we see a great deal of
friends who are growing old, like ourselves, but who seem never to
have been really young and whose moans and regrets, though genuine,
are not lifting to the spirits. So – to feel once again the excitement
and creative bustle of the theatre meant a great deal to us.

I was impressed anew by the skill with which you have captured so
much of *World of Wonders* and put it in a new form. There are things
in the book which are purely novelistic, and reflections that won't do
on stage, but you have seized all that is stageworthy, and given it a new
sort of life. You have a strong cast and reason for high hopes.

I spoke of the Magian World View* – "Everything has its astonishing, wondrous aspect, if you bring a mind to it that's really your own
– a mind that hasn't been smeared and blurred with half-understood
muck from schools, or the daily papers, or any other ragbag of reach-
me-down notions..... Phantasmagoria and dream-grotto." Perhaps
something about it might be shoe-horned into the text – especially as
you are doubtless going to use so much of the "flickering cavern-light"
in the production. There is also that observation that "We learn our

art at the price of our innocence,"* which Magnus might like to have, if it can be got in without unseemly lugging.

For some time I have been struggling to do a film treatment of *Fifth Business*, which Norman Jewison* asked me for. He thinks he might be able to get the rights away from the not very effective man who now has them. I am getting nowhere: I have no luck with trying to re-shape something I have written as a novel into another form. What would be your response if I suggested to Norman that you are a dab hand at such work, and that he might take a look at *World of Wonders* with an eye to a film? I believe he is, or was, a Board member and I know he has a warm feeling for the Festival.

We hope to get down to another rehearsal before we take off for the UK. Will of course check with you about times and suitability.

All good wishes

Rob.

To FRASER M. FELL

[Massey College
University of Toronto]
March 17, 1992

Fraser M. Fell (1928–   ), Canadian, chairman of Placer Dome Inc., was then chairman of the Committee of Management at the York Club. Davies had been a member since 1971.

[Dear Mr. Fell:]

I was sorry to see from your circular of March 3rd that we are losing Mr. Lapinski and also Raffaele,* because both of these men have been quite remarkable in establishing an excellent atmosphere in the club building. I see also that we are losing the chef, Paul Eng, and it is about this that I wanted to write to you.

The members of the York Club form a coherent group, most of whom have been aware from childhood of certain customs relating to food which are related to the seasons and to the Christian year. It would be very pleasant if the club took some recognition of this fact in its menu and I have been aware, for many years, that Mr. Eng belongs to a very different tradition. It would be agreeable, for instance, if it were possible to have pancakes on Shrove Tuesday, hot cross buns during Lent and possibly even a Simnel Cake at mid-Lent. Similarly it would be pleasant to see pumpkin pie on the menu at Michaelmas and Thanksgiving. It used to be that at the Christmas season the club served excellent mince pie, which was a fine seasonable dish, but I have not seen it now for two or three years.

I am sure you understand that I do not offer these suggestions in a cranky spirit but it does seem to me that nowadays we hear an extraordinary amount about "ethnic cuisine" and the dishes that I have mentioned above belong to the cuisine of the ethnic group to which virtually all of the members of the York Club belong. It would be a pity if we forgot about all our seasonable dishes.

I am delighted that Dan Boulton is taking on from Raffaele; he is a first-rate man and I am sure he will do an admirable job.

With good wishes,

Yours sincerely,

[Robertson Davies]

To BIRGITTA HEYMAN

Massey College
University of Toronto
April 22, 1992

Dearest Birgitta:

I am sorry you had trouble with the word "Murther" in the title of my latest book; it is simply an old spelling of Murder, and that pronunciation is still heard in Ireland; I used it because that is the way it is spelled in the quotation from which the title is taken. . . .

How tedious it is to grow old! I have been having a lot of work done on my teeth recently, and it is a nuisance. But as I am unquestionably getting old, I am trying to do a few things about it, and recently, on Brenda's strong advice, I bought a stationary bicycle and ride on it every day for about twenty minutes. It has handlebars that move back and forth, so that it gives me quite a good all-over workout. I like it because I really hate games and running and all that boring stuff, and this gives me the exercise I need fairly painlessly.

You speak of having "queer" winter weather; so have we. For most of the winter not much snow but intense cold; then, during March, heavy rains and ice storms that are very hard on the trees, tearing off big branches and carrying them long distances – very dangerous. We wonder if we are ever going to get any sun. Our daughter Miranda writes from England about daffodils and tulips and wonderful warm days, and we wonder what has happened. We go to England next weekend, for three weeks. The first week we shall spend motoring in Wales, because I have not been there for years, and we both love it. Then briefly to Oxford and on to London to see friends and see the theatre, and with any luck to have no work to do. But I shall have to sneak in and out of London without letting my publisher know, because he always wants me to do publicity jobs, which I really hate. I am beginning to think that I do not give a damn if I sell any more books or not – which I suppose is a sign of old age. But as for *writing* books – ah, that is something else! I cannot keep from doing it and next autumn I shall begin another novel [*The Cunning Man*] which is taking shape in my head at present – and as happens every time, I think it will be the best yet! For the past few months I have been writing a lot of ephemeral stuff – lectures and articles, and I want to get down to a solid piece of work.

I was fascinated to hear about your Club of friends who have been together for 46 years. How wonderful to keep friendships for so long! One of the things I have never been very good at is friendship. I have lots of friends, but they are not really intimate; that is to say, I do not think I could go to them if I got into real trouble, or met with a really desolating sorrow; they would help me, of course, but it would not be a close thing. I suppose this is part of what one must pay for a really happy marriage. And it is part of being a writer, as well. One becomes very fond of people, but never uncritically so, and in real friendship I do not imagine that there can be much criticism. *L'amitié est l'amour sans ailes*, says the French proverb, but I have never found that it is wholly true. . . .

Once again, dear Birgitta, I send you my love and every kind thought. Do write again when you feel like it, for your letters are always a joy. I always remember you exactly as you were when first I saw you, and as I am beginning to look more and more like the Apostle Paul after a bad encounter with the Romans, that is deeply refreshing.

Love,

Rob.

To DEREK HOLMAN

Massey College
University of Toronto
April 28, 1992

Derek Holman was writing the music and Davies the libretto for the oratorio Jezebel: The Golden Tale of Naboth and his Vineyard, and of King Ahab and his Wicked Queen. *(See 1 Kings 16 and 21, and 2 Kings 9.) It was performed by six principals, the Toronto Mendelssohn Choir, and the Toronto Symphony in Roy Thomson Hall on June 3, 1993.*

Dear Derek:

Here is the additional material that you called for and, as always, it is open to discussion and revision. It is all as you required except possibly the aria for Jehu, which is more in the nature of a song than a section of scripture. It seemed to me that it would lighten the character of Jehu which is a bit heavy as matters stand and would get away from the insistent praising of God, of which hearers – and I suspect God – get tired. I have also enclosed a new final chorus which allows all the principal singers, except Elijah, to have a say and gives at the end the kind of rowdy Anglican whoop-up which is almost obligatory for oratorios.

As I told you, I am going away on Saturday and will be in the U.K. until the end of May, but you told me that you also were going away so any discussion about this will have to wait until we can get together again, but I gather that there is still time.

If you want to assure your immortal fame why don't you do an oratorio based on C. G. Jung's superb book, *Answer to Job*, in which Job gives God a piece of his mind for having treated him so frivolously. The Time Spirit calls aloud for this and a really good new oratorio which rocked God back on his heels would be very much to the modern taste. You might try this on Nicki [Goldschmidt];* it will make his hair stand on end. . . .

Yours sincerely,

Rob . . . .

To NICHOLAS PENNELL

Windhover
Caledon East
August 2, 1992

> *Nicholas Pennell (1939–95) was the English actor who played Magnus Eisengrim in Elliott Hayes' adaptation of* World of Wonders *at the Stratford Festival. He acted at Stratford every season from 1972 through 1994.*

Dear Nicholas:

How good of you to send us flowers – quite needless but it is the needless courtesies in life that give the most pleasure. It was a very *great* pleasure to see you at dinner because as we said we have seen you so often over the years and admired you as a true theatre artist – not one of the personality-boys – and wanted to know you. But one does not like to intrude and fans, though welcome, can be exhausting. But it gave us a chance to thank you for your fine work in *World*

of Wonders; how often does an author see a character of his creation brought to a different sort of life with such truth to the original? WOW has been a thrill for me, because for so long I was a playwright (17 plays) without success, my peak being a Broadway failure* long, long ago. But now, vicariously and through Elliott's imaginative work, I have a vicarious success, to which you have contributed finely.....
So, again our thanks, and we hope we may meet with you again.

Rob. Davies

To SARA E. DUMONT

> Sara E. Dumont was an appreciative reader in New Haven, Connecticut.

Massey College
University of Toronto
August 5, 1992

[Dear Mˢ· Dumont:]

Thank you for your letter of January 22nd. I know that Miss Whalon has written to you apologizing for the delay but it did not reach me until July 28th. I am delighted that you get so much pleasure from my books and am sorry and apologetic that I cannot live forever and go on writing them, but I am sure you will understand that I am by no means unique in this respect. As for taking good care of my health, I do that, but health sometimes has a nasty way of ignoring one's kind attention.

One of the things that keeps me going, however, is kind letters like yours and again I thank you very much for it.

Yours sincerely,

[Robertson Davies]

To BIRGITTA HEYMAN

Windhover
Caledon East
August 24, 1992

Dear Birgitta:

The enclosed program offers an excuse for my delay in answering your last, splendid letter. To say that I have been *busy* with the play [*World of Wonders*] is not quite true for I have not taken a direct part in getting it on the stage. But its production involved me in a surprising amount of work, including two lectures that I gave about the problems involved in making a novel into a play; they were very well attended, to my surprise, because I did not think people would be greatly interested in such a subject, but they were and the questions they asked afterward were searching and probing in a surprising and complimentary way. . . .

Your letter gave me a good deal to think about. You are surprised that I say that I am a monarchist. I do not think you would be surprised if you had been living on this continent during the last few months. The Americans are about to elect a new President, and the television and the newspapers are full of the most nauseating stuff as the two opposing parties lie and throw dirt at one another. They declare that Ronald Reagan was a great man, that George Bush personally brought about the fall of the Soviet Empire, and even that the abominable Richard Nixon was a person to whom every American owes a debt of gratitude! This is what makes me a monarchist: a country must have some person who embodies the nation's ideal of honour and decency, and a king or queen does that not because of outstanding personal qualities but because of a myth and a long line of descent which embodies a nation's pride and ideals.

This happens at a time when we in Canada are having a series of conferences* among the prime ministers of all our ten provinces and also the Dominion Government, about the revision of our Constitution. Reform of the Senate, a new deal for Quebec as a special province of French-speaking people, a greater measure of self-government for our Indians and Inuit all have to be talked over and decisions reached. And this has been done with great difficulty and endless hours of discussion, and not one ugly word has been spoken, nobody has been called a crook, and although feeling has been hot, tempers have been kept in check. That's Canada, and although people call us dull and dowdy and worse than the Swiss, it is infinitely preferable to the horrible American way, with its hysteria and vulgarity. I watched the TV when George Bush made his speech accepting the presidential nomination. At the end of it, 220,000 red white and blue balloons were released over the huge auditorium, as Bush posed with his wife and his children and grandchildren as the Dear Old Daddy of his people. I nearly threw up! But I liked the balloons; I thought that they were symbolic of all the gas that is being released in American speeches at present.

This is very worrying to us in Canada, because whether we like it or not we are dragged at the American chariot wheel in many important matters, and they interfere in our affairs in the most crass fashion, not coarsely but simply because they don't know what they are doing. Quite recently an American bank decided to open a branch in Toronto, and had almost done so when they were told that no bank may be opened in Canada without government permission, because the government stands behind all our banks, so that people cannot be ruined if a bank fails – and so banks must be very careful not to fail or somebody will go to jail. The Americans were furious! They had never heard of such a thing! But they had to withdraw.

Next month I have to join in a public discussion of North American Culture (what a pompous title!) with Carlos Fuentes,* the Mexican writer (and a very fine one). Both Canada and Mexico know what it is like to live side by side with the USA, and to be taken for granted by its government and its people. I expect we shall have a lively time and I look forward greatly to meeting Fuentes.

So your farmers have been complaining about the dry weather? I wish we could send you some of our rain; this has been the wettest and coldest summer in a very long time and *our* farmers are complaining that the crops are rotting in the ground because the fields are too wet for harvesting. But it has been wonderful for the trees. Our small trees have done marvellously well, and our mature trees are still as green as they were in June, instead of getting on toward autumn colour.

I was greatly interested to hear about your grandson Niklas [Engdahl];* he must have been astonished by the USA. So he has decided that you are the world's best grandmother? That is quite a title. Brenda greatly enjoys being a grandmother but I sometimes wonder if I am not rather a disappointment as a grandfather; I find it so hard to talk to very young people; all I can think of to do is to give them money and books; I have just bought a really big dictionary for my eldest grandson [Christopher Cunnington] who sets out on university life this autumn. He wants to study, of all things, mathematics! God be with him; I was always a perfect fool at math.

Do write again soon, and I promise not to be so long replying. Next Friday I shall be 79! God, how awful! But just last week my brother [Arthur] was 89, so perhaps I have a few years left.

Love to you and all your family,

Rob.

To GORDON AND HELEN ROPER

Oaklands
Toronto
August 27, 1992

Dear Gordon (& Helen, of course):

What's all this I hear about being in hospital?* And you have not summoned Doctor Merryman? How can you expect to return to full health if you are so neglectful?.... But I hear from a well-informed source (M.W.) that you are on the mend and will probably be home by the time this reaches you. For which God be praised!

Moira [Whalon] keeps me abreast of Peterborough news, though my work never summons me in that direction. Indeed, this past year it has been summoning me to the west of Ontario, because the Stratford Festival mounted a dramatized version of my novel *World of Wonders* and performed it marvellously, to the great satisfaction of its audiences. The adaptation was done by a very able young man named Elliott Hayes, who took the book apart and reassembled it, leaving out whatever would not have worked on stage or what might seem to cloud or obstruct the story. It was a great lesson to me in what is dramatically usable and what is not. I think the great defect of my own plays, in the days when I used to write plays, was to try to get too much into the stage form of my story, so that they were rather over-written. Hayes kept firmly to the story of Magnus Eisengrim, though now and again he allowed one of his characters to fire off a one-liner that did not precisely fit into the dialogue, because it brought a laugh, or made the audience sit up. And sit up it did, for within the first ten minutes of the play the homosexual rape of little Paul was shown on stage, and it was done with so much discretion that the audience felt pity for the child, more than horror at what they were watching. A few people walked out, but that is rather good publicity than otherwise, as they say to their friends that the play is "dirty," and the friends rush to see it. The production also included a good many of Eisengrim's magical illusions, including the Brazen Head of Friar Bacon, which was tremendous. But I think the best trick of all was at the very end of the play, when the man who wants to make a television show of Eisengrim's life decides not to do so; Eisengrim takes his notes from him, throws them into the air, they float upward toward the ceiling of the theatre – and vanish! Brenda and I enjoyed it hugely, and were very grateful to the fine cast who gave it the most flattering sort of attention.

However, I took no part in the adaptation; the years have taught me not to meddle with other people's work, even when I might appear to have an excuse to do so. . . .

I wish I could say that we have been living quietly, but it would not be true. We yearn for quiet, but there seem to be so many things to which one cannot, for various reasons, say No. One of the foremost of these reasons is that in Canada at present there is a very strong feeling that anybody connected with the world of writing must be eager to engage in all sorts of political action; but even more pressing is the demand of young writers that they should be encouraged and boosted, even by people who know nothing about them, and as Moira will tell you I get far too many unsolicited manuscripts (is there such a thing as a *solicited* manuscript?) from people who have written something and think I could get it published. If the manuscripts showed any hint of promise, I could suggest that they talk to an agent, but the quality is drastic and the presentation to any possible reader is unappetizing. I am sure that when I rebuff these poor souls* they think I am jealous of their talent and am trying to keep them down, because their self-esteem is in direct contradiction of their abilities. Why do so many people think they can write? People are quite willing to admit that they have no talent for painting, or writing music, can't sing, can't dance – but the world is full of those who are convinced that they are splendid writers. It takes a lot of time and postage to get free of them. . . .

So – a quick recovery to you, and love from us both to you and Helen. The autumn colour cannot be far away. That should put you on your feet.

Rob.

PS: Judith Grant seems no nearer to producing her book. But I can read her mind: she wants me to die so she can end it properly. I hope to disappoint her.

To BASCOVE

Massey College
University of Toronto
September 15, 1992

Bascove is an artist known only by that name. A Jungian, she created distinctive cover designs which she describes as "woodcuts prints handcolored with watercolor and pencil" for the American Viking hardcover editions and Penguin paperbacks of Davies' books from 1981 on. She lives in New York.

Dear Bascove:

It was kind of you to send me the handsome artist's proof of your design for the jacket of the complete Cornish Trilogy. I am having it framed so that I can put it up over my typewriter and see it every day because, not only is it a very fine thing in itself, but it is linked for me with the picture which provided your inspiration; that is The Librarian, by Arcimboldo.* A large reproduction of that hangs over the door of my study and the sympathy between the two creates what I think of as an excellent literary joke.

My wife and I are both great admirers of Arcimboldo and I think that we have seen all of his pictures that now hang in European galleries. Also we have in the kitchen of our flat here in Toronto large reproductions of his four pictures of the seasons, all represented in fruits and flowers. I was delighted many years ago when my small grandson, who was about 5, pointed to the beautiful picture of Spring and said, "That's me"; and then, pointing to the hideous face of Winter, composed chiefly of knotted wood, said with great firmness, "And that's you."

Again thank you for your gift and I hope that we shall work together frequently in the future.

With good wishes,

Yours sincerely,

Robertson Davies

To HORACE W. DAVENPORT

Windhover
Caledon East
October 25: 1992

Dear Horace:

   Enclosed are a few verses, inspired by yours,* which I thought very
funny, but with the wry undertone that distinguished all your pieces
for the Long Christmas Dinner Society. I think of it with tenderness,
for it was one of the mainstays of our Oxford days, and we enjoyed
it in a manner which has almost wholly gone out of fashion it seems
to me – we enjoyed it simply for itself, for the happiness of the hours,
and without any ulterior motive or "good cause" or anything of that
sort in mind. It seems now that pleasure has always to be hitched to
the heavy wagon of Improvement, or some Good Cause, and of any
money that is spent, some portion has to be snatched for the Poor
and Needy (after the Government has had its grab).
   This has been rather a week. On Monday last (19th Oct.) I had my
eye operation, and it was as easy as anything of that kind can be, even
though my nervous temperament can make a drama out of cutting my
nails. (You know that the Welsh are reputedly the worst patients in the
world: they go into a hospital certain that they will never come out
alive.) But unhappily I was in a ward where there was a sneeping* draft,
and I had only one much-washed, thin blanket, and caught a chill, and
have had 'flu ever since; because of my asthma my doctor* gets very
shirty about chills, and immediately prescribed something called
Erythromycin, which charged toward my intestinal tract and made
great work, so that I was driven to have six great bowel movements in
thirty hours. For whom do they devise this stuff? People with granite
tripes? I have put it behind me, and am recovering under a cure suggested by a Scots doctor [Robert Laidlaw MacMillan]* who is an old
friend: a tablespoon of whisky every four hours. He says it does all that
any wonder drug can do, and won't kill you, which a wonder drug

may. But the eye is tremendous: the day after the operation I could read all but the last two lines on the doctor's illuminated chart, and he [John S. Speakman]* declared it "an exemplary success." And for the first time in two years I am free from shadows of things that aren't there, flashes of light from no source, and ghosts of God-Knows-Who appearing wherever there are shadows. All done with mirrors; for my dr. says that cataract acts somewhat like a mirror in certain lights.

On November 25 I am asked to speak to St. Catherine's Night at Balliol, and what do you think I am going to talk about? The LCDS, and your name will resound in the history of Elias Cabot. Have you ever heard from them? Last time I was there I told them you were too important a man to lose, and to make up the quarrel, whatever it was. If they haven't responded, I'll nudge them again.

We were deeply worried about Inge, and I think Brenda has written to her; it is splendid to hear that she is home again. Give her our love and assurance of our continuing goodwill (not Christian Science, but not trivial either, I think). Whatever else is to be said, I have said in the rhymes.

Rob.

To JOHN JULIUS NORWICH

Massey College
University of Toronto
November 3, 1992

Dear John Julius:

How very kind of you to send us *The Normans In Sicily*; we had already acquired a copy, and sent one to Brenda's sister [Maisie Drysdale] in Australia, but an inscribed copy is a treasure – and a fine book. A splendid story and you tell it admirably. How can it have gone so long without being better known? I suppose there was some pedantic awareness of it, but that is not at all the same thing. I have recently been taking a peep into Greene's *History** once again; it is admirable, but you write better.

We have seen you several times on the telly, in your Venice series. Good as it was, we wished you had been given more time to explain and introduce; there was rather a lot of atmospheric photography of waves in canals, and Murano in fog, and we would rather have had you talking about – well, what about Casanova, who always seems to me more Venetian than anything else. His Memoirs, by the way, I think too little known. So we have been very much aware of you, what with Venice and the Normans in Sicily. What a nailer you are!

Have no fear: Canada replied with a sharp No to the referendum,* and I am convinced for one excellent reason – the scheme as presented was too vague, but it was clear that it meant robbing the central government of too many powers, to put them in the hands of the provincial governments, who are understandably jealous and greedy. In a huge country like Canada, with a small population, a strong central government is absolutely obligatory, or we shall fall to bits. Nobody except a few half-wits want to lose Quebec, or deny her anything reasonable: nor does anyone of any intelligence want to continue our silly deal with the Indians and Inuit, who are capable of running their own show. (Though, like the tribes in Africa, money intended for the group tends to end up in the hands of a few lawyers and populist crooks.) But our Prime Minister [Brian Mulroney], who is a man of remarkable opacity of understanding coupled with the vanity of an opera star, has made a proper mess of things, and must go. The misery of it is that we have nobody of outstanding abilities to take his place. All three of our parties are suffering from a paucity of talent. A shame, because in our time we have found some men of great capacity to direct us.

The Booker: hmmm. Did I tell you that I was asked at the beginning of this year [if] I would head the selection committee? I moved with the speed of lightning to say no. That way madness lies. More and more I think that literary prizes are impossible things. Did you see the editorial in *The Times** about the Nobel? Very sound. The Nobel is becoming "politically correct" to a dangerous degree. I, by the way, was on the short list, as leaked to the press by the Swedish news agency, one suspects with collusion from the Academy. I had no reason at all to suspect that I would get it, being solvent, a citizen of an unfashionable and solvent country, of whitish complexion, and as a writer moderately comprehensible. But the foufara here was unpleasant, as the papers were already asking me what I would do with the lolly. Sartre was right;* one should not become a public monument. . . .

Brenda and I are going to be in London for a few days after November 22, and would dearly love to have you and Mollie as guests at dinner. I shall phone you when we arrive and see if anything can be arranged. We propose the Athenaeum, simply because it is the only London club we have, and despite the rude jeers of John Saumarez Smith, the grub is not bad (a rudish plenty, but rude in Greek, which makes a difference) and the wines are very far from rude. But if you choke at the notion, we can go elsewhere. Would you like the Penguins, Peter [Carson] and Eleo [Gordon],* if we can get them? I ask tentatively, because one never knows just how things stand between an author and one of his publishers. (Penguin did you proud on the Normans.) The last time they came to us at the Ath., their car was transfixed, or put in the cruel boot, or otherwise immobilized. What *do* they call those nasty things?

I *do* hope we can see you.

Love to you both & please forgive a messily proof-read screed in reply to your impeccable typing.

Rob. . . .

To *THE NEW YORKER*

Massey College
University of Toronto
December 15, 1992

Dear Sirs:

Will you please stop sending me cute notes asking why I have not renewed my subscription. I did indeed renew it in October, for two years, so will you now stop wasting time and postage on this matter.

For several months past you have been sending me three copies of every issue. Although I am happy to re-direct two of them to Old Folks' Homes and asylums for circulation managers who have lost their minds, I assure you that I really only need one copy. It will save you money if you will look into this matter.

Yours sincerely,

Robertson Davies

To RICHARD DAVIS

Windhover
Caledon East
December 27, 1992

Dear Rick:

Many thanks for your very kind Christmas greetings and the books; the one translated from the French* is truly horrifying. How many such unfortunate people are born now, do you suppose, when pre-birth examination can reveal so much? I can remember side-shows at fairs which exhibited such people – though not the worst,

I think – but they are long gone. Hunchbacks, dwarfs – hardly to be seen, but when I was a boy, living in the Ottawa Valley, they were common enough, and had a rotten life, I fear.

We spent a very quiet Christmas, because on December 3 I disgraced myself by having a heart attack, and being rushed off to the Toronto General, where they made some mistakes in examining me and there was some confusion as a result. But it is all sorted out now; the doctor* says it was *angina*, and I seem to be recovering satisfactorily, but I am not anxious to do it again in a hurry. I loathe hospitals; I have a real Welsh conviction that if once you are put in one, your chances of getting out are very slim.

I am beginning a new novel [*The Cunning Man*], as I think Moira [Whalon] has told you, and if I may I should like to turn to you for some expert advice. Would you like a note at the beginning saying: "I am indebted to Dr. Richard Davis for medical advice"? I will tell you what my problem is: I want to make use of a poison which is virtually instantaneous in its effect, and so far I have not been able to run one down. The situation is this: an old priest – over 80 – is celebrating Communion in his Anglican Church. As usual, he breaks the wafer and eats it, is overcome, and falls dead – or so near death that in the confusion nobody does the right thing, if indeed there is a right thing, and he dies. The wafer has been poisoned, but again in the confusion nobody finds it out. Now – what was the poison? It has to be something that the murderer – not an expert person – could get hold of pretty easily. My best solution so far is that the wafer has been poisoned with a strong extract of yew-twigs; they poison cattle, and if the extract was strong enough, they might poison an old man. But apparently it takes half an hour: in a man of 80 would it work more speedily? But fast enough? I can't tell, but perhaps you have an opinion, or some suggestion. Could we get together for lunch later in January, and talk about it? Meanwhile, keep it under your hat, or under the seal of your Aesculapian Oath, or whatever, as I don't want somebody else to pinch my plot.

We are in the country, and it is very beautiful. I sometimes wonder if Canada is not the most beautiful country in the world, when you get outside the towns. Friends who have visited us from all over are always astonished at how lovely it is, at all seasons except Spring, which is decidedly not our best.

Every good wish to you and your family for 1993

Robertson Davies

To GREG GATENBY

Massey College
University of Toronto
June 22, 1993

Greg Gatenby (1950–   ), Canadian, is the artistic director of the Harbourfront Reading Series in Toronto. He had printed Davies' playful speech at the Harbourfront Tribute for him in 1989 as a pamphlet, intending to sell signed copies to raise funds for the Series.

Dear Greg:

You are a merciless man and God will punish you in the next world. Have you any idea how much time it takes to sign 150 copies of anything, to say nothing of numbering them? I do not know how much time it will be but it will be quite a while and when the things are ready I will let you know.

Of course the Government is cutting the grant to Harbourfront; it is their well understood policy to quench every artistic venture in this province, hoping to achieve that end before they are defeated in the next election.

With good wishes – though I don't know why considering your unbearable cruelty toward me, I am

Yours sincerely,

Rob.

To ROGER AND FLORENCE
GALE

Roger Gale (1924–   ), Canadian, was
building superintendent at Massey
College from 1962 until he retired in
1989.

Massey College
University of Toronto
August 18, 1993

Dear Friends:

Please accept warmest congratulations from my wife and myself on your Fiftieth Wedding Anniversary. I am sorry that we are unable to be with you but you will understand that as we are quite a distance in the country it is not easy to get in on a Saturday.

Massey College, at its beginning, would not have become what it did without Roger's assistance and I very well remember the day when Colin Friesen* told me that, after having given his advice and help in getting started, he [Gale] decided to leave his work down town and join us at the College. It was, he said, because he had been so deeply impressed by the building. Since that time the building has cast its particular spell over several hundred people but I do not think that any of them could say that they had done more to establish the true quality of Massey College than Roger. His impeccable superintendence of the building and his recognition of and defence of everything that made the College good and individual were an enormous support to me and to everyone else connected with the place. Unquestionably anyone who is curious to know who the makers of Massey College were could not omit the name of Roger Gale. The Massey Foundation did a fine and generous thing in founding the College, but it had to be *made* by the devoted work of a body of people who put it above all other considerations, and among them Roger played a splendid part.

We send warm congratulations to you and to your children on this happy occasion and hope that there will be many happy anniversary celebrations in the future.

Yours sincerely

Robertson Davies

To BIRGITTA HEYMAN

Windhover
Caledon East
November 29: 93

Dear Birgitta:

It is a long time – a very long time indeed – since I wrote to you, and I have heard nothing from you for about a year. I hope that this does not mean that things are going badly for you; you have spoken often of your daughter's illness, and I most sincerely hope that is not darkening your life. Don't write if your hands are full and you don't feel like it, but sooner or later give me some news of yourself.

My news is chiefly concerned with growing old. But does that mean that I am sinking into an armchair, dozing and thinking of times past? It most certainly does not! I do not think I have ever been busier in my life. I am not looking for things to do. *They* are looking for *me*. I seem to make a great many speeches, and they all take time to prepare and I do not become any less nervous as I grow older. Since last summer it seems almost as if I had never shut up. But the last two ventures were entertaining. I went to Baltimore to the Johns Hopkins Medical Center, where they were having a series of meetings about old age; they asked me to speak about creativity in old age,* and as I am now eighty, and still working steadily, I was assumed to know something about it. What I told them was simply that if you have never been creative in your younger days you must not expect to write, or paint, or compose music simply because you have grown old. But if you have done these things when young, you will probably go on till you drop. Who ever heard of a "retired" painter?

The other affair, which I enjoyed greatly, was in New York, where the Morgan Library asked me to speak about Dickens' *A Christmas Carol*. It is a book I have loved since childhood and I was happy to say my say about it. The Morgan Library has Dickens' original manuscript of the book, which was the reason to celebrate the 150th anniversary. I spoke twice, and had large audiences, and loved every minute of it. Part of the fun was a Dickensian Christmas Dinner, at which we ate fried oysters, turkey with chestnut stuffing, and plum pudding with brandy, all washed down with some splendid wines and ending with hot spiced wine – which I avoided as I learned long ago that it is for younger drinkers than I.

It is some time since Brenda and I were in New York and we agreed that we would be perfectly happy never to go there again. There are lots of cities I should love to visit again – Rome, Lisbon, Vienna, Stockholm, Brussels – but New York is so noisy and angry that it is not a pleasure to visit it.

I look back over this letter with shame! What a lot of bad typing and misspelling! My typing grows worse every day and my secretary has her work cut out to make sense of it. I am working hard to finish a new book – before Christmas if I can – and the typescript is horrible.

This brings you all good wishes, and anxious hopes that you are not having a spell of bad luck.

Love from us both –

Rob.

Brenda Davies papers

SECTION
VIII

JANUARY 1994–OCTOBER 1995 – *THE CUNNING MAN* PUBLISHED; PLANNING OF
THE NEXT NOVEL BEGUN

he Cunning Man was published in Canada in September 1994, in the United States the following February, and in Britain in April, a rhythm which made for a protracted period of publicity. This interval was made more trying by the publication of my biography *Robertson Davies: Man of Myth*, about which Davies had powerful and mixed feelings. By April 1995, he (who was to turn 82 that August) began to mention ideas for a novel to complete the last trilogy, though in the end he made only a few pages of notes.

He continued to work at a pace which a much younger man would have found taxing. Apart from the readings, speeches, interviews, and travel associated with the publication of *The Cunning Man*, he continued to write articles, tributes, forewords for books, and speeches. He also agreed to prepare a substantial entry on the actor-manager Henry Irving for the new *Dictionary of National Biography*. And he gleefully undertook the writing of a libretto for a full-length opera on the subject of Apuleius' *The Golden Ass*.

He did one thing which made many aspects of his life as an author easier: at the beginning of 1994 he hired his daughter Jennifer Surridge as his research assistant. Nonetheless, his general health continued to worsen. In April and May 1995, home from the English publicity tour for *The Cunning Man,* he was slow to recover from a session of influenza and asthma. New tests revealed a leaky heart valve. As the medications he was given made him feel dull and shaky, he was delighted to be allowed to stop taking almost all of them that summer and to begin to feel himself again. But, late that October, back from speaking at Princeton, about to create a new ghost story for Massey College's annual Christmas celebration, still writing letters to readers in which he declared that he was "busy at the moment writing another novel," he contracted pneumonia. Before he recovered, he suffered a stroke, lapsed into a coma, and died on December 2.

To JOHN J. ESPEY

Massey College
University of Toronto
Feb. 8, 1994

Dear John:

The University of California Press has sent me a copy of *Minor Heresies** and a handsome volume it is, splendidly adorned with a poignant portrait of the author as a young missionary on the jacket. I took great pleasure in the illustrations, which gave reality to the mental pictures I had formed so many years ago when at Oxford you talked of your Chinese childhood. The compound seemed much bigger and less Somerset-Maugham in character than I had imagined it. But the surprise was the picture of your parents! I had imagined your father as a man of Jove-like proportions and very stern of mien. But your sister was much as I had imagined her, and looks (as a child) full of the devil. I hope the book has a large and appreciative reception; it tells of a kind of life that is rarely encountered in memoirs or fiction; missionaries are either made into figures of fun or denounced as crypto-sadists and child-abusers. (And speaking of that, isn't the R/C. Church taking a shellacking in these degenerate days? Here in Canada the Christian Brothers* are catching it from all quarters; they seem to have been so busy with the Sin of Sodom that I wonder how they found time to sow error and superstition, which was of course their principal *raison d'être*.)

Your Christmas circular told a terrifying story. Brenda and I read it with gasps of astonishment. What a moment it must have been when the wind changed and the fire took a turn and spared your house! I'll bet *that* shook your nullifidian soul, you unbeliever, you! California, which we are apt to regard as the Earthly Paradise (climate division), has certainly been getting its lumps. We read of your adventures while reading letters and reports from Brenda's sister in Australia, where they have been having horrendous forest-fires. Maisie (she is very grandly Lady Drysdale, being the widow of a well-known Australian painter, Sir Russell Drysdale) writes us that she had the car at the door, loaded with all the valuables (chiefly pictures) she could cram into it, ready to take off at the first signal from the fire-fighters; the fire came within a couple of miles of her house and played the devil with one of the suburbs of Sydney.

Reading of these terrors, we feel very lucky, though we have been having the worst winter since the 1920s, it appears. Weeks of sub-zero weather, storms, ice and every wintry delight. All there is to be done is to stay at home, build large wood fires and read Victorian novels. I have been reading *Anna Karenina* and I am no longer of an age when I have to be impressed and bend the knee to that pompous old fraud Tolstoy. *Anna* is a very great novel *in spite of* the facts that (1) It is too long by half, being padded out with the sophomoric reflections of Lyovin [Levin in many translations] about farming and the moral grandeur of the peasants; (2) Anna and Vronsky are marvellously described but they tend to be bores although Anna is a beauty and kind, and Vronsky is a gentleman and brave, because neither of them has enough brains to butter a biscuit – though in this they are very accurate portraits of people who have more emotion than gumption; (3) Tolstoy has not a crumb of humour and none of his people have any. A Russian friend of mine [George Ignatieff]* said to me "Russians have no humour – only a sort of facetiousness – but they imitate English humour as they imitate French taste." I maintain against all defiance that a writer without humour is not truly *great* because his insight (and Tolstoy is full of insight) lacks a dimension that Shakespeare (whom Tolstoy with Russian effrontery called a barbarian*) possessed and which enlarged his tragic perception. You know why; I don't have to enlarge on it.

Tolstoy put an awful spoke in the wheel of Brenda's parents.* They were (a) a Cambridge don (mathematics) utterly impractical, and (b) an Australian girl from a rich family who had never cooked anything or made a dishrag. These two, united in high-mindedness, obeyed Tolstoy's advice to get back to nature, and went apple-orcharding in Tasmania, and of course the marriage smashed to bits as he could not grow apples and she could not slave in a hovel with no running water and of course no plumbing. Brenda and I played a part in this mess because, twenty-five years later, we brought them together again and they were able to laugh about what a pair of Tolstoy-led simpletons they had been.

Tolstoy also wished upon Canada the Doukhobors, a primitive rabble of peasant Believers who were transferred here because even Russia could not stand them. They Believe, but not in Education (they burn schools) nor in taxes (they won't pay 'em) nor in any sort of national service. Tolstoy has much to answer for. But that is enough about him. . . .

Our best to you both.

Rob.

To HORACE W. DAVENPORT

Massey College
University of Toronto
Feb 8. 1994

Dear Horace:

At last I am able to sit down and address you with a mind that is not continually hopping sideways to look at some problem related to my book [*The Cunning Man*]. It has been many weeks, and you have been most considerate in respecting my silence, as you knew I was in an author's hysteria. But at last the thing is finished, or rather I should say that it has come as near completion as I can bring it. I have never written a book that troubled me more. Not, I think, because it is greatly different from what I have written before: indeed, I seem to be one of those authors who writes the same book over and over again. But why not? J. B. Priestley once complained to me that painters were allowed to paint the same subject until they thought they had got it right, or said all they had to say about it – but an author who repeated or took another look at the same subject was risking sharp critical rebuke. So I have been writing another of my *Bildungsromanen** and I think it will be my last novel. The reason it has cost me so much anxiety is simply old age: I cannot do the job now as readily as I did twenty-five years ago, and there is no great mystery in that.

But it is completed, and now begins the long wait until the publishers have done their work, and it should be ready for the bookshops some time in September.

Work complicated, as always at this time of year, by illness – mine and other people's. . . .

A few weeks ago Brenda and I took on our second daughter Jennifer [Surridge] as what I call on my tax return "a research assistant," which means that she does a lot of that sort of thing for me – filing, sorting, getting rid of junk, etc. – but also assists Brenda who is trying to get her papers (she is a compulsive saver of papers and has letters and whatnot from away back) into some sort of order. She is a whizz at such work, having been for many years the business manager of a small company, and what seems impossibly difficult for us is easy for her. She gave up her business job because the situation for small business in Canada at present is very difficult, and she did not want to go on denying creditors down one phone while nagging debtors down another.

The result is that work is a great deal simpler in one respect, and rather dismal in another, because I have now to try to get my affairs in order so that I shall not leave a mess when I die – which I have no intention of doing for a while, but which must eventually come about. . . .

When last you wrote you and Inge were having an especially thin time of it.* May I hope that things have improved? Do let me know and let us resume a correspondence which has been interrupted for too long..... As always, love to both of you, in which Brenda shares.

Rob.

P.S. Last week I had a talk with my grandson Piers [Cunnington], who tells me he "needs time to find himself" so is taking a semester off from the university to ski in British Columbia, where perhaps his true self will emerge from a cave.* I do not understand the modern young (Octogenarian Cliché No. 107086789): I never lost myself that I can remember, though there were times when I would have given much to get away from myself.

To THE EDITOR OF *THE GLOBE AND MAIL**

Windhover
Caledon East
[February 19, 1994]

[Sir:]

Pierre Berton, in your issue of Feb. 19, comments on an article that says "it is difficult to think of a Canadian writer of any prominence who at any time did not worship at the altar of funds," and Mr. Berton puts forward his own name and that of Farley Mowat as two to whom this comment does not apply. Permit me to offer my name as a third; I have never applied for a grant during 50 years as a writer.

Many writers who do apply for grants, to the Canada Council in particular, ask me to write in support of their applications, and in doing so they often use a form of words which puzzles me: they say they want money "to buy time" in which to write. There is no such thing as "buying time"; we all have whatever time there is to use as best serves us. For many years, when my earnings from my writing were small, I employed eight hours a day working at a job to support myself and my family; another eight hours, more or less, I slept; of the remaining eight hours I used two or three to write, for I am not one of those who can write for several hours at a time with any assurance of producing anything that would be publishable. I suppose the people who ask me to help them "buy time" know what they are doing, and I envy them their ability to write effectively for long hours. But when, I wonder, do they meet people, and take part in the ordinary concerns of life, which a writer must do if he or she is to have anything to write about? A job is wonderfully helpful in priming the creative pump.

[Yours faithfully,]

Robertson Davies

To JAMES CARLEY AND ANN
HUTCHISON

Windhover
Caledon East
April 22, 1994

James Carley (1946–   ) is a Canadian professor of medieval studies. He was abroad for a term as academic visitor at the London School of Economics. His wife, Ann Hutchison (1941–   ), is a Canadian medievalist and university teacher. James had been a junior fellow at Massey College from 1971–74, and he and Ann had been friends of the Davieses since the early 1980s.

Dear James & Ann:

Home at last and the delights of travel safely behind me for a while, and so I am able to write to you with a composed mind and the materials I am used to. I am sure you have observed how unfriendly all rented premises, hotels and other temporary accommodations are to any sort of writing, including writing letters. It is part of the mindset of landlords, in company with their conviction that nobody reads in bed, and that a forty-watt bulb in a cheap little lamp with a difficult button is all that anybody could possibly expect. Barbarians! But travellers must be content* as the Swan of Avon so despondently croaks.

The star in the crown of our visit was undoubtedly our dinner with you and the preceding visit to the MSS Dept of the British Museum. What a thrill! I was struck as near dumb as a Welshman ever gets, and had not much to say for myself about what I was shown. The alchemical MS in particular, which seemed to whisk me back into a world where all that could be said on its subject had to be disguised in a symbolism which seemed in so many cases to have taken over the reason of the alchemist and became an end in itself. I wanted to say something sensible about what I was seeing, and I gathered that neither Miss Backhouse nor Miss Jones* was especially "into" alchemy, and were inclined to take their tone from Ben Jonson.* Having got back to my books, I have found what I wanted to say in Jung,* in his splendid discussion of Goethe's *Faust* (which he called "the last and greatest work on Alchemy"). What he says is:

Goethe is really describing the experience of the alchemist who discovers that what he has projected into the retort is his own darkness, his unredeemed state, his passion, his struggles to reach the goal, i.e. to become what he really is, to fulfill the purpose for which his mother bore him and, after the peregrinations of a long life full of confusion and error, to become the *filius regius*, son of the supreme mother.

It was all there, in the beautiful, awesome manuscript, so lovingly presented, speaking of both the desire to communicate and the fear of the outcome if one succeeded. For Alchemy was, of course, a fearful heresy, and its complexity would have afforded the fierce lawyers of the Church a wonderful chance to show their quality. The rogue-alchemists of Jonson were another breed of cat.

Loved meeting the Bartons,* and delighted to find that he shared my doubts about Sam Wanamaker's Globe Theatre, which is being so much touted. But it must always be a curiosity – a museum theatre – and the *mana* of W.S. is not likely to mount from those sodden posts in the water and ennoble it.

And to dine at LSE!* Always a place of awe to me, for I have never understood economics, above the $5 level.

You treated us royal, that you did, and we bless and magnify the name of Carley!

Rob & Brenda

To HORACE W. DAVENPORT

Windhover
Caledon East
May 22, 1994

Dear Horace:

. . . It is good news that you and Inge are becoming more mobile,*
even if under restrictions. Especially that you are able to get to your
office and work in accustomed and encouraging surroundings. I envy
those people who can "write anywhere" – though I don't envy what
they write. More and more my writing needs a mass of reference books,
and I expect yours does, too. I am preparing a lecture on Lewis Carroll
and the Theatre,* and it gave me a great thrill to be able to turn up the
article he wrote on that subject *in my own library*. One cannot have
everything one needs immediately at hand, but one can at least try.

Have you ever taken a serious look at Lewis Carroll? The more I
find out about him, the odder he becomes. The oddest thing of all is
that he seems to have been, without a hint to the contrary, a *good man*
– really a Christian and a gentleman BUT, with a passion for photo-
graphing little girls naked, with their Mothers present. He would
never have made a President of the US; never dropped his pants and
demanded "oral sex" on any recorded occasion. As an author he was
a terrible fusser, worse than most of the breed, and drove his illustra-
tors almost to madness. *Hated* little boys; adored little girls. Why?
Probably sexually abused at school, as was very common in his day,
but no evidence exists. Loved the theatre and it is possible that he
became a deacon (because he had to be a clergyman or near to it to
be a don at Christ Church) but never proceeded to full ordination
because it would then have been forbidden for him to attend the
theatre, which was his passion. That, and photography..... Have you
ever read his novel *Sylvie and Bruno*, which he regarded as his finest
work? Don't; an embarrassing bore. But I am in this stuff up to my
neck and I must say enjoying it after the hassle of getting my own

book [*The Cunning Man*] ready for the press. It comes out here in September (and I shall send you a copy at once) and in New York in winter, and in London next early Spring. God knows what the outcome will be. Re-reading it I often felt that it was quite the worst novel ever written by anyone, but at my age what can you expect?

No more for the moment. But I promise that I won't be silent so long again.

Love to you both from us –

Rob.

PS: Judith Grant harasses me at least once a week about photographs.* Why is there no legal redress against literary (far worse than sexual) harassment?

To RICHARD BRADSHAW

Richard Bradshaw (1944–), English, is artistic director of the Canadian Opera Company.

Massey College
University of Toronto
June 21, 1994

Dear Mr. Bradshaw:

I am sorry to have been so long in replying to your letter of June 6th but I have been dashing about doing a great many things and am now trying to catch up. I was much interested in your suggestion that I might write an opera libretto for Jean Guillou;* I know nothing about him as a composer but I am sure you do, and if you think he is a man to write an opera that is a sufficient guarantee. There are problems, one of which is that I could not possibly write in French, but I could certainly supply him with the name of my translator [Lisa Rosenbaum] who is a lady who prepares first-rate versions of my books in French and knows my style of work.

I have an idea for a libretto – have indeed had it in my mind for many years – and it is an operatic version of that wonderful old story, *The Golden Ass*, by Apuleius.* You are probably acquainted with it; it is a marvellous tale of life in ancient Alexandria in which a man who is full of vanity falls into the hands of an enchantress and is, by mistake, turned into an ass. He has a number of adventures in this condition, becoming the drudge of a band of robbers and falling into the clutch of a rather strange woman who has a special interest in asses. Eventually he finds a way out of his dreadful predicament and, having gained wisdom, is made a priest of Isis. This story has considerable modern relevance, has a hint of Women's Lib about it, and is sufficiently dirty for modern taste without being gross. I would be glad to talk to you about it if we could get together sometime.

Meanwhile you might try it on M. Guillou. I think the opera could take quite a modern form, and be performed in an inventive and improvising manner. It should provide principal parts for a Narrator (a man or woman), a principal woman's role (Fotis) and the part of the hero, who could be a tenor or a countertenor as the composer thought fit. These and a few minor roles would do the trick. . . .

I think the opera that I am describing, and which has been rolling around in my mind for some years, could be both funny and profound, which for me is the ideal recipe for any work of art.

Yours sincerely,

Robertson Davies

To ROBERT FINCH

Windhover
Caledon East
July 13, 1994

Dear Robert:

Many thanks for your letter and the picture of Talma.* We both
agree entirely with you about Goya and Picasso. I cannot rid myself
of a feeling that Picasso is rather a faker; some of those ceramics,
though very clever, are cocking a snook at the gullible public? And I
have never warmed to *Guernica*.* Goya, on the other hand – ! Well
do I recall visiting the Prado and seeing – very badly displayed, in a
dark room – some of his little known pictures of the horrors of war
and the miseries of peasant life. As you say, he speaks directly; he does
not editorialize in paint.

But about Talma – I suppose you recall *Les Enfants du Paradis**
where he was played so finely by Pierre Brasseur – no, no, I'm wrong,
that was not Talma but Lemaitre – anyhow –. My first encounter with
Talma was in a school French class; we were reading one of those
books of extracts from famous writers and one of them – I forget
which – wrote about being taken to visit Talma in his dressing-room
and finding the great man *washing his chest*! This astonished us all
because we could not imagine why he did not wash all over. What
was so particular about his chest? But as I read more French literature I became accustomed to this partial washing. In Balzac* nobody
ever seems to take a bath, but bits of them are washed from time to
time. When Nana is preparing an elegant toilette for an evening with
one of her gentlemen, she washes her arms and her bosom, which I
suppose were the parts of her most prominently on display. Even
today I find the bathroom accommodation in any but the first-class
French international hotels, somewhat minatory, as if warning one
not to wash too much.

Further about Talma: I have always thought it was one of Napoleon's
clever strokes to employ Talma to show him how to behave like an

Emperor. How much better it would be if the present British Royals had undergone some such instruction. Democracy can be carried too far. Queen Victoria knew better; she employed Fanny Kemble* to teach her to speak and read and all her life she was admired for the beauty and charm of her speech – unlike some we could mention. I wonder if there might not be an essay on this subject of royal persons who have sought help from the stage in carrying off their ceremonial duties? . . .

Affectionate good wishes from us both.

Rob.

To JOHN IRVING

Windhover
Caledon East
July 31, 1994

John Irving (1942–   ) is an American writer who gained wide attention in 1978 with his novel The World According to Garp. *Davies and Irving had been friends since the early 1980s. This was Davies' third letter to Irving concerning his work. The other two – about* The Cider House Rules *(which he liked) and* A Prayer for Owen Meany *(which he did not) – have vanished.*

Dear John:

I realize with a sense of sick shock – how's that for classy prose? I really mean with a nasty twinge – that I have not written to you about *A Son of The Circus*, of which your publishers kindly sent me a proof copy. And here it is almost out! Here goes, then: it is a fine achievement and yet I think you must be glad to have it off your hands, for it is a huge work – what reviewers call "a large canvas" – and it must have been the devil's own work to keep everything in balance and to keep all the cast onstage when needed. These very big jobs are exhausting and I hope you are giving yourself time to breathe before publication and the onset of all the publicity work. I greatly admired your skill in dealing with India, about which you profess to know little. Well, who does know India? I had a friend – a nephew of Kipling* – who spent a lot of time in the diplomatic work there, and he told me that the deeper he went the more vast became the extent of what [he] did not and could not know. But you have done *just enough*, which is the great secret; you have suggested that there is a lot more in reserve, and thus the reader trusts you. It is the people who go in for frenzied "research" and then cannot bear to leave out anything they have discovered, who hang themselves in their own garters. But apart from my admiration for what you have done technically, I am delighted with your story and your atmosphere and the totality of your achievement. Well done, and I hope – and am indeed sure – that you will enjoy a commensurate recognition and reward.

As I expect you know from Janet,* my new book, *The Cunning Man*, comes out here in late September; in the US in February; in the UK next Spring. And I am already committed, as I am sure you are, to a lot of traipsing around, doing readings and making speeches. Readings are the devil; how does one cull a sufficient hunk out of a long novel to make a reading, complete in itself, and giving some hint of the quality of the whole work? I recall reading on one occasion with the late Anthony Burgess,* and to my surprise, he had no notion of how to tackle that problem, and read a story which he had written in Spanish, and which he translated as he read! It was about a meeting between Shakespeare and Cervantes, at some time when Shakes. was touring with actors in Spain, and as he was reading to an audience who had heard of Shakespeare and thought he had written the Bible, but who knew nothing of Cervantes, the reading was received with an enthusiasm which was, to put it mildly, muted. Everybody respected him, but nobody had *thrilled* to him..... So I have been sweating to prepare a reading, and also to write a speech titled *The Future of Fiction** which I am slated to give in several places while touring. . . .

. . . I suppose Janet may have told you that this autumn sees the appearance of a biography of me. Yes, a biography of a man whose life-story could be easily told on a half sheet of paper. I have had no adventures, never climbed Everest, never was caught in the Caliph's harem, never told Churchill what to do next, have known very few people of whom the world is aware and have been what Dr. Johnson calls "a reclusive drudge"* for lo, these eighty years. Yet the ineffable Dr. Judith Grant has written nine hundred pages about me, and has produced photographs of me at every stage of life, Sunday School certificates, analyses of blood and urine and lubricious records of every time I took a girl to a movie and fed her an ice-cream soda on the way home. This hangs over my head like the sword of Dan MacLise as the old Irish legend tells of it.

But I am falling into twaddle. I look forward to seeing you, when we meet to read together* if not before. Let's knock 'em out of their socks!

Love from us both to both of you –

Rob.

To JOHN JULIUS NORWICH

Windhover
Caledon East
August 1, 1994

Dear John Julius:

You mustn't think that I expect you to reply to my letters except when you really feel like it; I should hate to be one of those people who pout when they do not have a reply by return of post – though in the present state of post that could be quite a while. . . . I write to *you* when the spirit moves me, which means when I think of you so compellingly that only a letter will serve to put me right. I think of you often, however, but less demandingly.

Thought of you very strongly a few days ago when my researches (my grand name for fossicking about in books) put me into a consideration of macaronics, for which I have a weakness. After some years of taking pleasure in them I think my favourite is one by R. H. Barham;* I expect you know it:

What Horace says is,
  Eheu fugaces
  Anni labuntur, Postume, Postume,
Years glide away and are lost to me, lost to me!
Now, when the folks in the dance sport their merry toes,
Taglionis and Ellslers, Duvernays, and Ceritos,
Sighing I murmur, "*O mihi praeteritos!*"

The notion that you should do a book about the Richard II to Richard III century is surely attractive, but I urge you not to put off doing the book of memoirs for too long; good memoirs are among the very best books for they preserve the flavour of an age, which serious histories rarely do; you have lived in an age of great flavour, and have known many people who should be caught in a book by a writer with an appreciation of flavour. Of late I have been reading the letters and some autobiographical essays by Sylvia Townsend Warner,* and have been very happy in the depiction of people some of whom are quite unknown to me, and some whom I have known only through their writings, and above all in the wit and shrewdness of her observation. *Do* think seriously about the memoirs. I shall count the minutes until they appear, and I do not want to go on counting into astronomical figures.

My new novel, *The Cunning Man*, appears here in September, in the U.S. in February, and in the U.K. in the Spring. I shall send you a Canadian copy as soon as I have any, and I hope you will like it. I have tried in it to capture something of the Chekhovian quality of a certain kind of Canadian life, which appears as our population grows more and more un-British in origin and we are nagged by newcomers who are restless under British law and what continues to be British custom in government. Of course this is resisted, but inevitably there are those who regret the past loudly and plangently, and cannot see that it is a past that never was. These people interest me deeply and the change in this country from a colonial to another sort of colonialism – that dominated by the U.S.A. – is fascinating and one must fight down one's *Eheu fugaces* feelings and keep one's eye on what is happening. I mean it about U.S. colonialism. You may have seen something in the papers about the movement in Quebec to seek independence and become a country on its own. It won't work, I am ready to bet, because Washington would not put up with a fragmented Canada to its North. They have not yet ridded themselves of a dread that the Russkies are going to come over the Pole, squash Canada in seven minutes (they call us Seven Minutes in the Pentagon) and attempt to subdue the great republic and put its free citizens into peonage. Opium dream though this is, it has astonishing strength. So a word from the bankers of the US (to whom Quebec thinks it might look for support) will dispel all of that nonsense, though of course it will not silence the minority in Quebec which insists that our French brethren are spiritually and morally squashed.

But I must not prose on about the Quebec problem, which engages far too much time in Canada among our fruit salad of a population which the Québécois persist in referring to as Les Anglos. I wish we were a little more Anglo; I weary of turbanned taxi-drivers who don't know where anything is.

Our best love to you and Mollie. In October we set out on a longish tour of readings and speechifying, known to us privately as The Great Dog and Pony Show.

Rob.

To ALMA LEE

Massey College
University of Toronto
November 1, 1994

Alma Lee (1940–   ), Scottish-born Canadian, is the artistic director of the Vancouver International Writers Festival. Davies gave the Festival's Duthie Lecture on October 23 at the Arts Club Theatre on Granville Island, Vancouver.

Dear Mˢ· Lee:

Thank you for your Fax of October 31st. I sensed that you were somewhat surprised by the pressure that was put on me to support the cause of the Little Sister's Bookshop,* but I did not have an opportunity to discuss this matter with you later. What people like Ms. Fuller do not take into consideration is that if the uttermost freedom is given to originating and distributing any kind of writing in Canada, the doors are thrown open to a mass of hate literature and anti-Semitic literature which is, of course, undesirable and would involve the whole country in a miserable controversy. The pornographic business is so complex that I do not personally want to involve myself with it. Like virtually all writers, I dislike censorship but there are complex problems involved in total abandonment of all restrictions which would be much worse than the occasional troubles that afflict businesses like the Little Sister's Bookshop. I think that this arises from a very widespread misunderstanding of what the phrase "freedom of the press" means; as it was used by defenders like John Milton it meant simply the right to publish anything that you chose to publish and accept the consequences. Too many people assume that it means complete freedom to publish without any expectation of reprisal from people who disagree, and this is particularly cogent in the realm of pornography.

Just between ourselves I felt strongly that Ms. Fuller believed that if a woman cried at me I would melt: I do not melt so easily.

Yours sincerely,

Robertson Davies

To HERBERT WHITTAKER

Windhover
Caledon East
November 20, 1994

Dear Herbert:

Wonderful to hear from you. Yes, Barbara Hepworth* died in a fire which destroyed her studio, and made a very sad ending. The murmur was that she was drunk. Brenda and I knew a little about her because she was a friend – not an intimate one but she had few intimates – of Brenda's Aunt Elsa [Larking] who lived nearby at St. Ives where she was an etcher. I made free with Dame Barbara in my book, but not in a way that would annoy or distress anyone who knew her. I made much freer with quite a few other people, some of whom you may have recognized. I meet people now who assure me that the two artist ladies in the book were Miss Loring and Miss Lyall,* of Toronto; I have given up protesting that I never knew, or even saw, those ladies, because I learned long ago that when people know better than you do about your work it is fruitless to argue.

How many books do I read at once, you ask. More than is probably wise, for I suppose one ought to concentrate, but my work, like yours, demands that one's concentration be parcelled out; it can't be beamed in one direction for days at a time. I have been doing some rather weary reading lately because the revised *Dictionary of National Biography* has asked me to do the article on Henry Irving, which I take as a huge compliment. But it has meant that I have had to read* Laurence Irving's 700 pages with great care, and skim Brereton and Stoker, and read Gordon Craig carefully and try to drain the admirable good sense out of the gush. How I envy you having met Craig! A Truly Great Phoney, without whom the theatre would be infinitely poorer. What we owe to our phonies! The solemn-minded souls cannot understand how enriching they are..... And by the way, I apologize for that boner* about Byron and reading Shakespeare by flashes of lightning; of course it was Coleridge. But as James Agate wrote so bitterly, it is possible to peruse and scour a piece of writing until one is dizzy and then, in the end, some stupidity will have escaped notice. I checked that quote in the *Oxford Dic of Quotes*, and then put down "Byron." Alzheimer's, here I come!....

Also for Irving I have to search a lot of memoirs of people,* some of whom are more revealing than the serious biographers – Max Beerbohm, W. Graham Robertson, Eliza Aria and the like. A woman named Madeleine Bingham has written a book* about H.I. which is mostly scissors and paste from Brereton and Stoker but contains raunchy revelations about the love-affair between H.I. & Ellen Terry; untrustworthy, for she belongs to the Orgasm Is All generation, and is warming herself at fires which I think were much more carefully tended than she suggests. Ellen Terry, in her memoirs,* is as discreet as one would expect; they probably were lovers, but so what?

In such work one finds oneself stumped by trifles; some time in the late 1920s or early '30s Martin-Harvey unveiled a plaque on the house in Keinton Mandeville in which H.I. was born. Do you think I can find out the exact date?* I have searched and grubbed in vain. Do you know of any newspaper archive that might reveal the date? Not in Canada, I expect. I have a picture of J. M-H doing it, but it isn't dated. Drat!

Of course I'll sign *The Cunning Man*. I sign it for many people I don't know and of course I'd do it for an old friend. But I am a picky signer; I won't, as they say, "personalize" an autograph. When people approach me saying: Please sign it "With half a score of reechy kisses to Sugar Bunny" I turn them away with a fishwife's curse. But I'll sign yours with a real tribute to long friendship.

No I haven't given up the theatre. I am in the process of writing the libretto for an opera for a French composer [Jean Guillou] who is doing it for the Canadian Opera Company and also, it is hoped, for the Paris shop. Hard work. One must be so spare, so economical, because composers can squeeze so much out of a single short line. Give Verdi a chance to set "Mio padre!" to music and he won't hush up under a page and a half. I am finding this rather fun and, as they say A Challenge. And at my age one needs Challenges.

Age! As my nephew says, Old Age is not for sissies. My legs are going and I really think I shall have to take to a stick. Yesterday I tripped on a bit of stair carpet and fell with a trayful of glasses. Brenda picked me up, and never once breathed a word about the glasses! How's that for angelical femininity?

We must get together, perhaps over the Christmas season. I have a brief respite from the drudgery of being – not an author, but a man who has written a book and must therefore be seen by anyone who wants to take a gawp. . . . Specifically I have gone to Montreal, Ottawa, Toronto, Calgary, Vancouver, Victoria, Edmonton, Hamilton, London, Waterloo and on Dec. 1 I give tongue in Toronto again. Awful, but as Brenda reminds me, not as awful as not being asked to go anywhere.

Until we meet, but not, I trust, as the old hymn says,* at Jesus' feet.

Rob.

To HORACE W. DAVENPORT

Windhover
Caledon East
November 20, 1994

Dear Horace:

Thank you for your last letter – and that is more than a cliché opening, for you have said so much* about Judith Grant's book that I feel strongly but cannot quite bring myself to say to her. On the whole it is a creditable production, but I am vain enough to think that as a portrait of me it lacks *verve* and the failure to distinguish between the significant and the insignificant makes it a sad muddle; several friends have told me that they have essayed it, and have broken down in early pages. This is rubbed into me powerfully at present because, as I believe I have told you, I have been asked to prepare the new article on Henry Irving for the revision of the *Dictionary of National Biography* and I have to keep constantly before me the necessity to tell what is significant, and to add corroborative and lively detail, without producing an unreadable mess. I could use the whole of the space allotted to me to get down to cases on the Shaw–Irving quarrel but that cannot be and rightly so, because it was blown up by GBS into something vastly more important than it ever was. As you say, Judith's book will be a storehouse to be pillaged by future writers if there are any and what that might bring about I dread to think. Her version of my relations with my Mother is badly skewed; after I had grown up we were on the best of terms and I never failed in the duties a son brought up as I was owed to a parent. But I refused to bow the knee – as Irving did, I find – and thus I escaped being eaten alive. She has no notion at all of my Father, and I sometimes wonder if I did, either. These things cannot be captured by a third party when they are not clear to the principals. To compare small things to great, what was Johnson *really* like before Bozzy* imposed him on the world in a superb portrait – chiefly of the biographer. I tried many times to tell Judith that a biography was as much a portrait of the writer as of the subject, but she simply smiled the superior, kindly smile of the academic dealing with an untrained mind.

What you say about yourself* is profoundly true; but you are admirably documented and with a little bit of luck some future Davenport, writing medical history, will capture something of you – but not all.

Your strictures on Judith's sloppy usages* strike upon my heart. She really has no feel for language or she would not pour it out like a man emptying a sack of bird-seed. But who gives a damn about language? The folly which most burns me, because it is so common, is that of saying that something "is cut in half" when in fact it is either cut in halves or cut in two. Reduced to half, perhaps: cut in half, never.

Thanks for your reminiscences of Dreiser.* Did you see that Sir John Pope-Hennessy* died recently? His obit in *The Times* was enlightening; it appears that there was more innocent fun in Pea-Hen (as James told me he was called at Downside) than one might suppose.

But it is your last paragraph* that truly strikes upon my heart, in which you talk of suicide. I would not attempt, with sentimental gush, to dissuade you from such an action; if you chose to go after the high Roman fashion, nobody has a right to say you nay or deplore what they cannot comprehend. It would not do for me, for reasons that are clear in my books, but that is an irrelevance. You have indeed an extraordinary doctor and if the day should come, it may be that he will ease the way.

I hope that you will not regard it as an impertinence, or a folly or a mark of imbecility on my part, but I pray for you, my dear old friend. That is my way: yours must be your own. May God – whatever that abused, portmanteau term for the Unknowable and the Ineffable may mean – be with you.

Rob.

To HORACE W. DAVENPORT

Windhover
Caledon East
Holy Innocents', December 27, 1994

Dear Horace:

. . . But now, to stick my nose even further into your affairs. I do most fervently enjoin you to have nothing to do with psychiatric "help" or psycho-analysis.* You are (a) too old, and (b) too intelligent for that sort of thing. All my life I have been keenly interest in psycho-analysis and have come to know a fair amount about it, though I have never myself undergone the treatment. Reason? Dr. Jung's advice* to Laurens van der Post: "Do not undertake it unless something in your life is intolerable without it, for it is too demanding a process both for the patient and his immediate associates, to be undergone simply for the experience itself." I have known quite a few analysts, both Freudian and Jungian and have a daughter [Miranda] in the trade, and my advice is: *never – NEVER – put yourself in the hands of an analyst whom you do not feel certain is at least of equal intellectual and moral and spiritual stature with yourself.* The profession is crowded with self-seeking, duplicitous peewees. In such a case as yours this narrows the field gravely, and as Freud and Jung are both dead, don't trust anyone; I know one or two, in California, who might help, but they are very old and would probably confine their talks with you to three or four helpful conversations. As for psychotropic drugs, I have seen these at work and they are great causers of iatrogenic illness. I am shocked by the way doctors throw drugs around. A trivial instance: one of my quacks told me a while ago to take an aspirin tablet every night, to ensure that my blood pressure was kept in bounds. (My blood pressure, by the way, has always been that of a man younger than myself.) So I did that, and after a while began to feel quite queer. Asked my druggist about it. "Oh," said he, "they always over-prescribe that stuff; one child's dose three times a week is all you can helpfully absorb, as a continuing medication."... The vainglory of the medical profession is one of the wonders of our time; and to think that not much more than a century ago they made their calls through the back door!

Brenda and I spent Christmas alone, as we usually do now. The girls and the grandchildren come today for a dinner and a jollification. As you very well know, at our age it is not easy to find gifts for people who have everything they need and almost everything they want. So we gave ourselves a few operas on VCR and have been watching them. Last night it was *Il Trovatore* with a Met cast – Pavarotti, Sherrill Milnes,* et al. Musically very good but I had forgotten what an imbecilic plot that piece has. How Verdi can have written the music without laughing I cannot think. But I have long held the opinion that Verdi had no sense of humour. This production was in the old operatic mode: Pavarotti too fat to fight, so that the duels were comical; Leonora old enough to be Pavarotti's mother and fully as fat as he; a chorus which, when urged to battle, trudged off stage on sore feet, clearly unable to swat a fly.

I have undertaken to do a review of a book about Henry Irving for a publication associated with the University of Indiana. I was amazed to get a mimeographed direction to submit my review on disk, and workable on some contrivance made by IBM. I have replied saying that I am still in the quill pen stage of technology, and that if they want disks they will have to get them from somebody else. No wonder scholarship is going to hell. . . .

We approach 1995; hang in there, and don't get mixed up with shrinks. Most of them are not fit to wipe your boots and better your melancholy than their voodoo..... Our love to you and Inge.

Rob

To BIRGITTA HEYMAN

Windhover
Caledon East
January 8, 1995

Dear Birgitta:

. . . I *do* admire your lovely new computer! And how clever of you to be able to manage one of those alarming things! Luckily my daughter Jennifer does a lot of work for me, and she understands computers, and has one; her husband [Tom Surridge] designs computer programs for businesses, and is rather a whizz with them. But to me they are a dark mystery. What I should do without Jenny I don't know; she types all my speeches on her computer in big type, so that they are easy to read. The only sad thing is that my old secretary [Moira Whalon], who has been with me for almost forty years, feels a bit shoved aside; she isn't because I couldn't manage without her and she knows my ways perfectly and is a wonderful person, but like me she belongs to an earlier age. My secretary, by the way, is a splendid cook, and over Christmas we ate a good many of her wonderful lemon tarts.

Wonderful news about your daughter Agneta [Engdahl]! Long may her disease remain quiescent. So her son [Niklas] wants to be an actor? Well, who blames him. Didn't you? Didn't I? I am now heartily glad that I never achieved my ambition to remain on the stage, because I don't think I would ever have been really good; my temperament is wrong. I want to remain hidden, and an actor must *reveal*, or he will never succeed in a big way. Have I told you about the experience I had some years ago* with Marie-Louise von Franz, who was one of the greatest pupils of C. G. Jung? For years I have suffered from a recurrent dream that I am on a stage, my cue has been spoken, and not only do I not know what I should say, but I don't know what the play is! This is a terrifying dream. Well, quite a while ago Dr. von Franz came to Canada to give some lectures, and stayed with us at Massey College, and we became good friends. I told her about my dream. "That's an easy one to understand," said she; "it is telling you that you are not in the world to repeat what someone else has said, but to say what you have to say of your own!" I found this very helpful. Poor Marie-Louise is now very old and quite ill. "Old age is not easy," she writes. My older brother [Arthur], who is now 91, says the same thing. "Old age is not for sissies," he tells me. Poor man, he has to live in a wheel-chair, and the only good thing that can be said about his condition is that he has lots of money, a devoted man-servant, and a family of children who look after him like a treasure – which makes his situation about as comfortable as it could be, I suppose, but life is not much fun for him. . . .

Rob.

To SHIRLEY BAIN

Massey College
University of Toronto
January 10, 1995

Shirley Bain (1931–   ), Canadian retired school teacher, is a member and supply organist of St. James Presbyterian Church in Thamesville, Ontario. She was writing a history of the church's recently restored, 95-year-old organ.

Dear Mʳˢ· Bain:

Thank you for your letter of December 29th and for the photographs of St. James Church which I remember well, and of the house in which I was born,* now changed out of all recognition.

You ask about the organ in the church and all I can remember about it is that it had what was called "a tracker action"; this meant that the stops activated long rods which were connected with the pipes and opened and shut them. Although this is a very old way of constructing an organ it has its difficulties because sometimes the rods broke and at other times they stuck, in which case one note continued to sound until the trouble was put right, which could be quite a long time. In my parents' day this happened very often and my mother used to describe an occasion when the "ciphering" went on for some time and interrupted the sermon. My father, who was the choir master, and John Howat, who was the chief elder, crept behind the organ and proceeded to climb around its works to discover the source of the trouble. Unfortunately they forgot that everything they said could be heard plainly in the church and there was rather a lot of "Have you found anything?"; "Where are you?"; "I'm up here, where are you?" and this conversation brought the sermon, by the Reverend Arthur Boyd, to a somewhat miserable halt. It could take up to half an hour to find out which pipe was "ciphering."

I suppose now the action has been changed to electricity and this kind of low comedy no longer happens.

With good wishes, I am

Yours sincerely,

Robertson Davies

To PHILIP JOHN STEAD

Windhover
Caledon East
[April 1995]

Dear John:

Thanks for your letter of April 4, and your fine obit of Disher;* I shall renew my hounding of the *Oxford Comp. to the Theatre* and shall refer them to your piece in the Royal Society of Literature publication; shameful that he should be left out when weasel's turds like Jarry* get a big play.

As for Montague Summers, he is rather a speciality of mine, as I dote upon mountebanks in the scholarly world. Born a Methodist, or some such, he claimed to be an RC priest, though no record of his attainment of that rank can be found; he was a rancorous Catholic and his prefaces to his quite good work on Restoration drama are marred by rantings against the Reformation. And he was an old rogue; tumbled about Oxford in soutane and shovel hat, one foot on the pavement and the other in the gutter, always accompanied by (1) a pale, melancholy young man in black clothes or else (2) a big black dog, and rumour was that the two were one and MS's familiar. I knew his doctor, Dr. Raymond Greene* (brother of the novelist), who told me that he was once summoned – by dog or secretary – to MS's bedside, to find the old rascal tucked up with a huge folio of grotesques and monstrosities of the 17th century; he had it open at a picture of a woman with grotesquely deformed privy parts, and his query was: "Doctor, could there really be one *like that?*".... I used to recommend MS to my students as a change from the grey-faced nonentities whom they thought of as scholars.

I accept your judgement* of Judith Grant's book; I am the worst possible critic. Of course I am aware of how much she has missed of the self-doubting, maggoty-headed jackass that lies beneath the showy exterior. I was brought up a Calvinist and have never got over it.

Thank you for Speaight's book.* I never met him but knew Robert, and liked him immensely; a splendid talker and a mine of sound judgement on the theatre.

About Mr. Punch;* I want to make him central to my next – and probably my last – novel – as a special sort of spirit, not evil but outrageously derisive of stupidities and pretences, who sees no particular reason why a tiresome baby should not be thrown out of the window. There is much of Punch in me, as there is in you; a contempt for solemnity and Mrs. Grundy, especially when it is fashionable. Bye the bye, where do you stand on political correctness? I have recently been making some enquiries into Australian slang, assisted by the

invaluable Partridge,* and find some gems. Brenda is Australian, and
went to a posh girls' school in the mountains outside Melbourne;
when I ask her if the expression current among the girls and mistresses for voiding the bowels was "choking a darkie" she becomes
indignant; it would be great sport to try that one on some of the
pol-corr. gang..... But to return to Mr. Punch: I recall clearly an ornament to the magazine,* drawn I think by Richard Doyle, which
showed Mr. Punch as the central figure in what appears to be a
Bacchanalian procession; he is riding a donkey, and surrounded by
pretty girls in light garments who plainly adore him. And in his hand
he holds what might be some sort of staff or truncheon, but which
woundily looks like his erect pizzle, and his eye is cocked at it sug-
gestively. But – damn it – I can't find it! Have you ever seen it – it
appeared in *Punch* – and if so, how do you interpret it? I think I read
long ago that it caused a furore in the *Punch* offices because it reached
publication before anybody twigged quite what it was. What a job it
is to track down these recollections!

So you have business interests in Toronto? What a dark horse you
are! When next you are called to Hogtown to look after your affairs,
do let me know in lots of time and the red carpet shall be newly
empurpled and a bottle of my club's best claret shall be poured.....
Meanwhile, my respects to Judith; I am glad you thought Brenda got
a fair deal in the Grant book. But that is like Judith Grant – knows
very well how much wives matter, which so many biographers do not
seem to do.

Rob.

PS: Montague Summers had the amazing gall to preface his book
Essays in Petto with a photograph of himself in the full rig-out of a
Papal Prothonotary – which he wasn't. I marvel the Vatican did not
issue a *fatwa* on him.

To JOHN MCGREEVY

Massey College
University of Toronto
May 2, 1995

Dear John:

It was very kind of you to include us among your guests at Peter Ustinov's performance* on Monday night; we had a wonderful time and admired PU for many things that marked him as a really superior performer – and person.

For one thing, he has mastered the great secret of public performance, which is to "do less" – in the Stanislavsky manner.* I was happily reminded of Stephen Leacock's advice to humorists:* "Never be as funny as you can." How one has suffered from funny men who toil and strain to squeeze the last roar out of the last idiot in the audience, and lose all dignity and all decency in so doing. With PU we felt that he looked on us as sensible and intelligent people, and not simply as comedian-fodder – which is what such a lot of the TV people do. He complimented us, and we returned the compliment by regarding him as a man of quality, and not a clown.

Having gone through something of the sort – though of course on a lesser scale – in the U.K. recently I was delighted by his skill in charming and subduing an audience – making them friends rather than victims. And his extraordinary vocal technique! I decided that he must have a vocal range of at least two octaves, quite apart from his falsetto, and he used it with astonishing but discreet skill. This is what Forbes-Robertson said a really accomplished actor needed,* but it is very rare on the stage today. Unless one shuts off one's understanding of the words for a few minutes, and simply listens to the sound, one does not realize what an amazing range his voice has. He must surely be one of the most accomplished performers on the stage today – one of a very small number. And what a mimic! And how refreshingly indifferent to Political Correctness! I was enchanted by his impersonation of Charles Laughton, whom I have always thought of as an over-praised ham, making stage capital out of his personal nastiness. And his Gielgud! I laughed till I cried at his assumption of that extraordinary, splendid voice, saying rather ill-judged things.

But enough. It was a great evening and we thank you heartily.

Rob.

To JUDITH SKELTON GRANT

Windhover
Caledon East
May 26, 1995

Dear Judith:

By chance last night (May 25) I picked up the TV program *Imprint*,* which proved to be about literary biography, and as I watched it, with gaping mouth, I realised how gently and considerately you treated me in *Man of Myth* and I write once again to thank you for your forbearance. Prominent among the panelists – indeed Top of the Pops – was your old pal Elspeth Cameron, looking, I must say, splendid, elegantly dressed and coiffed and wearing in her face what Blake highly recommended* – "the lineaments of gratified desire." She declared in good set terms that the attitude between subject and writer in a lit. biog. was "adversarial" and hammered it home with great charm. Another panelist,* a man who is at work on deconstructing Graham Greene, was very hot on the theme that a writer has no "copyright" in his own life, which belongs to the public, who must look to the biographer to serve it up heavily spiced. The other two panelists were more reasonable, especially the woman, who was totally outshone by E.C., and was a picture of a public librarian – thin bang, unwise earrings, specs designed for a giant and the voice of a peewit.

I am sure you have heard the latest news of Elspeth. She has COME OUT OF THE CLOSET, and has discovered herself to be in the depths of her soul a Lesbian, and all the train of marriages and affairs behind her is but as piffle before the wind.* . . . The men of the literary world may now breathe more easily, but you Women of Letters had better watch your step.

I have now completed the travel and exhibitionism demanded by *The Cunning Man* and arrived home about a fortnight ago a total wreck, desolated by 'flu to which was added asthma as bad as I have ever had it. The doctors are severe. Must Go Easy. Must Cut Down. Must have some Regard For My Years. A Big Heart Man [Edward J. G. Noble]* wants to take home movies of my heart at work, suspecting it of some monkey business. But my G. P. [Jaroslav M. J. Polak] has photographed my heart and declares it to be a very nice article indeed. My asthma man [Christopher J. Allen] preserves a dignified reticence, insisting that he Knows What Ails Me. But I know better than any of them. "I have gone here and there/And made myself a motley to the view"* as a better writer than I has said and my whole being is in protest. I want to be quiet and write another book, which is kicking in my womb in lively style. So I have cancelled a jaunt to the Chichester Festival next October, and am refusing all sorts of invitations to give tongue, though I cannot escape them all.

I hope all goes well with you and your family. Tell John [A. G. Grant] that Lloyds and Barings have utterly destroyed my faith in Banking Nature, and I am burying my money under a stone in a coffee can. I hope we shall have a chance to talk soon.

Rob.

In the *United Church Observer* Martin O'Malley,* reviewing *CM*, denounces me as a snob. True, but if I had not been a snob I would never have met O'Malley, who was a Southam Fellow at Massey & thus the *crème de la crème* of Canadian journalism.

To MAISIE DRYSDALE

Windhover
Caledon East
July 22, 1995

*Mavis Drysdale (1915–   ), Australian, is
Brenda Davies' older sister. She was
successively married to two of Australia's
best-known painters, Peter Purves Smith
(1912–49) and Sir Russell Drysdale
(1912–81).*

Dear Maisie:

Your letter of July 1 was a surprise and a delight. So glad you heard
the broadcast;* I have rather given up that sort of thing but could not
resist Australia. The interviewer sounded v. solemn, and as it was by
a sort of telephone arrangement I had some trouble hearing her – as
I am getting rather deaf and she muttered. Glad you thought it was
all right; one never knows what questions will be asked or how seriously one is expected to answer, and I hate superficial drivelling,
which is what many interviewers think their public wants.

You ask about Mavis Gallant: I have not seen her for quite a while,
but she has been getting a lot of flattering attention lately, and I
wonder if it is making her proud? She comes the great lady of lit.
rather, and I think it shows in her work. I have just had to write a
piece to go with a new collection* of her stuff, and found it uphill
work; she is so touchy and what is one to say? Alice Munro* has been
enjoying an extraordinary, late success, and she is very good indeed;
she writes about the sort of people among whom I grew up, and for
whom I conceived a powerful dislike, and she has them dead to rights.
It is not "warts and all" but "Odorono* and all" that gets you down.

I did not meet _____, because I was unwell, but Brenda did him
proud – or proudish, for we gather he is rather grand. Wish I had seen
him because I am immensely interested in Ladies' Men, and anxious
to discover, if I can, what it is women like about them; to me they
rarely show anything above the agreeable commonplace, but I am
beginning to think I have been born without a dimension, as I appear
to have no homosexual element at all, and nowadays everybody
appears to have one. I have been reading a new biography of Thomas
Mann by somebody called Ronald Hayman, and he is determined to

equip Mann with gauzy wings and a fairy wand, despite the devoted wife and the six children.

To change the subject we have read recently of a picture of Tas's [Maisie's husband, Sir Russell Drysdale] selling for something like half a million, Canadian, of which of course you would not have got a red cent. I have often wondered why artists do not agitate for a copyright law, like writers, which would ensure them of a slice of anything their work sold for, for sixty years after their death. It would only be justice.

About Patrick White:* I cannot read him, though of course I have done so; but I mean I can't get next to him. Such a grim, sour quality. In which he was before his time, because that is all the rage now; the latest book by Childe Amis* is as bitter as he can make it, but he isn't in the White class as a lemon. I am betting his latest will get the Booker this autumn.

The Cunning Man is going well, and in funny places: I signed a contract for publication in Korea last week. Now what do Koreans want with a book like that? Or Israelis or for the matter of that Poles — Poles whine about their poverty and ask to be excused any royalty agreement as one is supposed to pity their sad state; I go along with this but I have known many Poles in my time and some of them were château-bottled shits.

I am very busy . . . . I am winding up to do a new novel, to follow *The Cunning Man* and I have what I think is a good plot, and must now cloak it in entertaining garb. I need information: have you, by any chance, any friends who know anything about the Barnardo Homes, how they operate and what they are like? If so, could you pump them and send me the pumpings? I cannot get a thing here.

We are having an extraordinary summer; torrential rains and a lot of damage over a wide area. But here we have not been too bad. B. slaves in the garden: your Mum [Muriel Ethel Newbold] lives again in her. I don't understand gardeners; they never *enjoy* what they have made; they fret and worrit and weed neurotically. B has created a huge and very handsome garden here, but it seems to oppress her; I am the one who walks about and enjoys it.

Why don't you write more often? Your letters are splendid but piteously infrequent.

By the way, I did not mention that the heart ailment assigned to me is called Mitral Regurgitation,* which I interpret as Puking of the Ticker; can this be right? How disgusting! And yet I have just been reading the Diary of John Cowper Powys* who sometimes had to have three enemas a day and his mistress had to help him or he got stuff on the ceiling. Ah, the literary life!

B will write shortly; at present she is sitting up with a sick cotoneaster.

Love from us both,

Rob.

To HORACE W. DAVENPORT

Windhover
Caledon East
August 27, 1995

Dear Horace:

Have been involved in a mixture of obligations and odd jobs and have neglected your last letter. . . . I have pondered a great deal about Judith Grant's book about me, and feel that she has used me well and very probably beyond my desert: but still there are things I would rather she had not said, and her portraits of some of the people I have known are all askew, because there is no way in which she could reconstruct old times and old unhappiness except in terms known to herself — which are quite other than mine. I have been asked to prepare a book of essays for next year, and I think I shall write a new one on the experience of being biographed, and the essential impossibility of either biography or autobiography. Look at Boswell: so much that he tells in adulatory terms might have been used to show Johnson as a narrow, egotistical old boor..... But enough of this.

I have completed my libretto for *The Golden Ass* and to my great relief the opera people and the composer [Randolph Peters]* like it very much, and a first-rate opera director, Colin Graham (he did *Ghosts of Versailles* at the Met and is a specialist in Benjamin Britten),* is eager to direct it. But nothing will happen till 1998. Can I hang on till 1998?

Perhaps; at last one of my doctors [Robert Laidlaw MacMillan] – the oldest and best – has given me a real run-down on my heart condition. Leaky valve; but he thinks it is an old injury, and it may go back to childhood when I had bad scarlet fever – which he said is now seen as a form of rheumatic fever – accounting for many things in my life which I never wholly understood. But if I have made it to 82 with whatever it is, he sees no immediate sign of my demise, and has taken me off all my pills except a diuretic. Result: I feel really well for the first time in months, dizziness and wobbly legs gone, and Brenda says I have resumed making jokes, which she had missed. It was the dizziness that really depressed me; I had to walk with a stick, not for style but for necessity.

I am getting on with an odd job; writing the entry in the *Dictionary of National Biography* about Montague Summers, the great scholar of Restoration Drama, but also an eccentric and whistletricker of the highest order. Astonishing what a lot of work one of these entries requires if one is not to mislead or omit vital facts within a limited space.

We took a couple of days off recently to go to Stratford, and saw a disappointing *Macbeth* but a superb production of *Amadeus** – better than the original production in London which we saw in 1980. We are both refreshed by first-rate theatre as by no other pleasure. Also saw a very fine production of *Long Day's Journey Into Night** but I cannot like that play. My Mother's father [William H. McKay]* was a morphine addict and I know something about what it is to have one of those people to cope with. Of course women respond differently: Mary Tyrone was wistful and dreamy and worried about what the Blessed Virgin would think; my grandfather was demonically eloquent, and now and then took after his wife with a large knife, so that at last he had to be "put away," poor soul. His downfall was that he was an asthmatic, and his doctor – also his brother-in-law – said to him "William, it is ridiculous for me to come here every time you have one of these attacks to give you an injection; I'll just leave you a syringe and an open prescription, and you can take care of yourself." And so poor William, armed with the monkey-pump, went to the dogs and supplied my grandmother with a grievance which lasted for the rest of her life. My father, who was not one of her fans, suggested that William took to the dope in order to be quit of Lavinia. But how trustworthy is the evidence of a son-in-law?

All good wishes to you both. The autumn approaches, my favourite season and this year, after all the rain, the colour ought to be spectacular.

Love

Rob. . . .

To TONY VAN BRIDGE

Massey College
University of Toronto
September 20, 1995

Tony van Bridge (1917–   ), an English actor and director, has been active in Canada since 1954. His book is Also in the Cast: The Memoirs of Tony van Bridge, *edited by Denis Johnston.*

Dear Tony:

It was a great pleasure to see you at the party to mark the publication of your book on Monday, and since then Brenda and I have read nothing else and have talked about it incessantly. It is a very good book, and I do not say that patronizingly but in sober truth; it is so direct, so spare, so good-humoured without being sentimental and so down-to-earth and sensible about the theatre and in these respects so unlike the general run of theatrical reminiscences. Good books of reminiscence by actors* are uncommon: Alec Guinness wrote an excellent one, but Olivier didn't; Gielgud covers his tracks in every line; Robert Morley simply gives a performance as himself. They can't write for beans and you are a very good writer. The book is a delight and will be a source for every history of the theatre in Canada.

I still smart a little in damp weather about *Love and Libel.** It should never have been a play in the first place; the plot wasn't a theatre plot. But when the Theatre Guild offered, I could not resist the chance. Before it went into rehearsal I went through great stress with Tony [Guthrie], who fancied himself as a playwright, though he never wrote a good play. I had three severe weeks with him in Ireland, writing and re-writing and trying to warp the material to suit his personal fancy. But that was just the beginning. Dennis King demanded countless changes and I still recall him glaring into my face and shouting, "If I haven't got six more *sure laughs* in that scene by tomorrow morning, *I walk out*." How, pray, does one create a sure laugh? One drags in cheese and mothers-in-law and other hallowed triggers of mirth. I wrote and re-wrote and wore myself out. Before we went to New York there were innumerable after-show meetings with the Guild . . . . Then Tony left rehearsals to have a tooth dealt with. The piece was doomed in spite of the false dawn in Boston. After the first night [in New York] Young Langner summoned me and declared furiously, "Unless I have an additional $10,000 by tonight we close!" I consulted my agent; he said, "It's a scam; don't fall for it." Later my father said he would happily have provided the money, but I told him it would have been throwing good money after bad. It was then that I gave up the theatre, as a mistress who had repeatedly rejected me, and took to novels. And novels have served me well, though I still long for the theatre. "You're stage-struck!" Tony said to me. Yes. That's it. The novelist is a solitary creature, and I long for the splendid geniality and excitement of the theatre.

What a lot of pleasure you have given to so many people! Brenda and me, among them. Particularly, I think the best and most complete Falstaff* in a long experience. Richardson was wonderful as the dark side of F., but he lacked the spacious geniality. You had it all, and were heart-rending in the scene with Doll Tearsheet when Falstaff murmurs that he grows old, and she comforts him; Shakespeare's genius never plunged deeper – no, not even in Lear – and as one grows old oneself the scene is ever more poignant.

Have you seen anything of this season's Stratford? . . .

But I become a bore. Again, congratulations and thanks and long life and happiness to you.

Rob. Davies

To ELEANOR SWEEZEY

Massey College
University of Toronto
September 25, 1995

Dear Eleanor:

It is a long time since I heard from you, and I hope that does not mean that you have been ill, or have run into some sort of difficulty. Has Parizeau* been making your life a misery because you are an Anglo? Claim dual citizenship at once and flee to Ontario.

I need your help. You have had a lot of experience with tours* and I should think that such tours included quite a few old people; what can you tell me about the sort of romances that develop on such tours (because I know that travel is a great provoker of romance). Are they real, sincere, romantic in any special way? I am particularly interested in old men because, as you will have already divined, I am writing a book to which this sort of thing is relevant. My suspicion is that old men, who are so often defined as lecherous old nuisances, are driven by a need for romance, understanding and companionship – sometimes so, because the old lechers are certainly to be seen. I feel that there is something pitiable about many of them, and I want to write about it: any words of wisdom from you would be keenly appreciated. Perhaps your hospital experience suggests something? I have a notion of old men lying in bed, with no resource but romantic fantasy or reverie, of romances that never were but which were painfully desired. Dig in your experience and please let me know what you think. . . .

... I am clearing the decks to get to work on a new novel, to round out my last trilogy. It will have a good deal to say about old age, on which I am becoming a reluctant expert. My poor brother Arthur has just become 92, which is something of a miracle as he was born a spina bifida child, and instead of dying young, has lived long and done a lot of interesting things – many of them for Queen's [University in Kingston, Ontario], which gave him an honorary doctorate a while ago; he watched over the building of a lot of their new places, found money and fought contractors. But now the poor man is in really bad shape – no illness but oppressive old age. He says he wishes he could die, but wishing won't make it so. I hope I don't come to that. We bred-in-the-bone Presbyterians have to stick it out, whatever the time it takes.

I repeat, I hope this finds you well, busy, much sought after and happy. And once again I ask for your words of experience.

Love,

Rob

To HORACE W. DAVENPORT

Windhover
Caledon East
October 16, 1995

Dear Horace:

I have been neglecting you, for which apologies. The past two weeks have been unusually demanding, as I keep getting myself involved in things which I should have the good sense to leave alone. A celebration of the establishment of a professorship to commemorate a good friend of mine – a geo-physicist [John Tuzo Wilson]* – who died recently. Some business involving Massey College, which

now has a new Master [John Fraser], a very good man who is making
positive moves to improve the college's financial position; government cuts have affected the coll. like every other part of the university. The request of a German magazine for an article* about Canada.
(This has been troublesome because I wrote a serious piece, which
they returned saying they wanted something light-hearted; I wondered whether I ought to resent this and be huffy, but decided that
as I am a professional writer who had undertaken a commission, it
was the professional thing to fulfil it, and not make a pompous fuss
like an amateur.) A request that I read a Ghost Story at the college's
Christmas Gaudy; they asked for one of the old ones, but I thought
a repeat not good enough, so have undertaken to write a new one,
which is a fair sized job as ghost stories do not shake out of my sleeve
– not ones of which I would not be ashamed. And I am off this week
to Princeton, to talk and attempt the impossible task of saying something sensible about writing. I am too busy, and it is nobody's fault
but my own, as Brenda and Jenny assure me, but I find it difficult to
say No to what appears to be a reasonable request.

I do say No to some things, however. France is preparing some sort
of literary jamboree next May and wants me to go. Can't and won't,
but they are very pressing. However I have promised to talk to the
Trollope Society in New York in May, and one job of that kind is
enough in a month when I want to be up here recovering from winter.

As for that, Brenda is insistent that we should go away in winter
for at least a month, to give my asthma a rest; I expect we shall go to
one of the Caribbean Islands. I do not yearn for winter holidays; my
Puritanism rebels against escapes from the weather to which I was
born. But common sense says otherwise.

I have been reading your recent pieces with pleasure. How well
you write! I still think a franker autobiography, even if you simply
confided it to an archive for later reading, would be a good idea. Your
life, like that of everybody who *is* anybody, is a Hero Struggle, a
contest with circumstances, and there is no better plot..... My poor
brother Arthur* is completing his Hero struggle, I fear, and I am committed to speaking about it at his funeral – a task I do not look forward

to, I can tell you. But unavoidable..... Our love to you and Inge. What news of Rob? All good, I trust.....

Rob.

To MRS. RENTOUL

Massey College
University of Toronto
October 17, 1995

> *Mrs. Rentoul's letter was forwarded to Davies by his London publishers. This reply was not the last letter he wrote. There was at least one more before he died, and there may be others, though not to any of his regular correspondents. Davies often wrote letters at home; usually no copies of those were kept.*

Dear Mrs. Rentoul:

Mr. Peter Carson of Penguin Books has sent me your letter of September 25, in which you express annoyance at the characterization of Mervyn Rentoul* in *The Cunning Man*, where he makes a brief appearance as an amateur actor. I am sorry you were disturbed by what seemed to be a reference to a relative of yours, who was indeed an actor. This is one of those mortifying things that happen to writers, and I apologize, and offer some explanation.

There was a time, in the nineteenth century, when characters in books were given names that labelled them, and which had no relationship to any name that could ever have been borne by anybody. If I had been writing then I should have called the man not Mervyn Rentoul, but Thespian Wouldbe or Gasper Garrick. But readers nowadays will not put up with that sort of thing, so names must be sought for characters which might conceivably occur in real life.

So – why Mervyn Rentoul? Rentoul, because it is the name of an estate in Scotland, and a Lord Rentoul appears in J. M. Barrie's *The Little Minister*.* (Canada is full of people with Scots names.) Mervyn, because it is a name which without being common is credible and

often heard. And as I could trace no person of that name anywhere
– telephone books, cast lists of plays done at Hart House,* etc. – I
thought it was safe.

But alas, there is no such thing as safety in the matter of names.
Every author knows what it is to hurt somebody's feelings, or even
to become involved in a libel suit, over a name which he thought
harmless. I can only say that I am sorry, and as I am busy at the
moment writing another novel, I shall hope for better luck – without
being in any way certain that I shall get it.

Yours sincerely

Robertson Davies

Editorial Note

The later letters of Robertson Davies have a characteristically handsome appearance. He wrote most of them on cream-coloured, 20-pound bond paper bearing his address at Massey College, at Windhover, or at The Oaklands. Most are typed, with the salutation, signature, date, and, in some instances, postscript, marginal corrections, and comments, added by hand. The handwritten parts provide a pleasant visual note, for Davies wrote in italic and varied the colour of the ink in his fountain pen from letter to letter – purple, green, red, black, blue. Generally he put the date at the bottom of a letter below his signature. If the letter was typed by his secretary, then the name and address of the recipient appear at the bottom of the letter. In this volume, however, I have put the date at the top of the letter under a simplified version of Davies' address. Correspondents' addresses have been omitted.

As this is the first edition of Davies' letters, their integrity has been respected as much as possible, particularly as it is not easy to consult the originals. (They are widely scattered, in the hands of recipients and in a number of public collections.) Omissions of repetitive material and of a few brief comments about living persons are marked by conventionally spaced ellipsis points.

Davies' enthusiasm for capital letters has been preserved, although his underlined passages appear here in italics. The one exception concerns abbreviations like Dr. Mr., Mrs. 2nd, 39th, Xtmas, where Davies underlined and elevated some letters when writing by hand. This characteristic has been preserved. Where necessary for clarity, his abbreviations have been expanded. Basic punctuation is as he wrote it, except for a few additional commas. From time to time he used strings of periods of variable length to indicate a minor break in thought, and these are represented here by five unspaced periods. Paragraph breaks occur where he established them, with the addition in a few places of an extra paragraph division for clarity's sake.

Davies often said that he preferred the way the British handle quotation marks. But in practice he was inconsistent, often changing style mid-quotation and mid-letter, or following the British practice in one letter, the North American in another. When preparing a typescript for publication, his secretary always standardized to North American style, and I have adopted her policy. Like most Canadians', Davies' vocabulary and spelling contained elements of both British and American usage, though he leaned more heavily than most toward the British. If his spelling was supported by *The Oxford English Dictionary* or a standard American dictionary, it stands here as he wrote it. He often invented variants on words (or created new ones), and I have presented these, too, as he wrote them. While generally an accurate speller, he occasionally made mistakes, and he used a few consistently idiosyncratic spellings like "accomodation" and "beseiged." Were he alive, he would certainly have insisted that such errors be corrected for publication, and so they have been. Typographical slips have likewise been dealt with silently and the variable use of the apostrophe in possessives has been regularized.

It was usually clear where Davies' marginal comments should be placed in the text, but in a few instances I have created a separate paragraph for them following the one to which they applied, or placed them in a bracketed sentence or two within the subject paragraph itself.

Square brackets denote my editorial additions (primarily names but also, occasionally, brief explanations). They also indicate a best guess about the form Davies may have used in his salutation and signature when a secretarial carbon copy of a letter was the only available source.

Brief biographical notes on Davies' correspondents are supplied at the head of the first letter to them. Endnotes identifying people mentioned in the letters are provided on the first occasion that they appear. Page references for these notes appear in bold under the name of the person in the index.

Page references to Davies' books are to the Penguin editions.

Works by Robertson Davies mentioned in *For Your Eye Alone*

Shakespeare's Boy Actors (criticism, 1939)
Fortune, My Foe (play, first performed 1948)
The Table Talk of Samuel Marchbanks (belles lettres, 1949)
Tempest-Tost (novel, 1951)
Leaven of Malice (novel, 1954)
A Mixture of Frailties (novel, 1958)
Love and Libel (play, first performed 1960)
A Voice from the Attic (essays, 1960)
Fifth Business (novel, 1970)
The Manticore (novel, 1972)
World of Wonders (novel, 1975)
One Half of Robertson Davies (speeches, 1977)
Pontiac and the Green Man (play, first performed 1977)
The Rebel Angels (novel, 1981)
Dr. Canon's Cure (libretto, first performed 1982)
High Spirits (ghost stories, 1982)
The Mirror of Nature (lectures, 1983)
What's Bred in the Bone (novel, 1985)
The Papers of Samuel Marchbanks (belles lettres, 1985)
The Lyre of Orpheus (novel, 1988)
Murther & Walking Spirits (novel, 1991)
Jezebel (libretto, first performed 1993)
The Cunning Man (novel, 1994)
The Merry Heart (miscellany, 1996)
Happy Alchemy (miscellany, 1997)
The Golden Ass (libretto, first performed 1999)

NOTES

SECTION I

p. 3: *Bear*: Novel by Canadian Marian Engel (1933–85), concerning a woman (humanity) enamoured of a bear (animal nature). RD's comment appeared on the jacket of the first printing.

p. 3: *Surfacing*: Novel by best-selling, influential Canadian poet, novelist, and critic Margaret Atwood (1939–).

p. 3: *Margaret Laurence and Adele Wiseman*: Laurence (1926–87) and Wiseman (1928–92), Canadian novelists, each known personally to RD from her year at Massey College as writer-in-residence at the University of Toronto.

p. 4: *my own recent experience*: The previous fall, Roy MacSkimming (1944–), Canadian writer and book reviewer, reviewed RD's novel *World of Wonders* in *The Toronto Star*, William French (1926–), Canadian critic, in *The Globe and Mail* [Toronto], and Brian Vintcent (1940–89), Canadian book reviewer, in *Books in Canada*.

p. 4: *Gordon Sinclair*: (1900–84), Canadian radio commentator, television panelist, and journalist.

p. 4: *Pierre Berton*: (1920–), Canadian journalist, popular historian, editor, media personality, and moderator of "The Great Debate," a public affairs program on Global TV.

p. 4: *Peter Newman*: (1929–), Canadian journalist, author, newspaper and magazine editor. He published the first volume of *The Canadian Establishment* in 1975.

p. 4: *Farley Mowat*: (1921–), best-selling, prolific Canadian author of books about Arctic peoples and animals.

p. 4: *Peter Gzowski*: (1934–), Canadian broadcaster, editor, and author.

p. 4: *Judy LaMarsh*: (1924–80), Canadian lawyer, Liberal politician, and broadcaster.

p. 5: *Wild Animals I have Known*: By Ernest Thompson Seton (1860–1946), naturalist and writer in Canada and the United States.

p. 6: *Sir John Martin-Harvey*: (1863–1944), English actor-manager who toured Canada with his company six times in the 1920s and early '30s, and the original of Sir John Tresize in *World of Wonders*.

p. 6: *The Corsican Brothers*: Translation by Irish playwright Dion Boucicault (1820–90) of a French dramatization of Alexandre Dumas *père's Les Frères Corses*. The play figures in *World of Wonders*.

p. 6: *The Only Way*: Dramatization by Freeman Wills (d. 1913) and Frederick Langbridge (1849–1922), Irish clergymen, of Dickens's *A Tale of Two Cities*.

p. 7: *Michael*: RD encountered Michael Martin-Harvey briefly in England during the fall of 1938 when both toured in Morna Stuart's play *Traitor's Gate*.

p. 7: *Nina de Silva*: (1868–1949) English actress of Spanish parentage.

p. 7: *Irving*: Sir Henry Irving (1838–1905) English actor-manager, first actor to be honoured with a knighthood.

p. 7: *Gordon Craig*: (1872–1966) English actor, director, scene designer, and theorist.

p. 7: *Reinhardt*: Max Reinhardt (1873–1943), Austrian actor, director, and impresario.

p. 7: *The Lyons Mail and The Bells*: *The Lyons Mail*: the name under which Irving produced *The Courier of Lyons*, a melodrama by English novelist and playwright Charles Reade (1814–84); *The Bells*: a melodrama translated and adapted by English solicitor and journalist Leopold Lewis (d. 1890) from Erckmann-Chatrian's *Le Juif polonais*. RD knew a great deal about Martin-Harvey's *Hamlet*, *Richard III*, *The Lyons Mail* and *The Bells*, but did not see them himself.

p. 7: *my novel*: *World of Wonders* 262–68.

p. 8: *your recollections*: Gielgud recounted how he and Terrence Rattigan were well along with preparations for staging Dickens's *A Tale of Two Cities* in 1935 when Martin-Harvey wrote insisting – effectively – that they desist as he was planning a farewell tour of *The Only Way*.

p. 8: *No Man's Land*: By English playwright Harold Pinter (1930–).

p. 8: *Israel Shenker*: (1925–), author and journalist, and, in the early 1970s, a reporter for the *New York Times*.

p. 8: *the Bollandists*: Small group of Jesuits in Antwerp, Belgium, who engage in the critical study and publication of the lives of the saints.

p. 9: *When I Was Young*: First volume of Raymond Massey's autobiography.

p. 9: *the succeeding volume*: *A Hundred Different Lives*.

p. 9: *Vincent Massey*: (1897–1967) Canadian politician, diplomat, governor general from 1952–59, Raymond's brother, and dominant member of the family which founded Massey College.

p. 10: *John Robert Evans*: (1929–), president of the University of Toronto from 1972–78, and Canadian doctor known for innovative reforms in medical education.

p. 10: *the Gordon Lectures*: Given in 1974–75, funded by the Walter and Duncan Gordon Foundation, and called the Massey College Lectures. They were published in 1976 as *Beyond Industrial Growth*, edited by Abraham Rotstein, with a preface by RD. This was probably the book RD promised to send.

p. 10: *Wealth of Nations*: Seminal work by Adam Smith (1723–90), Scottish moral philosopher and political economist. The bicentennial discussion had no connection with the "Gordon Lectures."

p. 12: *my speech on Canadian Nationalism*: "Canadian Nationalism in Arts and Science," given June 3, at the University of Wisconsin, Milwaukee.

p. 12: *a series of special lectures*: The Larkin-Stuart Lectures, given at Trinity College, November 15–18. See *One Half of Robertson Davies* 177–269.

p. 12: *Major Robert Rogers*: (1731–95) American frontiersman, author, able leader of the colonial Rangers during the War of the Austrian Succession, the Seven Years' War, and the American Revolution.

p. 12: *my wife [Brenda]*: (1917–) Australian-born Canadian, whose love, knowledge, and experience of theatre were almost as deep as RD's.

p. 13: *G. B. Shaw*: George Bernard Shaw (1856–1950), Irish dramatist, critic, and social reformer.

p. 14: *Hugh Anson-Cartwright*: (1930–) Toronto dealer in rare and second-hand books.

p. 14: *Samuel Marchbanks*: RD's pseudonym for his editorial page column in the *Kingston Whig-Standard* and *Peterborough Examiner* 1940–53, and for the books drawn from the column.

p. 14: *Trilby*: Dramatization by playwright Paul Potter (1853–1921) of the novel by George Du Maurier (1834–96). It tells how Trilby O'Ferrall, an artist's model in Paris, becomes a famous singer under the influence of the mesmerist Svengali, but loses her voice when he dies.

p. 14: *The Way of the World*: Comedy by English dramatist William Congreve (1670–1729).

p. 14: *Tree*: Herbert Beerbohm Tree (1853–1917), English actor-manager, who bought the rights to the play *Trilby* from Paul Potter, and had George Du Maurier contribute to its final adaptation for his London production.

p. 14: *My father Rupert Davies*: (1879–1967) Welsh-born Canadian, who rose from modest beginnings to own two Ontario regional newspapers, the *Peterborough Examiner* and the *Kingston Whig-Standard*.

p. 14: *Wilton Lackaye*: (1862–1932) English actor.

p. 15: *page 199*: In the first edition of *World of Wonders* (Toronto: Macmillan, 1975). See Penguin 179.

p. 15: *Edward Carrick*: (1905–) designer, author, and lecturer. The Old Vic did *The Taming of the Shrew* in March and April 1939.

p. 15: *Frank Moore*: Probably Frank More, who was Thomas Cranmer in *Traitor's Gate* while RD played the Duke of Norfolk. He appears under his own name in *World of Wonders* as a member of Sir John Tresize's troupe.

p. 15: *Ben Webster*: (1864–1947) Egeus in the Old Vic production of *A Midsummer Night's Dream* (December–January 1938–39) in which RD played

Snout. His daughter Margaret Webster (1905–47) was an English actress and director. *Importance* is *The Importance of Being Earnest* by the Irish wit, writer, and playwright Oscar Wilde (1854–1900).

p. 15: *Eric Jones-Evans*: (1898–1989) English actor, physician, and collector of theatrical memorabilia. RD exchanged a few letters with him and visited him once.

p. 16: *Your questions*: 1) "In what ways do you find Canadians to be significantly different from people from other countries, (e.g. European)?" 2) "Do you believe that Canadians, because of their background, lack an imagination, and also possess a 'guilt feeling,' (e.g. Dunny and Deptford)?" 3) "What do you feel constitutes a novel's 'Canadian' qualities?"

p. 17: *Miss Julie*: By Swedish dramatist August Strindberg (1849–1912).

p. 18: *Douglas Rain*: (1928–) Canadian actor, who played Jean.

p. 18: *Eric Steiner*: (1946–) Canadian freelance director, active in Toronto theatres during the 1970s and across Canada since then.

p. 19: *prostate job as well as the other*: Davenport had had a transurethral prostatectomy.

p. 19: *Shall we . . . river*: By Robert Lowry (1826–99), American Baptist pastor.

p. 19: *the production*: In the MacMillan Theatre, Edward Johnson Building, University of Toronto, October 26–November 5. It was the Drama Centre's contribution to the University's sesquicentennial celebrations.

p. 20: *the chapters on Good and Evil*: See 177–269.

p. 20: *Marie-Louise von Franz*: (1915–98) German-born Swiss authority on analytical psychology, a founder of the C. G. Jung Institute in Zurich, and colleague of C. G. Jung's 1933–61. She mentioned this incident when she stayed with the Davieses in March 1975, while in Toronto to speak.

p. 20: *Florence McKay Davies's*: (1870–1948) Canadian.

p. 20: *Calvinist upbringing . . . Anglican prating*: RD was raised a Presbyterian, but joined the Anglican Church in 1937 while at Oxford.

p. 21: *Inge*: Davenport's second wife, Ingeborg Luise Günther Davenport (1919–), a German-born American, whose training was as a nurse.

p. 21: *second operation*: Another prostatectomy.

p. 21: *people ask me to make speeches*: Calgary, February 9; Montreal, "The Lahey Lecture," Concordia University, February 13; authors' association, The Canadian Authors' Association, February 23, Sheraton Centre, Toronto; Black Forest, at the Canadian military bases at Lahr and Baden, March 6–10.

p. 22: *A play*: For the St. Lawrence Centre in Toronto. Nothing came of this.

p. 22: *Arthur Spring-Rice Pyper*: (1916–94) fellow student with whom RD took Latin tutorials in 1936, later headmaster of a preparatory school in Seaford, East Sussex.

p. 23: *To THE EDITOR . . . REPUBLIC*: Published in that magazine May 27: 3.

p. 23: *Joyce Carol Oates*: (1938–) prolific American author, professor of English at the University of Windsor in Ontario 1967–78, and at Princeton 1978– . Her review appeared in *The New Republic* April 15: 22–25.

p. 23: *Sydney Smith's query*: Smith (1771–1845), English cleric, wit, and writer. For his query, see his review of Adam Seybert's *Statistical Annals of the United States of America*, *Edinburgh Review* 65 (January 1820): 79.

p. 23: *The situation . . . Civil War*: RD viewed the struggle between Quebec and the balance of Canada, together with several other wrangles, as his country's civil war, a psychological one, whose resolution would produce a sense of national identity. See *One Half of Robertson Davies* 279–80.

p. 24: *a weekly book-reviewer of some influence*: As literary editor of *Saturday Night* 1940–42 and 1953–59, columnist for the *Toronto Star* syndicate 1959–62, and editor of the *Peterborough Examiner* 1942–63.

p. 25: *melodrama of the high kind – Byron*: Lord George Gordon Byron (1788–1824), English Romantic poet and dramatist. For high and low melodrama, see *One Half of Robertson Davies* 143–60 and *The Mirror of Nature*.

p. 25: *a natural for Penguin*: Elisabeth Sifton promptly sent RD the new Penguin *Notre Dame de Paris*, translated by John Sturrock.

p. 26: *spurn it . . . menstruous cloth*: "Ye shall defile also the covering of thy graven images of silver, and the ornament of thy molten images of gold: thou shalt cast them away as a menstruous cloth; thou shalt say unto it, Get thee hence." Isaiah 30:22

p. 26: *Readers–Writers Conference*: The Wesleyan–Suffield Writers' Conference, an annual week-long gathering, in Connecticut. In 1976, '77, and '78, RD co-taught six 90-minute sessions about fiction and counselled many aspiring writers individually.

p. 26: *Curtis Brown*: Curtis Brown, Ltd., RD's agents in New York.

p. 26: *Richard Barber*: (1940–) American, director of corporate public relations and editor at The Viking Press in New York.

p. 27: *your piece*: "The Golden Age of Canadian Writing Is Here, Says a Writer. Respect It," *The Globe and Mail*: 6.

p. 27: *visited the University of Freiburg*: During his visit to the military bases at Lahr and Baden.

p. 27: *Dr. Konrad Gross . . . Malcolm Ross*: Gross (1940–), then an assistant professor in the English department at the University of Freiburg. He introduced Canadian literature and Canadian Studies at the University of Kiel the following year. Malcolm Ross (1911–), Canadian, was then a professor of English at Dalhousie University and editor of the influential New Canadian Library reprint series.

p. 28: *Lady Audley's Secret*: Novel by English writer Mary Elizabeth Braddon (1837–1915), adapted for the stage by Douglas Seale.

p. 29: *birthday card*: RD was born August 28, 1913. He wrote Elisabeth Sifton (to whom he had sent a copy of his letter to *The New Republic*): "What do you think? Joyce Carol Oates has sent me a birthday card – a sour-funny one, but still a card. In return I have written asking her to come to dinner. We'll see what happens, and if there is any blood-letting I shall inform you at once."

(Oates never came to dinner, probably because she moved from the University of Windsor to Princeton at this time.)

p. 29: *Daphne Athas*: (1923–) American novelist and writer of short stories.

p. 31: *Chuzzlewit, Pecksniff, and Gamp*: Characters in *The Life and Adventures of Martin Chuzzlewit*.

p. 31: *Henry James*: (1843–1916) novelist and critic, scion of a prosperous American family.

p. 31: *Joseph Conrad*: Conrad (1857–1924) spoke Polish as his cradle tongue, learned French young, but began to absorb English, the language he used for his stories and novels, only at 20.

p. 32: *Paul Patterson*: (1947–) versatile English composer of contemporary classical music.

p. 32: *Old Ebenezer*: Ebenezer Scrooge, the curmudgeon in Dickens's *A Christmas Carol*.

p. 32: *Rosamond & John Cunnington and their four young*: Rosamond (1947–), RD's youngest daughter, was married to John Cunnington, a physician, from 1969 to 1983. Their children are Christopher (1969–), Piers (1971–), Erik (1977–) and Cecilia (1978–).

p. 32: *Chums*: Weekly British magazine for boys, which was gathered into annual volumes.

p. 33: *she has slain*: This grotesque Toronto murder took place on April 9, 1978, but it was in the news on December 15, 16, and 19 when the case came before the Supreme Court of Ontario. The girl was found not guilty by reason of insanity. RD refers to this murder again in his letter of August 7, 1986.

p. 33: *reviewing . . . Dark Lady*: See *The Globe and Mail* January 13, 1979: 43. A. L. Rowse (1903–97), famous English authority on Tudor history, was equally well known for his often wrong-headed criticism of Shakespeare. In particular, with no solid proof or likelihood, he contended that the "Dark Lady" of Shakespeare's sonnets was the English poetess Emilia Lanier (Aemilia Lanyer, 1569–1645).

p. 34: *Michael Davies*: (1936–) the older of Arthur's two sons, general manager, then publisher and eventually owner, of the *Kingston Whig-Standard* 1962–90.

p. 34: *the room at the Grand Theatre*: On June 1, the lounge of the newly renovated Grand Theatre in Kingston was named after Rupert Davies and a plaque was unveiled describing him as "publisher of *The Whig-Standard* from 1926 until 1951 and as a lover of the arts who spent many happy hours in this theatre."

pp. 34–35: *Jenny and Tom Surridge . . . Miranda Davies*: Jennifer Surridge: (1942–) the Davieses' middle daughter, an administrative assistant and a teacher of needlework; *Thomas Surridge*: (1930–) her husband, a Jamaican-born Canadian psychologist; *Miranda Davies*: (1940–) the Davieses' eldest daughter, then training to become a Jungian analyst in London, England.

p. 35: *to hand over to Michael Peterman*: Peterman (1942–), now professor and chairman, then a junior member of the English department at Trent University in Peterborough, Ontario. Roper had suffered a heart attack in February.

p. 36: *Nabokov*: Vladimir Nabokov (1899–1977), Russian-born American novelist, poet, and critic. For "shamanstvo" see Andrew Field, *Nabokov: His Life in Part* (New York: Viking, 1977) 268. RD had read this biography.

p. 37: *Helen*: Roper's wife Helen Denmark Caddy Roper (1910–98), Canadian, a nurse for several years.

SECTION II

p. 40: *To THE EDITOR . . . MAIL*: Not published.

p. 40: *Mr. Scott Symons*: (1933–) controversial, combative, avowedly bisexual Canadian novelist and journalist. See "The New Literature of Canada: GritLit," 7 (part of a series Symons was writing for the *Globe* about different aspects of Canada).

p. 42: *Alfred Knopf*: (1892–1984) the most literary of the major American publishers. He invited RD to write the book on reading which appeared under his imprint as *A Voice from the Attic* (1960).

p. 42: *Salvador Dali*: (1904–89) Spanish painter, leading figure in the surrealist movement.

p. 43: *invented the term Fifth Business*: For the origin of the term, see *Man of Myth* 471.

p. 44: *Morley Callaghan*: (1903–90) Toronto novelist and short-story writer.

p. 45: *The Queen of Spades*: (1949) British film based on Alexander Pushkin's story about an impoverished army officer who sells his soul to the devil in order to force an aged countess to reveal her secret of winning at cards, but she dies of fright and haunts him. *Yvonne Mitchell*: (1925–79) leading English actress, playwright and author.

p. 45: *The Guardsman:* (1931) American film of Ferenc Molnar's play in which a jealous actor tests his wife's fidelity. *Lynn Fontanne*: (1887–1983) English stage actress, married to *Alfred Lunt* (1892–1977), American actor. *Roland Young*: (1887–1953) English actor.

p. 45: *The Man from Blankley's*: (1930) amusing American film about a drunken aristocrat who goes to the wrong party and teaches those present, and himself, a thing or two. *John Barrymore*: (1882–1942) American actor. *Frederick Anstey*: pseudonym of Thomas Anstey Guthrie (1856–1934), prolific English writer of novels and dialogues, including *The Man from Blankley's*. *Charles Hawtrey*: (1858–1923) English actor-manager.

p. 46: *a cloud of witnesses*: "Wherefore seeing we also are compassed about with so great a cloud of witnesses, let us lay aside every weight, and the sin which doth so easily beset us, and let us run with patience the race that is set before us,/Looking unto Jesus the author and finisher of our faith." Hebrews 12:1–2.

p. 47: *Trudeausday*: That day, to RD's pleasure as a Liberal, the newspapers reported that Pierre Elliott Trudeau (1919–), Canada's Liberal prime minister 1968–79, had been returned to power in the previous day's election.

p. 48: *extraverted*: RD preferred the spelling used by the translator of *The Collected Works of C. G. Jung*. See his use of "extraversion" in his letter of August 27, 1984.

p. 48: *Sarah-Jane Edinborough*: (1956–), now Sarah J. E. Iley, Canadian, president and chief executive officer of the Council for Business and the Arts in Canada. She is the Edinboroughs' daughter, a graduate of Queen's, and was RD's god-daughter.

p. 48: *Gamaliel*: Great Jewish rabbi and teacher of St. Paul (Acts 22:3).

p. 49: *Rabelais*: François Rabelais (1494?–1553), French humanist, satirist, and physician.

p. 49: *Stephen Leacock*: (1869–1944) English-born Canadian humorist, writer, professor, and political economist. The Owls' Club epitomized all little associations whose executives sought out speakers, paid them nothing, and had a membership that rarely attended meetings. See Leacock's "We Have with Us To-night," in *My Discovery of England* or *The Leacock Roundabout*.

p. 49: *George Herbert Clarke*: (1873–1953) English-born professor of English, poet, editor of *Queen's Quarterly* 1944–53. He was one of RD's professors at Queen's 1932–35.

p. 50: *Sturge Moore*: Thomas Sturge Moore (1870–1944), English poet, dramatist, critic of art and literature, wood-engraver, and stage designer.

p. 52: *one of the Gospels*: The Book of Enoch.

p. 53: *our present mess*: Prime Minister Trudeau was seeking patriation of the British North America Act (Canada's constitution) from Britain, along with changes, including a Charter of Rights. The provinces were opposing his every move, mounting court challenges, and lobbying the British parliament in London.

p. 54: *The brouhaha at Stratford*: The Stratford Festival's board had failed to take decisive action to replace its retiring artistic director. Into the vacuum stepped two successive groups from among the Festival's directors and actors; the board issued press releases but no contracts. The 1981 season proposed by the second group was the basis of the usual request for funding from the Canada Council. The board then had second thoughts about its financial viability, said nothing to the proposers and hired a British artistic director. Indignant at the insult to its members, the Council of Canadian Actors' Equity voted, in effect, to boycott the Festival. Militant nationalist positions were taken – and opposed. The British director was denied a work permit. The Festival's December annual meeting was angry and vitriolic. The board then hired a Canadian director.

p. 54: *posturings of Scott Symons*: See RD's letter of April 23, 1979 and the note about it.

p. 55: *Dictionary of Angels: A Dictionary of Angels Including the Fallen Angels* by Gustav Davidson (1967).

p. 55: *Stoicheff:* Boris Stoicheff (1924–), Yugoslav-born Canadian physicist with a special interest in lasers, atomic and molecular spectroscopy and structure; senior fellow at Massey College 1978– .

p. 56: *The White Hotel:* Novel by English poet, novelist, and translator Donald Michael Thomas (1935–). The Viking Press published it in 1981.

p. 57: *shamanstvo:* See RD's letter of March 29, 1979.

p. 57: *To THE EDITOR . . . MAIL:* Published January 19: 6.

p. 57: *The Dumbells:* Canadian army entertainers during World War I, later a vaudeville troupe.

p. 57: *Chico Marx:* (1891–1961) one of the family of American comic actors – the Marx Brothers – that included Harpo, Groucho, and Zeppo.

p. 58: *Naughty Daughter:* The United States.

p. 59: *Mackenzie King:* William Lyon Mackenzie King (1874–1950), Canada's Prime Minister 1921–26, 1926–30, and 1935–48.

p. 59: *The Old Wise Woman:* Subtitled *A Study of Active Imagination* this book is by Rix Weaver (1902–), Australian student of Jung's thought.

p. 59: *put on . . . armour of God:* Ephesians 6:11.

p. 59: *I ruptured myself:* RD suffered a hernia.

p. 60: *Maisie Drysdale:* (1915–) Australian. Her husband, Sir Russell Drysdale (1912–81), was an Australian artist and colour photographer, especially known for his paintings of drought landscapes and Aborigines.

p. 60: *Perry H. Knowlton:* (1927–) American, president of Curtis Brown, Ltd., in New York.

p. 60: *theatre history of Canada:* He completed his piece on "The Nineteenth-Century Repertoire" in the fall of 1982, but the volume for which he prepared it – *Early Stages: Theatre in Ontario 1800–1914,* ed. Ann Saddlemyer – did not appear until 1990.

p. 61: *J. N. Patterson Hume:* (1923–) Canadian educator in physics and computer science, master of Massey College 1981–88.

p. 61: *Inge . . . better:* Inge Davenport had had a stroke the previous May.

p. 64: *Burton or Aubrey:* Robert Burton (1577–1640) was the English author of *The Anatomy of Melancholy,* a miscellany of learning which figures in *The Cunning Man.* John Aubrey (1626–97) was the English author of a collection of *Lives* of eminent persons which figures in *The Rebel Angels.*

p. 64: *Jean-Claude Parrot:* (1936–) president of the Canadian Union of Postal Workers. The 42-day postal strike ended on August 11.

p. 64: *his son Lionel:* Lionel Massey (1916–65), Canadian director of administration of the Royal Ontario Museum and member of the foundation that founded Massey College.

p. 66: *a party:* On June 16.

p. 67: *Little Dorrit*: Novel by Dickens.

p. 67: *Oxford English Dictionary* (1933, rpt. 1977) in 13 volumes, plus 4 supplements.

p. 67: *Memoirs of an Anti-Semite*: Novel by Gregor von Rezzori (1914–), author, broadcaster, and filmmaker who writes in German. This English translation was published by The Viking Press.

p. 67: *your Judge [Charles P. Sifton]*: (1935–) American, Elisabeth Sifton's husband and United States District Court Judge in the Eastern District of New York 1977– .

p. 68: *Lorenzo (da P.) . . . Salieri*: Lorenzo da Ponte (1749–1838), Italian-born American, was Mozart's librettist. Antonio Salieri (1750–1825), Italian conductor and composer, was said to have disliked Mozart and to have poisoned him.

p. 70: *what Liliane Frey-Rohn says*: Frey-Rohn (1901–??), Swiss analyst, colleague of Jung's, and author of "The Psychological View" in *Evil: Essays*, edited by the Jung Institute in Zurich. Ewing quoted her, in his September 25, 1981, letter to RD, as saying: ". . . knowledge of one's personal shadow is the necessary requirement for any responsible action, and consequently for any lessening of moral darkness in the world."

p. 70: *Boy Staunton*: Staunton, like his son David, is a character in RD's Deptford trilogy.

p. 71: *John Irving*: (1942–) American writer who gained wide attention in 1978 with his novel *The World According to Garp*. The book RD reviewed – generously and perceptively – was *The Hotel New Hampshire*. See "John Irving and His Traveling Menagerie," *Washington Post Book World* September 6, 1981: 1–2.

p. 73: *Douglas Gibson*: (1943–) Scot, publisher at Macmillan of Canada and RD's editor there.

p. 74: *Claude Bissell*: (1916–) Canadian professor of English, president of the University of Toronto 1958–71 when Massey College was founded and set going, senior fellow at Massey College 1971– , friend and appreciative reviewer of RD's early work.

p. 74: *Hugh MacLennan*: (1907–90) Canadian novelist and essayist, a defining voice in Canadian literature.

p. 74: *Judith Grant*: Judith Skelton Grant (1941–) Canadian, editor of two collections of RD's journalism and a university teacher, who had approached RD that May about writing his biography. When he agreed, I talked with him about the various kinds of private papers that would help me understand his life: diaries, manuscripts, letters, and the like. Not until 1983, when RD made a selective transcript of them for my use, did I learn that the "letters . . . from Oxford" were love-letters.

p. 74: *Eleanor Sweezey*: Eleanor Anne Sweezey (1915–) Canadian medical illustrator. RD dated and fell in love with her while they were students at Queen's University. See *Man of Myth* 150–60.

p. 74: *Parson Weems*: Mason Locke Weems (1759–1825), American Episcopal clergyman, author of *The Life and Memorable Actions of George Washington*, which is responsible for much of the Washington myth.

p. 74: *the letters I wrote to you*: Letters written in 1972, as RD proofread *The Manticore* and as *World of Wonders* began to take shape.

p. 75: *to have a library named after me*: The library at Massey College.

p. 75: *honour from the University of Toronto*: An honorary Doctor of Laws degree at fall convocation.

p. 75: *Malton*: Earlier name of Toronto International Airport.

p. 76: *Kroch and Brentano*: A bookstore.

SECTION III

p. 80: *the piece*: "The Inventor of Gods," February 8, 1982: 78–80.

p. 80: *Tyrone Guthrie*: (1900–71) English-born. Guthrie subsequently became the founding artistic director of the Stratford Festival.

p. 80: *heaping Pelléas on Mélisande*: RD here plays with the title of Claude Debussy's opera *Pelléas et Mélisande* and the expression "heaping Pelion upon Ossa" – a reference to the giants trying to scale heaven by placing Mount Pelion upon Mount Ossa for a ladder (*Odyssey* 11. 315).

p. 81: *Kenneth Galbraith*: John Kenneth Galbraith (1908–), Canadian-born economist, writer, activist liberal, and professor at Harvard. See "The World of Wonders of Robertson Davies," *New York Times Book Review*, February 4, 1982: 7, 30.

p. 81: *I hope they don't cut . . . like the above*: They didn't.

p. 81: *gnawing at my vitals . . . Spartan boy*: This story is drawn from Plutarch's life of Lycurgus. Exemplifying the stoicism inculcated by harsh Spartan training, it tells of a lad who stole a young fox, hid it under his cloak and, though it tore out his entrails with claws and teeth, died, rather than reveal it.

p. 81: *Alfred Tennyson*: (1809–92) the most famous English poet of the Victorian period.

p. 84: *Dunstan Ramsay's girlfriends*: *Fifth Business* 118.

p. 85: *your likeness struck*: Stead's friends in the Police Service subscribed to have his portrait painted and hung in the dining hall at Bramshill.

p. 85: *tankards of Haigh the Vampire*: John George Haigh (1909–49), murderer, dissolved the bodies of his victims in sulphuric acid, but not until he had drunk their blood (or so he claimed).

p. 85: *escape artist . . . Irving statue*: Behind the National Portrait Gallery in London. See *World of Wonders* 149–51, 154–55.

p. 86: *Somerset Maugham*: (1874–1965) English (born in Paris) novelist and dramatist. RD saw *Lady Frederick* on January 5, 1971.

p. 86: *something . . . computers*: Surridge was director of statistics for the Solicitor-General.

p. 87: *Jaroslav M. J. Polak*: (1936–) Czech-born Canadian, general practitioner, RD's doctor 1966–95.

p. 87: *Judith*: Judith Irene Stead (1921–), English.

p. 87: *the clipping*: The title page and pages 295 and 314 from Arthur Cleveland Bent's *Life Histories of North American Birds of Prey* Part 2 (Smithsonian Institution United States National Museum Bulletin 170). RD used the information in *What's Bred in the Bone* 53.

p. 89: *Ubukata*: Bruce Ubukata (1949–), Canadian pianist, organist, and accompanist.

p. 90: *the singers play instrumentally*: The singers each imitate a different instrument.

p. 92: *a Celt*: RD's father, Rupert, came to Canada from Wales; RD's mother, Florence, was born in Canada, but her father's family was Scottish in origin. (Her mother's family was German or Dutch, by way of the United States.)

p. 94: *fan letters*: Irving had long admired RD's work, but was not moved to write until RD reviewed *The Hotel New Hampshire* (see RD's letter dated Thanksgiving [Canadian Style] 1981) in a way which "meant a great deal" because of how much Irving "respected him as a writer."

p. 94: *Upper Canada College*: The most prestigious of Canada's private boys' schools. UCC is in Toronto and RD was there 1928–32.

p. 94: *wearing running-shoes*: Irving had broken a big toe while wrestling, and was wearing his son's wrestling shoes as the only comfortable footwear. But he was acutely conscious of the lapse in decorum.

p. 94: *Rusty*: Rustine Unger, married for a period to Thomas Guinzburg (1926–), American president of The Viking Press in New York, 1962–80, and president of Viking Penguin Inc., 1976–80.

p. 95: *a short movie*: Aired as "Writers and Places," BBC2-TV, August 7, 1983.

p. 95: *Dingley Dell*: Home of the hospitable Mr. Wardle in *Pickwick Papers*.

p. 96: *two of Australia's foremost painters*: Peter Purves Smith (1912–49), painter of bleak images of the outback and of several of the most formidable images in Australian post-war art, and Sir Russell Drysdale.

p. 96: *Waugh for writing Brideshead*: Evelyn Waugh (1903–66) was an English satiric, witty, sophisticated writer. *Brideshead Revisited* is one of his novels. Why she hated *Brideshead* is not known.

p. 96: *Elspeth Cameron*: (1943–) Canadian biographer, critic, and professor of English, author of the recently published *Hugh MacLennan: A Writer's Life*.

p. 96: *have shuffled off this mortal coil*: Hamlet 3.1.

p. 97: *correspondence between Bernard Shaw and Lord Alfred Douglas*: See *Bernard Shaw and Alfred Douglas: A Correspondence*, ed. Mary Hyde. Lord Alfred Douglas (1870–1945) was an English aristocrat, son of the Marquess of Queensberry, and Oscar Wilde's lover.

p. 97: *from the country*: The Ropers lived just outside Peterborough, Ontario.

p. 98: *Barry's call . . . birthday celebrations*: Morley Callaghan turned 80 on February 23. Barry Callaghan (1937–) is a poet, writer, journalist, professor of English, and Morley's son. Lorette was Morley Callaghan's wife.

p. 99: *long article*: "Playing the Davies Game." I have been unable to find *In Print*.

p. 99: *Katy Brooks*: Temporary editorial assistant at The Viking Press in New York.

p. 99: *Thornton Wilder*: (1897–1975) American novelist and playwright. See "Thornton Wilder," *Writers at Work: The Paris Review Interviews*, ed. Malcolm Cowley (New York: Viking, 1959): 102.

p. 99: *Woe unto me when all men praise me*: A teasing quotation, not, in fact, from T. S. Eliot's *Murder in the Cathedral*, but an application of "Woe unto you, when all men shall speak well of you," Luke 6:26.

p. 100: *Love Locked Out*: By Anna Lea Merritt (1834–1930), American-born English painter, muralist, and printmaker. The painting depicts Love at the door of a tomb.

p. 101: *The Canadian Society for Italic Handwriting*: This group flourished 1955–56. RD was its vice-president, and contributed several articles and brief reviews to its publication *Italic*.

p. 101: *not in the power of Morris West*: Morris West (1916–), Australian best-selling novelist. RD refers to his *The World Is Made of Glass*.

p. 101: *Jung, his wife and Toni Wolff*: Jung's wife was Emma Rauschenbach (1882–1955), a Swiss, a colleague of Jung's and an analyst; Antonia Wolff's dates were 1888–1953.

p. 102: *A fine tribute to Toni Wolff*: For this and Emma Jung's declaration of gratitude, see *Jung and the Story of Our Time* (New York: Pantheon, 1975) 169–77. Laurens van der Post (1906–) is a South African writer who was a friend of Jung's.

p. 102: *Anthony Burgess*: (1917–93) English novelist, best known for *A Clockwork Orange*.

p. 102: *Ernest Jones*: (1879–1958) Welsh psychoanalyst and follower, colleague, and biographer of Sigmund Freud.

p. 104: *University of Toronto Bulletin*: June 20, 1983: 9.

p. 105: *piece of really good advice*: Namely: "You may not be able to alter reality, but you can alter your attitude towards it, and this, paradoxically, alters reality."

p. 105: *Robert Ross*: Robert Baldwin Ross (1869–1918), literary journalist and art-critic. His great grandfather (William Warren Baldwin) and his grandfather (Robert Baldwin), both lawyers and politicians, worked for responsible government in what was to become Ontario, and Robert Baldwin was effectively the province's first premier, 1842–43 (and he served again, 1848–51). Ross moved to London with his family in 1871 and he made his career there.

p. 105: *Oscar was doom-eager*: Wilde, counselled to flee England when the Marquess of Queensberry accused him of posing as a sodomite and of enthralling his son Lord Alfred Douglas, chose instead to prosecute Queensberry for criminal libel. Unsuccessful, he was then charged with committing homo-sexual acts (a criminal offence), found guilty, and sentenced to two years at hard labour. The scandal ruined him financially: his wife, Constance, and their children had to leave the country, change their name, and accept the charity of her family.

p. 106: *We have not met for*: Over the years, they had seen each other briefly two or three times before or after RD gave a speech in Montreal.

p. 106: *Time's winged chariot*: "But at my back I always hear/Time's wingèd chariot hurrying near" (from "To His Coy Mistress" by the English poet Andrew Marvell [1621–78]).

p. 107: *your Margery Pinchwife*: In *The Country Wife* by William Wycherley (1640–1716), English restoration playwright. RD saw the play at the Avon Theatre in Stratford, Ontario, on August 27. It concerns the efforts of jealous Mr. Pinchwife to keep his young wife, Margery, from the temptations of London.

p. 107: *So what have you seen*: *Sydney Carroll*: (1877–1958) Australian director; *Lesley Wareing*: (1913–) English actress; *Athene Seyler*: (1889–1990) English actress outstanding in Restoration comedy; *Ruth Gordon*: (1896–1985) American actress; *Edith Evans:* (1888–1976) one of the great English actresses of her generation; *Julie Harris:* (1925–) versatile, powerful American actress; *Stratford production*: In 1964, in Stratford, Ontario; *Helen Burns*: English actress and director.

p. 107: *a common grayness silvered all*: From "Andrea del Sarto," by English poet Robert Browning (1812–89).

p. 108: *The Pilgrim's Progress*: Allegorical story of Christian's journey (and that of his wife and children) through such places as the Slough of Despond and the Palace Beautiful to the Celestial City, by John Bunyan (1628–88), English Nonconformist preacher.

p. 108: *Dostoevsky*: Feodor Mikhailovich Dostoevsky (1821–81), great Russian novelist, profound psychologist, and philosopher.

p. 108: *Zola and Flaubert*: Émile Zola (1840–1902), French novelist and journal-ist. *Nana* is one of 20 novels in his principal work, the natural and social history of the Rougon-Marquart family over five generations. Gustave Flaubert (1821–80) was a French realistic novelist. *Madame Bovary*, one of the great novels of the nineteenth century, portrayed the frustrations and adulteries of the wife of a dull provincial doctor.

p. 109: *God is not mocked*: Galatians 6:7.

p. 109: *The dog shall return again . . . wallowing in the mire*: 2 Peter 2:22.

p. 109: *As a man soweth, that shall he also reap*: Galatians 6:7.

p. 111: *Luigi von Kunits*: (1870–31) Viennese conductor of the TSO 1923–31. His concertmaster was Donald Hein. Frank Blachford (1879–1957), Canadian, violinist, teacher, conductor, and composer, played in the orchestra 1932–46, and was assistant concert master for part of that period.

p. 111: *Trollopian*: With reference to Anthony Trollope (1815–82), prolific English novelist and astute observer of English society. The clergy of the Church of England play a predominant part in his Barsetshire novels.

p. 111: *Lohengrin*: Wagner's opera about the tragic love of a Knight of the Holy Grail. The brilliant third act prelude introduces a fleeting moment of happiness.

p. 111: *Sir Ernest MacMillan*: (1893–1973) Canadian conductor of the TSO 1931–56.

p. 111: *Stanley Solomon*: (1917–) Canadian principal viola of the TSO 1949–83, and principal emeritus until 1988.

p. 112: *sugar scoops*: The balconies of the Hall are divided into scooplike sections.

p. 113: *Margaret Mitchell Sweezey*: (1912–83) Canadian daycare helper and nurse's aide volunteer, caregiver for her mother, had been failing seriously when she had a heart attack, was revived and sustained on life support systems, and lingered until November 22.

p. 113: *Harriet Mitchell Watson Sweezey*: (1887–1960) Canadian, wife and mother, at Queen's University 1933–34 studying philosophy. She invited RD to produce *The Importance of Being Earnest* for a New Year's party at her country house outside Kingston. See *Man of Myth* 149–50.

p. 114: *A pupil of Dr. Jung's told me*: RD made fictional use of this story. See *The Rebel Angels* 300.

p. 115: *John . . . Orwell*: George Orwell (1903–50), Indian-born English writer. His novel *Nineteen Eighty-Four* is a nightmare story of totalitarianism and one man's hopeless struggle against it. John is John A. G. Grant (1938–), Canadian economist and my husband.

p. 116: *Jonsonian*: With reference to English playwright Ben Jonson (1572–1637). In his *Volpone, or The Fox*, Volpone, a rich, childless Venetian, pretends that he is dying in order to elicit gifts from his would-be heirs.

p. 116: *a painter*: Judith Stead is a painter in oils, primarily of city scenes – Paris, London, and New York.

p. 117: *Surtees*: Robert Smith Surtees (1805–64), English author of humorous sporting novels. For Stead's article, see "Surtees: A Centenary Appreciation," *The Horseman's Year* [an annual], ed. Dorian Williams (London: Collins, 1965).

p. 117: *Phyllis Rose*: (1942–) American professor of English at Wesleyan University 1969– .

p. 117: *Lacenaire*: *The Memoirs of Lacenaire* (a French murderer who was tried before the Assize Court of the Seine in 1835). RD reviewed Stead's translation in the *Peterborough Examiner*'s "Bibliomania" column June 21, 1952:4.

p. 118: C. G. JUNG FOUNDATION: RD probably had this letterhead as one of the Foundation's Directors and Officers. The letter appears to have been typed on his own machine.

p. 118: *the Mirror of Nature*: *Hamlet* 3.2.22.

SECTION IV

p. 123: *For many years*: 1960–81.

p. 123: *Imam of Yemen*: Probably an inaccurate recollection of the murders in February 1948 of Imam Yahya (who ruled 1904–48), two of his sons, and a grandson. Yahya's eldest son Ahmed, who succeeded him as Imam in April, does not seem to have been involved. Newspaper reports at the time were confusing.

p. 123: *Ezra Pound*: (1885–1972) who lived in Italy from 1925 until the end of World War Two. During the war he broadcast Fascist propaganda over the Rome radio.

p. 124: *Hugh MacLennan*: MacLennan seconded Stead's nomination of RD.

p. 125: *the Gilman*: The Daniel Coit Gilman Lecture which RD gave at The Johns Hopkins Medical Institutions, Baltimore, on November 18, 1984. See *The Merry Heart* 90–110.

p. 125: *Death, thou shalt die*: RD quoted the whole, not just this concluding phrase, of *Holy Sonnet X* by John Donne (1571 or 72 to 1631), English cleric and metaphysical poet.

p. 126: *carpenter's son . . .* : A line (or perhaps two) appears to have been missed in the photocopy of the letter here; the original has vanished.

p. 126: *Aldous Huxley*: (1894–1963) English novelist and essayist. RD refers to the concluding passage of *Texts and Pretexts*: "People will accept certain theological statements about life and the world, will elect to perform certain rites and to follow certain rules of conduct, not because they imagine the statements to be true or the rules and rites to be divinely dictated, but simply because they have discovered experimentally that to live in a certain ritual rhythm, under certain ethical restraints, and as if certain metaphysical doctrines were true, is to live nobly, with style."

p. 127: *trouble with your eyes*: Degeneration of the optic nerve was gradually depriving Roper of his sight; his wife, Helen, had cataracts.

p. 127: *The first*: I have not been able to find this article, review, or letter.

p. 127: *a "paper" on Fifth Business*: See R. D. MacDonald, "Small Town Ontario in Robertson Davies' *Fifth Business*: Mariposa Revised?" *Studies in Canadian Literature* 9 (1984): 61–77.

p. 128: *to New York University*: In the week of October 14–20.

p. 128: *This summer*: May 30–June 2.

p. 128: *Douglas LePan*: (1914–98) Canadian poet, diplomat, professor of English, friend at Oxford, and senior fellow at Massey College 1970–98.

p. 129: *your pilgrimage*: The Davenports had combined a visit with RD and Brenda at Windhover and a jaunt to the Stratford Festival almost every year since the early 1970s.

p. 130: *John Hirsch*: (1930–89). RD saw six of the seven productions Hirsch directed while artistic director of the Stratford Festival.

p. 130: *John Neville*: (1925–) English actor, director, and manager.

p. 130: *Bartholomew Fair*: Play by Ben Jonson. RD does little justice here to either side of a complex mess. See *Man of Myth* 377–79.

p. 130: *Cyrano de Bergerac*: Play by French dramatist Edmond Rostand (1868–1918) which was performed at Stratford in 1962.

p. 130: *Kathryn Davies Bray*: (1939–) married to James Bray. Their three girls are Gillian, Virginia, and Jamesie. Frederic Rupert Mackay Davies (1902–54) was RD's oldest brother.

p. 131: *Sleeping Beauty*: On December 26 at the Shaw Theatre in Camden.

p. 131: *Starlight Express*: By Andrew Lloyd Webber (1948–), English theatre composer and song writer, at the Apollo Victoria Theatre on December 27.

p. 131: *Goethe's Faust*: Dramatic poem by lyric poet, dramatist, novelist, and scientist Johann Wolfgang von Goethe (1749–1832), Germany's greatest man of letters.

p. 131: *Like the fellow says*: See Ecclesiastes 1:9.

p. 132: *news about your book*: Earlier, the University of Michigan Press had turned down Davenport's *Fifty Years of Medicine at the University of Michigan, 1891–1941*, but now the University of Michigan Medical Schools decided to publish it.

p. 132: *Anthony à Wood*: (1632–95) English antiquarian, author of histories of the University and of the City of Oxford and of a biographical dictionary of Oxford writers and bishops.

p. 133: *Brueghel*: Probably the Flemish painter Pieter Brueghel (c. 1525–69).

p. 133: *Lotfi Mansouri*: (1929–) Iranian-born general director of the Canadian Opera Company 1976–88.

p. 133: *Faust*: Opera by Charles Gounod (1818–93).

p. 133: *Il Trovatore*: Opera by Italian composer Giuseppe Verdi (1813–1901).

p. 133: *Capriccio* and *Die ægyptische Helena*: Operas by German composer and conductor Richard Strauss (1864–1949).

p. 135: *Ye have the poor always with you*: See Matthew 26:11, Mark 14:7, John 12:8.

p. 136: *To THE EDITOR . . . MAIL*: Published March 16, 1985: 7.

p. 136: *Mr. Mulroney*: Martin Brian Mulroney (1939–), Canadian lawyer, Progressive Conservative member of parliament, prime minister of Canada 1984–93.

p. 137: *the book*: *Robertson Davies*, the book Roper began and Michael Peterman completed for Twayne's World Authors Series.

p. 138: *Moira . . . critical operation*: Probably her first cataract operation. The operation was risky because she suffered from glaucoma and her other eye also had a cataract.

p. 138: *Helen's operations . . . Milton's daughter*: Helen Roper had had both eyes operated on for cataracts. RD envisions her reading to Roper, now blind, as the daughters of the great English poet John Milton (1608–74) read to him once he became blind in mid-life.

p. 139: *the Apology of a Second-Class Man*: See *Annual Review of Physiology* 47 (1985): 1–14.

p. 140: *Osler*: Sir William Osler (1849–1919), renowned Canadian physician and educator, author of the authoritative *The Principles and Practice of Medicine*, first published in 1892. For the connection RD drew between Osler, "lung troubles," and "shit," see *Man of Myth* 532.

p. 140: *Colley Cibber*: (1671–1757) English playwright who was fiercely attacked by other writers when he was made poet laureate in 1730.

p. 140: *Goldsmith and Sheridan*: Oliver Goldsmith (1730?–74) and Richard Brinsley Sheridan (1751–1816), Irish playwrights whose plays are still performed.

p. 141: *Bascove*: New York artist known only by that name. A Jungian, she created distinctive cover designs which she describes as "woodcuts prints handcolored with watercolor and pencil" for the American editions and Penguin paperbacks of RD's books from 1981 on.

p. 142: *John Pearson*: (1915–58) Canadian. For the connections between Pearson and Parlabane see *Man of Myth* 527–28, 528n, and for Pearson himself 128–29.

p. 143: *Calithumpian parade*: See *Fifth Business* 94.

p. 144: *Grant Macdonald*: (1909–87) Canadian artist known for his sketches of theatrical celebrities, collaborator with RD and others on three books commemorating the opening years of the Stratford Festival, a friend since 1935. After a refrigerator fell on him in his home in Kingston, Ontario, in 1983, he was no longer himself. His pictures are still held by the Agnes Etherington Art Centre at Queen's University. His parents were Kenneth Jonathan Macdonald, a Presbyterian minister, and Rilla Gertrude McMahon.

p. 144: *Clair Stewart*: (1910–) Canadian designer.

p. 144: *Ben Cunningham*: Douglas Gordon Cunningham (1908–92), one of Kingston's leading lawyers, a good friend of Grant Macdonald and of RD's brother Arthur.

p. 145: *Nathan Cohen*: (1923–71) controversial Canadian theatre critic for CBC Radio and the *Toronto Star* 1946–71.

p. 146: *Borges*: Jorge Luis Borges (1899–1986), influential Argentine poet, critic, and short-story writer.

p. 146: *Robt. G. Lawrence*: See "Canadian Theatre in Robertson Davies' *World of Wonders*," in *Studies in Robertson Davies' Deptford Trilogy*, ed. Robert G. Lawrence and Samuel L. Macey.

p. 147: *Den Danske Skueplads*: See RD's letter of August 13, 1979.

p. 147: *Donald Maclean*: (1913–83) British Foreign Office official and Soviet spy who fled to Russia in 1951. For Alan Maclean, see RD's letter of August 13, 1979.

p. 147: *Lise-Lone Marker*: (1934–) fellow professor in the Drama Centre since 1970.

p. 147: *astrologers*: Hugh McCraig, a New York astrologer, cast RD's horoscope in 1958, and RD thought his observations astute then and later when events unfolded as predicted.

p. 148: *essay on Karsh*: This appeared first in the London *Spectator*, and later as "Karsh of Ottawa" in Richler's volume of essays *Home Sweet Home*.

p. 148: *Face of Destiny*: Karsh's *Faces of Destiny* appeared in 1946. The picture RD describes here (taken in 1977) is in *Karsh Canadians* (1978).

p. 149: *Marianne Florence Scott*: (1928–) Canadian, National Librarian 1984– .

p. 149: *Mills and McSweeney*: John Mills (1930–), English-born Canadian novelist, essayist, and professor of English. Kerry McSweeney (1941–), American-born Canadian critic and professor of English at McGill University in Montreal.

p. 149: *George Woodcock*: (1912–95) eminent Canadian literary journalist, historian, and man of letters.

p. 150: *Beckmessers*: Beckmesser was the name under which Wagner caricatured the critic Edward Hanslick in *Die Meistersinger von Nürnberg*.

p. 150: *The Way of the World*: For the quotation, see Act 4.

p. 151: *PEN*: Poets, Playwrights, Editors, Essayists, and Novelists. The 48th International PEN Congress met January 13–17.

p. 152: *Norman Mailer*: (1923–) American novelist and journalist whose works are frequently critical of modern American society.

p. 152: *Nadine Gordimer*: (1923–) South African writer of short stories and novels.

p. 152: *Percy Scholes . . . Elias Cabot*: Espey invited friends to his rooms to meet the English music critic Percy Scholes (1877–1958) when the latter came from Switzerland to deliver the manuscript of *The Oxford Companion to Music*. "The Myth" probably refers to Espey's pretence for English students at Oxford that he had lived "a completely Wild West life after leaving China." Elias Cabot was a fictitious New England poet with whom RD, Espey, and several friends duped the Balliol English Club. See *Man of Myth* 171–72 and Espey's *Two Schools of Thought* 43–45.

p. 153: *Post reviewed . . . me as Prospero*: See Michael Dirda, "Robertson Davies: Marvels and Mysteries," *The Washington Post Book World* November 17, 1985: 1, 12. Prospero is the magician (and exiled Duke of Milan) in *The Tempest*.

p. 153: *The review . . . Oppenheim*: The review criticizes *What's Bred in the Bone* for wallowing "in its own pretentious academic cleverness." See "Davies's Drippy Brush," *The Washington Book Review* 1.1 (January 1986): 17. Oppenheim (1955–), American, was then a graduate student, and later became an editor and writer.

p. 154: *whips and scorns of time*: See *Hamlet* 3.1.

p. 155: *book of criticism . . . Univ. of Victoria*: *Studies in Robertson Davies' Deptford Trilogy*, ed. Robert G. Lawrence and Samuel L. Macey.

p. 155: *Joseph Campbell*: (1904–87) American professor and writer interested in culture and mythology. See his *The Masks of God: Primitive Mythology* (Penguin, 1976) 339, 341.

p. 156: *Hakluyt's Voyages*: Richard Hakluyt (1553?–1616), English clergyman who collected and published several volumes of accounts of English explorations.

p. 156: *Sir Wilfrid Laurier and King George V*: Laurier (1841–1919), Liberal prime minister of Canada 1896–1911, figures in Part One of *What's Bred in the Bone*. King George V appears in *Fifth Business* 86–87.

p. 156: *no notes*: After RD completed *The Lyre of Orpheus*, he allowed me to read the Cornish notebooks.

p. 157: *Kleinian*: With reference to Melanie Klein (1882–1960), Austrian-born English psychoanalyst, who worked with emotionally disturbed children.

p. 157: *Doctor Dock*: *Doctor Dock: Teaching and Learning Medicine at the Turn of the Century* describes the diagnostic clinics Dock conducted for his fourth-year medical students at the University of Michigan 1899–1908.

p. 157: *American cousins*: Especially John Pierce Langs (1882–19??), lawyer, pianist, and composer, who was still living in the 1960s, in Niagara Falls, New York.

p. 157: *man who ate so many bananas*: The man's doctor had diagnosed him as suffering from worms. Dock pointed out that he had undigested bananas, not worms, in his stools, but neither the man nor his doctor would accept this, despite the ease with which it could be verified.

p. 157: *note about "whomever"*: In his letter to RD, Davenport described his anguish at discovering, too late, that his editor had changed his correct "whoever" to "whomever" in a sentence in his Preface to *Doctor Dock*.

p. 158: *Jacques Barzun's fine attack*: Barzun (1907–) American scholar (born in France), teacher, editor, critic. For his "fine attack" see "Behind the Blue Pencil" in his *On Writing, Editing, and Publishing* (1986).

p. 159: *your forensic work*: Davenport was receiving training in forensic pathology as part of his residency (1984–88) in the Department of Pathology at the University of Michigan, Ann Arbor. The Department performed autopsies for the County of Washtenaw. For the Department and in two other capacities he performed several hundred autopsies, and as Deputy Medical Examiner, Washtenaw County (1985–) he was involved in scene-of-death investigations.

p. 159: *Sir Bernard Spilsbury*: (1877–1947) English detective-pathologist, the dominant figure in English pathology for 35 years.

p. 159: *honey of a case . . . three years ago*: See RD's letter dated [end of December 1978].

p. 159: *Kenneth Garlick*: (1916–) English, Keeper of Western Art at the Ashmolean Museum, Oxford 1968–84, author of *Sir Thomas Lawrence* (1954), and at work on his *Sir Thomas Lawrence: A Complete Catalogue of the Oil Paintings* (1989). He was an acquaintance from Balliol College and in 1985 RD had sought his opinion about his portrait of Lady Clanricarde, reputed to be by the English portrait painter Sir Thomas Lawrence (1769–1830). It was not a Lawrence.

p. 160: *Back to Methuselah*: By George Bernard Shaw.

p. 160: *for my implant*: On June 9, 1986.

p. 160: *the book*: It was titled *Robertson Davies*. See RD's letter of March 29, 1979.

p. 161: *a mirror of nature*: *Hamlet* 3.2.22.

p. 161: *urged by a publisher*: Probably the English-born editor John Pearce (1947–), then editorial director of Irwin Publishing in Toronto, which brought out RD's *The Papers of Samuel Marchbanks* in 1985. The subject of memoirs arose in a casual conversation about diarists and autobiographical writing; Pearce was not trying to lure RD away from his traditional publishers. (Douglas Gibson is also a possibility: he too had urged RD to consider writing his memoirs, but he had moved to McClelland & Stewart earlier that year and, at this point, was no longer RD's editor and publisher.)

p. 162: *Margaret Drabble*: (1939–) English novelist. As edited by Sir Paul Harvey (1869–1948), *The Oxford Companion* went through four editions – 1932, 1937, 1946, and 1967.

p. 162: *your island*: The Ropers had a five-acre island in Stoney Lake near Peterborough, Ontario.

p. 162: *Peggy Atwood tells me*: Margaret Atwood also told RD that Laurence had only six months to live.

p. 162: *raving of the Moral Majority*: Laurence's books were attacked twice. In 1976 *The Diviners* was removed from the grade 13 curriculum in her home village of Lakefield, Ontario, and in 1985 a local councillor declared that *The Stone Angel* showed "disrespect for humanity."

p. 164: *a few people*: Michael Denison (1915–), English actor and friend from the Oxford University Dramatic Society, and his wife, the English actress and novelist Dulcie Gray (1919–).

p. 165: *Nature*: October 30, 1986: 754 (a page of correspondence about the difficulties in verifying or repudiating "miracles" scientifically).

p. 166: *said C. G. Jung*: See *The Collected Works* 6: para. 433 and 10: para. 326.

p. 167: *to New York for some nonsense or other*: On November 25–26 for a *Paris Review* interview (see RD's letter of April 14, 1989) and a reading at the Unterberg Poetry Center at the 92nd Street Y.

p. 167: *Nativity Play*: In December 1946, 1947, and 1948. See *Man of Myth* 297–98.

p. 167: *Father Moore*: Rev. Edgar Cecil Moore (1894–1974), American-born Anglican rector, incumbent of Peterborough South Diocese 1943–51.

p. 168: *Christmas parties*: On Boxing Day, in their house at 361 Park Street, Peterborough, in the 1950s. See *Man of Myth* 324–25.

p. 168: *Scott Young*: (1918–) Canadian sports journalist and author. Neil Young (1945–).

p. 168: *Muriel Ethel Newbold*: (1892–1976) Australian. Her maiden name was Larking. She was married twice, to Brenda's father Paul Mathews and to Claude Henry Newbold.

p. 168: *Tom Symons*: Thomas Symons (1929–   ), Canadian teacher, historian, author, founding president of Trent University in Peterborough, and brother of Scott Symons.

pp. 168–69: *Christmas . . . at my Grandfather Davies' house*: The house of Walter Davies (1851–1928) was in Brantford, Ontario; *Aunt Mary* (1887–19??) was Walter's daughter; *Aunt Elsie* (1881–19??) was also Walter's daughter; *Auntie Bess* was Elizabeth Beckingham Davies, wife of Walter's eldest brother; *Uncle John Robertson* was the brother of Walter's wife Janet Robertson. *The Holy City* is a song by Stephen Adams, pen name for Michael Maybrick (1844–1913), English composer and baritone; *The Mistletoe Bough*'s music is by English composer Sir Henry R. Bishop (1786–1855) and its words by the English composer, poet, and author Thomas Haynes Bayly (1797–1839); *Nazareth* is a song by Charles Gounod (1818–93), the French composer of opera.

SECTION V

p. 172: *group of pictures . . . the Rideau Club*: The group includes photographs of George Bernard Shaw, Ernest Hemingway, Tennessee Williams, Pablo Casals, and Winston Churchill. The Rideau Club is a private club in Ottawa.

p. 172: *what I said about Margaret Laurence*: Laurence died on January 5. RD's tribute was probably broadcast over CBC Radio, which often asked him to comment on the passing of prominent Canadians.

p. 173: *Undine*: Romantic opera by E. T. A. Hoffmann (1776–1822), German novelist, poet, critic, composer, conductor, theatre manager, and civil servant. The tapes were of the BBC Radio 3 broadcast on January 22.

p. 173: *Schumann & Schubert*: Robert Schumann (1810–56), German composer of songs and orchestral music; Franz Schubert (1797–1828), Austrian composer of songs, symphonic works, choral, and piano music.

p. 173: *in my book [The Lyre of Orpheus]*: See 94 and 445.

p. 173: *Weber*: Carl Maria von Weber (1786–1826), German composer, conductor, and pianist.

p. 173: *a book . . . by Murray Schafer*: *E. T. A. Hoffmann and Music* by R. Murray Schafer (1933–   ), Canadian composer, writer, and educator.

p. 174: *Donizetti and Bellini*: Gaetano Donizetti (1797–1848) and Vincenzo Bellini (1801–1835), both Italian opera composers.

p. 174: *Marschner*: Heinrich Marschner (1795–1861), German opera composer.

p. 174: *BIG DOINGS*: RD was presented with the 1987 Medal of Honor for Literature by the National Arts Club on February 24, and on the 26th he addressed the C. G. Jung Foundation in New York. See *Happy Alchemy* 299–321.

p. 174: *The Aged P.*: The Aged Parent, the phrase Wemmick uses when referring to his father in Dickens's *Great Expectations*.

p. 174: *Burgon Bickersteth*: John Burgon Bickersteth (1888–1979), Canadian (born and died in England), first warden of Hart House, centre for men students, University of Toronto (1921–47).

p. 175: *To the EDITOR . . . MAIL*: Published April 8, 1987.

p. 175: *Thomas M. Paikeday, in his letter of March 4*: Paikeday (1926–), Indian-born lexicographer, editor of many dictionaries. RD's and Paikeday's letters were part of an ongoing debate on English usage. RD had introduced the issue of the word "momentarily" in a letter published in *The Globe and Mail* February 18, 1987: A6.

pp. 175-76: *I had a wrangle . . . grammar*: See *The Papers of Samuel Marchbanks* 247.

p. 178: *the life of Robert Graves*: Graves (1895–1985) was an English poet, novelist, and critic, known for his fictionalized reappraisals of history and myth, and for his studies of the mythological sources of poetry. The biography – called *Robert Graves* – was by Robert Percival Graves.

p. 178: *Yeats*: William Butler Yeats (1865–1939), eminent Irish poet and playwright.

p. 178: *Old Man of the Sea*: With reference to the story of "Sindbad the Sailor" in the *Arabian Nights* in which the Old Man of the Sea clings to Sindbad's shoulders for many days and nights until Sindbad finally gets him off by making him drunk – thus, any burden that cannot be sloughed without the greatest exertion.

p. 179: *recent professorial criticism*: Probably Anthony Dawson's "Picking a Bone with R.D.," *Canadian Literature* 111 (Winter 1986): 147–54.

p. 179: *Wheatland people . . . Lord Weidenfeld*: The Wheatland Foundation was created in 1985 by Ann Getty and by Lord George Weidenfeld (1919–), Austrian-Jewish chairman of the London publishing house of Weidenfeld & Nicolson, to bring writers into conversation in luxurious surroundings at an annual conference. See RD's letter of May 29, 1987.

p. 179: *Shelley's phrase*: See *Prometheus Unbound* 3.4.204 by Percy Bysshe Shelley (1792–1822), English Romantic poet.

p. 180: *BBC material about Hoffmann*: Transcriptions of a talk by John Warrack in "Music Weekly," Radio 3, January 18, 1987, and of Clive Bennett's and Lionel Salter's introduction and narration of *Undine*, Radio 3, January 22, 1987.

p. 180: *Elsa Larking*: Louisa Larking (1898–1978), Brenda's Australian-born aunt, a painter who spent much of her life in St. Ives.

p. 180: *score of Undine . . . Edward Johnson building*: For the score, see the first 3 volumes of E. T. A. Hoffmann, *Ausgewählte Musikalische Werke* (Mainz: B. Schott's Söhne, 1971–). The University of Toronto's music library is in the Edward Johnson building.

p. 180: *significance . . . Lyre of Orpheus*: See 94 and 445.

p. 181: *Berlioz' sneer*: Louis Hector Berlioz (1803–69), French Romantic composer and conductor. His "sneer" is mentioned, for example, in R. Murray Schafer's *E. T. A. Hoffmann and Music* (Toronto: University of Toronto Press, 1975) 175, which RD had been reading – ". . . Berlioz disparagingly referred to Hoffmann's music (without, incidentally, having heard any of it) as 'writer's music'. . . ."

p. 181: *your commentary*: "Comment on 'Struggles with the "Other One"' by N. Eide-Midtsand," *Journal of Analytical Psychology* 32.2 (1987): 173–75.

p. 181: *including Fordham*: Michael Fordham (1905–95), English analyst, contributor to Jungian thought, director of the training in child analysis at the Society of Analytical Psychology in London when Miranda trained there.

p. 182: *Michael Holroyd*: (1935–) English biographer and editor, soon to publish his four-volume biography *Bernard Shaw* (1988–92).

p. 183: *grave Western critics*: See RD's letter of April 20, 1987.

p. 183: *Quaker Oats prose*: The Quaker Oats Company of Canada, maker of the rolled oats used for porridge and cookies, is located in Peterborough.

p. 184: *letters to Eleanor Sweezey*: See RD's letter of November 29, 1981. In only one of the letters – a despairing one – did RD's handwriting trail downward.

p. 184: *the work of Thomas Otway*: Otway (1652–85), English dramatist. His *Venice Preserv'd* is a tragedy in blank verse. Elizabeth Barry (1658–1713) was the celebrated English actress who "created" the role of Belvidera in *Venice Preserv'd*. For the quotations from Otway's letters to Elizabeth Barry, see *The Complete Works of Thomas Otway*, ed. Montague Summers, vol. 3 (London: Nonesuch, 1926) 241 and 245.

p. 186: *Agneta . . . Anders*: Agneta Engdahl (1948–) has multiple sclerosis. Anders (1950–) is the youngest of Birgitta Heyman's four children.

p. 188: *two-volume autobiography*: *The Confessions of a Caricaturist*.

p. 188: *given to my brother, Arthur*: Arthur himself recalled that Mr. Cameron, owner of a drug store in Renfrew where he had a Saturday job in 1921, gave him the book as a Christmas gift.

p. 189: *Lewis Waller*: (1860–1915) English actor-manager, a "matinee idol." See *What's Bred in the Bone* 221–22.

p. 189: *William Humble*: English scriptwriter for television and theatre.

p. 191: *Cupid and Venus of Bronzino*: For RD's description of "An Allegory of Time" by the Italian painter Agnolo Bronzino (1503–72), see *What's Bred in the Bone* 222–23.

p. 191: *Goethe did it onstage*: In Part 2 of *Faust*.

p. 192: *The Bowel Hymn*: By Isaac Watts (1674–1748), English writer of several popular hymns. The verse RD sent to Norwich begins "Blest is the man whose bowels move/And melt with pity for the poor" and ends "He in a time of general grief/Finds that his Lord has bowels too."

p. 192: *broadcast about ghost stories*: For *The Journal*, CBC-TV, December 25, 1987.

p. 192: *a gasping, new-deliver'd mother. Richard II* 2.2.65.

p. 192: *Dr. Johnson*: Samuel Johnson (1709–84), English wit, leading literary scholar and critic of his time, author of the famous *A Dictionary of the English Language*. The precise source of the quotation ascribed to him remains a mystery.

p. 193: *Felicity Bryan*: (1945–) English authors' agent who handled RD's literary affairs in Britain for Curtis Brown 1985–88. In 1988 she set up her own agency in Oxford and from 1993 represented him again. She is also Norwich's agent and introduced RD to Norwich.

p. 193: *Peter Mayer*: (1936–) British-born American book publisher. He was CEO of The Penguin Group 1978–96, and in 1987, his headquarters were in New York. Currently he is in charge of The Overlook Press in New York.

p. 193: *Graham Greene*: (1904–91) prolific English Catholic novelist and playwright.

p. 193: *the Conqueror Worm*: With reference to the poem of that title by American poet and short-story writer Edgar Allan Poe (1809–49), which concludes: "And the angels, all pallid and wan,/Uprising, unveiling, affirm/That the play is the tragedy 'Man,'/And its hero the Conqueror Worm."

p. 193: *Richard Winter*: (1937–) Canadian, junior fellow at Massey College 1963–64, the College's solicitor since 1969, and senior fellow since 1978. He specializes in corporation and estate law and was RD's lawyer from the late 1960s on.

p. 193: *grim wolf with privy paw*: From Milton's *Lycidas*, line 128.

p. 193: *the Choir Invisible*: With reference to the poem of that title by English novelist George Eliot (1819–80). It begins: "Oh may I join the choir invisible/Of those immortal dead who live again/In minds made better by their presence."

p. 193: *your work on Venice*: Probably his *A History of Venice* in two volumes.

p. 193: *one of a panel*: Comprised of John Polanyi (winner of the 1986 Nobel Prize in Chemistry), Anton Kuerti (pianist), Gordon Wilson (recent president of the Ontario Federation of Labour), Israel Halperin (see next note), and RD. Pierre Berton was moderator, and the dissident physicist Yuri Orlov, recently released from Siberia, was the featured speaker. The event took place on October 29 at the Ryerson Polytechnical Institute in Toronto.

p. 194: *Israel Halperin*: (1911–) Canadian professor of mathematics, involved in building an international movement to eliminate torture and oppression one case at a time.

p. 195: *Tauchnitz editions*: Famous library of paperback British and American books in English, published in Leipzig and circulated in continental Europe. RD had 90 volumes plus 5 more in the same bindings published by Dodd, Mead & Co. of New York.

p. 195: *Bayntun*: Bayntun's is an English firm of bookbinders, established in 1894 in Bath by George Bayntun (d. 1940). RD probably had other books bound by Bayntun's: the binder of his Trollope, however, was Charles E. Lauriat of Boston.

p. 196: *Folio Society*: London-based group which has, since 1947, offered nicely printed and bound editions of the world's great literature and curiosities to members. RD was a member from 1949 on.

p. 196: *John Saumarez Smith*: (1943–) English, manager and a director of G. Heywood Hill Ltd., sellers of old and new books, in London.

p. 196: *Dr. A. S. W. Rosenbach*: (1876–1952) American.

p. 197: *novelists will have to include*: Isaac Bashevis Singer (1904–91), Polish-born American; Saul Bellow (1915–), Canadian-born American; Budd Schulberg (1914–), American. These writers, like Norman Mailer and Mordecai Richler, are Jewish.

p. 198: *In What's Bred in the Bone*: See 27.

p. 198: *James Agate sadly remarked*: See *Ego 6* (London: Harrap, 1944) 48. James Agate (1877–1947) was a prominent English drama, literary, and film critic.

p. 198: *as Shakespeare said*: RD here plays with "at lovers' perjuries/They say Jove laughs" (*Romeo and Juliet* 2.2.).

p. 199: *Planché*: James Robinson Planché (1796–1880), versatile and prolific English writer and librettist.

p. 199: *Christ's First Miracle*: Turning the water to wine at the marriage in Cana (John 2:1–11).

p. 199: *Swanee Whistle*: See *Lyre* 54. RD's "note" ran – "see *The Oxford Companion to Music*; also called the Siren Whistle; a simple tubular whistle equipped with a plunger which, when extended or withdrawn produced a glissando, or whoop; much used in the 20s in Coon Bands; bet you've never heard of them, either."

p. 199: *helping . . . bookshop*: Briefly, during the Christmas rush.

p. 200: *Pär Lagerkvist*: (1891–1974) Swedish poet, dramatist, and novelist.

p. 200: Thomas Mann: (1875-1955) influential German novelist and essayist

p. 200: *Frej Lindqvist*: (1937–) Swedish actor.

p. 200: *Amadeus . . . Paul Scofield*: *Amadeus* is a play by the English dramatist Peter Shaffer (1926–), about the bitterness aroused in the composer Salieri by the success of Mozart. Paul Scofield (1922–), is an English actor.

p. 200: *Sonja Bergvall*: (1907–89) Swedish. She worked on marketing, public relations, and foreign rights for the publishers Bonniers Förlag, and was a brilliant translator of Dorothy L. Sayers, William Golding and Doris Lessing, among others.

p. 201: *Mrs. Märta-Stina Danielsson . . . Söderberg*: Mrs. Danielssohn (1930–), Swedish, was with the Bonnier group all her working life, retiring as Senior Editor/Editor in Chief in 1995; Anders Söderberg (1938–), Swedish, is publisher at Wahlström & Widstrand and gave up smoking in February 1998.

p. 202: *engineers stole it*: In 1993, thirty years after the event, the bell was finally returned through an intermediary.

p. 202: *Dr. Ramsey*: The Rt. Rev. and Rt. Hon. Arthur Michael Ramsey (1904–88), Archbishop 1961–74.

p. 202: *Bishop Wilkinson*: The Rt. Rev. Frederick Hugh Wilkinson (1896–1980), Canadian bishop of the diocese of Toronto 1955–66.

p. 202: *Ann Saddlemyer's*: Saddlemyer (1932–), Canadian, authority on the Irish dramatists J. M. Synge and Lady Gregory, professor of English and drama, master of Massey College 1988–95.

p. 203: *Tanya Moiseiwitsch and Robin Phillips*: Moiseiwitsch (1914–), English designer of the Stratford Festival's thrust stage and of many Festival productions; Phillips (1942–), English director active in Canada since 1973, artistic director of the Stratford Festival 1974–80, and director of productions there subsequently.

p. 205: *lightning descent upon London*: Publicity trip from September 24 to October 2 for *The Lyre of Orpheus*.

p. 205: Mollie: Mollie Philipps, English, Norwich's wife.

p. 205: *Rev. Richard Harris Barham . . . Ingoldsby Legends*: Barham (1788–1845) was English and a minor canon of St. Paul's cathedral. With their inventive rhymes, lively rhythms, and their comic and grotesque treatment of medieval legends, his *Ingoldsby Legends* were immensely popular. The story about Young Norval also appears in the first volume of *The Life and Letters of the Rev. Richard Harris Barham* by His Son (London 1870): 120–21.

p. 206: *Edmund Wilson*: (1895–1972) American literary and social critic and author. The piece appeared in *The New Yorker* November 21, 1970.

p. 209: *Partridge's*: Eric Honeywood Partridge (1894–1979), prolific New Zealand author interested in the English language, especially slang.

p. 209: *Liddell and Scott*: *A Greek-English Lexicon*, compiled by Henry George Liddell and Robert Scott, first published in 1869 and still in print.

p. 209: *Murray's method*: Guide to pronunciation developed by Sir James A. H. Murray (1837–1915), the Scottish first editor of *The Oxford English Dictionary*.

p. 210: *a song current in our youth*: "My Sin" by B. G. DeSylva, Lew Brown, and Ray Henderson, c. 1921.

p. 210: *John Napier Turner*: (1929–) English-born Canadian politician, lawyer, Liberal prime minister in 1984, leader of the opposition going into this election. Why RD uses this nickname is a mystery. Turner had opposed capital punishment during the previous year's parliamentary debate on restoring the death penalty. Brian Mulroney won the election.

p. 210: *Barnacle's name*: English reviewer?

p. 211: *John Metcalf*: (1938–) English-born Canadian writer of short stories and novels, editor, and teacher. He is relentlessly derisive of the Canadian literary establishment.

SECTION VI

p. 214: *Long Christmas Dinner Society*: Dining club (named after Thornton Wilder's play) which met in Oxford, 1936–38. Its members were RD, Espey, William L. Sachse, and Horace W. Davenport.

p. 214: *Christopher J. Allen*: (1950–) Canadian and British respirologist and associate clinical professor of medicine at McMaster University in Hamilton, Ontario. RD consulted him professionally on five occasions. The connection was through his wife Marilyn Craven (now a medical doctor) who was a doctoral student at the Drama Centre 1972–77.

p. 215: *fantasy of sexual intercourse with H.M.*: See *The Satanic Verses*, "Ellowen Deeowen" 3.

p. 215: *your memoir*: About Espey's experience at Oxford. It was published in *Impromptu*, an occasional publication of Occidental College in Los Angeles. Later it became the first chapter of Espey's *Two Schools of Thought*.

p. 215: *Ridley*: Rev. M. Roy Ridley (1890–1967), English fellow and tutor in English Literature at Balliol 1920–45, editor of the New Temple Shakespeare, and RD's chief tutor at Balliol 1935–38. He was known for the liberal glasses of sherry laced with gin that he poured for himself and students.

p. 216: *James Joyce . . . Fielding*: Joyce (1882–1941) was an Irish writer best known for his novel *Ulysses* and for his experiments with stream of consciousness technique. Henry Fielding (1707–54) was an English novelist and dramatist, best known for his novel *Tom Jones*.

p. 216: *Bryson*: John Norman Bryson (1896–1976), Irish, RD's lesser tutor at Balliol. When Balliol made RD an honorary fellow in 1986, RD was asked to fill out the library's holdings of his books, and did so.

p. 216: *Jacobus De Wett*: Almost certainly Jacobus Stephanus De Wet (1913–95), the South African who was a Rhodes Scholar at Balliol 1935–37 (when RD was there) and who became Balliol's Fellow and Tutor in Mathematics 1947–71, then Dean of Science at the University of Cape Town.

p. 216: *to see you again*: At UCLA on January 23, during the publicity tour for *The Lyre of Orpheus*.

p. 216: *Tom*: Thomas Landis Davenport (1952–89), American computer programmer, the older of Davenport's two sons, died suddenly during a grand mal seizure. Unaware of the gravity of his son's condition, Davenport was completely unprepared for his death.

p. 216: *loss of an eldest son . . . my Father*: RD's eldest brother, Frederic Rupert Mackay Davies, was killed near Nassau in the Bahamas when his car went out of control and hit a tree.

p. 217: *Paris Review piece*: "The Art of Fiction CVII: Robertson Davies," *Paris Review* 110 (1989): 34–60. This was based on an interview Elisabeth Sifton conducted with RD in November 1986.

p. 217: *article of mine . . . in Harper's*: See "Signing Away Canada's Soul: Culture, Identity, and the Free-Trade Agreement," *Harper's Magazine* January 1989: 43–47; and also "NB: ¿Aca nada?" *Times Literary Supplement* September 30–October 6, 1988: 1070–80.

p. 218: *your life chez Knopf*: Elisabeth Sifton moved to Alfred A. Knopf as executive vice president 1987–92. (RD remained with Viking Penguin, so she was no longer his New York editor.)

p. 218: *Things fall apart . . . hold*: From "The Second Coming" by William Butler Yeats.

p. 218: *old Mr. Dent*: Probably Hugh R. Dent, son of Joseph Malaby Dent (1849–1926), founder of the English publishing house J. M. Dent & Sons.

p. 219: *your review of Ritual Slaughter*: "The Trendy Hasid," *Globe and Mail*, May 20, 1989: C19. *Ritual Slaughter* is a novel by Sharon Drache.

p. 220: *offprint of your article*: See "Robertson Davies and the Cornish Trilogy," *Journal of Canadian Studies* 24.1 (1989): 140–45.

p. 221: *lilies of a day . . . brooks*: For "the lilies of a day" see Ben Jonson's Pindaric Ode "To the Immortell Memorie, and Friendship of that Noble Paire, Sir Lucius Cary, and Sir H. Morison." For "as the hart . . . brooks," see Psalms 42:1.

p. 221: *years ago . . . some remarks of J. B. Priestley's*: J. B. Priestley (1894–1984), prolific English novelist, dramatist, and critic. RD met him in London (probably in 1954) after Priestley read *Tempest-Tost* and invited him to visit, and again in Toronto when Priestley came to lecture in 1956.

p. 221: *(Schnak) . . . (Monica)*: Hulda Schnakenburg is the gifted young composer in *The Lyre of Orpheus* who completes the score of an opera begun by E. T. A. Hoffmann. Monica Gall, the young heroine of *A Mixture of Frailties*, after thorough training becomes an accomplished professional singer.

p. 221: *his reach . . . grasp*: With reference to the rueful self-judgement of Robert Browning's "Andrea del Sarto."

p. 222: *Jung and the Writer*: See *Happy Alchemy* 331–51.

p. 223: *The Ancient Landlubber*: RD here plays with the title and opening lines of "The Rime of the Ancient Mariner" by Samuel Taylor Coleridge (1772–1834), English Romantic poet and critic.

p. 223: *Choral Festival*: RD wrote a two-page piece "The Only Creatures in All Creation Who Sing Are Birds and Mankind" for its souvenir program *The Joy of Singing: 1989 International Choral Festival*.

p. 224: *Helmuth Rilling*: (1933–) German conductor, chorus master, and organist.

p. 224: *macabre articles*: See "How to Please the Antivivisectionists," *Gastroenterology International* 2.4 (1989): 236–37.

p. 224: *legs giving up*: Progressive arthritic overgrowth of the bone in Davenport's lower spine was gradually destroying his ability to control his legs and to know what his legs were doing. In time it would put him in a wheelchair, and affect much else, including his hands and arms.

p. 224: *first wife, Virginia*: Virginia Chapin Dickerson (1912–68), American physiological chemist.

p. 224: *place names*: Of Cape Cod. Published by Sachse and Eugene Green as *Names of the Land* (1983).

p. 225: *great-great-great-grandfather's*: Samuel Davies (1823–85). See *Man of Myth* 33–35, 53, 235, 493, 620.

p. 225: *Nancy*: Sachse's wife Nancy Davis.

p. 225: *chapter on Gastrointestinal physiology*: In *Handbook of Physiology, Section 6: The Gastrointestinal System, Vol IV: Intestinal Absorption & Secretion*, ed. Michael Field et al. (Washington DC: The American Physiological Society, 1990) 1–101.

p. 226: *Dogs, Trojans, niggers*: As in the expressions "You have been working like a dog," "working like a Trojan," and "working like a nigger," all current in RD's youth and used by him, on occasion, all his life.

p. 226: *Soma Weiss*: (1899–42) Hungarian-born noted research physician at Boston City Hospital and Peter Bent Brigham Hospital, one of Harvard's major medical teaching centres. Weiss was admired for his diagnostic acumen.

p. 226: *Semmel Weiss*: Ignatz Philipp Semmelweiss (1818–65), Hungarian physician who imposed antiseptic methods on physicians working with maternity patients and who prevented many deaths from childbed fever. Irascible, impatient and tactless, he was expelled from the first obstetric clinic in Vienna. He died in an asylum, of an infected dissection wound, prey to the very disease he had fought so long.

p. 226: *troubled by my tripes . . . what ailed us*: When RD was growing up, he and his father both suffered from indigestion, probably the result of tension and disagreements at family meals. Nervousness on social occasions tended to bring on hiccups while RD was young, and later, acid indigestion and loose stools.

p. 226: *in the hands of a man*: Herbert V. Dobson, specialist in internal medicine in Peterborough, Ontario.

p. 226: *Our jaunt*: From September 5 to October 13. RD became so ill that Brenda feared for his life. Their time-shared flat in London was on Pont Street, not far from Harrods.

p. 228: *A Satyr on the Players . . . Montague Summers*: *Satyr on the Players* appears in *Roscius Anglicanus* by John Downes and edited by the prolific English scholar Montague Summers (1880–1948).

p. 229: *those books for Christmas*: A reprint of *Anomalies and Curiosities of Medicine* (1896) by George M. Gould and Walter L. Pyle and *Recollections of Death: A Medical Investigation* (1982) by Michael B. Sabom.

p. 229: *C. G. Jung's description*: See the opening pages of Chapter 10 "Visions" in Jung's *Memories, Dreams, Reflections*, ed. Aniela Jaffé.

p. 230: *To . . . GLOBE AND MAIL*: Published February 14, 1990: A6.

p. 232: *anniversary card*: For RD and Brenda's 50th wedding anniversary on February 2.

p. 232: *in The Shrew*: The Old Vic production of *The Taming of the Shrew*, March 28–April 29, 1939. It was directed by Tyrone Guthrie, Frederick Bennett played Grumio, the English actor Edward Chapman (1901–86) acted Christopher

Sly, and RD performed four roles: the Widow, Curtis, the pedant and a zany.

p. 232: *went to Ireland*: The Guthries' home was in County Monaghan.

p. 232: *Judy*: Judith Guthrie (1903–72), English-born, Guthrie's wife.

p. 233: *our Club*: The York Club, a private club on St. George St. in Toronto, not far from Massey College.

p. 234: *her first book . . . working on another*: The first book was *Jungian Child Psychotherapy: Individuation in Childhood*, ed. Mara Sidoli and Miranda Davies (1988). In the end she did not co-edit the second, she contributed two papers to it. See *Incest Fantasies and Self-Destructive Acts: Jungian and Post-Jungian Psychotherapy in Adolescence*, ed. Mara Sidoli and Gustav Bovensiepen (1995).

p. 237: *Espey's most recent book*: *Strong Drink, Strong Language*.

p. 237: *you-know-who and . . . Swift*: Oscar Wilde and Jonathan Swift (1667–1745), Irish clergyman and satirist.

p. 237: *that poem*: See "The Bells of Shandon," by Francis Mahony (1804–66), English poet and writer.

p. 238: *that awful Macbeth in Oxford*: The Oxford University Dramatic Society's *Macbeth* of February 1937. It was directed by Hugh Hunt, stage managed by RD, and had special effects by Davenport.

p. 238: *Home*: By David Storey (1933–), English playwright and novelist.

p. 238: *The Ring*: Richard Wagner's *The Ring of the Nibelung* embraces four operas: *The Rhinegold, The Valkyrie, Siegfried*, and *The Twilight of the Gods*, which tell of the struggle for power between the Nibelung dwarfs, the Giants and the Gods of German mythology.

p. 238: *Der Rosenkavalier*: Opera by Richard Strauss, performed by the Canadian Opera Company at the O'Keefe Centre in Toronto.

p. 240: *eye operation*: For a cataract.

p. 241: *Bayreuth*: Town in Bavaria where Wagner's operas are performed annually in the theatre Wagner designed.

p. 241: *Georg Solti*: (1912–) eminent Hungarian-born English conductor, known especially for his interpretations of Wagner, Verdi, Mahler, and Richard Strauss.

p. 241: *we are not going . . . Mozart*: But see RD's letter of May 22, 1991.

p. 241: *Uruguay and Argentina*: Birgitta Heyman instructed a group of Swedish lawyers (who were learning about law in different countries) in effective court behaviour and speech. The same trip took her to Brazil, and others to Malaysia, Egypt, and Madeira.

p. 242: *your sister*: Ingrid Rydbeck-Zuhr (1905–), painter and editor of a major art magazine.

p. 242: *His book*: Senator W. Rupert Davies, *Far-Off Fields* (privately printed in 1962).

p. 243: *A psychiatrist*: Robert Gillespie (1897–1945), Scottish physician for psychological medicine at Guy's Hospital in London. RD had a series of sessions with him in 1936–37. See *Man of Myth* 182–85.

p. 243: *extraordinary production*: Tyrone Guthrie's imaginative Victorian production, first presented at the Old Vic in November–December 1937, and revived
December 26, 1938–January 21, 1939 with RD as Snout.

p. 244: *from Greenland's . . . India's coral strand*: From the hymn "From
Greenland's Icy Mountains" by Reginald Heber (1783–1826), English cleric,
bishop of Calcutta 1822–26.

p. 245: *The Satanic Verses*: Novel by Salman Rushdie.

p. 246: *Hesse Lecture at the Aldeburgh Festival*: RD gave the Prince of Hesse
Memorial Lecture on June 11 (see *Happy Alchemy* 207–26) at this Festival of
music and other arts held in Aldeburgh, on the Suffolk coast of England.

p. 246: *Heraclitus*: Greek philosopher who lived c. 540–c. 480 B.C.

p. 246: *to give two lectures on Reading and Writing*: On February 20 and 21. See
The Merry Heart 213–56.

p. 247: *quotation from Samuel Butler (1613–80)*: Butler was an English poet and
satirist, best known for his poem *Hudibras*, a satire against the Puritans. For
the quotation see Samuel Butler, *Prose Observations*, ed. Hugh de Quehen
(Oxford: Clarendon, 1979) 159.

p. 247: *Lady Day*: Annunciation of the Virgin Mary and day marking the end of
the first quarter of the year.

p. 248: *Christine Pevitt*: (1945–) British senior vice president and publisher at
Viking Penguin in New York and RD's editor there 1988–91.

p. 249: *BUT TO RESOOM – as Artemus Ward says*: RD had written to Davenport
just two days earlier. Artemus Ward was the pseudonym of American humorist
Charles Ferrar Browne (1834–67). He purports to describe the experiences of
a travelling showman, and uses his own phonetic spelling.

p. 249: *the foul rag-and-bone shop*: From "The Circus Animals' Desertion," where
Yeats laments the desertion of the themes that had occupied him in youth and
middle age, reducing him to "the foul rag-and-bone shop of the heart."

p. 249: *your piece about Rudolf Heidenhain . . . a "vitalist."*: "Was Rudolf
Heidenhain a Vitalist?" *Gastroenterology International* 3.4 (1990): 192–93.
Davenport uses the definition of vitalism from *The Oxford English Dictionary* –
"The doctrine or theory that the origin and phenomena of life are due to or pro-
duced by a vital principle, as distinct from a purely chemical or physical force."

p. 251: *my health*: In a letter written April 27, RD mentioned being prey to a "particularly venomous kind of 'flu" since mid-January.

p. 252: *Gervinus*: Georg Gottfried Gervinus (1805–71), noted German historian
and Shakespearean scholar.

p. 252: *Balliol . . . Honorary Fellow*: In 1986.

p. 252: *Encaenia*: Annual commemoration of founders and benefactors at Oxford.

p. 252: *your fascinating story*: See RD's letter of July 17, 1989.

p. 253: *Evgeny Kissin*: (1971–) Russian concert pianist. Davis had given RD a
two-CD set of Kissin's Carnegie Hall debut concert.

p. 253: *Alfred Brendel*: (1931–) Austrian pianist.

p. 253: *Chopin*: Frédéric Chopin (1810–49), Polish (of French descent) pianist and composer primarily for the piano. Much of his music was influenced by Polish folk music.

p. 254: *piece in the New Yorker*: A thoroughgoing consideration of Separatism in Quebec. See "A Reporter at Large," September 23, 1991: 40+.

p. 254: *our Civil War*: See RD's letter of May 1, 1978.

SECTION VII

p. 261: *Crime & Punishment and The Brothers Karamazov*: Novels by Dostoevsky.

p. 261: *translations I know best are those of Constance Garnett . . . and Magarshack*: Constance Garnett (1861–1946), English, known as a distinguished translator of the Russian classics. David Magarshack (1899–1977), English (Russian-born), biographer and translator, working on Russian literature and writers. Nabokov's slighting comments about Constance Garnett appear primarily in his chapter on Tolstoy and in *Vladimir Nabokov: The American Years* by Brian Boyd.

p. 261: *Nabokov's opinion of Dostoevsky*: See Nabokov's chapter on Dostoevsky in *Lectures on Russian Literature* (1981), ed. Fredson Bowers. Much of this passage is influenced by it. "Poshlust," according to Nabokov, means "[c]orny trash, vulgar clichés, Philistinism in all its phases, imitations of imitations, bogus profundities, crude, moronic, and dishonest pseudo-literature" (George Plimpton, ed., *Writers at Work: The Paris Review Interviews: Fourth Series* [New York: Viking, 1976] 101).

p. 261: *learnt much from Dickens*: Dostoevsky's letters reveal that he admired Dickens and saw Mr. Pickwick as one of the precursors of his own Prince Myshkin in *The Idiot*, but I can find no general "assertion that he learnt much from Dickens."

p. 261: *George Ignatieff (Michael's father)*: George Ignatieff (1913–89), Russian-born Canadian diplomat. Michael Ignatieff (1947–), Canadian writer, historian, and broadcaster.

p. 261: *My favourite line*: From Act 2 of the play *The Three Sisters* by Anton Pavlovich Chekhov (1860–1904).

p. 262: *Pevear and Volokhonsky*: Richard Pevear (1943–) and Larissa Volokhonsky, translators of *Crime and Punishment* and *The Brothers Karamazov*. Pevear is an American poet and writer.

p. 262: *to give tongue*: RD read from *Murther & Walking Spirits* on January 12 at the Unterberg Poetry Center of the 92nd Street Y.

p. 263: *horrid illness*: Cancer of the uterus, which entailed a hysterectomy and lengthy radiation treatment.

p. 263: *Hodgkin's Disease*: Cancer of the lymphatic system, at that time usually fatal. See *Man of Myth* 253–55.

p. 265: *Harold Nahabedian*: (1939–) Canadian (of Armenian extraction), junior fellow at Massey College 1965–66.

p. 265: *Colin Graham*: (1931–) English artistic director of the Opera Theatre of St. Louis. When RD first met him in August 1986, he was head of the opera division of the Banff Centre School of Fine Arts. RD was in Banff, Alberta, to receive the Centre's National Award and to serve as writer in residence for a week.

p. 265: *John Corigliano*: (1938–) American composer in a relatively conservative, largely tonal, and accessible style.

p. 265: *Beaumarchais*: Pierre-Augustin Caron de Beaumarchais (1732–99) French playwright whose comedies *Le Barbier de Séville* and *Le Mariage de Figaro* were the basis of operas by Rossini and Mozart. Gioacchino Antonio Rossini (1792–1868) was an Italian operatic composer.

p. 266: *two Canadians*: Teresa Stratas (1938–), soprano; and Gino Quilico (1955–), baritone.

p. 266: *Like Shakespeare*: See Sonnet 110.

p. 267: *as the Good Book says*: Proverbs 17:22.

p. 267: *Magian World View*: See *World of Wonders* 313 and 287–88.

pp. 267–68: *"We learn . . . innocence"*: See *Fifth Business* 259.

p. 268: *Norman Jewison*: (1926–) Canadian film producer and director. He was a member of Stratford's Board of Governors 1983–88.

p. 268: *Mr. Lapinski and also Raffaele*: Jan Lapinski was the club's secretary-manager and Raffaele Santasola its chief steward. As things fell out, Santasola was not succeeded by Dan Boulton as RD suggested at the end of his letter.

p. 272: *Nicki Goldschmidt*: Nicholas Goldschmidt (1908–), Czech-born Canadian conductor, administrator and organizer of festivals.

p. 273: *a Broadway failure*: *Love and Libel* in 1960. See RD's letter of September 20, 1995.

p. 274: *a series of conferences*: These produced the Charlottetown Accord which included distinct-society status for Quebec, a reformed Senate, a larger House of Commons, native self-government, and expanded provincial powers. Although the Accord was approved on August 28 by the federal government, all ten provincial and both territorial governments, and four native organizations, it was rejected in a referendum in October.

p. 275: *Carlos Fuentes*: (1928–) novelist, editor, and diplomat. Fuentes and RD gave the third annual Walter Gordon Memorial Lecture at the University of Toronto on September 23.

p. 276: *Niklas Engdahl:* (1974–) then a student, now becoming an actor.

p. 276: *in hospital*: Gordon Roper had had a heart attack.

p. 278: *rebuff these poor souls*: RD returned many unsolicited manuscripts with polite notes, but over the years he read and commented on a surprising number.

p. 279: *Arcimboldo*: Giuseppe Arcimboldo (1537–93), Milanese painter known for his symbolical figures composed of fruits or animals or landscapes or implements – and in the case of The Librarian, books.

p. 280: *a few verses, inspired by yours*: Davenport's verses opposed rueful reflections on aging with warm recollections of Long Christmas Society Dinners and old friends (especially RD). RD's verses countered Davenport's gloomy view of old age with a positive one and then celebrated the Long Christmas Dinner Society with a drinking song. Both were to be read at a special meeting of the LCDS – cancelled when Davenport's wife collapsed suddenly and proved to have a serious heart disease.

p. 280: *sneeping*: nipping, biting.

p. 280: *my doctor*: Christopher J. Allen or Jaroslav M. J. Polak. Erythromycin is commonly prescribed in such cases.

p. 280: *Robert Laidlaw MacMillan*: (1917–) Canadian of Scottish descent, internist specializing in cardiology and professor of medicine at the University of Toronto.

p. 281: *John S. Speakman*: (1928–) Canadian ophthalmologist and professor. He operated on the cataract on RD's right eye in 1986.

p. 282: *Greene's History*: Probably the classic *A Short History of the English People* by English historian John Richard Green (1837–83). Published first in 1874, it had been reprinted most recently in 1992 by the Folio Society and RD had acquired it in this form.

p. 282: *No to the referendum*: In the national referendum held on October 26, six provinces and the Yukon territory rejected the Charlottetown Accord (see RD's letter of August 24, 1992).

p. 282: *editorial in The Times*: "Crown of Dynamite," October 9, 1992: 15.

p. 283: *Sartre was right*: Jean-Paul Sartre (1905–80), French existential philosopher, novelist, playwright, and critic, was quoted in *The Times'* editorial as declining the Nobel Prize on the ground that "A writer must refuse to allow himself to be transformed into an institution."

p. 283: *Peter Carson and Eleo Gordon*: Peter Carson (1938–), British editor-in-chief of Penguin in the United Kingdom 1989–98, directly responsible for RD's books. Eleo Gordon [Carson] (1947–), British. In 1992 she was a senior editor at Viking and Penguin in the United Kingdom.

p. 284: *the one translated from the French*: A book about freaks, as Davis recalls.

p. 285: *the doctor*: A doctor in the emergency ward at the Toronto Hospital.

p. 287: *Colin Friesen*: (1922–) Canadian, Bursar of Massey College 1962–88.

p. 288: *to speak about creativity in old age*: See *The Merry Heart* 301–15.

SECTION VIII

p. 292: *Minor Heresies*: *Minor Heresies: Major Departures; A China Mission Boyhood*. Espey was the son of a Presbyterian missionary in Shanghai.

p. 293: *R/C. Church . . . Christian Brothers*: A lay order of the Roman Catholic Church, the Christian Brothers are dedicated to Christian education of youth.

In the late 1980s and early 1990s, Brothers at an orphanage in Newfoundland and two Ontario schools were accused and found guilty of sexual and physical abuse of boys in their care.

p. 294: *George Ignatieff:* See RD's letter of December 2, 1991.

p. 294: *Tolstoy . . . called a barbarian:* Perhaps a general recollection of *Tolstoy on Shakespeare,* where Tolstoy mounts a thoroughgoing attack on Shakespeare.

p. 294: *Brenda's parents:* Muriel Ethel Newbold (1892–1976) and Paul Mathews (1892–1985).

p. 295: *Bildungsromanen:* German term for novels that show the growth and development of a protagonist in relation to the society of his or her times.

p. 296: *you and Inge . . . thin time of it:* The previous September Davenport had been fitted with leg braces and was able to move only with difficulty. He was dependent on his wife for many things, driving among them. Later that September, she broke her femur and faced months of rehabilitation. At this point Inge was walking with a stick and Davenport had learned to drive a car fitted with hand controls.

p. 296: *true self will emerge from a cave:* According to Piers, it did, and he is pleased with it.

p. 297: *To THE EDITOR . . . MAIL:* Published February 24, 1994: A24. The letter from Pierre Berton which prompted this one was headed "Two, for Starters" and appeared on page D7.

p. 298: *travellers must be content:* See *As You Like It* 2.4. RD and Brenda had been in London April 5–20, staying at their time-shared flat on Pont Street and visiting their daughter Miranda.

p. 298: *neither Miss Backhouse nor Miss Jones:* Janet Backhouse (1938–), English curator of illuminated manuscripts at the British Library, and Shelley Jones (1936–), Welsh, in the conservation department at the British Library.

p. 298: *their tone from Ben Jonson:* In Jonson's play *The Alchemist* a rascal impersonates an alchemist in order to delude and cheat people.

p. 298: *found what I wanted to say in Jung:* See *The Collected Works* 16: para. 407.

p. 299: *the Bartons . . . Sam Wanamaker's Globe Theatre:* John Bernard Adie Barton (1928–), English associate director of the Royal Shakespeare Company in London 1964–91, and still its Advisory Director, and Anne Barton (1933–), American-born professor of English at Cambridge University. Sam Wanamaker (1919–93) was an American actor, director, and producer for stage and film, and the moving force behind the building of a replica of Shakespeare's Globe Theatre in London.

p. 299: *And to dine at LSE:* In the private dining room off the Senior Common Room at the London School of Economics.

p. 300: *you and Inge . . . more mobile:* Davenport was now able to drive short distances – to the grocery store, the bank, the swimming pool, his office, and the library.

p. 300: *lecture on Lewis Carroll and the Theatre*: Lewis Carroll, pseudonym for Charles Lutwidge Dodgson (1832–98), English, lecturer in mathematics at Oxford and author of many books, including *Alice's Adventures in Wonderland* and *Through the Looking Glass*. RD gave his lecture on July 10, 1994, in the Festival Theatre, Stratford, Ontario (see *Happy Alchemy* 80–103). *Alice Through the Looking Glass* was one of Stratford's offerings that season.

p. 301: *about photographs*: For *Man of Myth*, which was being prepared for the printer at the time.

p. 301: *Jean Guillou*: (1930–) French composer, organist, and pianist. In the end, RD worked with Randolph Peters. See RD's letter of August 27, 1995.

p. 302: *operatic version . . . Apuleius*: Lucius Apuleius (c. 124–c. 170), a North African writer, satirist, and rhetorician. An opera on the theme of *The Golden Ass* was created and performed in RD's novel *A Mixture of Frailties* (1958).

p. 303: *Talma*: François-Joseph Talma (1763–1826), French actor and splendid speaker of verse.

p. 303: *Goya . . . Guernica*: Francisco José de Goya y Lucientes (1746–1828), great Spanish painter and etcher, many of whose paintings hang in the Prado in Madrid. Guernica, a town in northern Spain, was bombed by German planes during the Spanish civil war, an event which inspired one of Picasso's most celebrated paintings.

p. 303: *Les Enfants du Paradis*: 1944 film directed by Marcel Carné, which evokes the rich and colourful theatrical society of nineteenth-century Paris. As RD realized, Pierre Brasseur (1905–72), French stage and screen actor, played not Talma but Antoine-Louis-Prosper Lemaître (1800–1876), the great French Romantic actor known as Frédérick.

p. 303: *Balzac*: Honoré de Balzac (1799–1850), one of the great French masters of the novel.

p. 304: *Fanny Kemble*: (1809–93) English actress.

p. 305: *a nephew of Kipling*: Graham McInnes (1912–70), Canadian (born in England and raised in Australia). He was first secretary in New Delhi in the early 1950s. McInnes's mother, the writer Angela Thirkell, was a cousin of the English writer Rudyard Kipling (1865–1936), who is best known for his stories about India, the jungle and its beasts, and the army.

p. 305: *Janet*: Janet Turnbull Irving (1954–), Canadian, Irving's wife and president of Curtis Brown Canada Ltd. (and thus the Canadian arm of RD's New York agent).

p. 305: *reading . . . Anthony Burgess*: On May 13, 1987, at Massey Hall in Toronto.

p. 305: *The Future of Fiction*: See *The Merry Heart* 353–71.

p. 306: *a reclusive drudge*: Probably a play on Johnson's famous definition of "lexicographer" in his *Dictionary* – "A writer of dictionaries; a harmless drudge, that busies himself in tracing the original, and detailing the signification of words."

p. 306: *when we meet to read together*: On December 1, at Convocation Hall, University of Toronto.

p. 307: *one by R. H. Barham*: Macaronics are verses in which two or more languages are jumbled together. This one is usually titled "Epigram" and included in the Third Series of Barham's *The Ingoldsby Legends*. Barham here plays with Odes 2, 14, 1 by the Roman poet Quintus Horatius Flaccus (65–8 B.C.) – *Eheu fugaces, Postume, Postume,/Labuntur anni; nec pietas moram/Rugis et instanti senectae/Adferet, indomitaeque morti*, which has been translated by the Victorian scholar John Conington (1825–69) as "Ah! Postumus, they fleet away/Our years, nor piety one hour/Can win from wrinkles and decay/And Death's indomitable power."

p. 307: *letters . . . Sylvia Townsend Warner*: Warner (1893–1978), English novelist and poet. RD was reading her *Letters*, edited by William Maxwell. What he meant by "autobiographical essays" is less clear – possibly *The Diaries of Sylvia Townsend Warner*, edited by Claire Harman or *Sylvia Townsend Warner: A Biography*, by Claire Harman, for both contain autobiographical passages and both are in his library.

p. 309: *the cause of the Little Sister's Bookshop*: Little Sister's Book and Art Emporium (a gay and lesbian bookstore in Vancouver) had brought a case before the British Columbia Supreme Court, challenging the constitutionality of book seizures by Canadian Customs officials. Janine Fuller is the manager of Little Sister's.

p. 310: *Barbara Hepworth*: (1903–75) English abstract sculptor.

p. 310: *Miss Loring and Miss Lyall*: Frances Norma Loring (1887–1968) and Florence Wyle (1881–1968), both born in the United States, both sculptors, shared a studio in a converted Toronto church for more than 50 years. See RD's letter on the subject – "The Cunning Man," *Globe and Mail* 14 Oct. 1995: D7.

p. 310: *I have had to read*: *Henry Irving: The Actor and His World* (1951) by Laurence Irving; *The Life of Henry Irving* (1908) by Austin Brereton; *Personal Reminiscences of Henry Irving* (1906) by Bram Stoker; and *Henry Irving* (1930) by Gordon Craig.

p. 310: *that boner*: See *The Cunning Man* 263. Agate wrote several passages on this theme in the nine volumes of his extended autobiography *Ego*. This is probably a paraphrase of one in *Ego 6* (London: Harrap, 1944) 48.

p. 311: *memoirs of people*: See Max Beerbohm (1872–1956) *Around Theatres, Last Theatres 1904–1910*, and *More Theatres 1898–1903*; W. Graham Robertson (1866–1948) *Life Was Worth Living: The Reminiscences of W. Graham Robertson*; and Eliza Aria (1866–1931) *My Sentimental Self*.

p. 311: *Madeleine Bingham has written a book*: *Henry Irving and the Victorian Theatre* (1978).

p. 311: *Ellen Terry, in her memoirs*: Ellen Terry (1847–1928), Irving's leading lady at the Lyceum Theatre in London 1878–1902. RD had both *The Story of My Life* (1908) and *Ellen Terry's Memoirs* (1933).

p. 311: *the exact date*: October 31, 1925 (as Jennifer Surridge discovered a day or two later).

p. 312: *as the old hymn says*: "Till we meet at Jesus feet" is part of the refrain (usually omitted in modern hymnals) of "God Be with You till We Meet Again," by the American Congregational minister Jeremiah Eames Rankin (1828–1904).

p. 312: *said so much*: Davenport's assessment was positive (except for his strictures on style). He commented on the biography's usefulness to scholars and on what it revealed about RD's industriousness and about the idiocy of editors and publishers.

p. 313: *Bozzy*: James Boswell (1740–95), Scottish author of the great *Life of Samuel Johnson*.

p. 313: *say about yourself*: "I am cited surprisingly frequently, but no portrait is attempted." Davenport also described what he had done to provide resources for a future biographer.

p. 313: *sloppy usages*: "One does not *loan* something; one *lends* it. T.G.[Tyrone Guthrie] *enthuses* on successive pages, and immediately after something *transpires*. Plants transpire; events occur. A task, as on page 508, is inevitably an *unenviable* one. On page 496 your relation with your father had changed 'now that death had intervened between them.' What does she think *intervene* means?"

p. 313: *Dreiser*: Theodore Dreiser (1871–1945), American novelist.

p. 313: *Sir John Pope-Hennessy*: (1913–94) English art historian, older brother of the writer James Pope-Hennessy (1916–74) whom RD knew at Balliol in 1935–36. Downside is the school the brothers attended.

p. 313: *your last paragraph*: "I am terrified by the approach of winter, and I wonder whether, if spring does come as promised, what state I will be in, if any state at all, to greet it. After more than forty years of self-referral I now have a primary physician. . . . Recently, after we had discussed my medical problems he asked: 'Have you ever thought of harming yourself?' A rather delicate way of putting the question, but one the ordinary run of physicians would not ask. I replied: 'Oh, yes. Of course.' and we talked about the possibility of my suicide. I said I could never do it so long as my wife is alive, and I have said the same thing to Inge. But what happens when I am no longer able to take care of her or indeed of myself?"

p. 314: *psychiatric "help" or psycho-analysis*: There had been some thought that Davenport might find psychotherapy or psychotropic drugs helpful as he coped with his deteriorating body.

p. 314: *Dr. Jung's advice*: RD's source remains elusive.

p. 315: *Sherrill Milnes*: (1935–) American baritone.

p. 317: *some years ago*: See RD's letter of November 10, 1977.

p. 317: *the house in which I was born*: 145 Elizabeth Street. RD lived there from 1913 until 1919 when his family moved to Renfrew, Ontario.

p. 318: *Disher*: Maurice Willson Disher (1893–1969), English critic, theatrical historian, and playwright.

p. 319: *Jarry*: Alfred Jarry (1873–1907), French dramatist, writer of witty, blasphemous, scatological, surrealistic verse stories, known for his eccentric and dissolute behaviour.

p. 319: *Raymond Greene*: (1901–82) English, RD's doctor when he was at Oxford.

p. 319: *your judgement*: This was "entirely laudatory."

p. 319: *Speaight's book*: *The History of the English Puppet Theatre* by George Speaight. RD met his brother, the English actor and author Robert Speaight (1904–76), in 1949 when, as adjudicator for the Dominion Drama Festival, he praised RD's direction of the Peterborough Little Theatre's *The Taming of the Shrew* and described RD's *Fortune, My Foe* as "one of the most subtle and original" contemporary plays he had seen.

p. 319: *Mr. Punch*: RD had mentioned Mr. Punch because Stead was an expert on Punch and Judy shows. See Stead's *Mr. Punch* (1950).

p. 320: *invaluable Partridge*: See RD's letter of November 10, 1988.

p. 320: *ornament to the magazine*: Stead recommended that RD consult *The History of "Punch"* by M. H. Spielmann (where the ornament appears on pages 47 and 48).

p. 321: *Peter Ustinov's performance*: Ustinov (1921–), English actor, director, and writer, was in Toronto for ten days, presenting his one-man show *An Evening with Sir Peter Ustinov* at the Royal Alexandra Theatre.

p. 321: *the Stanislavsky manner*: With reference to Konstantin Sergeivich Stanislavsky (1863–1938), Russian actor, director, teacher of acting, and cofounder of the influential Moscow Art Theatre. Stanislavsky rejected the declamatory style of acting of the time, and urged actors to use their bodies and voices naturally.

p. 321: *Leacock's advice to humorists*: RD's source remains elusive.

p. 321: *Forbes-Robertson said . . . actor needed*: See Johnston Forbes-Robertson's *A Player Under Three Reigns*, chapter 3. Forbes-Robertson (1853–1937), the English actor-manager, was famous for his perfect elocution.

p. 322: *TV program Imprint*: On TVOntario.

p. 322: *what Blake highly recommended*: See "What Is It Men in Women Do Require," in Poems from the Notebook c. 1791–92, by the English poet William Blake (1757–1827).

p. 322: *Another panelist*: Michael Shelden (1951–), American biographer, reviewer, writer of essays, professor of English and author of *Graham Greene: The Man Within*.

p. 323: *piffle before the wind*: Phrase from chapter 5 of Daisy Ashford's *The Young Visiters*.

p. 323: *Edward J. G. Noble*: (1931–) Canadian consultant cardiologist at the Toronto Hospital and assistant professor at the University of Toronto. RD was referred to him in May by Dr. Polak. The "home movies" he had in mind were coronary angiograms (cardiac catheterization of the heart), to ascertain the degree of disease in the coronary arteries.

p. 323: *I have gone . . . motley to the view*: See Shakespeare's Sonnet 110.

p. 323: *United Church Observer Martin O'Malley*: See *The United Church Observer* May 1995: 39. Martin O'Malley (1939–), Canadian journalist, free-lance writer, and author, was a Southam Fellow at Massey College in 1972–73.

p. 324: *the broadcast*: An interview about *The Cunning Man* with Romona Koval for "Books and Writing," Radio National, Melbourne, recorded June 6 and probably broadcast June 23.

p. 324: *Mavis Gallant . . . a new collection*: Gallant (1922–), Canadian writer who published most of her stories in the *New Yorker*. RD wrote the Afterword for the New Canadian Library edition of Gallant's *Across the Bridge* (1997).

p. 324: *Alice Munro*: (1931–) Canadian writer of short stories.

p. 324: *Odorono*: A deodorant and antiperspirant.

p. 325: *Patrick White*: (1912–90) English-born Australian novelist.

p. 325: *latest book by Childe Amis*: Martin Amis (1949–), English novelist and son of the novelist Kingsley Amis who won the Booker Prize in 1986, when RD was on the short-list. Martin Amis did not win that year's Booker Prize.

p. 326: *Mitral Regurgitation*: In 1992–93, an electrophysiologist had noted aortic valve insufficiency with only mild mitral insufficiency and evidence of a pre-vious myocardial infarction (heart attack). Similar tests ordered by Dr. Noble in 1995 showed moderate mitral regurgitation, which could be described as "Puking of the Ticker."

p. 326: *Diary of John Cowper Powys*: Powys (1872–1963), English novelist, poet, critic, philosopher, and lecturer had been a favourite with RD since the early 1930s. RD had been reading *Petrushka and the Dancer: The Diaries of John Cowper Powys 1929–1939*, edited by Morine Krissdóttir and published that year.

p. 327: *Randolph Peters*: (1959–) Canadian composer for orchestra, chamber groups, voice, and film, and of the opera *Nosferatu*. The Canadian Opera Company gave *The Golden Ass* its debut in April 1999.

p. 327: *Benjamin Britten*: (1913–76) English composer, conductor, and pianist, known especially for his vocal music.

p. 327: *Amadeus*: See RD's letters of [Fall 1981] and [April 1988].

p. 327: *Long Day's Journey Into Night*: Autobiographical play by American dramatist Eugene O'Neill (1888–1953), about a miserly actor father, his mor-phine-addicted wife (Mary Tyrone), and their two sons.

p. 327: *William H. McKay*: (1848/9–1918) Canadian builder. See *Man of Myth* 42. His wife was Lavinia C. Langs McKay (1845–1924), also Canadian.

p. 328: *books of reminiscence by actors*: These actors are all English. Of their reminiscences, RD had on his shelves: Alec Guinness (1914–) *Blessings in Disguise*; Laurence Olivier (1907–89) *Confessions of an Actor*; John Gielgud (1904–) *Early Stages, Stage Directions*, and *An Actor and His Time*. RD appears not to have possessed the memoirs of Robert Morley (1908–).

p. 329: *Love and Libel*: RD's adaptation of his novel *Leaven of Malice* for the Theater Guild, a New York producing company. RD worked on it at Guthrie's home in Ireland in the summer of 1959. In the fall of 1960, under Guthrie's direction, the play opened in Toronto, moved on to Detroit and Boston, and closed in New York after five performances. The English-born actor and singer Dennis King (1897–1971) played the eccentric organist Humphrey Cobbler. For a full discussion of *Love and Libel*, see *Man of Myth* 390–95.

p. 329: *most complete Falstaff*: In both parts of *Henry IV* at the Stratford Festival, Ontario, in 1965. RD saw the English stage and film actor Sir Ralph Richardson (1902–83) in both parts of *Henry IV* when the Old Vic visited New York in 1946.

p. 330: *Parizeau*: Jacques Parizeau (1930–), Canadian Québécois economist, politician and separatist, leader of the Parti Québécois 1987–95, premier of Québec 1994–95. Eleanor Sweezey lives in Montréal, in the province of Québec.

p. 330: *experience with tours*: Eleanor Sweezey had been taking two trans-Atlantic trips a year since 1984, for pleasure. Earlier, as a medical illustrator, she had been attached to a veterans' hospital. Neither sort of experience produced the insights RD was hoping for.

p. 331: *John Tuzo Wilson:* (1908–93) Canadian important for his explanation of plate tectonics, senior fellow at Massey College 1962–93.

p. 332: *a German magazine for an article*: The magazine was *GEO*. The article was cut when the magazine's special issue on Canada had to be shortened "for various business reasons."

p. 332: *My poor brother Arthur*: Arthur outlived RD by almost a year, dying on November 11, 1996, in his 94th year.

p. 333: *characterization of Mervyn Rentoul*: See *The Cunning Man* 157–59 and 176–79.

p. 333: *J. M. Barrie's The Little Minister*: J. M. Barrie (1860–1937), Scottish novelist and dramatist, best known for *Peter Pan*. *The Little Minister* is a play.

p. 334: *Hart House*: RD drew on recollections of the University of Toronto's Hart House Theatre in creating The Players' Guild and its activities in *The Cunning Man*.

Acknowledgements

The copyright for all of Davies' letters is held by Brenda Davies, and my first and greatest debt is to her and to her daughter Jennifer Surridge. They both gave great time and energy to this project, suggesting people who might have interesting letters, checking Davies' diaries for elusive dates, and searching his bookshelves for the references he consulted in the last few years of his life. They also read successive drafts of this book with great care. In short, their contribution was invaluable.

After them, my chief debts are to the many recipients of Davies' letters who searched their files, forwarded copies and supplied details of themselves, their letters, and their relationship with him. Their contributions are evident in the head and endnotes. Several of Davies' regular correspondents – Horace W. Davenport, Miranda Davies, Arnold Edinborough, John Espey, Birgitta Rydbeck Heyman, Elisabeth Sifton, John Stead, and Eleanor Sweezey – were especially helpful. Also, many individuals who are mentioned in the letters kindly responded to queries. The information they supplied enriches the endnotes.

Less evident are the contributions of those who searched for letters on my behalf or who suggested where they might be found – Nancy Bartlett and Anne Frantilla, reference archivists at the Bentley Historical Library, Ann Arbor, Michigan; Lisa Brant, Archivist, and Brigitte Lawson, of the Director's Office, at the Stratford Festival, Stratford, Ontario; Dr. Bernadine Dodge, University Archivist at Trent University, Peterborough, Ontario; Catherine Downey of the Office of the President and Anne Robertson in the Development Office at Trent University; Anne Goddard, Manuscript Division of the National Archives of Canada, Ottawa; Janet

Turnbull Irving at Curtis Brown Canada, Toronto; Birthe Jörgensen at the Joan Baillie Archives of the Canadian Opera Company, Toronto; Fred Kerner of the Academy of Canadian Writers, Toronto; Geoffrey Massey, son of Raymond Massey; Apollonia Lang Steele, Special Collections at The University of Calgary, Calgary, Alberta; Gail Stewart, Assistant to the Publisher at McClelland & Stewart Inc., Toronto; Dr. Richard Verr, Curator of Manuscripts at McGill University, Montreal.

Several friends and colleagues solved conundrums or gave me advice – in particular the classicist Joan Bigwood who suggested Plutarch's life of Lycurgus as the source of the story about the Spartan boy, Ramsay Derry who suggested lines of inquiry about several elusive individuals, Peter S. Grant who helped with Warner/Chappell Music, Georgia Hershfeld who tracked down a couple of ephemeral American periodicals, Susan Howson who told me how to reach Sir John Gielgud, Robin and Heather Jackson who solved the reference to Semmel Weiss, Marie Korey who dealt quickly with queries about denizens of Massey College, Michael Laine who supplied advice about editorial practice, and Abraham Rotstein who recalled details about the Gordon Lectures.

In addition, I would like to thank Brigitte Barkley who explained why *GEO* failed to publish an article by Davies, Pramila Bennett of the *Journal of Analytical Psychology* who suggested approaches to several Jungian questions, Julie Berger who answered my questions about her husband Jacques, the Hon Mr. Justice J. D. Cunningham who supplied information about his father Ben, Unn Palm of Wahlström & Widstrand in Stockholm who solved several Swedish references, Rosemary Spring-Rice Pyper who furnished facts about her husband Arthur, and Grace Wherry who forwarded information about Perry Knowlton.

A number of people found letters that I have not been able to include, but I am grateful to have been able to consider them when making my selection: Hugh Anson-Cartwright, Bert Archer, J. E. Belliveau, Russell Brown, Felicity Bryan, Jack A. Carr (Archives, The Arts and Letters Club, Toronto), Michael Davies, Michael Denison, Cheryl Ennals (University Archives, Mount Allison University, Sackville, New Brunswick), Constance Fisher (Co-ordinator: Opera Division, Faculty of Music, University of Toronto, Toronto), Ian Gentles, Kenneth Garlick, Konrad Gross, John

Jones (Dean and Archivist, Balliol College, Oxford University, Oxford), John H. Lutman (Special Collections, The University of Western Ontario, London, Ontario), Eluned MacMillan, Donald Moggridge, Tanya Moiseiwitsch, Claire Northrop, Christopher G. Petter (Special Collections, University of Victoria, Victoria, British Columbia), Fern A. Rahmel, Shelley Sweeney (Archivist, University of Regina, Regina, Saskatchewan), Ian E. Wilson (Archivist of Ontario, Toronto), and Richard Winter.

Some letters proved to be elusive at this time, but I appreciate the efforts of the many who searched their files and reported back to me – Sue Bradbury, Peter Brigg, Gwen Brown, C. Abbott Conway, John Kenneth Galbraith, Colin Graham, Douglas Rain, and Lucinda Vardey. I am also grateful to those who checked their memories and their collections and wrote to say that they had no letters.

Finally, I would like to thank those people who forwarded letters written prior to 1976 or who helped with them in one way or another. Their assistance will be acknowledged more fully when Davies' early letters are published.

The originals of many of the letters in this volume are still in private hands. Those to the following recipients are with their papers –

Margaret Atwood's, Robert Finch's, and William J. Keith's in the Thomas Fisher Rare Books Library, University of Toronto, Toronto.

Horace Davenport's in the Michigan Historical Collections, Bentley Historical Library, University of Michigan, Ann Arbor, Michigan.

Leon Edel's in the Department of Rare Books and Special Collections of the McLennan Library, McGill University, Montreal.

Timothy Findley's and Yousuf Karsh's in the National Archives of Canada, Ottawa.

Robert Fulford's and Jack McClelland's in the Archives and Research Collections of McMaster University, Hamilton, Ontario.

Elliott Hayes's and Nicholas Pennell's in the Stratford Festival Archives, Stratford, Ontario.

Margaret Laurence's, Harry Rasky's, and Herbert Whittaker's, in the Archives and Special Collections, Scott Library, York University, Toronto.

Mordecai Richler's in the University of Calgary Libraries Special Collections, Calgary, Alberta.

Gordon Roper's in the Trent University Archives, Peterborough, Ontario.
The copies of Davies' business correspondence that were created by
his various secretaries are in the National Archives in Ottawa, except for
those for 1991 to 1995.

INDEX